Visualizing Information Using SVG and X3D

Vladimir Geroimenko and Chaomei Chen (Eds)

Visualizing Information Using SVG and X3D

XML-based Technologies for the XML-based Web

**With 125 Figures
including 86 Colour Plates**

 Springer

Vladimir Geroimenko, DSc, PhD, MSc
School of Computing, University of Plymouth, Plymouth PL4 8AA, UK

Chaomei Chen, PhD, MSc, BSc
College of Information Science and Technology, Drexel University,
3141 Chestnut Street, Philadelphia, PA 19104-2875, USA

British Library Cataloguing in Publication Data
Visualizing information using SVG and X3D:XML-based
   technologies for the XML-based web
   1. Information visualization 2. computer graphics 3. SVG
   (Document markup language) 4. XML (Document markup language)
   5. Semantic Web
   I. Geroimenko, Vladimir, 1955– II. Chen, Chaomei, 1960–
   005.2'76

ISBN 1852337907

CIP data available

ISBN 1-85233-790-7 Springer London Berlin Heidelberg
Springer is a part of Springer Science + Business Media
springeronline.com

Typeset by Gray Publishing, Tunbridge Wells, UK
34/3830-543210   Printed on acid-free paper   SPIN 10942703

Contents

Foreword

Correcting the Great Mistake

People often mistake one thing for another. That's human nature. However, one would expect the leaders in a particular field of endeavour to have superior abilities to discriminate among the developments within that field. That is why it is so perplexing that the technology elite – supposedly savvy folk such as software developers, marketers and businessmen – have continually mistaken Web-based graphics for something it is not.

The first great graphics technology for the Web, VRML, has been mistaken for something else since its inception. Viewed variously as a game system, a format for architectural walkthroughs, a platform for multi-user chat and an augmentation of reality, VRML may qualify as the least understood invention in the history of information technology. Perhaps it is so because when VRML was originally introduced it was touted as a tool for putting the shopping malls of the world online, at once prosaic and horrifyingly mundane to those of us who were developing it. Perhaps those first two initials, "VR", created expectations of sprawling, photorealistic fantasy landscapes for exploration and play across the Web. Or perhaps the magnitude of the invention was simply too great to be understood at the time by the many, ironically even by those spending the money to underwrite its development. Regardless of the reasons, VRML suffered in the mainstream as it was twisted to meet unintended ends and stretched far beyond its limitations.

VRML was originally intended to be a platform for delivering, presenting and executing interactive 3D graphics – period, full stop. This meant any graphical application, ranging from the prosaic to the fictional, from fully photorealistic to purely synthetic. What attracted me to work on VRML in 1994 was its potential to transform the human–computer interface from a 2D window- and page-based metaphor into a 3D metaphor of objects and spaces. Such objects and spaces might be photorealistic and verisimilar; they might just as easily be abstract and fantastic. The point is: they are intended to convey information.

The great mistake of Web media is that the developers and marketing machines of high-tech companies believe and actively promote the idea that the primary use for graphics is as "art rather than information": the stuff of banner ads, games, walkthroughs and avatars. This misguided notion ignores the reality that computers are still largely used for managing, sharing and communicating textual and numeric data. Take a look at today's 2D computer applications. How many of them are oriented toward managing abstract entities – numbers, words or folders full of files – versus real-world images and sounds? You will discover that an overwhelming majority of these applications are intended for the former. Granted, images, sounds and video account for a growing amount of the data stored on personal computers and shared over the Web. However, even that data is presented via an organizing principle known as the user interface: an abstract thing, generated from underlying relationships in the data – not painted by artists.

The Web is a fine place for sharing family photo albums, displaying ads and playing games. However, I predict that these applications of Web graphics will be dwarfed in comparison by its absorption into the mainstream in the form of simpler and more intuitive interfaces, rich media presentations, interactive training manuals and animated multidimensional charts. Ultimately, the percentage of 2D and 3D Web graphics created by artists compared with that generated using data visualization techniques will probably be close to the percentage of PC users who own a licensed copy of Photoshop, and the mix of applications roughly what we see on today's desktop computers. As in the real world, art will constitute a minority of the use of the Web.

This book is for those of us who wish to take advantage of the rich palette of objects provided by SVG and X3D – two new standards for delivering interactive 2D and 3D graphics and animations over the Web – but have neither the requisite skills nor the luxury of time to create original artwork and hand-crafted objects. We have data; we want to see and understand it. *Visualizing Information Using SVG and X3D* presents a range of techniques and tools for realizing that desire in code and in context. System programmers can use the information in this book to develop complex client–server frameworks for presenting and navigating data using rich media interfaces; application writers can integrate the results of that work to convey meaning for particular kinds of datasets; developers of authoring environments can provide drag-and-drop tools for creating easy to navigate user interfaces at the touch of a button. Together, these building blocks enable us to understand and interpret our information better and instantly share the results with everyone on the Internet.

SVG and X3D are based on XML, the common glue that binds together the next generation of Web data. XML promises to be the foundation of a "Semantic Web": a web where information is given meaning. Although art will play an important role in the unfolding of this new Web, that role will not be fundamental. The Semantic Web will be built upon data, reified in graphics and sounds generated by programs. The software developers and information designers working in data visualization today are the architects of a new and brilliant medium for understanding our world. This book provides an entry point for joining that revolution. It also represents a vital course correction for Web graphics: maybe now we can stop chasing the butterflies and get back to changing the world.

Tony Parisi
San Francisco, California
18 May 2004

Preface

Vladimir Geroimenko and Chaomei Chen

Information visualization is one of the most important and well-established areas of research and development. In recent decades, it experienced remarkable achievements, especially in enhancing the visual appearance of the Web in order to make it more attractive and useful for the user. As has happened with many other areas, the Web has become one of the few ubiquitous driving forces behind the current development of information visualization.

The Web is undergoing revolutionary changes – its second generation is emerging. The key player in the new generation is not HTML but XML (this is why it is also known as "the XML-based Web"). If the appearance of Web pages is a major concern in the first generation, then the meaning (or semantics) of information on the Web is the focus of the second generation, which is why it is also called the "Semantic Web". The fundamental idea of the Semantic Web is to enable computers to deal with the Web information in a much more meaningful and practical way as if they are able to understand it to some extent. This phenomenon will be achieved by marking up the meaning of the data with domain-specific XML tags, by describing further relationships between the hierarchical system of meanings using specialized technologies such as RDF (Resource Description Framework) or OWL (Web Ontology Language) and by adding many other technological and conceptual layers required to enable computer programs to handle Web data properly without human intervention.

Rome was not built in a day. According to Tim Berners-Lee, the inventor of the current Web and the Semantic Web, it may take up to 10 years to complete the building of the second generation of the Web by continuing to add new layers. To achieve the revolutionary transition, there is a lot of work to do and a lot of discrepancies and conflicts to resolve. Given the indispensable role of Web graphics in today's Web, it is a natural starting point for a journey that may join some of the most visionary routes and promising techniques.

On the Semantic Web, almost everything will be written in XML-based plain text format and will include metadata (data about data) that make the data understandable by computers. Web graphics are not an exception. Both two- and three-dimensional graphics will be presented in XML-based formats, called SVG (Scalable Vector Graphics) and X3D (Extensible 3D Graphics), respectively.

This book is the first research monograph that explores the opportunities of designing and using Web graphics in the broader context of XML. It focuses on the use of SVG and X3D in generic Web applications and the applications of these novel technologies to specific problems. All these areas are considered in the broader context of the XML family of technology and the emerging Semantic Web. SVG and X3D are leading-edge technologies primarily because they are native to the XML-based Web. This means that they can be easily and seamlessly integrated with practically any other XML technologies, including those dealing with semantics, ontologies and metadata. Moreover, XML desperately needs these native technologies for representing Web data in a visually rich form since one of the fundamental principles behind XML is the separation of data from presentation rules. Basically, XML documents contain nothing else but pure data, and therefore the use of additional technologies is required to go beyond graphically primitive representations of XML data.

Taking these radical changes into consideration, it becomes obvious that information visualization is going to experience new and exciting life on the Second-generation Web. It will deal with two- and three-dimensional graphics that are written in plain text format, understandable by computers, integrated with dozens and dozens of other XML technologies, vitally important for the visually rich representation of "nothing-but-pure-data" XML documents, and so on. This is the first book that directly addresses these significant and fascinating areas of this new terra incognita. It is also a conceptual sequel to our pioneering book *Visualizing the Semantic Web: XML-based Internet and Information Visualization*, published by Springer in 2003 (ISBN-1-85233-576-9). We hope that this new monograph will stimulate and foster more studies and more books on the SVG/X3D-based visualization of the new version of the Web.

The book is arranged as follows.

Chapter 1, "SVG and X3D in the Context of the XML Family and the Semantic Web", explores the place of SVG and X3D technology within the architecture of the second-generation Web.

Chapter 2, "The Foundations of SVG", is a concise but comprehensive introduction to the scalable vector graphics language. It covers both the SVG 1.0 and 1.1 specifications and aspects of the SVG 1.2 specification that are unlikely to change significantly after the publication of this book.

Chapter 3, "X3D Fundamentals", provides the reader with high-level exposure to many of the fundamentals of the international standard for 3D graphics on the Web. From basic scene construction to incorporation of simple behaviours, it attempts to walk the reader through enough of the syntactical requirements while keeping a high-level overview perspective on the underlying infrastructure support that makes X3D possible.

Chapter 4, "SVG as the Visual Interface to Web Services", describes the relationship between XML data, Web services and SVG as a visual interface. It provides the definition of a Web service and identifies its core components and the workflow of a typical Web-based visualization or application. Also, it points out the technological gaps in providing a solution today and showcases the tools being provided from such vendors as Corel Corporation that will close the gap and make this a viable solution.

Chapter 5, "X3D Graphics, Java and the Semantic Web", shows the reader how to use the Java programming language to manipulate X3D graphics scenes. First, it reviews the X3D Object model and the concept of fields and nodes that compose the building blocks used to create an X3D scene. Then, it examines how we can utilize more advanced manipulation of an X3D with Java and ECMAScript to make more interesting content. Finally, it looks at how X3D can be leveraged in the framework of an XML-based Web for dynamic representation and interaction of information in a Web services context.

Chapter 6, "Distributed User Interfaces: Toward SVG 1.2", focuses on the SVG 1.2 working draft that offers a number of very compelling pieces that will have a direct impact on the way that we build large-scale, distributed applications. It looks more specifically at some of the changes implicit within the SVG 1.2 working draft that it is hoped will provide a meaningful answer to how such applications can and will be written.

Chapter 7, "Publishing Paradigms for X3D", reviews the literature on interactive 3D visualizations and enumerates criteria to design successful and comprehensible visualizations. It focuses on modular approaches to X3D scene design and production and examines how XSLT can be used to transform and deliver XML data to X3D visualizations within current publishing paradigms.

Chapter 8, "Visualizing Complex Networks", explores networks as one of the most powerful means of abstracting and analysing an extremely wide range of complex phenomena. It introduces the latest advances in complex network theory, followed by a survey of the most representative network visualization techniques. In particular, the chapter focuses on the need for modelling and visualizing the growth of complex networks. It examines a number of well-known examples of network growth models and their underlying theoretical expectations. The role of available standards and techniques, such as VRML, SVG and X3D, is presented in this context. Challenging issues are identified with respect to the future of X3D and other 3D graphics initiatives.

Chapter 9, "Applying SVG to Visualization of Chemical Structures and Reactions", explores some of the possibilities available to the chemical educationalist for developing learning materials and experiences that use SVG for the visualization of organic compounds and reaction mechanisms. It shows how SVG might be used as a vehicle for the introduction of numerical and computing "key skills" into student work and reviews some tools available for creating chemical structure graphics in SVG format.

Chapter 10, "Using Metadata-based SVG and X3D Graphics in Interactive TV", starts with the presentation of digiTV's essentials and its convergence with the third generation of Web-based multimedia. New audiovisual content models are presented and software architecture for consumer devices is shown. Television tells narratives in a virtual story space, with which the consumer can interact. This leads to new service types and application scenarios of graphics in digiTV, especially by involving SVG and X3D graphics.

Chapter 11, "Knowledge Visualization Using Dynamic SVG Charts", describes the relationship between rating data and generated charts used for SVG-based data visualization. The main focus in this chapter is to explain how SVG technology may be used to visualize rating data that is collected in the context of a knowledge management application. The case study discussed in this chapter shows how the visualized data may support consultants in their daily work: the charts are useful to analyse and identify weak points, strengths and forthcomings within an organization. Another advantage is the support of different kinds of devices – dynamically generated SVG charts can be used both on a standard computer and on personal mobile devices.

Chapter 12, "Using SVG and XSLT to Display Visually Geo-referenced XML", focuses on SVG as a means of displaying geographical information that allows us to display XML data visually on a map. The chapter gives examples of how XSLT can be used to merge data from different XML files by using a combination of the document() function and the key() function. Since the document() function can be used for combining several XML files, the examples can be expanded to allow the use of an intermediary file such as a gazetteer or a postcode reference file.

Chapter 13, "Using Adobe Illustrator to Create Complex SVG Illustrations", first investigates the advantages for using SVG files. Then it takes the reader through two thorough tutorials that focus on using Adobe Illustrator to create SVG images.

Chapter 14, "X3D-Edit Authoring Tool for Extensible 3D (X3D) Graphics", deals with X3D-Edit – an authoring tool for X3D graphics scenes developed using IBM's Xeena, an XML-based tool-building application. With this tool, XSLT stylesheets provide rapid translation of XML-based X3D scenes into VRML97 syntax or pretty-print HTML pages. The chapter shows that use by several dozen students, and the development of numerous examples have led to the development of context-sensitive tooltips and demonstrated good effectiveness overall. It concludes that the use of XML for both scene design and tool construction provides numerous benefits, including improved author productivity and content stability.

Contributors

Timothy Adams (UK)
Independent GIS Consultant, UK
Web site: www.tim-adams.co.uk
Email: tim@tim-adams.co.uk

Shane Aulenback (Canada)
Former Director of Development – Smart Graphics, Corel Corporation, Ottawa,
Ontario, Canada
Web site: www.smartgraphics.com/About.shtml
Email: shaneaul2004@yahoo.com

Curtis Blais (USA)
Research Associate in the Modeling, Virtual Environments and Simulation
(MOVES) Institute, Naval Postgraduate School, Monterey, CA, USA
Email: clblais@nps.navy.edu

Don Brutzman (USA)
Associate Professor in the Modeling, Virtual Environments and Simulation
(MOVES) Institute, Naval Postgraduate School, Monterey, CA, USA
Web site: http://web.nps.navy.mil/~brutzman
Email: brutzman@nps.navy.edu

Kurt Cagle (USA)
Chief Technical Architect, Seattle Book Company
Editorial Director, Center for XML and Web Services, City University, New York, USA
Web site: www.metaphoricalweb.com
Email: kurt@kurtcagle.net

Chaomei Chen (USA)
Associate Professor, College of Information Science and Technology,
Drexel University, Philadelphia, PA, USA
Web site: www.pages.drexel.edu/~cc345
Email: chaomei.chen@cis.drexel.edu

Vladimir Geroimenko (UK)
Senior Lecturer in Computing, School of Computing, University of Plymouth,
Plymouth, UK
Web site: www.tech.plym.ac.uk/soc/staff/vladg/
Email: vgeroimenko@plymouth.ac.uk

James Harney (USA)
US Naval Postgraduate School, Modeling, Virtual Environments and
Simulation (MOVES) Institute
Monterey, CA, USA
Email: dunblane74@msn.com

Alan Hudson (USA)
Project Manager X$_j$3D
Web site: www.xj3d.org
Email: giles@oz.net

Seppo Kalli (Finland)
Professor, CEO Ortikon Interactive Ltd.
Digital Media Institute, Signal Processing Laboratory,
Tampere University of Technology, Tampere, Finland
Web site: www.cs.tut.fi, www.ortikon.com
Email: seppo.kalli@tut.fi

John Leaver (UK)
Lecturer in Computing, University of Derby College, Buxton,
Derbyshire, UK
Web site: www.chem-svg.org.uk
Email: john@chem-svg.org.uk

Natasha Lobo (USA)
Graduate Research Assistant, College of Information Science and Technology,
Drexel University, Philadelphia, PA, USA
Email: lobonata@yahoo.com

Artur Lugmayr (Finland)
Project Coordinator, Researcher, Digital Media Institute, Signal Processing
Laboratory, Tampere University of Technology, Tampere, Finland
Web site: www.lugy.org, www.digitalbroadcastitem.tv
Email: lartur@acm.org

Nicholas F. Polys (USA)
Media Amoeba & CTO, VirtuWorlds LLC, Blacksburg, VA, USA
Web site: www.3DeZ.net
Email: npolys@virtuworlds.com

Sara J. Porter (USA)
Assistant Professor, Computer Graphics Technology, Purdue University,
Kokomo, IN, USA
Web site: www.tech.purdue.edu/cg/facstaff/sporter/
E-mail: sjporter@purdue.edu

Nikolas A. Rathert (Germany)
Research Associate, Fraunhofer Institute for Computer Graphics,
Fraunhoferstrasse 5, Darmstadt, Germany
Web site: www.igd.fraunhofer.de/~nrathert
Email: nikolas.rathert@igd.fraunhofer.de

PART 1
Using SVG and X3D in Generic Web Applications

Chapter 1
SVG and X3D in the Context of the XML Family and the Semantic Web

Vladimir Geroimenko

1.1 From HTML to XML and the Semantic Web

The First-generation Web was based on HTML (Hypertext Markup Language). The emerging Second-generation Web utilizes XML (Extensible Markup Language) and related technologies. Why were changes necessary? What was wrong with HTML and what are the main advantages of XML? HTML was created as a means of presenting information of the Web. It is about the spatial layout of a presentation, styling fonts and paragraphs, integrating multimedia elements, enabling user interactivity and the like. Only humans are able to understand the content of such presentations and to deal with them. Computers have played a passive and an inadequate role in this process – just as the technical means of display, something similar to TV sets or data projectors. They had no real access to the content of a presentation because they were not able to understand the meaning of information on HTML pages. On the other hand, the growth of e-commerce created a need for a language that could deal not only with the design (things such as "font colour" or "image size") but also with the content (things such as "item price" or "sale offer") of a presentation. In other words, there was need for a markup language that would go beyond HTML limits in the following aspects: first, it should describe not only the style but also the content of a Web documet; second, it has to mark up this content in such a meaningful way that it would be understandable not only by human beings but also (to a certain extent) by computers; third, it should be sufficiently flexible to describe specific areas of interest of any of the millions of existing and future businesses, companies and organizations.

XML was introduced in early 1998 as a new markup language and was intended as the foundation of the next generation of the Internet. It has very quickly spread through all the major areas of Web-related science, industry and technology – and the XML revolution began (for more information about the XML revolution and its semantic approach, see Hellman, 1999; Lassila et al., 2000; Hill, 2002; Goldfarb and Prescod, 2002).

The XML syntax is easy to read and to write. A real-world example of an XML document is shown in Figure 1.1. Since XML is a plain text format, an XML document can be created using any available text editor and then saved as a file with an extension " .xml". In the document illustrated, the first line, called the "XML declaration",

```
<?xml version="1.0" encoding="UTF-8"?> ←──────── XML declaration
<!-- This is a sample XML document --> ←──────── Comment
<Catalog> ←──────────────────────────── Root element
  <Book ISBN="1-85233-576-9">
    <Title>Visualizing the Semantic Web</Title>
    <Editor> ←──────────────────────── Start tag
      <FirstName>Vladimir</FirstName>
      <LastName>Geroimenko</LastName>
    </Editor> ←──────────────────────── End tag
    <Editor>
      <FirstName>Chaomei</FirstName>
      <LastName>Chen</LastName>
    </Editor> ←──────────────────────── Element content
    <Publisher>Springer-Verlag</Publisher>
    <PubDate>November 2002</PubDate>
    <Pages>212</Pages> ←──────────────── Element name
    <Price currency="USD">79.75</Price> ← Element with
    <BookCover image="1852335769.gif"/> ← an attribute
  </Book>                                  Empty element
  <!-- More books can be added here -->
  <Book></Book> ←────────────────────
  <Book></Book> ←──────────────────── Empty elements
</Catalog>
```

Nested elements

Element with an attribute

Figure 1.1   The anatomy of an XML document.

is always to be included because it defines the XML version of the document. In this example, the document conforms to the 1.0 specification of XML. The rest of the file is easily understandable, even if the reader has never heard about XML. It is obvious that the file describes a book in a book catalogue. XML uses "tags" (words or phrases in angle brackets) to mark up the meaning of the data it contains. To show precisely what piece of data they describe, tags usually appear in pairs, "start tag – end tag". The start tag and the end tag must match each other exactly (since XML is case sensitive) except for a forward slash that has to be included in every end tag after the opening angle bracket. The combination "the start tag – the content – the end tag", called "an element", is the main building block of an XML document. Some elements include "attributes" in order to add more information about the content of an element. Attributes are "name-value" pairs enclosed within the start tag of an element. In our example, the element "Book" has an attribute with the attribute name "ISBN" and the attribute value "1-85233-576-9". Some elements may contain no content at all and store data only in their attributes (such as the element "BookCover" in our example: `<BookCover image = "1852335769. gif"/>`). They are called "empty elements" and combine the start and end tags in one, as shown above. (More information about XML can be found in Harold, 1999; Birbeck et al., 2000; Dick, 2002; Pappamikail, 2002; Bates, 2003; Geroimenko, 2004.)

It is important to emphasize that XML is not a language but a metalanguage, i.e., a high-level language specially intended for creating and describing other languages. For a deeper understanding of the nature of XML as a metalanguage, let us look at some contradictory uses of terms. It seems to be common and normal to talk about specific documents that "they are written in XML". Strictly, however, it is impossible to write even a single document in XML because XML *is not* a language. As a metalanguage, it has no tags at all for describing any specific content and therefore can be used only as a language-definition tool. This means that one has to develop first a specialized XML-based language (something like "MyML") and only after this to have the possibility of creating documents that are written, strictly, not in XML but in MyML (using XML syntax, of course).

Since XML is a metalanguage, it allows a company, organization or even an individual to create their own domain-specific markup languages, giving them considerable flexibility and functionality. At the same time, this most useful feature of the technology can lead to a paradoxical conclusion that the use of XML technology is in principle hardly possible. Indeed, if every company uses its own XML-based language for its specific business, any meaningful communication between them will be out of the question. For example, Company 1 describes its customers and staff using XML tags <first_name> and <last_name>, Company 2 uses <given_name> and <surname> and Company 3 goes for <Given_Name> and <Surname>. From a human point of view, these metadata tags convey the same meaning, but for computers they are different, even in the case of the languages developed by Company 2 and Company 3 (since XML is case sensitive). To avoid a "Tower of Babel" scenario, significant efforts are required in order to compensate for the unlimited freedom of creating everyone's own markup languages. Basically, there are two possible solutions to this problem. The first is to create special applications that serve as translators between corporate markup languages of interest. The second is to use existing XML vocabularies developed for horizontal or vertical industry as an intermediary language to allow communication and mutual understanding.

Although XML will form the basis of the new generation of the Web, it is not a replacement for HTML. They are designed for different purposes: XML for describing data, HTML for displaying data. XML cannot throw HTML aside because it needs HTML as a means of presenting the data it describes. At the same time, XML forces HTML to change itself. Everything on the future XML-based Web tends to be written or re-written using the XML syntax. And HTML is not an exception. A new generation of HTML called XHTML (Extensible HTML) began its life as a reformulation of the latest version of HTML, namely HTML 4.0, in XML. That is, HTML will be replaced by XHTML, not by XML. The last two languages will complement one another very well on the future Web. XML will be used to structure and describe the Web data, whereas XHTML pages will be used to display it. Table 1.1 compares some of the main features of XML, HTML and XHTML.

Since XML incorporates a revolutionary new approach to the future of the Web, it has numerous advantages and benefits. Here are just a few of them:

- XML is an open industry standard defined by the World Wide Web Consortium (W3C). It is a vendor-independent language, endorsed by all the major software producers and market leaders.
- XML is a text format. Since practically all relevant software and devices are able to process text, XML is good for all platforms, devices, programming languages and software. XML is based on a new multilingual character-encoding system called "Unicode" and because of this it permits exchange of information across national and cultural boundaries.

Table 1.1   Main features of XML, HTML and XHTML

XML	HTML	XHTML
Metalanguage	SGML-based language	XML-based language
Intended for describing and structuring data	Intended for formatting and displaying data	Intended for formatting and displaying data
No predefined set of tag	Predefined set of tags	Predefined set of tags
Case sensitive	Case insensitive	Case sensitive. Tag and attribute names must be written in lower case
XML documents must be well formed	HTML documents do not need to be well formed	XHTML documents must be well formed
All non-empty elements require end tags	Some end tags are optional	All non-empty elements require end tags
Empty elements must be terminated, e.g. <img/>	Empty elements are not terminated, e.g. <img>	Empty elements must be terminated, e.g. <img/>
Attribute values must be quoted	Unquoted attribute values are allowed	Attribute values must be quoted
No attribute minimalization is allowed	The minimal form of an attribute is allowed	No attribute minimalization is allowed
Tags must be nested properly, without overlapping	Tags may be nested with overlapping	Tags must be nested properly, without overlapping

- XML separates the content of an XML document from its presentation rules. As a result, the content or any of its fragments can be presented in many desired forms on a variety of devices, such as computers, mobile phones, personal digital assistants or printers.
- XML contains self-describing and therefore meaningful information. Metadata tags and attributes allow not only humans but also computers to interpret the meaning of XML data.
- XML is both Web-friendly and data-oriented. It enables us to integrate data from any legacy, current and future sources such as databases, text documents and Web pages.

XML forms the technological basis of the Second-generation Web. Since XML is intended for describing the meaning of Web data (or, in other words, their semantics), the emerging XML-based Web is also called the "Semantic Web". The concept of the Semantic Web is based on a vision of Tim Berners-Lee, the inventor of the World Wide Web and the Director of the World Wide Web Consortium. In particular, this vision was expressed in his *Semantic Web Road Map* document (Berners-Lee, 1998), his book *Weaving the Web* (Berners-Lee, 1999), and his speech at the XML2000 Conference (Berners-Lee, 2000). Recently, many online and magazine articles have appeared which provide a more or less clear explanation of what the Semantic Web actually is (see, for example, Bosak and Bray, 1999; Decker et al., 2000; Dumbill, 2000, 2001; Cover, 2001; Berners-Lee, et al., 2001; Heflin and Hendler, 2001; Palmer, 2001; Daconta et al., 2003; Davies, 2003; Fensel et al., 2003; Passin, 2003; Geroimenko, 2004). Some Web sites are specially devoted the Semantic Web and

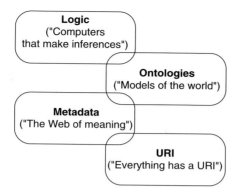

Figure 1.2 Conceptual building blocks of the Semantic Web.

its key technologies (for instance, www.semanticweb.org, www.w3c.org/2001/sw/ and www.xml.com).

The main idea of the Semantic Web is to delegate many current human-specific Web activities to computers. They can do them better and quicker that any individuals. However, to enable computers to do their new jobs, humans need to express Web data in a machine-readable format suitable for completely automate transactions that do not require human intervention. This can be achieved by (1) identifying all Web and real-world resources in a unique way; (2) adding more and more metadata to Web data using XML, RDF and other technologies; (3) creating general and domain-specific ontologies using RDF Schemas, OWL and similar technologies; and (4) enabling computers to use simple logic in order to deal with Web data in a meaningful way (see Figure 1.2). For example, computers should "understand" not only what a bit of data means but also that other pieces of data, located somewhere on the Web, mean the same even if they look different (for instance, <last_name> and <surname>). The idea of the "sameness" of Web data will provide a new solution to many current problems, such as more meaningful searches on the Web. For example, if you are looking for "Wood" and specifying this word as a person's last name, you will get back only topics related to people, not timber, firewood or forest. The use of RDF, OWL or other high-level metadata technologies can make Web searches even more powerful and therefore more successful. Computers will be able to convert automatically complex expressions from one domain-specific XML language into another in order to process them.

Although it is hoped that the above considerations will provide the reader with some general understanding of the concept, the question "What is the Semantic Web?" is not a simple one to answer. Computer scientists and Web developers in different fields (e.g., e-commerce, networking, knowledge management or artificial intelligence) tend to have contradictory views. The new generation of the Web will be so complex and multifaceted that it will allow people with almost any background to find all that they need or want to see. For one group of researchers and developers, the Semantic Web is a brain for humankind (Fensel and Musen, 2001), for another it is a database for communicating invoices, timetables and other similar information in XML. The spectrum of such views becomes even more diverse when the matter in question is how to implement the concept of the Second-generation Web, what technologies to use and in what direction to move. Indeed, there are many ways of constructing the Web and many technologies that can be employed.

It is interesting to analyse the conceptual basis of the Semantic Web from a methodological point of view because it helps in developing a deeper understanding of the nature of this new-generation Web. As is generally known, semantics is a branch of linguistics concerned with meaning. The Semantic Web, in contrast to the current HTML-based Web, is all about the meaning of data. For instance, if 100 means £100 it can be described in XML as `<Price currency="GBP">100 </Price>`. But if 100 means a speed it might be marked up as `<Speed><mph> 100</mph></Speed>`. Obviously, in these cases the same syntax ("100") has different semantics. It is not just a number any more, it is something meaningful and therefore much more useful. It is important to keep in mind that we are talking here about data that is meaningful not only for humans but in the first instance for computers. Human beings do not need any markup metadata tags for understanding current Web pages. For them, the existing Web is already the semantic one. However, for machines it is meaningless, and therefore non-semantic (perhaps the only exception is the `<meta>` tag that can be placed in the head section of an HTML page in order to add non-displayable information about the author, keywords and so on). Consequently, a question is arising about the point from which the Web becomes meaningful for computers (in other words, becomes "semantic") and the extent to which it can be possible.

A fairly common opinion is that the point where the Semantic Web actually starts is not XML (since this language is "not semantic enough"), but RDF, RDF Schema, OWL and other more specialized metadata technologies. The proposed architecture of the Second-generation Web will be discussed later in this chapter. Our view is based on a multilevel conceptual model of a machine-processable Web. In our opinion, since XML allows us to add meanings to Web data and these meanings can in principle be understandable by computers, we can talk about XML as the first level of the Semantic Web (see also, for example, Patel-Schneider and Simeon, 2002). This new generation of the Web begins where XML and its companion (XHTML) are replacing HTML. Of course, XML is far from being sufficient to construct the Semantic Web as such. The human system of meanings, and even the current Web recourses, is not so simple that they can be described using XML alone. Therefore, the architectures of the Semantic Web need to add more and more new levels on top of XML. It is impossible to say what kind of technology will be successfully implemented in the future in order to construct a complex hierarchical system of multilayered semantic information that would enable computers to understand a little bit more after adding each new layer. As of today, for example, RDF and OWL seem to be the most suitable technologies for adding more meanings to the Web data and resources. At the same time, XML Topic Maps also look like a promising candidate for this job.

Hence the Semantic Web originated in XML, that provides a minimal (but not zero) semantic level, and this version of the Web will be under development for a long time ahead by adding extra levels of meaning and by using new specialist technologies for doing this. As a result, computers will be able to "understand" more and to put this to good use. Although it will work, in reality we can talk about meanings, understandable by computers, only in a metaphorical sense. For machines, any XML element is still meaningless. For them, the element `<Price in_GBP="100"/>` makes no more sense than, for example, the element `<Kdg9kj Drdsf="100"/>`. Paradoxically, adding new levels of semantics (using

RDF, OWL or any other future technologies) does not change the situation. As long as computers do not possess a very special feature, similar to human consciousness, they are not able to understand any meanings at all. However, by using computers, the creators of the Semantic Web will be able to simulate some human understanding of meaningful Web data and, what most important, to force machines to make practical use of this.

1.2 The Architecture of the Semantic Web

The first attempt to give a high-level plan of the architecture of the Semantic Web was made by Tim Berners-Lee in his *Semantic Web Road Map* (Berners-Lee, 1998) and refined in his subsequent publications and presentations (Berners-Lee, 1999, 2000; Berners-Lee et al., 2001). According to him, the Semantic Web will be built by adding more layers on the top of the existing ones and may take around 10 years to complete. Figure 1.3 shows Semantic Web architectural relationships. It is based on the famous "layer cake" diagram presented by Tim Berners-Lee at the XML2000 conference (Berners-Lee, 2000).

Most of the current Semantic Web technologies belong to the XML family and it is almost certain that all future layers will also be XML based. XML is the foundation of the new generation of the Web. XML is powered by the URI, Namespaces and Unicode technologies. URIs are intended for identifying arbitrary resources in a unique way; they may or may not "point" to resources or serve for their retrieval. Together with XML Namespaces, they allow everyone to identify uniquely elements within an XML document, without the danger of a name collision. Unicode, as a multilingual character-encoding system, provides opportunities for describing Web resources in any natural language and therefore allows exchange of information across national and cultural boundaries.

XML documents form the most substantial layer of the Semantic Web because they embrace, strictly not only documents with the domain-specific content (such as product catalogues) but also almost all "technological" documents written in XML (such as XSLT, RDF or OWL). XML is a universal format for storing and exchanging data and metadata on the new version of the Web.

Trust	
Proof	Signature & Encryption
Logic	
OWL and other ontology languages	
RDF & RDF Schema	
XML Schema and vocabularies	
Domain-specific XML documents	
XML-based GUI: XHTML, SVG, X3D, SMIL etc.	
XML (Metalanguage), Namespaces, Infoset	
URI	
Unicode	

Figure 1.3 The architecture of the Semantic Web.

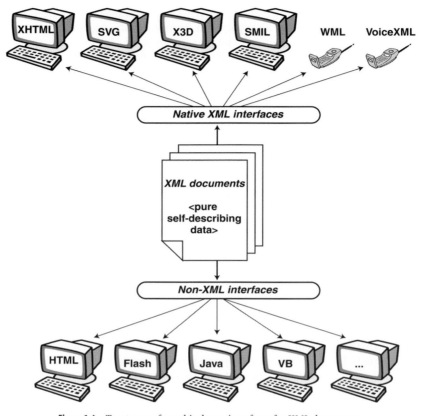

Figure 1.4 Two types of graphical user interfaces for XML documents.

The XML document layer has to interface with the two main types of Semantic Web users: humans and computers. Although an XML document, as a rule, says nothing about how to present its content to an individual, this is not a problem because plenty of formatting and rendering technologies (both legacy and XML based) are available for displaying XML data in human-readable form (for example, Flash, Java, HTML, XHTML, XSLT, SVG, X3D; see Figure 1.4). Interfacing with computers and especially autonomous software agents is a much more difficult problem. To make XML documents "understandable" and processable by computers, a hierarchy of special layers should be added in order to achieve the only goal – to make meanings of data clear to non-human users of the Web. No one knows how many extra layers will be needed in the future and what kind of new technologies should be implemented.

RDF seems to be one of the main building blocks of the today's Semantic Web, giving a domain-neutral mechanism for describing metadata in a machine-processable format (see, for example, Hjelm, 2001). RDF is built around three concepts: resources, properties and statements. Resources can be anything that can be referred to by a URI (from an entire Web site to a singe element of any of its XML or XHTML pages). A property is a specific characteristic or relation that describes a resource. RDF statements are composed of triplets: an object (a resource), an attribute (a property) and a value (a resource or free text). They are the formal implementation of a simple idea expressed in the natural-language sentences of the following type: "Someone is the *creator/owner/etc.* of something else". RDF statements describe additional facts about an XML vocabulary in an explicit, machine-readable format, and therefore allow computers to understand meanings in context. In this way, they act for human abilities of implicit common-sense understanding of the underlying real-world concepts.

RDF Schemas provide appropriate data typing for RDF documents by defining domain-specific properties and classes of resources to which those properties can be applied. These classes and properties are organized in a hierarchical way by using the basic modeling primitives of the RDF Schema technology: "class" and "property" definitions and "subclass-of" and "subproperty-of" statements.

Topic Maps are a standard defined by the International Organization for Standardization (ISO). Like RDF, they are intended to annotate Web resources in order to make them understandable by computers (see, for instance, Lacher and Decker, 2001). Topic Maps technology can be used to build a semantic network above information resources (some sort of "GPS of the information universe") and thus to enhance navigation in very complex data sets. A topic map is an XML document that based on the fundamental concepts of "topics, associations and occurrences". Similarly to an entry in an encyclopaedia, a topic can represent any subject and therefore almost everything in a Topic Map is a topic. Topics are connected by associations and point to resources through occurrences. An association expresses a relationship between topics. A topic can be linked to one or more occurrences – information resources that are somehow related to this topic. For example, "the Semantic Web" and "the Web" are topics that have an association "is a new version of" and several assurances (places where they are mentioned, including not only text but also images) in this book. The relationship between RDF and Topic Maps technologies is not simple. On the one hand, Topics Maps are in competition with RDF. They provide an effective knowledge-centric approach to metadata in contrast to the resource-centric RFD technique. On the other hand, Topic Maps may be used to model RDF and vice versa.

Ontologies are another fundamental technology for implementing the Semantic Web (Ding, 2001; Fensel, 2001; Fensel et al., 2001; Gomez-Perez and Corcho, 2002; Kim, 2002). They establish a common conceptual description and a joint terminology between members of communities of interest (human or autonomous software agents). An ontology is an explicit specification of a conceptualization (Gruber, 1993). An XML Schema can be regarded as a primitive ontology. The construction of the new Web requires ever more expressive languages for describing and matching a variety of "horizontal" and "vertical" ontologies. The latest development in this area includes, on the one hand, generating a variety of ontologies within vertical marketplaces – such as Dublin Core, Common Business Library (CBL), Commerce XML (cXML), Open Catalog Format (OCF), and RosettaNet – and, on the other, creating new, improved languages that extend the RDF Schema by richer sets of modelling primitives for representation of Boolean expressions, property restrictions, axioms, etc. – such as OIL (Ontology Inference Layer) and DAML + OIL (DARPA Agent Markup Language + OIL).

At present, the leading Semantic Web technology is OWL (Web Ontology Language), which is a revision of the DAML + OIL Web ontology language. It is based on XML, RDF and RDF Schema but goes beyond these languages by providing more facilities for expressing the semantics of Web data. OWL extends RDF

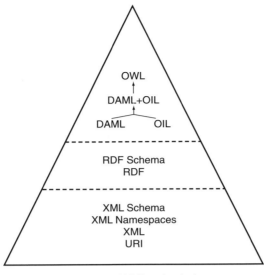

Fundamental XML technologies

Figure 1.5   The genesis of OWL and its relationships to other XML technologies.

Schema with a richer OWL vocabulary that provides advanced inferencing capabilities. OWL relationships to other XML technologies are shown in Figure 1.5.

The highest layers of the Semantic Web are yet to be fully developed. The logic layer will contain logical rules that allow computers to make inferences and deductions in order to derive new knowledge. The proof layer will implement languages and mechanisms for distinguishing between Web resources with different levels of trustworthiness. The logic and proof, together with the XML Digital Signature, will enable us to construct the "Web of Trust", where autonomous software agents will be able and allowed to undertake important tasks such as finding and buying expensive goods without any human intervention.

Hence the Semantic Web will make maximal use of both Web resources and computers. Computers will not be just devices for posting and rendering data, but will deal with resources in a meaningful and competent way. Current technologies for adding multilayered machine-processable semantics and heuristics make this development possible.

1.3 The XML Family

As a metalanguage, XML is simple and therefore easy to learn and use. However, there are countless numbers of "big" and "small" languages written in XML. It is called the family of XML-based languages. The members of the XML family can be described and classified in several different ways (see, e.g., Bain and Shalloway, 2001; Salminen, 2001; Vint, 2001; Sall, 2002; Turner, 2002). Our approach is shown

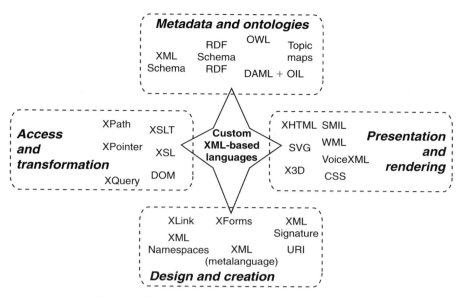

Figure 1.6 The structure and main members of the XML family.

in Figure 1.6. The core of the family is formed by numerous custom XML-based languages, such as NewsML and SportXML. Actually, this is the most important part of the XML family since custom languages describe the content of XML documents. In other words, they are intended for marking up the meaning of domain-specific web data such as "car price". Any organization and even any individual are free to create their own XML-based languages.

Besides the custom languages, XML has a considerable number of specifications that help to realize its potential. This type of XML-related languages (also known as the XML family of technologies) is mostly being developed by the W3C. Since this area is evolving extremely quickly, the only possibility of finding out its state of the art is to visit the Consortium Web site (www.w3.org) in order to comprehend the situation as it develops literally day by day. It is good to know that all results of W3C development activities are presented as *Technical Reports,* each of which can reach one of the following levels of its maturity (from lower to higher): *Working Draft, Candidate Recommendation, Proposed Recommendation* and *Recommendation.* A *Recommendation* represents consensus within W3C and is a de facto Web standard.

The XML family of technology can be divided into four groups, in accordance with their main functionalities: (1) enabling the design and creation of XML-based languages and documents; (2) providing a means of accessing and transforming XML documents; (3) enabling efficient presentation and rendering of XML data; (4) describing the meaning of XML data using metadata and ontologies. The overview of the XML family provided below is very condensed and just describes their main purpose and meanings of acronyms:

1. XML technologies involved in the **design and creation** of XML-based languages and their documents:
   - *XML* – a metalanguage that allows the creation of markup languages for arbitrary specialized domains and purposes. This is XML as such.

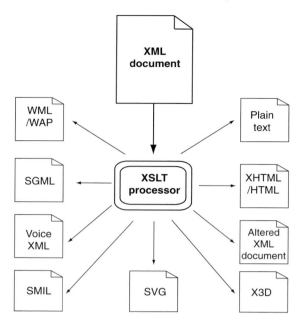

Figure 1.7   Transforming an XML document into other formats using XSLT.

- *XML Namespaces* prevent name collision in XML documents by using qualified element and attribute names. A qualified name consists of a namespace
  name and a local part. The namespace name is a prefix identified by a URI
  (Uniform Resource Identifier) reference.
- *XLink* provides facilities for creating and describing links between XML documents, including two-way links, links to multiple documents and other types
  of linking that are much more sophisticated than in HTML.
- *XForms* specifies the use of Web form technique on a variety of platforms,
  such as desktop computers, television sets or mobile phones.
- *XML Signature* provides syntax and processing rules for XML digital
  signatures.
2. XML technologies that are mostly intended for **accessing and transforming**
   XML documents:
   - *XSL (Extensible Stylesheet Language)* consists of *XSL-T (XSL Transform-
     ations)* and *XSL-FO (XSL Formatting Objects)* and is a language for trans-
     forming XML documents into other XML documents and for rendering
     them, for example, into HTML, Braille, audible speech and many other forms
     on a variety of platforms and devices, as shown in Figure 1.7.
   - *DOM (Document Object Model)* is an application programming interface
     that describes an XML document as a tree of nodes and defines the way the
     nodes are structured, accessed and manipulated.
   - *XPath* specifies how to address parts of an XML document.
   - *XPointer* extends XPath by defining fragment identifiers for URI references.
   - *XQuery* is a language for querying XML data that considers an XML file as a
     database.

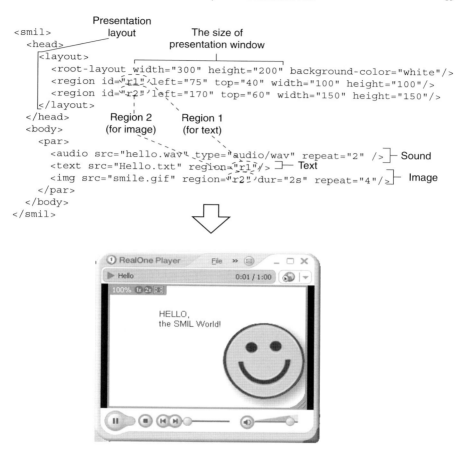

Figure 1.8 An example SMIL document and its visual rendering.

3. XML technologies responsible for **presenting and rendering** XML documents:
   - *CSS (Cascading Style Sheets)* is a simple language for specifying style sheets for rendering XML documents.
   - *XHTML (Extensible HTML)* is a reformulation of HTML 4.0 into XML.
   - *SVG (Scalable Vector Graphics)* is a language for describing two-dimensional vector and mixed vector/raster graphics in XML.
   - *X3D (Extensible 3D)* is a markup language that allows VRML (Virtual Reality Markup Language) content to be expressed in terms of XML.
   - *SMIL (Synchronized Multimedia Integration Language)* is used to create multimedia Web presentations by integrating, synchronizing and linking independent multimedia elements such as video, sound and still images; see Figure 1.8 for an example.
   - *WML (Wireless Markup Language)* is a language for presenting some content of Web pages on mobile phones and personal digital assistants. Figure 1.9 illustrates the use of WML.
   - *MathML (Mathematical Markup Language)* deals with the representation of mathematical formulae.

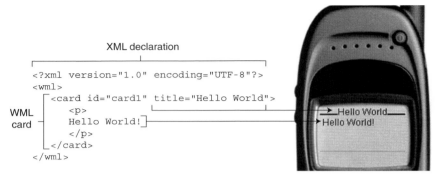

```
                        XML declaration
                    ┌──────────┴──────────┐
                  ┌─                           ─┐
                    <?xml version="1.0" encoding="UTF-8"?>
                    <wml>
                  ┌─   <card id="card1" title="Hello World">
                  │        <p>
         WML   ┤          Hello World!
         card  ─┤        </p>
                  └─   </card>
                    </wml>
```

Figure 1.9   A simple WML document and its view in a mobile phone browser.

4. XML technologies that are specially intended for expressing **metadata and ontologies:**
   - *XML Schema* defines types of elements an XML document can contain, their relationships and the data they can include. A schema can be used for both creating and validating a specific class of XML documents. An XML document must be "well formed", i.e., conform to the syntactic rules of XML, and additionally it can be "valid," i.e., conform to the rules of a schema if it has one.
   - *RDF* (*Resource Description Framework*) is one of the cornerstones of the Semantic Web. It defines a simple data model using triples (subject, predicate, object), where subject and predicate are URIs and the object is either a URI or a literal. It allows one to describe and to retrieve Web data in a way that is similar to using catalogue cards for describing and finding books in a library.
   - *RDF Schema* is a key technology that defines classes, properties and their interrelation with the RDF data model in order to enable computers to make inferences about the data collected from the Web.
   - *DAML + OIL* (*DAPRA Agent Markup Language + Ontology Inference Layer*) are languages for expressing ontologies that extend RDF Schema.
   - *OWL* (*Web Ontology Language*) is the latest language for defining and instantiating Web ontologies to permit machine-processable semantics. It can be used to represent explicitly the meaning of terms in a vocabulary and the relationships of those terms. OWL is a revision of the DAML + OIL Web ontology language. It is based on XML, RDF and RDF Schema but goes beyond these languages by providing more facilities for expressing the semantics of Web data.
   - *Topic Maps* is a technology that allows one to build a structured semantic network above information resources using topics and topic associations. This permits the description and retrieval of Web data in a way that is similar to using the index of a book to find the pages on which a specific topic is covered.

1.4 The Role and Advantages of SVG and X3D

SVG and X3D are the main members of the XML family of technologies intended for authoring two- and three-dimensional web graphics, respectively. They allow developers to create visually rich and functionally smart interfaces to XML documents of different kinds. As was shown in Figures 1.3, 1.4 and 1.6, other languages and

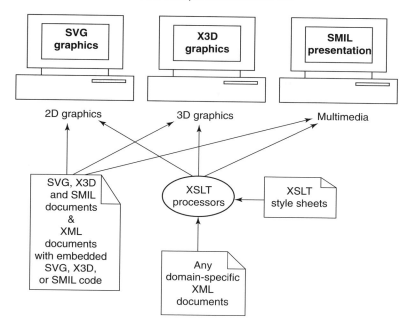

Figure 1.10 Visualizing XML data using SVG, X3D, SMIL and XSLT.

technologies can also be used for the visualization and rendering of Web data. Some of them are based on XML (such as XHTML and SMIL) and some are not (such as Flash and Java). Why are SVG and X3D unique? They are the principal XML-based technologies for 2D and 3D graphics. Moreover, they can be used together with practically any other members of the XML family, providing unprecedented new opportunities for Web graphics.

Since most members of the XML family are still under development, the opportunities provided by their mutual use are yet to be explored. However, theoretically any XML document (including SVG and X3D ones) may be embedded or transformed into another document, because all of them are written in the same language. Figure 1.10 shows different ways of presenting domain-specific XML documents in 2D, 3D and multimedia form.

SVG and X3D play a central technological role in visualizing the Semantic Web (Geroimenko and Geroimenko, 2000, 2002b; Cleary and O'Donoghue, 2001; Geroimenko and Chen, 2002). On the one hand, metadata and Web ontologies can be embedded into SVG and X3D files, turning them into "smart", machine-understandable graphics. On the other hand, SVG and X3D can effectively be used for visualizing metadata, ontologies and other conceptual structures of human meanings (Geroimenko and Geroimenko, 2000, 2002a). This "two-way" relationship is illustrated in Figure 1.11.

Many advantages of the SVG and X3D technologies are thoroughly explored in the following chapters of this book. Here we just name some of beneficial features of SVG and X3D graphics:

- high-quality Web graphics with precise structural and visual control
- dynamically generated graphics driven by real-time XML data

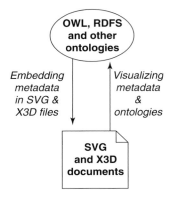

Figure 1.11   Relationships between SVG/X3D and metadata/ontologies.

- interactive and scriptable graphics utilizing XSLT, JavaScript, DOM, Java, Visual Basic, etc.
- graphics tightly integrated with other members of the XML family
- personalized graphics easily customizable to all users
- graphics automatically optimizable for mobile phones, PDAs, etc.
- easily updateable graphics (since design is separated from content)
- custom-zoomable graphics that allow users to drill down to additional levels of details
- graphics that enable internationalization and localization (the use of many world's languages)
- graphics in text-based human-readable format
- Open, royalty-free standards.

X3D is a successor to VRML (Virtual Reality Modelling Language) that provides Web developers with many new features, including extensibility, modular architecture, improved APIs and additional data encodings. It allows the use of 2D and 3D graphics, spatialized audio and video, animation, user navigation and interaction, user-defined objects, scripting and networking.

Since both SVG and X3D are written in XML, they might be integrated with each other. For example, SVG can be extended into three dimensions. In this case, some surfaces within an X3D world will be able to act as rendering canvases for SVG graphics. Theoretically, the mix of SVG and X3D syntaxes opens new possibilities for developers to create really exciting and useful "all-in-one" visualization applications.

SVG and X3D are the two current Web graphic standards that will play increasingly important roles in visualizing information and creating graphical interfaces for the next generation of the Web. They are XML-based graphics of choice for the emerging XML-based Web, since they allow dynamic visualization of XML documents, tight and seamless integration with each other and numerous XML-based technologies and the use of metadata, ontologies and other Semantic Web technologies.

References

Bain SL and Shalloway A (2001) *Introduction to XML and its Family of Technologies*. Net Objectives.
Bates C (2003) *XML in Theory and Practice*. New York: Wiley.

Berners-Lee T (1998) *Semantic Web Road Map*. Available: http://www.w3.org/DesignIssues/Semantic. html

Berners-Lee T (1999) *Weaving the Web*. San Francisco: Harper.

Berners-Lee T (2000) *Semantic Web – XML2000*. Available: http://www.w3.org/2000/Talks/1206-xml2k-tbl/

Berners-Lee T, Hendler J and Lassila O (2001) The Semantic Web. *Scientific American*, May. Available: http://www.scientificamerican.com/2001/0501issue/0501berners-lee.html

Birbeck M, et al. (2000) *Professional XML*. Wrox Press.

Bosak J and Bray T (1999) XML and the Second-generation Web. *Scientific American*, May. Available: http://www.scientificamerican.com/1999/0599issue/0599bosak.html

Cleary D and O'Donoghue D (2001) Creating a Semantic-Web interface with Virtual Reality. *Proceedings of the SPIE – The International Society for Optical Engineering*, **4528**, 138–146.

Cover R (2001) *XML and 'The Semantic Web'*. Available: http://www.coverpages.org/xmlAnd SemanticWeb.html

Daconta MC, Obrst LJ and Smith KT (2003) *The Semantic Web: a Guide to the Future of XML, Web Services, and Knowledge Management*. New York: Wiley.

Davies J (2003) *Towards the Semantic Web: Ontology-driven Knowledge Management*. New York: Wiley.

Decker S, et al. (2000) The Semantic Web: the roles of XML and RDF. *IEEE Internet Computing*, **4**(5), 63–73.

Dick K (2002) *XML: a Manager's Guide*, 2nd edn. Addison Wesley Professional.

Ding Y (2001) A review of ontologies with the Semantic Web in view. *Journal of Information Science*, **27**, 377–384.

Dumbill E (2000) *The Semantic Web: a Primer*. Available: http://www.xml.com/lpt/a/2000/11/01/ semanticweb/index.html

Dumbill E (2001) *Building the Semantic Web*. Available: http://www.xml.com/pub/a/2001/03/07/ buildingsw.html

Fensel D (2001) *Ontologies: a Silver Bullet for Knowledge Management and Electronic Commerce*. Berlin: Springer.

Fensel D, et al. (2003) *Spinning the Semantic Web: Bringing the World Wide Web to Its Full Potential*. MIT Press.

Fensel D and Musen M (2001) The Semantic Web: a brain for humankind. *IEEE Intelligent Systems*, **15**(2):24–25.

Fensel D, et al. (2001) OIL: an ontology infrastructure for the Semantic Web. *IEEE Intelligent Systems*, **16**(2), 38–45.

Geroimenko V (2004) *Dictionary of XML Technologies and the Semantic Web*. Berlin: Springer.

Geroimenko V and Chen C (eds) (2002) *Visualizing the Semantic Web: XML-based Internet and Information Visualization*. Berlin: Springer.

Geroimenko V and Geroimenko L (2000) Visualizing human consciousness content using Java3D/X3D and psychological techniques. In *2000 IEEE Conference on Information Visualization. An International Conference on Computer Visualization and Graphics*, pp. 529–532.

Geroimenko V and Geroimenko L (2002a) Interactive interfaces for mapping e-commerce ontologies. In Geroimenko V and Chen C (eds), *Visualizing the Semantic Web*. Berlin: Springer, pp. 168–179.

Geroimenko V and Geroimenko L (2002b) SVG and X3D: new technologies for 2D and 3D visualization. In Geroimenko V and Chen C (eds) *Visualizing the Semantic Web*. Berlin: Springer, pp. 90–96.

Goldfarb CF and Prescod P (2002) *Charles F. Goldfarb's XML Handbook*, 4th edn. Englewood Cliffs, NJ: Prentice Hall.

Gomez-Perez A and Corcho O (2002) Ontology languages for the Semantic Web. *IEEE Intelligent Systems*, **17**(1), 54–60.

Gruber TR (1993) A translation approach to portable ontologies. *Knowledge Acquisition*, **5**:199–200.

Harold ER (1999) *XML Bible*. Hungry Minds.

Heflin J and Hendler J (2001) A portrait of the Semantic Web in action. *IEEE Intelligent Systems*, **16**(2), 54–59.

Hellman R (1999) A semantic approach adds meaning to the Web. *Computer*, December, 13–16.

Hill A (2002) The XML revolution. *Financial Technology*, **1**(14), 5–6.

Hjelm J (2001) *Creating the Semantic Web with RDF*. New York: Wiley.

Kim H (2002) Predicting how ontologies for the Semantic Web will evolve. *Communications of the ACM*, **45**(2), 48–54.

Lacher MS and Decker S (2001) RDF, Topic Maps, and the Semantic Web. *Markup Languages: Theory and Practice*, **3**, 313–331.

Lassila O, et al. (2000) The Semantic Web and its Languages. *IEEE Intelligent Systems*, **15**(6), 67–73.

Palmer S (2001) *The Semantic Web: an Introduction*. Available: http://infomesh.net/2001/swintro/

Pappamikail P (2002) *XML by Stealth: A Manager's Guide to Strategic Implementation.* New York: Wiley.

Passin T (2003) *Semantic Web Field Guide.* Greenwich, CT: Manning Publications.

Patel-Schneider PF and Simeon J (2002) Building the Semantic Web on XML. In *The Semantic Web – ISWC 2002. First International Web Conference. Proceedings*, pp. 147–161.

Sall KB (2002) *XML Family of Specifications: a practical Guide.* Addison Wesley Professional.

Salminen A (2001) *Summary of the XML family of W3C languages.* Available: http://www.cs.jyu.fi/ ~airi/xmlfamily-20010806.html

Turner R (2002) *The Essential Guide to XML Technologies.* Englewood Cliffs, NJ: Prentice Hall PTR.

Vint D (2001) *XML Family of Specifications.* Greenwich, CT: Manning Publications.

Chapter 2
The Foundations of SVG

Kurt Cagle

2.1 Introduction

The premise that underlies HTML is at once both simple and compelling – that, using a basic, open, declarative vocabulary, one can describe a comprehensive subset of all hyperlinked documents. Scalable Vector Graphics (SVG) takes this same underlying concept and applies it to the realm of vector graphics. What results is a language that provides far more than simply another graphic format. Specifically, SVG makes possible the following:

- **Named Graphical Entities.** Everything in SVG can be named and, because of this, can be referenced. This differs from other vector graphical languages which may let one name groups or layers but seldom gives one the level of control to manipulate individual pieces that SVG does.
- **Animations.** An animation involves changing a portion of a graphic (its position, a fill colour, text, etc.,) over time. SVG incorporates the Synchronized Multimedia Integration Language (SMIL) to provide control over various graphic properties and the definitions of paths, even audio and video.
- **Text.** The ability to work with text at both the individual line and glyph level and at higher levels of organization bridges the difference between graphic and written content. SVG includes support for embedded HTML and the next generation of SVG includes the ability to work with flow diagrams and pages.
- **Interactive Programming.** Like HTML, SVG supports a native Document Object Model (DOM), which is an abstract interface that can be implemented in any language and allows for sophisticated manipulation of the SVG scene graph. Although JavaScript is perhaps the most widely used language, SVG processors capable of working with Java, C++, Perl, Java and PHP are now available.
- **Linked Resources.** SVG handles resource management by linking graphics or graphic elements (such as fills) into other graphics. These resources can include other SVG content (even from external files), making library-based graphics (and functional classes) feasible.
- **Metadata.** Because SVG is XML based, it is possible both to include metadata about specific pieces within a graphic and to bind those pieces to external metadata. In essence, this makes SVG graphics much more self-aware, even when they do not have interactivity bound to them.

This combination of graphical description, time- and event-based animation and metadata makes SVG fairly unique among even graphical languages, in that this functionality is generally more associated with a full user interface API such as

Microsoft's DirectX or GDI architecture or The Xfree Server used by Linux. However, the fact that it is also an XML language gives it a number of advantages that other descriptive graphical languages, such as Postscript, cannot match.

For instance, it is possible using languages such as XSLT to transform an XML document (such as sales figures) into one or more graphical image representations through SVG, solely through node template matches independent of a graphical interpreter. This means that the transformation could occur on a server but the image itself will only be realized on the client.

Similarly, because SVG exists as an XML document, a significant portion of the manipulation of SVG can be accomplished through the generalized XML DOM interfaces, rather than requiring a separate (and sometimes fairly esoteric) manipulation API to be able to work with the technology. This, of course, is not just an advantage for SVG – any XML document can be manipulated in this way, regardless of the semantics associated with the particular XML schema.

The use of DOM provides additional advantages because the same tools that can be used to manipulate the SVG XML can also be used for any additional embedded namespaces at play within an SVG document. Effectively, this means that rather than performing separate manipulations on each entity according to arbitrarily defined interface conventions, XML DOM manipulations are the same at all levels, minimizing the amount of separate classes that have to exist to make XML-based languages work.

This chapter is intended as an introduction to the Scalable Vector Graphics language, and covers both the SVG 1.0 and 1.1 specifications and aspects of the SVG 1.2 specification that are unlikely to change significantly after the publication of this book. The SVG 1.0 recommendation, located on the W3C website at http:// www.w3.org/TR/SVG, was formally approved in November 2000 and the SVG 1.1 recommendation (http://www.w3.org/TR/SVG11) was approved in February 2003. A roadmap of the SVG specifications and expected publication dates for future standards can be found at http://www.w3.org/Graphics/SVG. Several books on SVG are also available (Frost et al., 2001; Cagle, 2002; Eisenberg, 2002; House and Pearlman, 2002; Watt and Lilley, 2002).

This chapter assumes that the reader has basic familiarization with vector graphics in general, XML DOM manipulation and at least one high-level language (JavaScript is used here as the baseline reference, but the examples should be easy to follow for anyone with a computer science background). It is not intended to be exhaustive.

2.2 Structural Pieces of SVG

Scalable Vector Graphic documents have a number of structural elements which, although not necessarily producing a specific graphic effect, nonetheless provide a great deal of organization, coordinate control and interactivity.

2.2.1 <svg>

The principal container for an SVG document is the root <svg> element. This element performs a number of different actions, depending on its position within a document (an <svg> document can have multipled descendent <svg> elements).

The first role that the <svg> element performs is to act as the vehicle for declaring to critical namespaces – the svg namespace itself:

```
xmlns:svg="http://www.w3.org/2000/svg"
```

and the xlink namespace, which is used heavily throughout the language for referential entities:

```
xmlns:xlink="http://www.w3.org/1999/xlink"
```

For the sake of both clarity and brevity in subsequent code samples, this author is making the explicit assumption that the default namespace in fact corresponds to the svg namespace, specifically:

```
xmlns="http://www.w3.org/2000/svg"
```

unless otherwise contraindicated.

SVG makes use of the concept of defining user coordinate systems (indicated with unitless numbers in places where units might be expected). Thus the width and height attributes on an <svg> elements indicate the size of the <svg> element based on some absolute unit measure (inches or points), some hardware-denominated unit (pixels), percentage of a coordinate system (100%, for instance) or the units of the SVG's container.

For instance, if you wanted to create an SVG document that was displayed as being 500 by 300 pixels, you would do so as follows:

```
<svg xmlns:svg="http://www.w3.org/2000/svg"
   xmlns:xlink="http://www.w3.org/1999/xlink"
   width="500px" height="300px">
<!-- svg content here -->
</svg>
```

These units will also become the intrinsic units used for the SVG document, unless a viewBox attribute is also specified. The viewBox provides a relative coordinate system in user units, based on the ratios of the displayed areas, as a space-separated attribute tetrad indicating (xorigin yorigin width height). Thus, you could create a coordinate system that was 1000 by 600 user units with the origin at the upper-left-hand corner as

```
<svg xmlns:svg="http://www.w3.org/2000/svg"
   xmlns:xlink="http://www.w3.org/1999/xlink"
   width="500px" height="300px"
   viewBox="0 0 1000 600"
   >
<!-- svg content here -->
</svg>
```

It is not strictly necessary that the width and height of the coordinate system be proportional to that of container, although obviously angle measures in such a coordinate system are no longer isogonal. Similarly, the origin of the viewBox can be changed. For instance, if you wanted to have the viewBox use as its origin the point (200,300) for the upper-left-hand corner, the viewBox would be given as

```
<svg xmlns:svg="http://www.w3.org/2000/svg"
   xmlns:xlink="http://www.w3.org/1999/xlink"
```

```
width="500px" height="300px"
viewBox="200 300 1000 600"
>
<!-- svg content here -->
</svg>
```

The one limitation that the <svg> element has in establishing viewports is that it is not possible to set either width or height negative, which would otherwise have the effect of changing the x and y orientation. As this can be handled through the use of coordinate transforms of subordinate groups, this is typically not a major limitation.

As previously mentioned, it is possible for one <svg> element to contain another one (either as a child or as a greater descendant, or through linkages). These subordinate <svg> elements similarly describe viewports for their respective contents, essentially masking the content so that it fits within the width and height of the child <svg> element (again with the understanding that width and height are given in the coordinate system of the container). Thus, in the following example, the containing <svg> document is as that given above, whereas the second <svg> document provides a rectangular window that provides a unit coordinate system for a circle that is 500 × 500 user units in the other coordinate system:

Listing 2.1. Illustrating how <svg> elements can be embedded within other <svg> elements (svgs.svg)

```
<svg xmlns:svg="http://www.w3.org/2000/svg"
   xmlns:xlink="http://www.w3.org/1999/xlink"
   width="500px" height="300px"
   viewBox="0 0 1000 600"
   >
   <svg width="500" height="500" viewBox="-1 -1 2 2">
   <circle cx="0" cy="0" r="1.1" fill="red"/>
   </svg>
</svg>
```

In this particular case, the *cx* and *cy* attributes indicate the centre of the circle (at 0,0 in the new coordinate system) with a radius of 1.1 in that system. Relative to outer <svg>, however, the red circle so displayed will be rendered as a circle 50 units from the upper-left-hand-corner, with a radius of 50 units. Notice that because the radius is greater that the internal viewBox, the edges of the circle are all truncated, as shown in Figure 2.1.

The *preserveAspectRatio* attribute for the <svg> element indicates what happens when the aspect ratio of the *width* and *height* attribute differs from that of the viewBox. If the value of this attribute is "meet", then the SVG processor attempts to fit the graphic within the smaller of the two dimensions relative to the aspect ratio. This means that the graphic will always be displayed, but may be smaller than specified in order to ensure that this happens.

If the value of *preserveAspectRatio* is "slice", then the graphic will fill to the largest possible dimension in one dimension, even if it means that a part of the graphic is sliced off. In both of these situations, it is possible to fine tune this with additional qualifiers.

Setting *preserveAspectRatio* to "none" indicates to the SVG viewer that the graphic should be distorted so that it fits exactly in the indicated space. If preserving

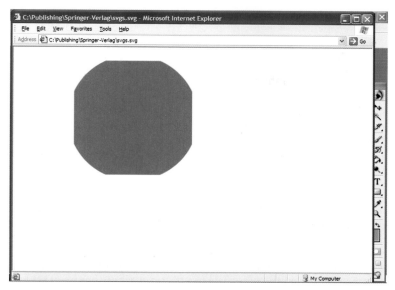

Figure 2.1   The <svg> container can be used within another <svg> to create a localized viewport.

angles are not an important consideration, this value is the one most likely to meet people's expectations, although it should obviously not be used for isogonally exact graphics.

2.2.2 <defs> and <use>

The <defs> section provides a way to define objects that can later be referenced via a <use> statement. This is useful for creating symbol objects (using <svg> and an associated *id* attribute) that can be called later, and also for defining static patterns, masks, filters and related graphical effects.

For instance, the circle element as it is defined within SVG assumes that one will start with a centre point (given by *cx* and *cy*) and a radius. However, there are times when it is more useful to define a circle as a shape that will just fit within a square or rectangle (becoming elliptical in the latter case). In Listing 2.2, the <svg> symbol defined within the <defs> with id of "rectCircle" is not rendered directly. Instead, it is invoked through the <use> attribute by setting the *xlink:href* attribute (note the xlink: prefix) to a pointer to rectCircle, as indicated by the hash mark (xlink:href = "#rectCircle"):

Listing 2.2.   A symbolic reference (defAndUse.svg)

```
<svg xmlns="http://www.w3.org/2000/svg"
  xmlns:xlink="http://www.w3.org/1999/xlink"
  width="500px" height="300px"
  viewBox="0 0 1000 600"
  >
```

```
<defs>
  <svg viewBox=" -1 -1 2 2" id = "rectCircle"
    preserveAspectRatio="none">
  <circle cx="0" cy="0" r="1" opacity="0.5"/>
  </svg>
</defs>
<circle cx="100" cy="200" r="50" fill="red"/>
<use xlink:href="#rectCircle" x="100" y="200"
  width="100" height="100" fill="green"/>
<use xlink:href="#rectCircle" x="400" y="200"
  width="200" height="100" fill="blue"/>
<circle cx="100" cy="200" r="5" fill="black"/>
</svg>
```

The red circle is shown drawn at the point (100,200) and centred there (the black dot indicates this point more precisely). The first <use> element, on the other hand, references the #rectCircle object defined earlier in the defs section, setting the x position, width and height of the circle as a separate entity, and setting the fill colour to green. Note that the *preserveAspectRatio* attribute has been set to "none", which has no effect in the case of the green circle, but which converts the blue circle into a blue ellipse with a major axis of 100 and a minor axis of 50.

One important consideration when working with elements (or aggregate groups of elements) defined in a <defs> section is that attributes that are explicitly defined in an element are treated as being invariant. For instance, if the fill attribute of the circle were set to yellow, then if a <use> statement used a fill attribute of any other colour, this would be ignored in favour of the yellow. By not including an attribute in the <defs> element, one can assign it elsewhere with impunity.

The <use> element essentially acts as a clone agent. It creates a clone of the element in question and inserts it into the render tree at the point where the <use> element was located, assigning attributes from the <use> as appropriate. Note that the one attribute that is not cloned is the *id* element – a <use> element can both reference an element with an *id* (through the *xlink:href* attribute) and have an *id* of its own.

The <use> element's *xlink:href* attribute must always point to an indexed item (that is, one that has an *id* attribute), but there is no restriction stating that the item must be in the same folder. For instance, suppose that one had an external file called circle1.svg, which contained a definition of a repositioned circle:

Listing 2.3.   Circle1.svg is an external library (circle1.svg)

```
<svg xmlns="http://www.w3.org/2000/svg">
    <defs>
        <svg viewBox = "-1 -1 2 2" id =
            "rectCircle" preserveAspectRatio="none">
            <circle cx="0" cy="0" r="1"
                opacity="0.5"/>
        </svg>
    </defs>
</svg>
```

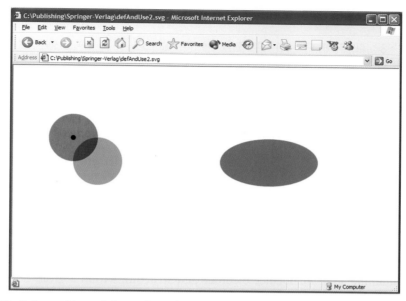

Figure 2.2 Define within a <defs> section only enough to specify the general fixed characteristics of a shape.

This definition could then be removed from the previous SVG file and then referenced through a file index (see Figure 2.2):

Listing 2.4.   defAndUse2.svg

```
<svg xmlns="http://www.w3.org/2000/svg"
  xmlns:xlink="http://www.w3.org/1999/xlink"
  width="500px" height="300px"
  viewBox="0 0 1000 600"
  >
  <circle cx="100" cy="200" r="50"
    fill="red"/>
  <use xlink:href="circle1.svg#rectCircle"
    x="100" y="200"
    width="100" height="100"
    fill="green"/>
  <use xlink:href="circle1.svg#rectCircle"
    x="400" y="200"
    width="200" height="100"
    fill="blue"/>
    <circle cx="100" cy="200" r="5"
      fill="black"/>
</svg>
```

Note that the cloning of elements or symbols is not the ideal way to do more sophisticated forms of inheritance, such as buttons with custom text. Alternative methods are dealt with in much greater detail later in this chapter.

2.2.3 <g>

The <g> element can alternatively be thought of a "g" for group or "g" for "graphicContext", although it is referred to in the SVG Recommendation as the group symbol. The <g> element has three distinct uses:

- **Grouping Related Content.** This is perhaps the most common usage, with the <g> element acting essentially like parentheses holding together other graphical elements into a cohesive unit. Significantly, <g> elements can retain their own *id* attributes, so these collections can be referenced from a <use> statement or from DOM.
- **Event/CSS Trap.** Applying a CSS attribute on a <g> element will apply the same attribute on all elements contained within the <g> element. This property is immensely useful in interactivity, where one can place an event handler on the <g> element containing a number of subordinate elements, and the contained elements will activate the event handler for the appropriate event.
- **Transformations.** One can apply matrix (affine) transformations on a <g> element, shifting its coordinate system. This is covered in more detail in Section 2.3.

As a simple grouping mechanism, the <g> element works remarkably well in maintaining some semblance of order and structure within a given document, especially because it can be labelled (through the *id* attribute).

2.2.4 <symbol>

A <symbol> is similar in most ways to <svg> except that whereas the contents of the <svg> element are automatically rendered, the contents of the <symbol> tag are only rendered through a <use> call. This makes the <symbol> element ideal for creating entities that need to be flexible (i.e., need to be defined outside the <defs> section) yet at the same time should not be initially rendered.

For instance, in symbol.svg, a smaller rotating diamond spins within a square, as shown in Figure 2.3:

Listing 2.5.   symbol.svg

```
<svg xmlns="http://www.w3.org/2000/svg"
  xmlns:xlink="http://www.w3.org/1999/xlink"
  width="500px" height="300px"
  viewBox="0 0 1000 600"
  >
  <symbol id="diamond" viewBox="-71 -71 142 142"
    preserveAspectRatio="none">
    <g transform="rotate(45)">
      <animateTransform attributeName =
        "transform"
        attributeType="XML"
        type="rotate" values="360;0"
        repeatCount="indefinite" dur="5s"/>
      <rect x="-50" y="-50"
        width="100" height="100"/>
    </g>
```

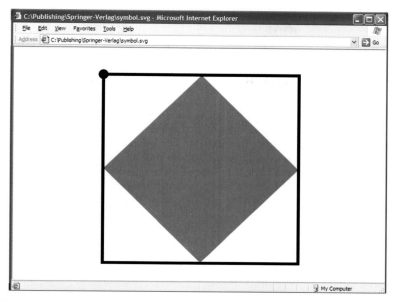

Figure 2.3 A <symbol> is a discrete XML group that can be defined without being immediately displayed.

```
</symbol>
    <use   xlink:href="#diamond"
        x="500" y="200"
        width="200" height="200"
        fill="red"/>
    <rect x="500" y="200"
        width="200" height="200"
        fill="none" stroke="black"
        stroke-width="3"/>
    <circle cx="500" cy="200" r="5"
        fill="black"/>
</svg>
```

Note that the coordinates for the <use> element and the <rect> are exactly the same. By taking advantage of the *preserveAspectRatio*="none" property that allows scaling, the symbol will automatically fit any rectangle that is specified by its *width*, *height*, *x* and *y* attributes.

2.2.5 <title>, <desc> and <metadata>

One of the more significant aspects of SVG is the ability to store contextual information at all levels of a particular document, information that effectively provides abstract motivation questions such as "What is this graphic supposed to be used for?", "How does this relate to other pieces in the library?" and "What does this particular sub-piece represent?"

The <title> element is perhaps the simplest of the three. With a text node content, <title> provides user-significant label to a graphic or sub-graphic. From the standpoint of the SVG document, the title provides a first-order abstraction that can be extracted by other applications. The SVG specification itself is careful not to enumerate how such a title is utilized, however, although it suggests that user agents may do things such as display tool tips during a mouse over or setting the title of the window showcasing the document (if the graphic is displayed independent of any external container such as an HTML document).

The <desc>, or *description*, element provides a useful tool for incorporating more complex documentation, particularly that which includes additional XML-based markup. For instance, suppose that you had an SVG document embedded within an HTML document (in this case illustrated with the Adobe SVG Viewer and special code, as few browsers yet support this). The description element can then be retrieved by any application that can parse this content.

The <metadata> element serves a similar, although not identical, purpose. The <desc> element provides a field for human-legible markup code (or resources), but the specific semantics within that code are up to the user. On the other hand, the <metadata> element is specifically set aside to provide metadata abstract information through a specific known metadata language such as the Resource Description Framework (RDF), most typically through the associated Dublin Core schema. This framework provides a specific set of tags that an RDF aware parser could use to retrieve specific information about a file.

The example shown in Listing 2.6 (Metadata.svg) illustrates the use of all three elements: <title>, <desc> and <metadata>. The example is a (starkly simple) traffic light that shifts between the three go/caution/stop lights. Notice how the title and the description provide basic usable information, but that the deeper information is kept within Dublin Core (dc: namespace) attributes:

Listing 2.6.   Metadata.svg

```
<svg
      xmlns="http://www.w3.org/2000/svg"
      xmlns:xlink="http://www.w3.org/1999/xlink"
      width="500px" height="500px"
      viewBox="0 0 500 500"
      preserveAspectRatio="none">
      <title>Stoplight</title>
      <desc>
          <div class="abstract"
            xmlns="http://www.w3.org/1999/xhtml">
          This is a stoplight object that rotates
            through the various states.
          </div>
      </desc>
      <metadata>
      <rdf:RDF xmlns:rdf="http://www.w3.org/1999/02/
          22-rdf-syntax-ns#"
              xmlns:rdfs="http://www.w3.org/2000/01/
                rdf-schema#"
              xmlns:dc="http://purl.org/dc/elements/
                1.1/">
```

```
            <rdf:Description about="http://example.
              org/myfoo"
            dc:title="Stoplight"
            dc:description="This is a very simple
              animated Stoplight"
            dc:publisher="Metaphorical Web
              Publishing"
            dc:date="2003-10-25"
            dc:format="image/svg+xml"
            dc:language="en"
            dc:creator="Kurt Cagle"/>
        </rdf:RDF>
    </metadata>
    <defs>
        <rect width="120" height="300"
            fill="#C08020" stroke="black"
            id="trafficLightBackground"/>
        <circle cx="60" cy="60" r="30"
            id="light"
            stroke="black" stroke-width="3"/>
    </defs>
    <g transform="translate(50,50)"
      onclick="alert(printNode(>
        <use xlink:href="#trafficLightBackground"
          x="0" y="0"/>
        <use xlink:href="#light" x="0" y="0"
          fill="maroon">
            <set attributeName="fill"
              attributeType="CSS"
                to="red" dur="2s"
                id="redLightOn"
                begin="yellowLightOn.end" />
        </use>
        <use xlink:href="#light" x="0" y="90"
          fill="#C0C000">
        <set attributeName="fill" attributeType="CSS"
          to="yellow" dur="2s"
          id="yellowLightOn"
          begin="greenLightOn.end"/>
        </use>
        <use xlink:href="#light" x="0" y="180"
          fill="darkGreen">
            <set attributeName="fill"
              attributeType="CSS"
                to="#80FF00" dur="2s"
                id="greenLightOn"
                begin="0s;redLightOn.end"/>
        </use>
    </g>
</svg>
```

Metadata content within SVG will have profound utility, as it will be possible to imbue semantics and abstraction into graphics at levels beyond the visual. At a bare minimum, it becomes possible to search graphics on the basis of non-graphical characteristics (find all graphics created by this person, all graphics updated from this date forward, all graphics that have these keywords in a specific keyword description field and so forth). It makes it much easier as well to create an audit history of changes to graphics, something that is key in areas such as cartography, and also interface design.

2.3 Manipulating Coordinate Systems

One of the more intriguing aspects of SVG was a conscious decision to make user coordinate systems possible not just for the root environment, but for any subordinate graphics. Put another way, the root document could define one coordinate system (say dividing the viewport into a square 1000 units on a side) while an inner <g> element could rotate this map by 45°, such that a unit square in the inner coordinate will appear as a diamond in the outer system. This succession of maps works well because of the encapsulated nature of XML – everything save the document node (the node itself, not just the first element encountered) has some parent that "owns" it, and hence could concievably share its coordinate system.

This advantage is not just a convenience of bookkeeping. Rotational and skew coordinate systems can often be computationally expensive to work with. A simple example illustrates this. Suppose that one wanted to draw a clockface. To do so in a purely rectangular system would require multiplying the position of each point by a set of four trigonometric values (six if you were attempting a skew). What is more, these values often do not have a lot of obvious intrinsic meaning, making it more difficult to maintain the code in the future.

On the other hand, if one is able to simply set the coordinate system for one element (say the tick mark indicating an hour), then perform rotations on that coordinate, this whole process emerges much more readily. Listing 2.7 and Figure 2.4 illustrate how this is accomplished:

Listing 2.7.   Rotation.svg

```
<svg
     xmlns="http://www.w3.org/2000/svg"
     xmlns:xlink="http://www.w3.org/1999/xlink"
     width="7in" height="7in"
     viewBox="0 0 1000 1000"
     preserveAspectRatio="none">
     <defs>
        <radialGradient id="clockBackFill">
            <stop offset="0%" stop-colour="blue"/>
            <stop offset="100%" stop-colour="navy"/>
        </radialGradient>
     <line x1="0" y1="0" x2="0" y2="-100"
        fill="none"
        id="clockLine"/>
     <circle cx="0" cy="0" r="100"
```

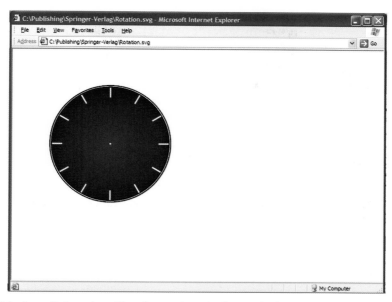

Figure 2.4 Controlled rotation of key elements in a circular coordinate can be accomplished with the rotation transformation.

```
    id="clockBack"/>
</defs>
<symbol id="clock"
    preserveAspectRatio="none"
    viewBox="-110 -110 220 220">
    <use xlink:href="#clockBack"
        stroke="black"
        stroke-width="3"
        fill="url(#clockBackFill)"/>
    <g stroke-dasharray="1 80 18 1"
        stroke="white"
        stroke-width="2">
        <use xlink:href="#clockLine"
            transform="rotate(0)"/>
        <use xlink:href="#clockLine"
            transform="rotate(30)"/>
        <use xlink:href="#clockLine"
            transform="rotate(60)"/>
        <use xlink:href="#clockLine"
            transform="rotate(90)"/>
        <use xlink:href="#clockLine"
            transform="rotate(120)"/>
        <use xlink:href="#clockLine"
            transform="rotate(150)"/>
        <use xlink:href="#clockLine"
            transform="rotate(180)"/>
```

```
                    <use xlink:href="#clockLine"
                        transform="rotate(210)"/>
                    <use xlink:href="#clockLine"
                        transform="rotate(240)"/>
                    <use xlink:href="#clockLine"
                        transform="rotate(270)"/>
                    <use xlink:href="#clockLine"
                        transform="rotate(300)"/>
                    <use xlink:href="#clockLine"
                        transform="rotate(330)"/>
                </g>
                <use xlink:href="#clockBack"
                    stroke="black"
                    stroke-width="4"
                    fill="none"/>
                <use xlink:href="#clockBack"
                    stroke="white"
                    stroke-width="1"
                    fill="none"/>
            </symbol>
            <use xlink:href="#clock" x="100" y="100"
                width="400" height="400"/>
</svg>
```

This illustrates a number of basic principles. Perhaps the first (and one not immediately obvious when dealing with the SVG specification) is that often the best way to understand an SVG document is to start from the bottom and work your way up. The next to-last line,

```
<use xlink:href="#clock" x="100" y="100" width="400"
    height="400"/>
```

draws a "clock" (although currently one without hands and just tick marks at the numbers' locations). The clock is defined to appear at position (100,100) relative to the local coordinate system, one which defines a $7'' \times 7''$ field as a 1000-unit square. Moreover, the width and height are both specified as 400 units. In other words, you get a pretty good indication here that the clock in question is scalable (and you would be right) – this in turn implies the use of either an <svg> element or a <symbol> element, with the latter being much more likely.

The <symbol id = "clock"> block in turn actually defines the clock:

```
<symbol id="clock"
    preserveAspectRatio="none"
    viewBox="-110 -110 220 220">
```

This specifies that the clock is scalable in both directions independently, and that the viewport is a box that starts at (-110, -110) and goes to (110,110) by adding 220 to each coordinate value. This describes a square centred on the origin and 220 user units wide and tall. Since the line involved is 100 pixels long, the overage is used to ensure a margin of width for the stroke; otherwise, the sides nearest the intersection of the square and the contained circle can appear unusually flat.

There are three <use> elements that all reference the #clockBack element, which is itself simply a circle centred on the origin with a radius of 100 units. In essence, this element (defined earlier in Section 2.2.2) provides only the geometry, with the custom elements that identify its presentation given with each <use> element. Three layers are in fact defined; the first draws the background of the clock, using a predefined radial gradient as a fill. The second and third use no fills, but specify two concentric strokes (or line characteristic), one black and 4 units wide, the second white and 1 unit wide.

The hour has marks are all contained within a <g> element that is used here to pass certain properties to all children that do not currently have those properties defined, such as setting a stroke-dasharray attribute and the stroke colour to white.

```
<g stroke-dasharray="1 80 18 1" stroke="white">
```

The stroke-dasharray attribute, by the way, is very useful. It lets you specify the patterns of drawn and skipped portions of a dashed line. In this particular case, the dasharray indicates that 1 pixel should be drawn, then 80 skipped, then 18 drawn, then 1 skipped, before the pattern repeats. This is a quick and rough way of specifying one line of a given length (here 100 pixels, a radius length), then customizing the line for drawing hash marks, an hour hand and a minute hand:

```
<g stroke-dasharray="1 80 18 1"
   stroke="white"
   stroke-width="2">
<use xlink:href="#clockLine"
   transform="rotate(0)"/>
<use xlink:href="#clockLine"
   transform="rotate(30)"/>
<use xlink:href="#clockLine"
   transform="rotate(60)"/>
..
<use xlink:href="#clockLine"
   transform="rotate(330)"/>
```

Each <use> statement then applies its own transformation. The first rotates the line (centred at the origin) by 0°, in essence performing an identity rotation, the second rotates by 30°, the third by 60°, and so forth to 330°.

This is the first instance encountered of the "transform" attribute. This powerful attribute changes the coordinate system of the object or of a group of objects if applied to a <g> element. This means that for

```
<use xlink:href="#clockLine"
   transform="rotate(30)"/>
```

the tick line is drawn in its own relative coordinate system as being a straight line, but the coordinate system itself is then transformed by a 30° rotation. The internal coordinate system does not know anything about this, by the way. This would be something akin to a classical physics problem where a person within a spaceship in orbit rotates around the Earth – the internal orientation of the person within the spaceship does not change (and the astronaut would not perceive any change), although from the outside, that person and the spaceship would appear to be rotating slowly as dictated by the orientation to the Earth.

2.4 Building Shapes and Paths

The graphical portion of SVG can effectively be broken down into three facets – geometric shapes, coordinate transformations and presentation (painting and stroking). The geometric piece of any graphic in turn can be thought of as either being simple shapes (such as rectangles or circles) and complex shapes (just about everything else). Within SVG, the simple shapes exist as a convenience mechanism – one can in fact do everything with a <path> element (the principle complex shape generator) including generating all of the more primitive shapes, but rectangles, circles, ellipses and the like are both common enough (and sometimes complex enough) that it is often easier to use custom interfaces for them.

2.4.1 Primitive Shapes

Primitive shapes usually have the advantage of being named shapes (such as rectangles or circles) and typically have a specialized interface that makes it easy to generate them in XML. For instance, a rectangle has six specialized geometric properties: *x*, *y*, *width*, *height*, *rx* and *ry*, with the last two specifying the x and y radii of ellipses used for rectangles with rounded corners. The same thing could be accomplished with the more general path statement, but the specific arc information would have to be passed into the path for the rounded corners, adding considerably to the complexity of the shape.

There are six primitive shapes in SVG: rectangles, circles, ellipses, lines, polylines and polygons. All six are shown in Listing 2.8 and Figure 2.5.

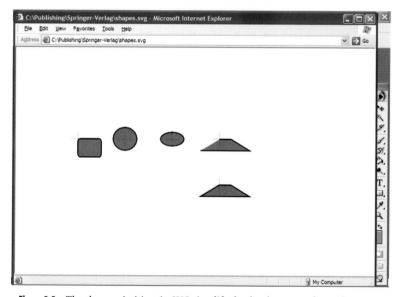

Figure 2.5   The shape primitives in SVG simplify the development of specific pieces.

Listing 2.8.   Shapes.svg.

```
<svg
     xmlns="http://www.w3.org/2000/svg"
     xmlns:xlink="http://www.w3.org/1999/xlink"
     width="1000" height="750"
     viewBox="0 0 1000 750" >
     <defs>
         <g id="crosshair" stroke="black" fill="none"
            stroke-width="1">
            <line x1="-30" y1="0" x2="30" y2="0"/>
            <line x1="0" y1="-30" x2="0" y2="30"/>
         </g>
     </defs>
     <g fill="red" stroke="black" stroke-width="4">
     <g transform="translate(100,100)">
         <rect x="0" y="0" width="100" height="80"
            rx="10" ry="15"/>
         <use xlink:href="#crosshair"/>
     </g>
     <g transform="translate(300,100)">
         <circle cx="0" cy="0" r="50"/>
         <use xlink:href="#crosshair"/>
     </g>
     <g transform="translate(500,100)">
         <ellipse cx="0" cy="0" rx="50" ry="30"/>
         <use xlink:href="#crosshair"/>
     </g>
         <g transform="translate(700,100)">
         <polyline points="0,0 50,0 130,50 -80,50"/>
         <use xlink:href="#crosshair"/>
     </g>
     <g transform="translate(700,300)">
         <polygon points="0,0 50,0 130,50 -80,50"/>
         <use xlink:href="#crosshair"/>
     </g>
     </g>
</svg>
```

The <line> element lets you specify the starting and ending points of the line (x1,y1)–(x2,y2). The circle, of course, provides the centre point as (cx,cy) and a radius r. Ellipses allow one to provide both a centre point (cx,cy) and the major (rx) and minor (ry) radii.

The difference between the <polyline> and <polygon> elements is more subtle. A <polyline> is defined to be opened, whereas the <polygon> is closed. This means that if you define a set of points where the starting point and the ending point are not the same, a <polygon> will automatically draw the line to complete the curve, whereas a <polyline> will not. Note that both will still fill the region the same.

This distinction can get you into trouble in the case where the starting and ending points do overlap. With a <polygon>, the curve will be joined together depending on the stroke-linejoin attribute (which will be "mitre", "round" or "bevel"), whereas with a polyline the points will be rendered with line-caps ("butt", "round" or "square"). Thus, if a polyline's starting point/ending point occurred at a non-right-angle, the end-points may appear to be barbed and otherwise not meet precisely (except for a "round" line-cap), whereas a polygon will meet properly in either a mitred edge or bevelled edge. Polylines and polygons have limited utility, and should generally be deprecated in favour of paths even if they are simpler to write.

2.4.2 Paths

The <path> element can provide all of the same functionality as any of the primitive shapes, although at the cost of more complexity (or the benefit of more control) in drawing the shapes. A path consists of a series of drawn lines, curves and skips which can include multiple enclosed regions and overlapping areas, and can be set to be both open and closed.

The key attribute of the path element is the *d* attribute (d for data), which in turn contains a sequence of space-separated coordinate pairs and commands. This particular format was chosen arguably because of the ease of parsing such strings compared with the equivalent XML nodes (although this argument is somewhat specious, in the author's opinion). This in turn creates a secondary language within SVG for specifying the datapoints.

A simple path is shown in Listing 2.9 and Figure 2.6:

Listing 2.9. simplePath.svg.

```
<svg xmlns="http://www.w3.org/2000/svg"
   xmlns:xlink="http://www.w3.org/1999/xlink" width="1000"
   height="750" viewBox="0 0 1000 750">
```

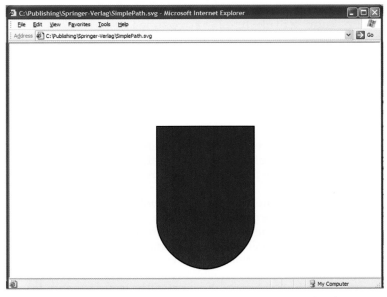

Figure 2.6   A simple path is one that does not break discontinuously.

```
<g transform="translate(100,100)">
    <path d="M0,0 L100,0 100,100 C100,125 75,150
       50,150 25,150
             0,125 0,100 L0,100z"
          fill="blue" stroke="black" stroke-
          width="1"/>
</g>
</svg>
```

One of the central concepts with paths is the notion of the "current point"(this is, in fact, a major aspect of SVG in general, but with paths it is most obvious). The current point prior to a path's beginning is the origin of the current graphical context. After each command (such as a move or the drawing of a line or curve), the new current point will be the resulting point of the command. Upon completion of the path, the current point returns to the graphic context origin.

It is noteworthy that most commands have both an absolute mode (given by an uppercase character) and a relative mode (lowercase). In the absolute mode, the coordinates given are the coordinates relative to the local coordinate system. In relative mode, however, the values provided are deltas, positions relative to the current point. Thus, a square would be rendered in absolute coordinates as

```
<path d="M0,0 L100,0 100,100 0,100 0,0z"/>
```

whereas the same path rendered in relative coordinates would be given as

```
<path d="m0,0 l100,0 0,100 -100,0 0, -100z"/>
```

Path *d* attributes can become fairly large, containing hundreds or even thousands of commands, and because of the complexity (and tedium) of building them, paths are usually best generated by some external application.

It is worth emphasizing that paths do not have to be connected. For instance, in ComplexPath.svg (see Listing 2.10 and Figure 2.7), the path consists of the tab from Listing 2.9 along with a second interior circle, drawn clockwise rather than counterclockwise. This direction change (also known as the winding) is used by SVG to compute whether or not a given point falls within or outside of a region, with clockwise windings being given a +1 and counterclockwise a −1; adding all of the windings between the "outside" the fill (that is, outside its bounding box) and the inside will determine whether a region is filled (typically with a non-zero winding) or empty (typically with a zero winding total).

Listing 2.10.   ComplexPath.svg.

```
<svg xmlns="http://www.w3.org/2000/svg"
   xmlns:xlink="http://www.w3.org/1999/xlink"
   width="1000" height="750" viewBox="0 0 1000 750">
       <g transform="translate(100,100)">
          <path d="M0,0 L100,0 100,100 C100,125 75,150
50,150 25,150 0,125 0,100 L0,100z
          M20,80 C20,95 35,110 50,110 65,110 80,95
80,80 80,65 65,50 50,50 35,50 20,65 20,80z"
```

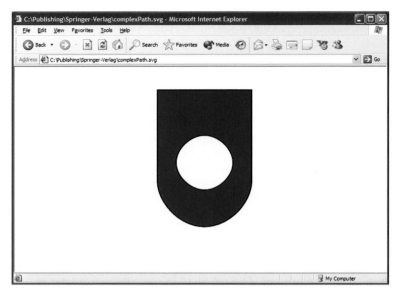

Figure 2.7   Within a complex path, you have the ability to set multiple disconnected regions.

```
          fill="blue" stroke="black" stroke-width="1"/>
     </g>
</svg>
```

Paths are important not just for creating simple shapes, but also for defining masks, filters and paths of animation, and indeed are the foundation upon which almost all graphics within SVG are actually accomplished. However, paths only provide the geometry – the presentation, accomplished through painting and drawing, turns that geometry into art.

2.5 Painting and Drawing

The principle means of adding presentation to this geometry comes through the use of three primary attributes, in addition to subordinate characteristics of these – the "fill", for painting the interior of a region, the "stroke", which determines the characteristics of the border of the region, and "opacity", which determines the degree of transparancy of the figure.

2.5.1 The "fill" Attribute and Paint Servers

The fill attribute determines what goes into the interior of a shape, regardless of whether than shape is closed or not. The fill goes beyond simply setting the colour of the region. Instead, the fill attribute makes use of Paint Servers to generate the contents of the displayed region. This server is in essence a program of some sort that generates content, such as a gradient fill or repeated pattern. By working with a paint server, the internal fill can actually be animated or respond interactively, making it far more dynamic than setting a static property would be.

The most basic such servers are the implicit colour servers; these define colours via a standardized set of names (such as "blue" or "aqua"), through a hex triplet (such as #00FFFF for that aqua), or through the use of the rgb() function [such as rgb(0,255,255) for the aforementioned aqua], as shown in Listing 2.11:

Listing 2.11.   Colors.svg

```
<svg xmlns="http://www.w3.org/2000/svg"
  xmlns:xlink="http://www.w3.org/1999/xlink"
  width="1000" height="750"
  viewBox="0 0 1000 750">
  <defs>
    <rect width="100" height="100" stroke="black"
      id="box"/>
  </defs>
  <use xlink:href="#box" x="100" y="100"
    fill="aqua"/>
  <use xlink:href="#box" x="300" y="100"
    fill="#00FFFF"/>
  <use xlink:href="#box" x="500" y="100"
    fill="rgb(0,255,255)"/>
</svg>
```

Up to SVG 1.1, colours were considered a special case where one did not need explicitly to invoke a server. However, the flipside to this is that it is marginally more difficult to define a new colour (although hardly impossible – one could just use a single-value gradient). SVG 1.2 defines a new element called <solidColor> that serves precisely this purpose, while additionally giving you better control over colour spaces. For instance, in Colors12.svg (Listing 2.12), the SVG document defines a solid colour called lime-green that can then be referenced indirectly via the url() function:

Listing 2.12.   Colors12.svg

```
<svg xmlns="http://www.w3.org/2000/svg"
  xmlns:xlink="http://www.w3.org/1999/xlink"
  width="1000" height="750" viewBox="0 0 1000 750">
    <defs>
      <rect width="100" height="100" stroke="black"
        id="box"/>
      <solidColor solid-colour="#12FFA0"
        id="limeGreen"/>
    </defs>
      <use xlink:href="#box" x="100" y="100"
        fill="url(#limeGreen)"/>
</svg>
```

2.5.2 Gradients

You can create more complex fills through the use of linear and radial gradient paint servers. A gradient server lets you create a sequence consisting of varying colours and opacities (called stops) that define the end-points and mid-points of blended colours. By parametrically locating these colours as offsets from 0 to 100%, you can precisely locate where these stops occur. For instance, Gradient1.svg in Listing 2.13 defines a blue/white gradient of varying opacities:

Listing 2.13.   Gradient1.svg

```
<svg xmlns="http://www.w3.org/2000/svg"
  xmlns:xlink="http://www.w3.org/1999/xlink" width="1000"
  height="750" viewBox="0 0 1000 750">
    <defs>
        <rect width="100" height="100" stroke="black"
          id="box"/>
        <linearGradient id="gradient1">
            <stop offset="0%" stop-colour="blue"
              stop-opacity="0.8"/>
            <stop offset="50%" stop-colour="white"
              stop-opacity="0.3"/>
            <stop offset="100%" stop-colour="navy"
              stop-opacity="0.6"/>
        </linearGradient>
    </defs>
    <use xlink:href="#box" x="100" y="100"
      fill="url(#gradient1)" stroke="black"/>
</svg>
```

One can similarly create radial gradients, with an offset of 0% corresponding to the centre of the circle and 100% being the distance to the bounding box edge, such as shown in Gradient2.svg (Listing 2.14):

Listing 2.14.   Gradient2.svg

```
<svg xmlns="http://www.w3.org/2000/svg"
  xmlns:xlink="http://www.w3.org/1999/xlink" width="1000"
  height="750" viewBox="0 0 1000 750">
    <defs>
        <rect width="100" height="100" stroke="black"
          id="box"/>
        <radialGradient id="gradient1">
            <stop offset="0%" stop-colour="blue"
              stop-opacity="0.8"/>
            <stop offset="50%" stop-colour="white"
              stop-opacity="0.3"/>
            <stop offset="100%" stop-colour="navy"
              stop-opacity="0.6"/>
        </radialGradient>
    </defs>
    <use xlink:href="#box" x="100" y="100"
      fill="url(#gradient1)" stroke="black"/>
</svg>
```

In addition to specifying stops, one can also specify a gradient transform. Such a transform acts only on the gradient itself, rather than on the shape to which the gradient belongs. Its principal purpose is to provide a means for rotating linear gradients, but it can also be used to generate offsets. Gradients are assumed to be generated on a unit square, so if you wished to shift the origin of a gradient (radial or linear) over by half the width, you would use an expression such as *gradientTransform = "translate(0.5,0)"*; see Listing 2.15:

Listing 2.15.   Gradient3.svg

```
<svg xmlns="http://www.w3.org/2000/svg"
   xmlns:xlink="http://www.w3.org/1999/xlink" width="1000"
   height="750" viewBox="0 0 1000 750">
     <defs>
         <rect width="100" height="100" stroke="black"
            id="box"/>
         <linearGradient id="gradient3" gradient
            Transform="rotate(50)">
             <stop offset="0%" stop-colour="red"
                stop-opacity="0.6"/>
             <stop offset="50%" stop-colour="yellow"
                stop-opacity="0.3"/>
             <stop offset="100%" stop-colour="maroon"
                stop-opacity="0.6"/>
         </linearGradient>
     </defs>
     <use xlink:href="#box" x="100" y="100"
        fill="url(#gradient3)" stroke="black"/>
</svg>
```

Currently, SVG defines only two gradients – linear and radial. It is possible to do shaped gradients by superposition of shapes (although this can be expensive in terms of memory), but there is no built-in provision to do this. However, it is possible to build composites of multiple semi-opaque gradients by using the <pattern> element. In the file gradientsCombined.svg (Listing 2.16 and Figure 2.8), the three gradients defined previously are placed into unit squares within a <pattern> element, creating a "gradient" with a much more organic feel to it.

Listing 2.16.   gradientsCombined.svg

```
<svg xmlns="http://www.w3.org/2000/svg"
   xmlns:xlink="http://www.w3.org/1999/xlink" width="100%"
   height="100%" viewBox="0 0 1000 750"
preserveAspectRatio="none">
     <defs>
         <rect width="100" height="100" stroke="black"
            id="box"/>
         <linearGradient id="gradient1">
             <stop offset="0%" stop-colour="blue"
                stop-opacity="0.8"/>
```

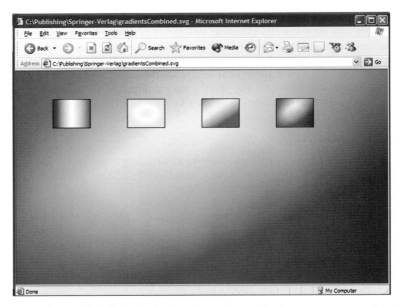

Figure 2.8 Gradients with differing levels of opacity can be combined to create more complex effects.

```
<stop offset="50%" stop-colour="white"
  stop-opacity="0.3"/>
<stop offset="100%" stop-colour="navy"
  stop-opacity="0.6"/>
</linearGradient>
<radialGradient id="gradient2">
  <stop offset="0%" stop-colour="yellow"
    stop-opacity="0.4"/>
  <stop offset="50%" stop-colour="white"
    stop-opacity="0.5"/>
  <stop offset="100%" stop-colour="orange"
    stop-opacity="0.3"/>
</radialGradient>
<linearGradient id="gradient3" gradient
  Transform="rotate(50)">
  <stop offset="0%" stop-colour="red"
    stop-opacity="0.6"/>
  <stop offset="50%" stop-colour="yellow"
    stop-opacity="0.3"/>
  <stop offset="100%" stop-colour="maroon"
    stop-opacity="0.6"/>
</linearGradient>
<pattern id="gradientFill" patternUnits=
  "objectBoundingBox" patternContentUnits=
  "objectBoundingBox">
  <rect x="0" y="0" width="1" height="1"
    fill="url(#gradient1)"/>
```

```
        <rect x="0" y="0" width="1" height="1"
          fill="url(#gradient2)"/>
        <rect x="0" y="0" width="1" height="1"
          fill="url(#gradient3)"/>
      </pattern>
  </defs>
  <rect x="0" y="0" width="1000" height="750"
    fill="url(#gradientFill)" stroke="none"/>
  <use xlink:href="#box" x="100" y="100"
    fill="white" stroke="black"/>
  <use xlink:href="#box" x="100" y="100"
    fill="url(#gradient1)" stroke="black"/>
  <use xlink:href="#box" x="300" y="100"
    fill="white" stroke="black"/>
  <use xlink:href="#box" x="300" y="100"
    fill="url(#gradient2)" stroke="black"/>
  <use xlink:href="#box" x="500" y="100"
    fill="white" stroke="black"/>
  <use xlink:href="#box" x="500" y="100"
    fill="url(#gradient3)" stroke="black"/>
  <use xlink:href="#box" x="700" y="100"
    fill="white" stroke="black"/>
  <use xlink:href="#box" x="700" y="100"
    fill="url(#gradientFill)" stroke="black"/>
</svg>
```

Although not in the current SVG 1.2 Working Draft, other gradients (such as stellar gradients, shaped gradients and cone gradients) are under consideration, and it is possible that the next Working Draft will more thoroughly specify a mechanism for implementing non-standard gradient (and other) paint servers.

2.5.3 Strokes and Drawing

Controlling line characteristics is essential in numerous different applications. SVG provides a number of central line properties, under the heading of strokes. Strokes can be applied to any line or shape, and are distinct from the fill properties.

The base *stroke* attribute sets the colour of the stroke, using the same kind of colour/paint servers as are used by fills. Although this means that you can colour strokes using the standard colour notations, it also means that you could use gradients and patterns to draw (and potentially animate) fills. These use the same url() functions as illustrated in the gradients section. In stroke1.svg (Listing 2.17 and Figure 2.9), this is shown by using the blue/white linear gradient:

Listing 2.17. Stroke1.svg

```
<svg xmlns="http://www.w3.org/2000/svg"
  xmlns:xlink="http://www.w3.org/1999/xlink"
  width="100%" height="100%" viewBox="0 0 1000 750"
  preserveAspectRatio="none">
```

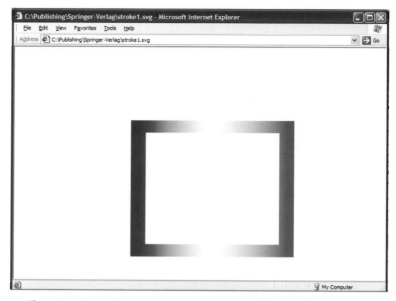

Figure 2.9   It is possible to apply gradients and other fill properties to a stroke.

```
<defs>
    <rect width="100" height="100" id="box"/>
    <linearGradient id="gradient1">
        <stop offset="0%" stop-colour="blue"
            stop-opacity="0.8"/>
        <stop offset="50%" stop-colour="white"
            stop-opacity="0.3"/>
        <stop offset="100%" stop-colour="navy"
            stop-opacity="0.6"/>
    </linearGradient>
</defs>
<use xlink:href="#box" x="100" y="100"
    fill="white" stroke="url(#gradient1)"/>
</svg>
```

Stroke width (via the *stroke*-width attribute) is defined such that the half-width of the stroke starts from the mid-point of the line, as would be expected, have any line will always be half within and half outside the boundary of a given shape. When one establishes the stroke-width, this width will be defined both vertically and horizontally in the appropriate coordinate system. Consequently, if one has a coordinate system where one unit of width is half the measure of one unit of height, the line will be wide in a vertical direction and narrow in a horizontal one.

The stroke-dasharray, covered Section 2.3, provides the sequence of drawn versus skipped segments of a line. Significantly, one can animate this sequence to create the marquee (or crawling ants) effect that signifies selection is many graphical applications.

The stroke attributes in general assume a fixed-width line. Although it is possible with subsequent versions of SVG that a line-width server could be created, in general variable line-widths currently would need to be accomplished via shaped fills.

2.5.4 Opacity and Visibility

Opacity controls the degree of transparency of a particular element or group of elements, and ranges from a value of 0.0 (completely transparent) to 1.0 (completely opaque). The *opacity* attribute, used on any visible element, will determine the opacity for all aspects of that element, with partially transparent elements showing some portion of the underlying graphics behind (in general before in the XML tree) this particular element.

Opacity can be subdivided further into *stroke-opacity*, which controls the opacity only of the stroke attribute, and *fill-opacity*, which controls the opacity of the fill. Note that such opacities are defined as multiplier on any internal opacity – thus, if a gradient fill is created with a *stop-opacity* of 0.8 and the element using that fill has an *opacity* of 0.4, then the total *stop-opacity* at that point in the gradient would be 0.8×0.4 or 0.32.

Opacity does not change the behaviour of events acting on the region of a shape. Thus, if you set the fill-opacity of a shape to 0.0 and the fill colour to "white", the fill will be completely transparent, but clicking on the fill region will still initiate an onclick event. On the other hand, if the fill colour is set to "none", then regardless what the fill-opacity is, the onclick event will pass through this particular shape to the next receptive region.

A related property to *opacity* is the *visibility* attribute. This can take on the value "visible" or "hidden", with the first being displayed and the second not. The *visibility* attribute does explicitly set mouse behaviours – an element with *visibility* of "visible" will receive mouse events, whereas one with a visibility of hidden will not.

The ability to work with text is a critical feature of any graphics language, especially one with as strong a metadata capability as SVG offers. The features of SVG 1.0 and 1.1 provide control over single lines of text at a time, although it is possible to create blocks of text through positioning of subtext elements. SVG 1.2 will offer much richer capabilities with respect to text manipulation, to the extent of providing text wrapping, text filling specific shapes and text flowing from one region to another.

2.6 The Core Text Elements

Text capabilities in SVG are controlled via the <text> element, which provides a general container for textual data. This element serves both as a unit for specifying text characteristics (although it can also inherit them from <g> containers) and as a wrapper that indicates that the only content contained within is text.

Text content in turn may be given either as a sequence of text characters (or CDATA delimited characters) or as a collection of <tspan> or <tref> elements (or both). In general, after a character or subordinate block is rendered, the next character in the sequence will appear next in line to what was just drawn, until all characters within the <text> element are given.

This is illustrated in Listing 2.18 and Figure 2.10. The main text block contains a sequence of characters, a <tspan> element, a <tref> element and another sequence of characters, all of which are rendered (using different styles) on the same line.

Listing 2.18.   Text1.svg

```
<svg xmlns="http://www.w3.org/2000/svg"
    xmlns:xlink="http://www.w3.org/1999/xlink"
    width="100%" height="100%" viewBox="0 0 1000 750"
    preserveAspectRatio="none">
        <def>
            <text id="referred">This is a referred block
                of text.</text>
        </def>
        <g transform="translate(100,100)">
            <rect x="0" y="0" width="500" height="400"
                fill="none" stroke="cyan"/>
            <text>This is a block of text.
                <tspan font-weight="bold">Here is another
                    block of text.</tspan>
                <tref xlink:href="#referred" font-
                    style="italic"/>
                A final bit of text.
            </text>
        </g>
</svg>
```

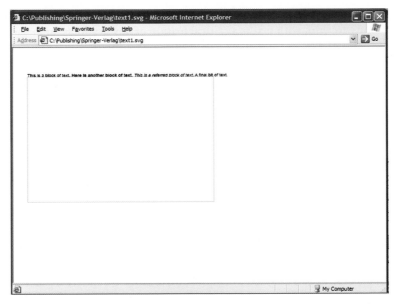

Figure 2.10   Text within a <text> element flows toward the ending side of the viewbox.

The <tspan>, or text span, element serves as a way to change the specific characteristics of a given sequence of characters within a text block, such as setting the font-weight of the font to bold only within the span. The <tref> element, on the other hand, retrieves its content from the text of some previously defined (and named) <text> block, possibly residing within a <defs> block. Both the <tspan> and <tref> elements can take individual x and y attribute values that allow you to position these blocks as appropriate.

2.6.1 Text and CSS

All text within SVG makes use of the CSS text attributes, although it also defines a number of new ones for tighter and more detailed control of text presentation. Table 2.1 provides a list of the primary CSS text attributes applicable to fonts, showing how they are used.

Table 2.1 CSS text attributes related to fonts

Attribute name	Examples	Description
font-size	font-size = "24" font-size = "0.25in" font-size = "32pt"	Sets the x-height size of the font to the given value. If no units are given, user coordinates are assumed
font-family	font-family = "Arial" font-size = "Arial, Helvetica"	Sets the font used. Subsequent fonts are queried until a match is found
font-variant	font-variant = "normal" font-variant = "small-caps"	Determines whether small-cap fonts are used on text
font-weight	font-weight = "bold" font-weight = "600" font-weight = "bolder"	Defines the weight (blackness) of a given font, using either comparative values (bold), numeric analogues (700 on a scale of 900) or relative measures ("bolder" than the current font weight)
font-stretch	font-stretch = "normal" font-stretch = "condensed" font-stretch = "expanded"	Expands or compresses the rendering of the font and the spaces in between according to the attribute directive
font-size-adjust	font-size-adjust = "10"	Sets the height for secondary fonts
font	font = "bold italic 0.25in Helvetica"	Combines multiple font directives in a single statement
kerning	kerning = "auto" kerning = "0"	Indicates whether the font should use kerning (spacing) that is part of the font-table, or to disable it and use a manual space (typically 0)
letter-spacing	letter-spacing = "0" letter-spacing = "5pt" letter-spacing = "−5pt"	Indicates the amount of additional space to add (or remove) between letters beyond that specified by kerning
word-spacing	word-spacing = "0" word-spacing = "5pt" word-spacing = "−5pt"	Indicates the amount of additional space to add (or remove) between words within the text expression

(continued)

Table 2.1   (*continued*)

Attribute name	Examples	Description
text-decoration	text-decoration = "underline" text-dec. = "overline" text-dec. = "line-through" text-dec. = "blink" text-dec. = "none"	Sets the text decorations (line behaviours for specific text), sets text blinking (although not on all systems) or disables this
text-anchor	text-anchor = "start" text-anchor = "middle" text-anchor = "end"	Determines where the text begins from within the bounding box of that text. This is useful for positioning in buttons and related code
baseline	baseline = "alphabetic | ideographic | hanging | mathematical | central | middle | text-before-edge | text-after-edge | before-edge | after-edge | top | text-top | bottom | text-bottom"	Determines how the text is displayed with respect to the current coordinate point when the graphics are rendered
dominate-baseline	as above	Sets the characteristic baseline location for text in the current context
alignment-baseline	as above	Sets how the text aligns with its parent
direction	direction = "ltr" direction = "rtl"	For bidirectional (bidi) text, sets the direction of that text
Unicode-bidi	unicode-bidi = "normal" unicode-bidi = "embed" unicode-bidi = "bidi-override"	Sets whether the text involved responds to bidirectional control
baseline-shift	baseline-shift = "baseline" baseline-shift = "sub" baseline-shift = "super" baseline-shift = "80%"	Used for placing subscripts or superscripts within text

The text characteristics fall into two basic groups. The attributes *text-anchor* and *baseline* (and its extensions *dominant-baseline* and *alignment-baseline*) control the position of the text within the text's bounding box. In particular, a *text-anchor* value of "start" indicates that the text is positioned to the left of the bounding box specified by the <text> element's width, *if* the text goes from left to right. If the text is oriented in the other direction (as is the case with certain Arabic languages), then the start value will be the rightmost point. A *text-anchor* of "middle" will centre the text within the specified width, making this value useful for creating buttons and other centred content.

The *baseline* attributes, on the other hand, control the vertical positioning of the text, with respect to the baseline used to render content. A baseline of "alphabetic", for instance, assumes that text is drawn so that the line at the y position is drawn so that it passes through the base of a lowercase 'x'. A baseline of 'central' will place it so that the text is centred within the bounding box of the text. Thus, if you wanted to create a box with text centred within the box, you could use a combination of baseline and text-anchor to control it is position, as shown in Text2.svg (see Listing 2.19 and Figure 2.11):

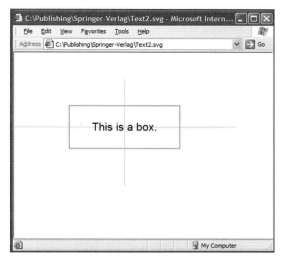

Figure 2.11 Use of the *text-anchor* and *dominant-baseline* attributes lets you control the relative position of text within its environment.

Listing 2.19.   Text2.svg

```
<svg xmlns="http://www.w3.org/2000/svg"
  xmlns:xlink="http://www.w3.org/1999/xlink"
  width="1000" height="750"
  viewBox="0 0 1000 750">
    <g transform="translate(100,100)">
      <rect x="0" y="0" width="200" height="80"
        fill="white" stroke="black"/>
      <line x1="-100" y1="40" x2="300" y2="40"
        stroke="lightBlue"/>
      <line x1="100" y1="-50" x2="100" y2="150"
        stroke="lightBlue"/>
      <text x="100" y="40" text-anchor="middle"
        dominant-baseline="mathematical"
        font-size="20">
        This is a box.
    </text>
    </g>
</svg>
```

This places the text so that if you drew a line through the mid-points of each side of the bounding box, the centre would also pass through the weighted centre of the text's mid-point.

The second set of CSS attributes actually affect the presentation of the font itself. Many of these attributes correspond directly to CSS presentation attributes used by HTML – *font-weight*, *font-family*, *font-size*, and so forth, although font-size in particular should be clarified in SVG to include user units – font-size = "12" will set the x-height (the height of a lower case "x") to 12 user units, which may be any absolute size depending on the user coordinate system. On the other hand, a font-size of "12pt" will be 12 points (one-sixth of an inch) regardless of the current coordinate system.

The set of CSS attributes also includes attributes that affect the spacing of letters and words – *font-stretch* will expand or contract the characters (and spaces) of the font itself, while *kerning* will set the space between letters – setting kerning to *auto* will tell the system to utilize the built in kerning table that is associated with many fonts, but one can also override this and set it to a specific value (setting it to zero essentially disables kerning outright).

2.6.2 Glyphs

One of the more intriguing aspects of SVG comes from the fact that a font definition is simply a set of path instructions for specifying the boundaries of the letter, along with spacing and kerning information for that set of paths. SVG consequently makes it possible to define individual font-characters, known as *glyphs*, and also whole fonts from these glyphs, which can then be referenced like any other font.

Unlike a symbol, a glyph can only be defined in the context of a font, although it is not necessary to define all possible characters in that font. A small sample of a font can be seen in Listing 2.20 and Figure 2.12.

Listing 2.20. Glyphs.svg (fragment)

```
<svg xmlns="http://www.w3.org/2000/svg"
   xmlns:xlink="http://www.w3.org/1999/xlink"
   xml:space="preserve" width="8.5in" height="11in"
   viewBox="0 0 8500 11000">
<defs>
```

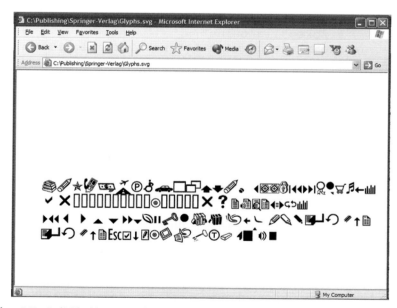

Figure 2.12   Individual letters, or glyphs, can be created and assigned for use in any text block.

```
<!-- define the font Bookdings -->
<font id="FontID0" fullFontName="Bookdings"
  fontVariant="normal" fontWeight="400">
<!-- identify the name of the font-face -->
   <font-face font-family="Bookdings">
   </font-face>
<!-- create a glyph for those letters that aren't
  in the font definition -->
<missing-glyph><path d="M0 0z"/></missing-glyph>
<!-- glyph for capital A -->
<glyph unicode="A" horiz-adv-x="1001"><path d="M963
  174l-246 -222c-3,-6 -6,-15 -15,-27 -9,-9 -21,-15
  -33, -12 -6,0 -15,3 -24,9l-561 147c-6,9 -18,24
  -30,45 -6,21 -9,39 -6,60 3,27 9,48 21,60 6,6 15,12
  27,21l3 15c-3,6 -12,18 -18,36 -6,15 -6,30 -6,48 0,
  21 6,45 18,63 12,18 33,33 63,45l3 15c-21,12 -30,33
  -30,66 0,18 12,39 42,60l18 0 3 12 285 114 399 -165
  0 -18 -18 -6c3,-9 3, -18 6,-33 0,-9 3,-18 6,-30
  3,-6 6,-9 12,-15l21 3 3 -30 -18 -6c-3,-12 -3,-24
  -3,-30 3,-15 9,-24 15,-27 6,-3 12,-6 21,-6l9 -33
  12 -24 -21 -18c0,-6 3,-21 3,-36 3,-9 3,-15 6,-24
  0,-6 3,-12 9,-18 3,-3 9,-6 18,-9l6 -30zm-117
  264c-3,6 -6,12 -9,21 -3,9 -3,24 0,42 0,6 0,15
  3,27l-249 -114c-3,-6 -6,-18 -9,-30 -3,-18 0,-33 6,
  -45 3,-6 9,-12 18,-18l240 117zm-33 117l-330 147
  -240 -102 345 -156 225 111zm78 -216c-3,3 -6,6
  -12, 12 -6,6 -12,15 -15,27 -3,9 -6,18 -6,30l-210
  -126c-9, -27 -15,-45 -12,-60 3,-15 9,-27 18,-42
  6,-6 15,-15 27,-24l210 183zm33 -153c-6,0 -12,6
  -21,12 -3,3 -9,12 -15,30 0,6 -3,15 -9,30l-189
  -165c-3,-6 -6,-15 -12,-27 -3,-15 0,-33 6,-51 3,-9
  9,-21 18,-33l222 204zm-375 240l-360 147c-3,0 -9,
  -6 -18,-12 -9,-12 -12,-21 -9,-33 0,-6 3,-9 6,
  -18l375 -171c0,6 0,18 -3,33 0,18 0,30 3,36 0,6
  3,12 6,18zm81 -276c-3,6 -12,15 -21,33 -9,15 -12,
  36 -12,57 3,12 6,30 12,51l-483 126c-3,-6 -12,
  -21 -18,-42 -6,-21 -9,-36 -6,-45 3,-9 9,-21 18,
  -33l510 -147zm-384 270l-69 30 -21 -12 90 -18zm432 -
  471c-6,9 -12,21 -21,36 -3,18 -9,33 -9,48 0,15
  0,39 6,66l-525 147c-6,-6 -15,-18 -30,-36 -6,-15
  -12,-33 -12,-54 0,-15 6,-33 15,-57l567 -159 9 9zm81
  600l-159 -66 -15 12 84 45 -18 6 -105 -42 -18 12
  66 54 -18 12 -90 -42 -12 6 45 54 -15 6 -96 -36 -9
  9 63 45 -18 6 -93 -33 -9 6 129 63 288 -117zm-453
  -45l-3 -12 -90 30c0,6 0,9 0,12 3,3 6,6 9,9l84 -
  39zm273 -255l-441 105c-3,6 -3,12 -3,15 0,3 3,9
  6,12l438 -111 0 -21zm33 -165l-6 -9 -483 99c0,12
  0,21 0,27 3,6 6,12 12,21l477 -138z"/></glyph>
<!-- glyph for capital B -->
<glyph unicode="B" horiz-adv-x="955"><path d="M786
  582c-21,12 -51,27 -90,48 -33,9 -66,18 -99,27l-138
```

```
        -27 -132 -57 -21 42 3 108c18,9 39,21 69,36 42,18
        69,27 87,27 9,0 24,0 42,0 18,-3 33,-3 45,-3 39,0
        96,-21 168,-66l66 -135zm12 -27l0 -339 -27 -33 -57
        -36 -6 -45 -141 -6 -90 24 -18 33 -69 6 -51 60 -3
        342c36,18 84,36 144,60 9,3 51,9 120,24 24,-6 63,
        -18 117,-36 21,-12 48,-30 81,-54zm144 -555l-30 0
        -168 141 12 3 186 -144zm-48 0l-60 0 -120 114 0 27
        18 -9 162 -132zm-567 255l-33 27c0,-30 -6,-45 -
        21,-45 0,0 -3,3 -3,3 -18,15 -27,39 -27,78l-117
        87c-6,-9 -12,-15 -15,-15 -3,0 -3,3 -3,3 -9,6 -15,
        21 -21,39l-42 36 0 33 105 96 147 117 -3 -105 33
        -51 0 -303zm-96 33l-99 81 3 18 93 -72 3 -27zm303
        -288l-36 0 -459 444 6 3 489 -447zm-69 0l-90 0 -357
        441 12 3 435 -444zm267 642l-48 69 -126 0 6 -36c21,0
        51,-6 93,-12 18,-6 42,-12 75,-21zm-177 108c0,15 -6,
        21 -21,21 -15,0 -21,-6 -21,-21 0,-12 6,-21 21, -21
        15,0 21,9 21,21zm189 -423l0 225 -117 57 0 -276 117
        -6zm-222 348l-6 33 -168 -9 -9 -54 21 -33c15,9 42,
        24 78,39 21,6 51,15 84,24zm81 -345l0 276 -132 -39
        0 -246 132 9zm156 -87c0,15 -9, 21 -21,21 -15,0 -
        21,-6 -21,-21 0,-15 6,-21 21,-21 12, 0 21,6 21,
        21zm0 45l0 15 -105 -9 -60 0 -159 6 -3 -18 162 -12
        63 0 102 18zm-504 258l0 99 -42 -33 0 -78 42 12zm285
        -306c0,15 -6,21 -21,21 -15,0 -21,-6 -21,-21 0,-15
        6,-21 21,-21 15,0 21,6 21,21zm-345 288l0 72 -27 -21
        0 -57 27 6zm108 12l-246 -66 0 0 243 45 3 21zm-153
        30l-21 -18 0 -42 21 6 0 54zm-33 -24l-36 -24 0 -24
        36 12 0 36zm186 -225l-234 141 24 -18 207 -135 3
        12zm423 195l-84 30 0 24 84 -33 0 -21zm-3 -54l-78
        24 -3 21 81 -21 0 -24zm0 -54l-75 15 0 21 75 -18 0
        -18zm-141 144l-99 -27 0 18 99 30 0 -21zm138 -
        195l-75 9 0 15 75 -9 0 -15zm-138 132l-90 -18 0 15
        90 21 0 -18zm-3 -39l0 -21 -87 -12 0 15 87 18zm3
        -84l-87 -9 0 15 87 15 0 -21z"/></glyph>
    <!-- glyph for capital C -->
    <glyph unicode="C" horiz-adv-x="692"><path d="M681
        441l-207 -153 78 -243 -207 150 -210 -150 81 243
        -207 153 255 0 81 246 78 -246 258 0zm-66 -21l-192
        0 -78 -75 270 75zm-270 -75l0 285 -60 -189 60
        -96zm159 -234l-60 180 -99 51 159 -231zm-159 234l
        -279 78 165 -123 114 45zm0 -126l0 123 -153 -228
        153 105z"/></glyph>
    <!-- additional glyphs defined for remaining
  characters -->
</font>
    <!-- Create a style association for ease of binding -->
<style type="text/css">
    <![CDATA[
        @font-face { font-family:"Bookdings";src:url
        ("#FontID0") format(svg)}
```

```
        .fil0 {fill:#1F1A17}
        .fnt0 {font-weight:normal;font-size:333;
          font-family:Bookdings}
   ]]>
</style>
</defs>
<g id="Layer 1">
   <!-- Use the font invoked through the class -->
  <text x="559" y="2663" class="fil0
   fnt0">ANCDEFGHIJKLMNOPQRSTUVWXYz</text>
  <text x="559" y="3011" class="fil0
   fnt0">abcdefghjikl;mnopqrstuvwxyz</text>
  <text x="559" y="3358" class="fil0
   fnt0">1234567890!@#$%^&amp;*()-_=+[{</text>
  <text x="559" y="3706" class="fil0 fnt0">-
   _=+[{]}\|;:&apos;&quot;,,&lt;.&gt;/?</text>
</g>
</svg>
```

The <font> element here differs considerably from the HTML <font> element, which existed pre-CSS to provide some basic hints for formatting HTML content. In SVG, the <font> tag serves to identify a complete font definition. In this particular case, it identifies the name of the font "Bookdings" and indicates that it is a normal (as opposed to italic or oblique) font, and that it corresponds to a fontWeight of 400 (which is defined as normal, compared with bold at 700). This section also identifies the font-family with which this font is associated, which is useful if you have an italic, bold or extra-heavy (usually referred to as "black") font in addition to your default "medium" font – all of them would have the same font-family, even though the name of the font itself may change:

```
<font id="FontID0" fullFontName="Bookdings"
   fontVariant="normal" fontWeight="400">
<!-- identify the name of the font-face -->
     <font-face font-family="Bookdings">
     </font-face>
```

Once this has been defined, the next stage is creating a glyph representing characters that are not within the listed glyphs. This is accomplished with the <missingGlyph>, which lets you specify a shape (or even a null path such as d="m0,0"):

```
<missing-glyph><path d="M0 0z"/></missing-glyph>
```

The <glyph>elements themselves identify the character with which each glyph is associated, and also the character-set of which this is a part, then specifies one or more graphical elements (they will usually be path sets if autogenerated, but this is not a strict requirement). For the letter "A", a specific glyph might look as follows:

```
<glyph unicode="A" horiz-adv-x="1001"><path d="M963
   1741-246 -222c-3,-6 -6,-15 -15,-27 -9,-9 -21,-15 -33,
   -12 -6,0 -15,3 -24,91-561 147c- ..."/></glyph>
```

The Unicode character will either be a letter or a numeric entity (such as a) which will then be given in the <text> section later in this form as well. Note that if you map named entities to specific characters through a DTD, then you can actually use glyph entities to replace more complex graphical entities, especially relating to inline graphics.

The ability to work with glyphs gives you the ability to create fonts that are portable between platforms. It is also noteworthy to consider that such fonts can be made to be animatable (and interactive) at the glyph level, opening up the possibilities of intelligent letters and other truly unique "artforms" that have not yet been explored because there was no real technology to do so.

2.7 Animating Graphics and Interactivity

Animation in SVG was something of a novelty that has nonetheless radically affected the development of the language for good and ill. Animation should be thought of as a short-hand term for a set of five distinct capabilities that SVG has supported from the beginning:

- **Movement and Distortion.** Changing the location, rotation, scale or other coordinate-based property either continuously or discretely based on time.
- **Property Change.** Changing certain CSS properties, such as opacity, to different values either continuously or discretely over time.
- **Colour Animation.** Being able to set colours for fills, strokes, gradients, etc.
- **Image Animation.** Repeatedly changing referenced images over time.
- **Interactivity.** Performing some other animation based on user input devices such as the mouse or keyboard.

2.7.1 The Flavors of Animation

One of the more novel aspects of SVG animation is the fact that it is accomplished predominantly via XML. In essence, an animation is a child element that is added to a given shape element or group. For instance, Listing 2.21 and Figure 2.13 illustrate the effects of animating position, movement along a path, rotations and changing of colours:

Listing 2.21.   animatedSquares.svg

```
<svg xmlns:svg="http://www.w3.org/2000/svg"
  xmlns:xlink="http://www.w3.org/1999/xlink"
  width="1000" height="750" viewBox="0 0 1000 750"
  preserve-aspect-ratio="none"
  >
<defs>
    <rect x="-50" y="-50" width="100" height="100"
      stroke="black" id="box"/>
    <rect x="-50" y="-50" width="100" height="100"
      stroke="black" id="box"/>
    <path d="m0,0 m-133.33,-133.33 l133.33,-133.3
      0,266.67z" id="triangle"/>
```

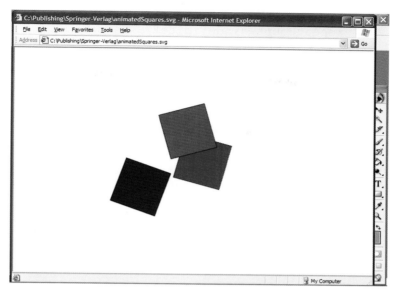

Figure 2.13 Combine offsets in timing with variable durations to provide the illusion of "random" motion.

```
    </defs>
      <g transform="translate(100,100)">
        <use xlink:href="#box" x="0" y="0" fill="red">
          <animateTransform attributeName="transform"
            attributeType="xml" type="rotate"
            begin="0s" dur="1s" from="0" to="360"
              repeatCount="indefinite"/>
          <animateMotion path="m0,0 C100,0 150,100 150,150
            150,200 200,250 250,250 275,250 300,200 300,150
            300,100 250,50 200,50 L50,50 C25,50 0, 25 0,0z"
            begin="0s" dur="4s" repeatCount="indefinite"/>
          <animateColor attributeName="fill"
            attributeType="CSS" values="red;blue;green;
            yellow;red" begin="0s" dur="6s"
            repeatCount="indefinite"/>
        </use>
        <use xlink:href="#box" x="0" y="0" fill="blue">
          <animateTransform attributeName="transform"
            attributeType="xml" type="rotate"
            begin="0s" dur="1s" from="360" to="0"
              repeatCount="indefinite"/>
          <animateMotion path="m0,0 C100,0 150,100 150,150
            150,200 200,250 250,250 275,250 300,200 300,150
            300,100 250,50 200,50 L50,50 C25,50 0,25 0,0z"
            begin="3s" dur="5s" repeatCount="indefinite"/>
          <animateColor attributeName="fill"
            attributeType="CSS" values="blue;green;
```

```
        yellow;red;blue" begin="2s" dur="6s"
        repeatCount="indefinite"/>
    </use>
    <use xlink:href="#box" x="0" y="0" fill="green">
        <animateTransform attributeName="transform"
          attributeType="xml" type="rotate"
          begin="0s" dur="1.5s" from="360" to="0"
            repeatCount="indefinite"/>
        <animateMotion path="m0,0 C100,0 150,100
          150,150 150,200 200,250 250,250 275,250
          300,200 300,150 300,100 250,50 200,50
          L50,50 C25,50 0,25 0,0z" begin="4s"
          dur="7s" repeatCount="indefinite"/>
        <animateColor attributeName="fill"
          attributeType="CSS" values="green;yellow;red;
          blue;green" begin="3.5s" dur="6s"
          repeatCount="indefinite"/>
    </use>
  </g>
</svg>
```

In this particular drawing, three rotating squares perform an intricate dance, following a custom path, each changing colours and positions according to its own schedule.

All of these are specializations off the two primary animation elements – <set> and <animate>. The set control provides one time animation based on some external event or interaction. For instance, suppose that you wanted to have a square change its fill colour, first to blue from red after 3 seconds, then to yellow from blue after 6 seconds. Ignoring the <svg> declarations, this would look something like the following:

```
<rect x="0" y="0" width="100" height="100" fill="red">
    <set attributeName="fill" attributeType="CSS"
      to="blue" begin="3s" fill="freeze"/>
    <set attributeName="fill" attributeType="CSS"
      to="yellow" begin="6s" fill="freeze"/>
</rect>
```

The <set> element is used to perform discrete transitions from one state to another. The example given here sets the fill of the rectangle first to blue and then to yellow. Note the use of the *fill* attribute within the <set> element itself. This use of *fill* has nothing to do with the fill property that established the paint server for a given shape; instead, it is actually inherited from the SMIL *fill* attribute which can take the value of either "freeze" or "restore". If set to "freeze", this property indicates that the object (or group) being changed should retain this state until it is next explicitly changed, whereas if *fill* is set to "restore", then once the animation completes, the state should revert to what it was prior to the animation being called.

The <animate> element handles continuous transitions between states of a given property. As with the <set> element, the attribute to be changed is given in the *attributeName* field. The *attributeType* is more problematic. Its intent is to signal whether the attribute to be changed is a CSS attribute (and hence has some immediate effect upon the environment) and an XML attribute, which may not have the same effect. In practice it is something of a nuisance, although it can be useful when changing attributes that are not specifically tied the SVG Document Object Model.

For instance, the following would cause the opacity of a square to go from 1 to 0 and back to 1 over a course of 6 seconds:

```
<rect x="0" y="0" width="100" height="100" fill="red">
    <animate attributeName="opacity" attributeType=
        "CSS" values="1;0;1" begin="0s" dur="6s"
        fill="replace"/>
</rect>
```

The key here is the *values* attribute. You can set transitional values in an animation by giving each value in turn separated by a semicolon. These will be set at evenly spaced intervals, although other properties can modify this.

The elements <animateColor>, <animateMotion> and <animateTransform> utilize these same properties, with a few additional ones as appropriate. For instance, the <animateTransform> element has you set the *attributeName* to "transform" (or "gradientTransform" if transforming a gradient fill) and then uses the second attribute *type* to indicate the type of transformation – translation, rotation, scaling, skew and so forth.

The <animateMotion> element lets you specify a given path (or path reference) for motion along this path. This can be seen in Listing 2.21, part of which is repeated here:

```
<use xlink:href="#box" x="0" y="0" fill="red">
<animateTransform attributeName="transform"
    attributeType="xml" type="rotate"
    begin="0s" dur="1s" from="0" to="360"
      repeatCount="indefinite"/>
<animateMotion path="m0,0 C100,0 150,100 150,150
    150,200 200,250 250,250 275,250 300,200 300,150
    300,100 250,50 200,50 L50,50 C25,50 0,25 0,0z"
    begin="0s" dur="4s" repeatCount="indefinite"/>
<animateColor attributeName="fill" attributeType=
    "CSS" values="red;blue;green;yellow;red"
    begin="0s" dur="6s" repeatCount="indefinite"/>
</use>
```

In this case, the *path* attribute contains a complex path that illustrates the motion of the square over a 4-second period. The path is not rendered, but instead just serves as the trajectory that the animated element takes. Significantly, the path need not be completely continuous – if you a path broken into disconnected sections (through the use of the "m" directive), the object will appear to jump to that new trajectory.

2.7.2 Linking and Cursors

There are three vehicles for adding interactivity into SVG graphics – the use of the <a> tag, SMIL events and scripted event handlers, each of which provides different capabilities.

The <a> tag acts in a manner similar to that of the <a> tag in HTML, although the attributes vary somewhat. In essence, the <a> tag provides a link to another resource, as indicated by the *xlink:href* attribute. Anything contained within this element will be considered to be a part of the link (although an <a> tag internal to this one will override the link). An example of this is shown in Listing 2.22:

Listing 2.22. hyperlink.svg

```
<svg xmlns="http://www.w3.org/2000/svg"
  xmlns:xlink="http://www.w3.org/1999/xlink"
  width="1000" height="750" viewBox="0 0 1000 750">
    <a xlink:href="newPage.htm">
      <rect x="100" y="100" width="100" height="100"
        fill="red" id="rect1"/>
    </a>
</svg>
```

When the cursor is moved over the rectangle, it will change shape to indicate that the rectangle is a live link, and pressing the link will replace the current SVG document with the newPage.htm page. It is possible to change the shape of the cursor with the *cursor* attribute, which can have the added benefit of hiding the I-bar text selection capability. The cursor can either be set to one of a range of standard shapes (cursor, pointer, move, text,wait, help) and can also be set to an external resource (up to 32×32 pixels in height), such as a PNG file, as illustrated in Listing 2.23, cursor.svg:

Listing 2.23. cursor.svg

```
<svg xmlns="http://www.w3.org/2000/svg"
  xmlns:xlink="http://www.w3.org/1999/xlink"
  width="1000" height="750" viewBox="0 0 500 375">
    <a xlink:href="myPage.htm">
      <rect x="100" y="100" width="100" height="100"
        fill="blue" id="rect1" cursor= "url(#myCursor)"/>
    </a>
    <cursor x="16" y="16" xlink:href="Dana_Cursor.png"
      id="myCursor"/>
</svg>
```

2.7.3 SMIL Interactivity

The <a> element is a coarse interactive tool – it permits the use of linked inter-active pages or external graphics, but it is considerably less useful for activating animations. To make this happen, SVG provides a second interactive vector – SMIL Interactivity.

The key to SMIL Interactivity is the use of the begin and end attributes within animations. Typically, such animations are keyed to begin or end based on the passing of a specific time interval. However, one can use the name of a particular type of event as the starting or ending point of an animation.

For instance, in Interactive1.svg (Listing 2.24), when the mouse rolls into the indicated square, the opacity of the square will decrease to 0, then increase back to 1 within the space of 3 seconds.

Listing 2.24.   Interactive1.svg

```
<svg xmlns="http://www.w3.org/2000/svg"
  xmlns:xlink="http://www.w3.org/1999/xlink"
  width="1000" height="750" viewBox="0 0 500 375">
    <rect x="100" y="100" width="100" height="100"
      fill="blue" id="rect1" cursor="url(#myCursor)">
      <animate attributeName="opacity" attributeType=
        "CSS" begin="mouseover" end="mouseout" dur="3s"
        fill="restore" values="1;0;1"/>
    </rect>
</svg>
```

The SVG space currently supports the "mouse" activities – mouseover, mouse-move, mouseout, mousedown and mouseup and click, in addition to focusin and focusout and activate, the last used principally by most. The click event will only fire if a mouseup event is fired first. The SVG 1.2 recommendation will probably have additional information concerning keyboard events, although most implementations for 1.1 currently offer their own.

2.7.4 Event Handlers and the <script> Block

The final piece of XML-based SVG is the use of the <script> block and event handler functions. In this case, event handlers are provided that can catch external events, and from there be used to launch an external command.

Script support in SVG is much like support within HTML, with the same issues of compatibility. Typically, JavaScript or EcmaScript are supported by most SVG versions, but this is not a hard and fast requirement, and one should test this fact out before relying upon scripting within a given implementation.

In Listing 2.25 and Figure 2.14, both the circle and the rectangle include an onlick event handler. When the event gets called (someone clicks on the graphic), it calls the *getInfo* handler, passing to it an event object.

Listing 2.25.   Event Handlers.svg

```
<svg xmlns="http://www.w3.org/2000/svg"
  xmlns:xlink="http://www.w3.org/1999/xlink"
  width="1000" height="750" viewBox="0 0 1000 750">
    <script type="text/javascript">
function getInfo(evt){
    var target=evt.target;
    alert(target.nodeName);
    }
    </script>
    <rect x="100" y="100" width="100" height="100"
      fill="blue" id="rect1" onclick="getInfo(evt)"/>
    <circle cx="300" cy="100" r="50" fill="red"
      id="circle1" onclick="getInfo(evt)"/>
</svg>
```

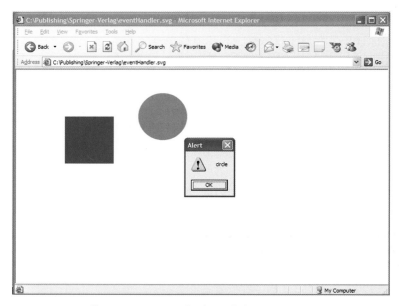

Figure 2.14   An example of an onlick event handler.

This event object is useful to determine which element was selected, as the example shows. The object that received the event (contained within the parameter *evt*), can then be referenced to retrieve the appropriate values, in this case the evt.target property. Once this object is received, it too can then be processed, as is illustrated in the getInfo() section.

2.8 Summary

This chapter has been, by necessity, principally an overview of the SVG language. The interactivity that was covered in the previous section ties in directly with the SVG DOM, which is covered in much more detail later in this book. Moreover, neither filters nor masks were covered here, because although they are very important, they are covered in much more detail in later chapters.

However, this chapter lays the foundation for more advanced programming of SVG, and also illustrates that one can do a great deal of activity without needing to break into procedural programming. Because of this, SVG has the flexibility to work from the very simplest levels of a graphic description language all the way to an extraordinarily rich user interface environment.

References

Cagle K. (2002) *SVG Programming: the Graphical Web.*: Berkeley, CA: APress.
Eisenberg D (2002) *SVG Essentials.* Sebastopol, CA: O'Reilly.
Frost J, Goessner S and Tindale I (2001) *Foundation SVG.* Indianapolis, IN: Sams
House L and Pearlman E (2002) *Developing SVG-based Web Applications.* Englewood Cliffs, NJ: Prentice
    Hall PTR.
Watt A and Lilley C (2002) *SVG Unleashed.* Indianapolis, IN: Sams.

Chapter 3
X3D Fundamentals

Don Brutzman, James Harney and Curt Blais

3.1 Introduction to X3D

This chapter will provide the reader with high-level exposure to the newly proposed Extensible 3D Graphics (X3D) specification. We will demonstrate basic scene construction and behaviour authoring. It is assumed that the reader has a basic understanding of the Extensible Markup Language (XML) to grasp more quickly the concepts introduced. 3D scene authoring experience is not necessary, but will aid the reader in understanding some of the concepts. Chapter 5 will build on concepts introduced in this chapter to show how the Java API, ECMAScript and other Application Program Interfaces (APIs) can be employed in the emerging XML-centric Semantic Web.

X3D is an emerging software standard for defining various interactive Web-based 3D content that can be integrated with multimedia across a variety of hardware platforms. X3D is the next-generation International Standards Organization (ISO) standard for Web-based 3D graphics, extending the earlier Virtual Reality Modelling Language (VRML) and VRML97 standards. It improves upon these standards by adding new features that could not be supported easily in the early days of the low-speed dial-up Internet. Additionally, it incorporates advanced applications programming interfaces, additional data encoding formats, stricter conformance enforcement and a componentized architecture allowing a modular approach extensible across the varieties of hardware to which content authors deploy in the modern Web. Since X3D is represented by the XML, it is intended to be a universal interchange format for integrated 3D graphics and multimedia (X3D ISO Specification).

3.1.1 X3D Architecture

Before getting started on the fundamentals of X3D as a markup language for 3D graphics, let us briefly review the architecture and runtime execution model. The architecture of each X3D application is defined independently of any physical devices or any other implementation-dependent concepts (e.g., display or input device types or even the existence of a mouse). Conceptually, every X3D application contains graphic and/or aural objects that can be loaded from local storage or over the network. These objects can be dynamically updated through a variety of means based on the delivery context and the content developer's design. X3D applications:

- Establish a world coordinate space for all objects defined and included by the application.

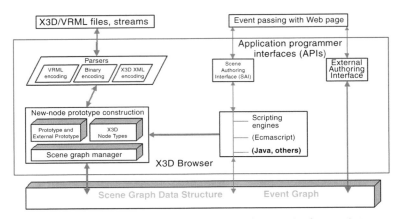

Figure 3.1   X3D system architecture for an example viewer implementation.

- Define and compose sets of 2D and 3D multimedia objects.
- Allow specification of hyperlinks to other files and applications.
- Allow object behaviours to be defined.
- Allow connection to external modules or applications via various well-defined scripting and programming languages.

The conceptual X3D system architecture is depicted in Figure 3.1.

An important thing to remember throughout this discussion of the fundamental design, layout and use of X3D is that backwards compatibility with the existing ISO VRML97 specification is encouraged to allow content authors to reuse existing work where it makes sense. In addition, authors are provided with new functionality and capabilities through the X3D specification to create even more complex and compelling 3D worlds on the Web.

Common to VRML97 and Java 3D, the basic unit of the X3D runtime environment is the scene graph. Scene graphs are directed, acyclic graphs containing the objects in the 3D world, in addition to relationships among the objects. Relationships among objects consist of (1) the transformation hierarchy describing spatial relationships and (2) the behavioural hierarchy describing runtime connections of fields and event flows in the 3D world. Nodes within the scene graph contain descriptive fields and can contain one or more child nodes, each of which may contain nodes, or instances of nodes, and so forth to produce the desired hierarchy of objects in the scene.

The X3D runtime environment is responsible for maintaining and updating the scene graph by effecting changes to applicable children in response to instructions from the event model's behavioural system. The runtime environment is also responsible for interfacing with the parent application for delivery of files, hyperlinking and any externally defined programmatic access.

3.1.2 X3D Components

X3D is organized as a set of components, where each component is a set of related functionality consisting of various X3D objects and/or services. In the initial X3D

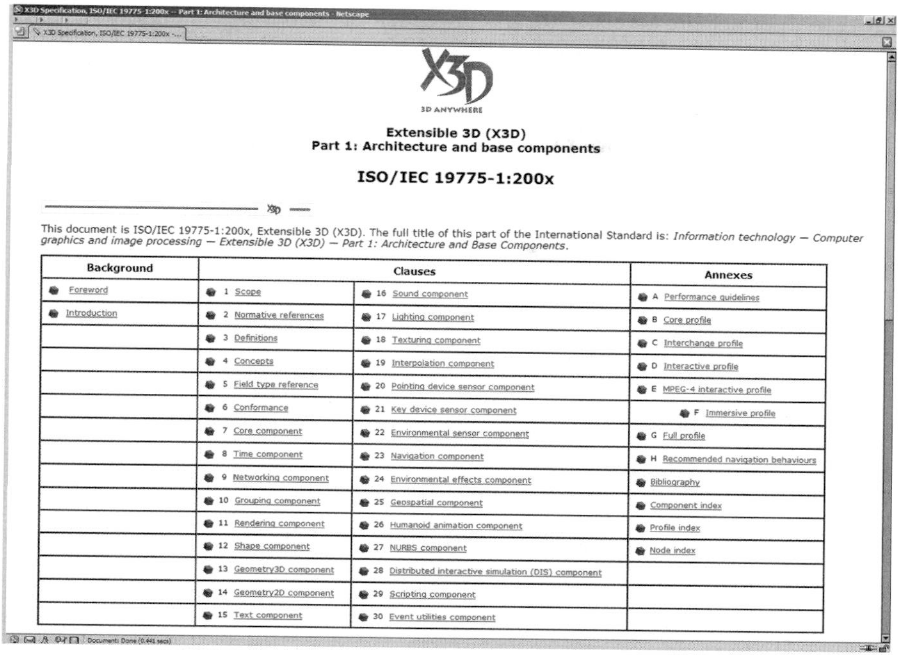
X3D Specification, ISO/IEC 19775-1:200x -- Part 1: Architecture and base components - Netscape

X3D 3D ANYWHERE

Extensible 3D (X3D)
Part 1: Architecture and base components

ISO/IEC 19775-1:200x

This document is ISO/IEC 19775-1:200x, Extensible 3D (X3D). The full title of this part of the International Standard is: *Information technology — Computer graphics and image processing — Extensible 3D (X3D) — Part 1: Architecture and Base Components.*

Background	Clauses		Annexes
Foreword	1 Scope	16 Sound component	A Performance guidelines
Introduction	2 Normative references	17 Lighting component	B Core profile
	3 Definitions	18 Texturing component	C Interchange profile
	4 Concepts	19 Interpolation component	D Interactive profile
	5 Field type reference	20 Pointing device sensor component	E MPEG-4 interactive profile
	6 Conformance	21 Key device sensor component	F Immersive profile
	7 Core component	22 Environmental sensor component	G Full profile
	8 Time component	23 Navigation component	H Recommended navigation behaviours
	9 Networking component	24 Environmental effects component	Bibliography
	10 Grouping component	25 Geospatial component	Component index
	11 Rendering component	26 Humanoid animation component	Profile index
	12 Shape component	27 NURBS component	Node index
	13 Geometry3D component	28 Distributed interactive simulation (DIS) component	
	14 Geometry2D component	29 Scripting component	
	15 Text component	30 Event utilities component	

Figure 3.2 Organization of base components in the X3D architecture (identification of numbered clauses from the X3D Draft International Specification).

specification, defined components are typically inter-related collections of various X3D nodes. The architects also envision components containing different file encoding formats, application program interface (API) services or other features as yet undefined. As we shall see, by design X3D is modular, allowing various levels of service to be provided and thereby giving the content creator greater flexibility for deployment of 3D graphics to a variety of hardware platforms (desktops to handheld devices).

Hence, when looking at X3D from a high level view in Figure 3.2, we see diverse components which provide broad, complementary functionality.

3.2 X3D Profiles

Profiles are built from components: "a profile is a named collection of functionality and requirements which shall be supported in order for an implementation to conform to that profile" (X3D Specification). Profiles provide layers of functionality that authors can opt to employ to achieve most efficient implementation of desired capabilities on the target hardware. The X3D Specification identifies six supported profiles, ranging from the Interchange profile targeted at the absolute minimum set of functionality to the Immersive profile supporting fully immersive virtual worlds with full navigation and environmental sensor control and also backwards compatibility with the VRML97 standard. Other available options provide intermediate levels of detail (in order of increasing complexity): Core, Interactive, MPEG-4 Interactive, CAD3D (for Computer-Aided Design) and Full.

Here is a portion of an example X3D file showing the file header and various other housekeeping information (HelloWorld.x3d):

```
1) <?xml version="1.0" encoding="UTF-8"?>
2) <!DOCTYPE X3D PUBLIC
"ISO//Web3D//DTD X3D 3.0//EN"
"http://www.web3d.org/specifications/x3d-3.0.dtd"
3) <X3D profile='Immersive'>
4) <head>
5) <meta name='filename' content='HelloWorld.x3d'/>
<meta name='description' content='Simple X3D example'/>
<meta name='created' content='30 October 2000'/>
<meta name='revised' content='24 August 2002'/>
<meta name='author' content='Don Brutzman'/>
<meta name='url'
content='http://www.web3d.org/x3d/content/examples/
HelloWorld.x3d'/>
<meta name='generator' content='X3D-Edit,
http://www.web3d.org/x3d/content/README.
  X3D-Edit.html'/>
</head>
<Scene>
```

The familiar XML declaration is shown in line (1). Line (2), the DOCTYPE declaration, identifies the Document Type Definition (DTD) file governing the structure of our X3D (XML) document. The declaration identifies both an online and a local definition for the DTD. The identified DTD (x3d–3.0.dtd) defines the rules for a valid X3D instance document. The reader might want to verify the applicable X3D DTD file online at http://www.web3d.org while the specification is undergoing the standardization approval process.

Line (3) is the X3D start tag, here shown with an optional attribute identifying the profile (Immersive) that will be enforced throughout the remainder of the X3D application. Line (4) is the head tag, which is a container for various metadata content shown in part (5). The metadata section allows a scene author to document the file clearly with descriptive data such as filename, creation date, revision date, author, online URL and other information. This is an important improvement over VRML, which provided syntax for scene comments but not as structured data as enabled through the use of XML tags.

3.2.1 Creating Our First X3D Scene

Let us now create an X3D scene to display a 3D representation of the Earth utilizing several scene graph components from the Immersive profile. We will then view a VRML97 rendering of the defined X3D scene. This example will enable us to look at some of the intricacies of direct XML or X3D file editing using a basic text editor, in contrast to the use of an XML editing tool such as X3D-Edit (Chapter 14). Our first scene is depicted in Figure 3.3.

Figure 3.3 HelloWorld.x3d styled to VRML97 and rendered in the Open Source exemplar VRML97 and X3D browser (Xj3DBrowser) under development concurrently with the X3D specification (http://www.xj3d.org and http://www.web3d.org/x3d).

3.2.1.1 Basic 3D Shapes via the Geometry3D Component

After the document header we discussed earlier, scene elements are contained as children inside the <Scene> </Scene> X3D tag. Before getting into more detail, let us see how we drew the basic sphere representing the Earth. We use the Sphere primitive defined as part of the Geometry3D component in X3D. By default, the sphere primitive has a radius of one 3D unit, which by convention is considered to be in metres, and is centred at (0,0,0) in the local coordinate system. Accepting these defaults, the basic default sphere can be represented as follows:

```
<Shape>
  <Sphere/>
</Shape>
```

Readers familiar with VRML97 syntax will find the convention of not explicitly declaring default values within a geometry definition to be the same in most cases with X3D. Since we did not add an appearance node from the Shape Component, the sphere will be given the default colour scheme, namely RGB value 1 1 1 (white), with an ambient intensity of 0.2 and a shininess factor of 0.2, and with neither emissive nor specular colour, nor transparency (Figure 3.4).

In Figure 3.3, a texture was applied to the sphere to give it the appearance of the Earth. The texture is applied by the underlying rendering engine in the following manner (Figure 3.5): (1) it covers the entire surface of the shape; (2) it wraps counterclockwise from the back of the sphere when viewed from the top in the default

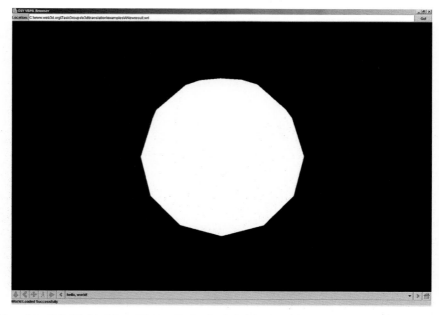

Figure 3.4 HelloWorld.x3d modified to display the default look and feel of the sphere primitive shape.

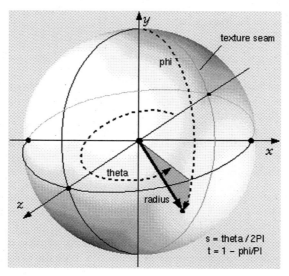

Figure 3.5 Representation of the default texture mapping on the Sphere primitive shape. (X3D Specification).

position; and (3) there is a seam at the back where the YZ-plane intersects the sphere and Z values are negative. The Texturing Component defines a Texture Transform with which we can modify and animate the coordinates of the texture to be applied to a shape. The Earth map texture applied in our example is shown in Figure 3.6.

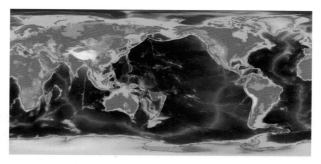

Figure 3.6   Earth-Topo Image is applied to the Sphere shape as an ImageTexture.

Here is the complete declaration of the Shape node in the HelloWorld.x3d file providing the texture mapping of the Earth's surface:

```
<Shape>
  <Sphere/>
  <Appearance>
  1) <ImageTexture url='"earth-topo.png" "earth-topo-
     small.gif"
  "http://www.web3d.org/x3d/content/
     examples/earth-topo.png"
  "http://www.web3d.org/x3d/content/
     examples/earth-topo-small.gif"'/>
  </Appearance>
</Shape>
```

In (1), note the use of multiple Universal Resource Locators (URLs) to access the image used in the scene. A standard convention practiced for extensibility and reuse of one's content is to provide a locally available location for an image or other resource first (in our case earth-topo.png), followed by an alternative local file type if applicable (here we see the alternative inclusion of the image in Graphical Interchange Format, i.e., earth-topo-small.gif), followed by online resources if the scene or content is being loaded live over the Internet or delivered as part of a Web service.

With all primitive shapes in the Geometry3D component (Box, Cylinder, Cone), rendering results are undefined when viewing the scene from the inside of the shape. Although the primitive shapes can be a powerful authoring tool to create content quickly, they do have drawbacks for many applications, such as making buildings that the user can view from the inside. We will look at an example of this in a later section.

3.2.1.2 X3D Text Component

Let us take a look at how we were able to draw the text "HelloWorld" in our scene. In X3D, text is treated as a shape object, or geometry. Just as we did with the sphere, we use a Shape tag, but with a <Text> element as its child:

```
<Shape>
1) <Text string='"Hello" "world!"'/>
<Appearance>
```

```
2) <Material diffuse Color='0.1 0.5 1'/>
</Appearance>
</Shape>
```

The Text tag (1) has two quoted strings ("Hello" and "world!") as the two-line value of the *string* attribute. The maximum number of strings that we can add here is unbounded, but obviously limited by the display size and other computing constraints not incorporated into the standard. Other attributes for the Text element are *fontStyle*, *length* per string of text and the *maxExtent* of the text. Additionally, the FontStyle Object allows us to declare the font type (dependent on fonts available on the client machine, defaulting to SERIF), whether the text is horizontal or vertical, the string justification (beginning, end, first, middle), language, leftToRight (true/false), text size (from 0 to infinity), text spacing (0 to infinity), a style (PLAIN, BOLD, ITALIC, BOLDITALIC), and topToBottom (true). Default values for these attributes are horizontal=true, justify=BEGIN, leftToRight=true, size = 1.0, spacing = 1.0, style = plain and topToBottom=true. The reader is referred to the X3D specification and the references at the end of the chapter for more detail on the various combinations and effects one can apply to text in X3D.

One authoring tip: although personal computer processing speed continues to increase significantly over time, real-time updating and setting of Text objects in X3D and VRML97 remain an expensive operation for computer memory. An alternative to this is the replacement of the Text shape object with transparent images overlaying text on other geometry, or the use of pixel texturing for creating a custom text library at reduced rendering cost, but at a loss of some functionality.

We have seen that Objects that are shapes can explicitly declare an appearance (we do not want an all-grey world!), and within the Appearance element we can also describe a Material. In our example, we are applying a diffuse colour of 0.1 0.5 1 to the text (red–green–blue values between 0 and 1).

3.2.1.3 *Material and Lighting Components*

Before moving on, it is important to digress for a moment to explain more about the Material and Lighting Components in X3D. In Figure 3.4 we showed a Sphere shape with no Material declaration. As a result, there was no emissive colour applied to the shape. The default value for the diffuse colour is (0.8, 0.8, 0.8). In the text example, we declared a Material element as a child of the Appearance element resulting in the X3D lighting model being activated. This is important to remember, since the Material and Texture nodes determine the diffuse colour for the lighting equation used for the parent Shape element. For example, the Material's diffuse Color field sets the colour in the texture being applied to the geometry. If we use a diffuseColor of white (i.e., undeclared explicitly), then the pure colour of the texture will be applied to the geometry. If we set diffuseColor to black (0, 0, 0), then the texture colour will be totally overridden and the shape will be black in appearance. The Material's transparency value modulates the alpha characteristic of an applied texture (i.e., the transparency factor), with similar behaviours for values of 0 or 1 as with the diffuse colours.

The Lighting Component in X3D allows for three types of lights to be defined within a scene: (1) DirectionalLight, (2) PointLight and (3) SpotLight. The PointLight and SpotLight illuminate all world objects that are contained within the lighting influence volume no matter what their location is within the transformation hierarchy.

PointLight interprets this volume to be a sphere centred at the light defined by a radius, whereas SpotLight defines the volume of influence as a solid angle which is resolved by a radius and cutoff angle. DirectionalLight illuminates only the objects that are children of the same common grouping node as the light, including other descendent scene graph children of that same parent node. The default declaration for a DirectionLight would be similar to the following:

```
<DirectionalLight ambientIntensity="0"color="1 1 1"
direction="0 0 -1" intensity="1" on= "TRUE"/>
```

The direction is unbounded and all other values are bounded between 0 and 1 inclusive. PointLight has attributes for attenuation and radius; SpotLight has attributes for beamWidth and cutoffAngle.

3.2.1.4 Grouping Component

Next, we move to Grouping Component nodes in X3D. All nodes in this component have a field containing a list of children nodes and define a coordinate space for their respective children. This space is relative to the coordinate space of the parent node of the respective group. Looking at our scene graph structure as a tree hierarchy, the transformations are accumulative as one proceeds down the graph. Grouping nodes include Anchor, Billboard, Collision, Group, Inline, LOD, Switch and Transform. The two that we will look at here are the Group and Transform nodes.

```
1)  <Group>
3)  <Viewpoint description='hello, world!'
    orientation='0 1 0 1.57' position='6 -1 0'
    centerOfRotation='0 0 0'/>
4)  <NavigationInfo type= 'EXAMINE ANY'/>
<Shape>
<Sphere/>
<Appearance>
<ImageTexture url='"earth-topo.png" "earth-topo-
    small.gif"
"http://www.web3d.org/TaskGroups/x3d/translation/
    examples/earth-topo.png""http://www.web3d.org/
    TaskGroups/x3d/translation/examples/earth-topo-
    small.gif"'/>
</Appearance>
</Shape>
2)  -<Transform rotation='0 1 0 1.57'
translation='0 -2 1.25'>
<Shape>
<Text string='"Hello" "world!"'/>
<Appearance>
<Material diffuseColor='0.1 0.5 1'/>
</Appearance>
</Shape>
</Transform>
</Group>
```

The Group node (1) in X3D is a container for a list of children. The Group node also maintains a bounding box around the child geometry within the scene. A convenient authoring practice involves placing child geometry in a Group node to copy and paste the scene objects easily elsewhere in the scene graph.

The Transform node (2) is a grouping node which defines a local coordinate system for its children relative to the coordinate system of its parent or ancestors. It has additional fields for positioning the child geometry, namely scale, translation, rotation, and centre. These attributes allow us to position, orient and scale objects statically and as we shall see later, dynamically for animation. The rotation values are in radians, represented by a vector describing the axis of rotation and the rotation angle about the axis (e.g., 0 1 0 1.57 represents a 90° counterclockwise rotation about the Y axis). Hence we can see these values applied directly in our example file from above where we specify rotation and translation of the displayed text inside the Transform node.

3.3 Viewing Our Worlds – The Navigation Component

The last elements to review from our HelloWorld example are the Viewpoint node and the NavigationInfo node from the Navigation Component. In older VRML scenes that one encounters on the Web, these capabilities are often neglected even though they are key techniques for user interaction with our scenes.

Navigation enables users to interact with the X3D browser using their available input devices to affect their view of the scene. A large part of what differentiates 3D from 2D is the ability to inspect the scene from different viewpoints. The content author has the opportunity to use one or more Viewpoint nodes to provide predefined viewing perspectives to make the content more easily and clearly observed. The NavigationInfo node further allows the user to change position and orientation within the world to exercise his own control over viewing perspectives. Figure 3.7 shows an example of Browser presentation of selectable navigation modes and viewpoints.

The NavigationInfo node defines characteristics of the navigation behaviour for the user, while leaving the interface semantics to the browser implementation layer. Fields contained within this node are *avatarSize* (in metres ranging from 0 to infinity; default values are 0.25, 1.6, 0.75 designating collision distance from viewpoint location to geometry in the scene, viewer height above ground, and height of objects the avatar can "walk" over, respectively), *headlight* (default TRUE), *speed* (default 1.0 m/s ranging from 0 to infinity inclusive), *type* (defaults are "EXAMINE", "ANY", with EXAMINE, NONE, FLY, LOOKAT, ANY as other options), *visibilityLimit* (ranging from 0 to infinity) and *isbound* (TRUE/FALSE). The *speed*, *avatarSize* and *visibilityLimit* values are all scaled by the transformation being applied to the currently bound Viewpoint node. NavigationInfo is called a *bindable* node in X3D. That is, we can have multiple coexisting ones, but there is a NavigationStack in which only one can be active at time. For this reason, when utilizing multiple scene components within one primary scene, authors must pay attention to values such as *visibilityLimit* (determines how far the user can see in a given scene) and *speed* (think of the difference in walking versus flying a jet aircraft). If one wants a consistent visibility limit within a given scene, then one would need to make sure all X3D or VRML97 dependencies utilized have the same limit defined or the user's experience can be adversely affected. Separately, the field values for *type* determine the navigation paradigm that has to be enforced by the X3D browser. A typical

Figure 3.7   Depicts how navigation modes and predefined viewpoints may be exposed to the end-user by the browser author.

navigation setting while developing a scene is "EXAMINE ANY FLY", which allows the greatest capability for navigation and inspection by the user. However, this combination might not be the best deployment choice for a first-person shooter game or a 3D tetris game. In line (4) of the example above, we see that NavigationInfo is set to: <NavigationInfo type="EXAMINE ANY"/>. This setting gives the user a great deal of freedom in navigating the scene. In large scenes, the more exposure one gives to the end-user for freedom of navigation can result in a greater loss of scene performance. This is perhaps not a serious issue for the latest hardware, but can be a consideration if one is not sure of the user's hardware capabilities.

As we stated, the Viewpoint node specifies predefined locations and viewing orientations in our world to enable the user to observe the scene readily. Viewpoints, similar to NavigationInfo, are considered bindable nodes, and have their own stack defined by the X3D browser. Only one Viewpoint is bound at a time. Viewpoints also exist in their parent node's coordinate system and, when placed as a child of a Transform Grouping node, can be animated at runtime to provide an augmented viewing experience for the user. Some fields that are exposed in the Viewpoint node are *centerOfRotation, fieldOfView* (default is 0.785, ranging from 0 to infinity non-inclusive), *jump* (default = TRUE), *orientation* (default is 0, 0, 1, 0), *description* (default is a null string; can be any description separated by whitespace), *bindTime* (SFTime type) and *isBound* (TRUE/FALSE).

3.4 Introducing the X3D Event Model

Now that we have had a chance to look at the HelloWorld example in detail, we will examine the X3D Event Model and review a simple example for implementing behaviours within our scene.

3.4.1 X3D Event Model and Scene Behaviours

As mentioned in our previous discussion of the X3D application architecture, the X3D scene graph also contains a behavioural hierarchy defining runtime connections and event flows in the system. Behaviours include the ability to change some aspect of a portion of our scene graph over time, whether a change in position, reaction to user interaction with the scene or any other syntactically legal change. The X3D/VRML browser implementer coordinates the processing of events within the behavioural portion of our X3D scene. Before examining an example, we need to have a better understanding of events in the scene graph.

By specification definition, an X3D event consists of "a message sent from one node to another as defined by a ROUTE". A ROUTE can be thought of as the abstract connection between a node sending an event and the node receiving the event. These can be used in many ways, such as providing a driver for time-stepped simulations or animations, detection and handling of various object picking and detecting collision and user movement through a scene. Although the event model without an external API appears simple, it is possible to define fairly complex scenes with only X3D native events.

There are several ways to modify the fields of an object. Using one of the X3D file formats, an author can declare a set of nodes, the initial state of their fields and interconnections between the fields called *ROUTEs*. X3D uses an event propagation or *dataflow* model to change the values of fields at runtime. As part of its abstract specification, the behaviour of a node in response to events sent to its fields and the conditions under which its fields send events out are described. It is possible to create a scene with runtime behaviour using only this event propagation model. The following example (Figure 3.8) demonstrates some simple translation

Figure 3.8   Simple incorporation of behaviours with a Dolphin in the 3D scene.

and orientation behaviours changing over time while introducing a few more
node types:

```
<X3D profile='Immersive'>
<head>
<meta name='filename' content='TestBehavior.x3d'/>
<meta name='description' content='Simple scene
  displaying basic X3D scene graph behaviors with
  routes.'/>
<meta name='author' content='James Harney'/>
<meta name='created' content='11 December 2002'/>
<meta name='revised' content='11 December 2002'/>
<meta name='generator' content='X3D-Edit,
http://www.web3d.org/x3d/content/README.
  X3D-Edit.html'/>
</head>
<!--
_____

Index for DEFs: DolphinClock, DolphinOrientationInter
polator, DolphinPositionInterpolator, DolphinTransform.
_____
-->
<Scene>
<NavigationInfo type='EXAMINE ANY'/>
6) <Background backUrl='"ocean_3_back.jpg"
"http://www.web3d.org/WorkingGroups/media/textures/
  panoramas/ocean_3_back.jpg"'
bottomUrl='"ocean_3_bottom.jpg"
"http://www.web3d.org/WorkingGroups/media/textures/
  panoramas/ocean_3_bottom.jpg"'
frontUrl='"ocean_3_front.jpg"
"http://www.web3d.org/WorkingGroups/media/textures/
  panoramas/ocean_3_front.jpg"'
leftUrl='"ocean_3_left.jpg"
"http://www.web3d.org/WorkingGroups/media/textures/
  panoramas/ocean_3_left.jpg"'
rightUrl='"ocean_3_right.jpg"
"http://www.web3d.org/WorkingGroups/media/textures/
  panoramas/ocean_3_right.jpg"'
topUrl='"ocean_3_top.jpg"
"http://www.web3d.org/WorkingGroups/media/textures/
  panoramas/ocean_3_top.jpg"'
/>
<Viewpoint description='Side View of Dolphin'/>
<Viewpoint description='Top View of Dolphin'
  orientation='1 0 0 -1.57' position='0 10 0'/>
1) <TimeSensor DEF='DolphinClock' cycleInterval='5'
  loop='true'/>
2) <PositionInterpolator DEF='DolphinPosition
  Interpolator' key='0 .5 1' keyValue='0 -1 0, 0 1 0,
  0 -1 0'/>
```

```
3) <OrientationInterpolator
   DEF='DolphinOrientation Interpolator' key='0 .25 .75
   1' keyValue='0 1 0 0, 0 1 0 .57, 0 1 0 -.57, 0 1 0 0'/>
<Transform DEF='DolphinTransform'>
4) <Inline url='"Dolphin.wrl"
"http://web.nps.navy.mil/~brutzman/Savage/Biologics/
   Dolphin.wrl"'/>
</Transform>
5) <ROUTE fromNode='DolphinClock' fromField=
'fraction_changed' toNode='DolphinPositionInterpolator'
toField='set_fraction'/>
<ROUTE fromNode='DolphinPositionInterpolator'
fromField='value_changed' toNode='DolphinTransform'
toField='set_translation'/>
<ROUTE fromNode='DolphinClock' fromField=
'fraction_changed' toNode = 'DolphinOrientation
Interpolator'toField='set_fraction'/>
<ROUTE fromNode='DolphinOrientationInterpolator'
fromField='value_changed' toNode='DolphinTransform'
toField='set_rotation'/>
</Scene>
</X3D>
```

This example reuses some of the concepts that we introduced in the HelloWorld example earlier, but we also utilize basic components of the available behavioural graph components exposed to us for content creation. The scene slowly animates a dolphin up and down the verticle Y axis while applying a rotation about this same axis over a repeating period of 5 seconds.

In this case, we use a TimeSensor (1) as the driver of our simple behavioural system. This sensor is part of the Time Component in X3D. Its primary duty is to generate events as time passes once it is loaded by the X3D runtime environment. In our case, we are using it to drive continuously our simple dolphin animation. TimeSensors may also be used to control periodic activities or to trigger single occurrence events. When the TimeSensor is initiated, it outputs a *fraction_changed* event which consists of a floating point value in the closed interval range of [0,1]. This value can be routed to Interpolators to create changes in different types of values. The TimeSensor *fraction_changed* event starts at 0 and ranges through 1.0 at the completion of its *cycleInterval*. There are also other exposed fields for this node that allow a clock to be started upon a predefined action or selection by the end user. One note of warning with respect to TimeSensors and other X3D/VRML types: until the X3D specification is more widely adopted than the older VRML97 standard by browser manufacturers, we can only rely on floating-point accuracy when dealing with the X3D event model. This generally does not create a problem, but when it does the general convention has been to normalize the data to avoid having the browser implementation perform an incorrect rounding of our data.

Now that we have a general idea on what a TimeSensor does, consider the PositionInterpolator (2) and OrientationInterpolator (3) nodes. In the X3D Interpolator Component there are eight options from which to choose: ColorInterpolator, CoordinateInterpolator, CoordinateInterpolator2D, NormalInterpolator, Orientation-Interpolator, PositionInterpolator, PositionInterpolator2D and ScalarInterpolator. For most purposes, we generally just need to animate the position and orientation of an

object in our virtual world. Following regular object-oriented design patterns, the
defined Interpolator nodes are based on an abstract X3Dinterpolator node for reuse of
common components. The interpolators are designed for linear, key-framed animation based on the concept of a key (relative time mark) and corresponding key value.

On receipt of a *set_fraction* input routed from a TimeSensor, the corresponding
interpolator node function will compute a *value_changed* output event with the
same timestamp as the *set_fraction* input. The biggest difference in the various types
of interpolators lies in the data typing of the *keyValue* and *value_changed* fields. For
our simple PositionInterpolator (2) in the above example, we define three key values
of 0, 0.5 and 1 which correspond to three predefined positions (0 −1 0, 0 1 0, 0 −1 0).
Between key values, the interpolator performs linear interpolation between these
position values. The OrientationInterpolator (3) is similar in function, except that in
place of 3-tuple location coordinates it has the applicable values for effecting changes
to orientation (axis and angle 4-tuples).

Section (5) of the example contains the routes used to connect the various nodes
through their event interfaces. The TimeSensor (DolphinClock) drives the interpolators (DolphinPositionInterpolator and DolphinOrientationInterpolator) which
provide values to the translation and rotation fields of the Transform node
(DolphinTransform) positioning the Dolphin geometry. Note that the Dolphin geometry is added to the scene as a child to the Transform node using an Inline node that
identifies the file containing the Dolphin model.

Not all field values of nodes can be changed at runtime using X3D routes. Node
fields have the following access settings: inputOnly, outputOnly, initializeOnly or
inputOutput. Hence, an illegal declaration would be to route an outputOnly field to
another outputOnly field (would need to route to a field with inputOnly or
inputOutput access). When using the X3D-Edit authoring tool (see Chapter 14 on
X3D-Edit), these field access permissions are indicated in the authoring tooltips in
addition to a shortcuts guide provided through http://www.web3.org.

One of the primary advantages to using ROUTEs is that a scene author can create fairly complex scenes by declaratively connecting the output events of a node to
input events of other nodes without having to learn or use a declarative or procedural programming API. It should be kept in mind that ROUTEs are not nodes, just
constructs for effecting the connection(s) between specified fields of nodes. Also,
when dealing with defined components in the draft specification, it must be recog-
nized that the data type of a destination field must be the same as the source type
unless there is an extension to the rule. Finally, the X3D runtime environment
ignores duplicate routes contained in the scene graph. In summary, the runtime
environment for this example scene follows the following basic execution order:

1. Update the camera based on the currently bound Viewpoint's position and
   orientation.
2. Evaluate input from sensors.
3. Evaluate routes.

When using an external API to effect changes within our scene graph, there can
be intermediate steps added between each of these sub-steps.

3.4.2 Environmental Effects Component

The last portion of the Dolphin TestBehavior.x3d scene that we will look at is the
Background node (6). The Background node is a member of the Environmental

Effects Component of the X3D Specification. This component contains three nodes currently: Background, TexturedBackground and Fog. Typically, these nodes are used to specify a colour or textured backdrop which simulates the ground and sky. Like Viewpoints and NavigationInfo, Background nodes are bindable children nodes (yet another stack managing our currently active background within the X3D scene graph). We typically use the Background node in one of two ways: (1) we define the ground and sky colours and angles to draw a gradient effect similar to those with which we may be familiar in Adobe Photoshop or Illustrator, or (2) to texture-map panoramas on an imaginary cube that bounds our scene geometry. Option 2 is the approach that we took with the Dolphin example, but there is nothing wrong with defining both so that if one experiences a networking delay for content being delivered over the Web there will be less delay rendering some colour close to that of the desired texture. This is more visually appealing than displaying the default black background, possibly obscuring the desired features and confusing the user.

Consider the *skyColor* field in (6). Its first value represents the colour of the sky straight up from the viewer (represents the zenith). The *skyAngle* is bounded between 0 and π, and defines the next angle from zenith at which the next defined colour in *skyColor* will be applied. The browser linearly interpolates between the two colours across the given angle. The same idea holds for ground colour except that we start off looking straight down and proceed upwards in the range of 0 to π/2 radians, inclusive. There also must be one more *groundColor* value than *groundAngle* values. One last note with Background nodes is that if an author decides to use the Environmental Component Fog, then if a Background Node is bound at the same time the Fog effects will not change the visual appearance of the Background.

The following sample scene using the Background node is shown in Figure 3.9.

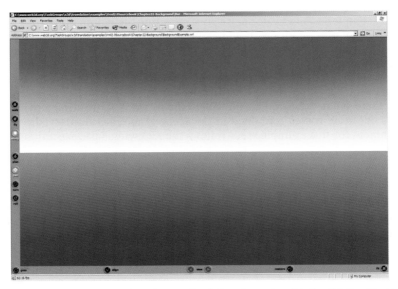

Figure 3.9   Use of a background node with ground and sky colours viewed in Parallel Graphics Cortona VRML Client (http://www.parallelgraphics.com).

```
<Scene>
<!-- Note that navigation mode doesn't matter here,
since you cannot approach the background, it always
stays at maximum (horizon) distance -->
<!-- At least EXAMINE mode lets you easily look
up/down/around. --> <NavigationInfo type='EXAMINE ANY'
/>
<Background groundAngle='1.309, 1.571' groundColor='0.1
0.1 0, 0.4 0.25 0.2, 0.6 0.6 0.6' skyAngle='1.309,
1.571' skyColor='0 0.2 0.7, 0 0.5 1, 1 1 1'
/>
</Scene>
```

3.5 User-initiated Behaviours

So far, we have walked through a basic X3D scene, and then touched on how to put behaviours in our world. Next, we shall show how to trigger desired behaviours from user interactions using the Pointing Device Sensor Component in X3D. This component consists of five node types: CylinderSensor, PlaneSensor, SphereSensor, TouchSensor and the Anchor node. Each node detects user actions in a scene. These sensors share several capabilities in common:

1. They are activated when the user places the pointing device (e.g., mouse) over the geometry in the scene influenced by that sensor.
2. These sensors affect all geometry descended from its parent node, except the Anchor node, which is considered to be a parent group by itself.
3. Pointing Device Sensors are normally siblings under a common parent node to the geometry that they are intended to influence.
4. Transparent qualities of geometry have no affect on these sensors. They consider all geometry under their influence to be opaque.
5. For any one instance of user activation, the lowest enabled sensor in the hierarchy is activated with all others above in the hierarchy being ignored. If there are many at the same lowest level, then we consider them "tied", and each are allowed to be activated simultaneously and independently. This allows for combinations such as TouchSensors and various PlaneSensors to operate simultaneously in a given scene.
6. If a pointing device sensor is not enabled when it is activated, it will not generate events until it is enabled. If this happens, for example, while we are dragging the mouse across the screen, then it will not be enabled until the dragging is completed.

Furthermore, these sensors can be partitioned conceptually. Drag sensors consist of a subset of the above-mentioned ones, namely CylinderSensor, PlaneSensor and SphereSensor. These have two eventOuts: *trackPoint_changed* and *value_changed*. The nodes send events for every change of the activated pointing device according to the "virtual" geometry that they are mimicking (evident by the name of the node). We typically use these nodes to restrict the movement of a piece of geometry within a scene, i.e., to a given plane or planes with PlaneSensor or to a given virtual shape with Sphere and CylinderSensors. The actions can be used to help the user from becoming lost in our scenes.

The pointing device (usually a computer's mouse) will maintain control of a pointer in our virtual world. When we activate a PointingDeviceSensor, it generates events as we move the pointing device about the scene until the sensor is deactivated. If for some reason the pointing device indicates that it is selecting two different pieces of geometry that are controlled by separate sensors, then our X3D browser should select the closest one in the scene to the pointing device.

In the upcoming example, we will use the TouchSensor. This node keeps track of the location and state of the pointing device (i.e., for a computer mouse the state of the mouse buttons). The node detects when the user points the device at the geometry that is contained by its parent group. One way to save this small overhead is to route our TouchSensor node an enabled or disabled TRUE or FALSE event. When disabled, it will not perform the tracking of the user input or send any events.

There are a number of options for the type of events that the TouchSensor can generate to allow us to effect changes or initiate behaviours in our virtual world. One is the *isOver* field, which reflects whether the pointing device is over the associated geometry or not. When it is, an *isOver* TRUE event is generated that can be used for routing within our scene. When it is not, the *isOver* event changes to FALSE. These events are not generated if we are not moving the pointing device even if the geometry is animated underneath it. Other events that also occur while *isOver* is TRUE are *hitPoint_changed*, *hitNormal_changed* and *hitTexCoord_changed*. The *hitPoint_changed* value contains the 3D point on the geometry over which the user has moved the pointing device, *hitNormal_changed* contains the surface normal vector at this point and *hitTexCoord_changed* contains the texture coordinates (if any) at this same point (referred to as the *hitPoint*).

The browser uses field *touchTime* to generate events when the any of the following three conditions occur:

1. Our pointing device was pointing at the geometry when activated (i.e., *isActive* is TRUE).
2. The device is still pointing at the geometry (*isOver* is TRUE).
3. The pointing device is deactivated (*isActive* FALSE).

With these mechanisms, we can now place a touch sensor at the same level as the dolphin geometry in the previous example, and only trigger its simple behaviours of slowly rising and falling while twisting slightly to each side when the user activates the touch sensor on the dolphin geometry. Let us change the scene slightly and put these techniques in practice (Figure 3.10).

X3D source for Figure 3.10:

```
<X3D profile='Immersive'>
<head>
<meta name='filename' content=
  'TestBehaviorWithShark.x3d'/>
<meta name='description' content='Simple scene displaying
basic X3D scene graph behaviors with routes.'/>
<meta name='author' content='James Harney'/>
<meta name='created' content='11 December 2002'/>
<meta name='revised' content='11 December 2002'/>
<meta name='generator' content='X3D-Edit,
http://www.web3d.org/x3d/content/
  README.X3D-Edit.html'/>
```

Figure 3.10 Example of scene behaviours triggered by user actions. By clicking the initial geometry of the shark in the scene, the same simple behaviour utilized in the Dolphin example is triggered, causing the shark to rise and fall once while twisting slowly from side to side.

```
</head>
<!--
```

Index for DEFs: behindShark, SharkClock,
SharkOrientationInterpolator, SharkPositionInterpolator,
SharkTouchSensor, SharkTransform.

```
-->
<Scene>
<NavigationInfo type='EXAMINE ANY'/>
<Viewpoint DEF='behindShark' description='"Behind Lefty
  Shark"'
 orientation='0.00390132 -0.999986 0.0034463 1.44711'
position='-1.5071 0.358747 0.17578'/>
<Background backUrl='"ocean_3_back.jpg"
"http://www.web3d.org/WorkingGroups/media/textures/
  panoramas/ocean_3_back.jpg"'
bottomUrl='"ocean_3_bottom.jpg"
"http://www.web3d.org/WorkingGroups/media/textures/
  panoramas/ocean_3_bottom.jpg"'
frontUrl='"ocean_3_front.jpg"
"http://www.web3d.org/WorkingGroups/media/textures/
  panoramas/ocean_3_front.jpg"'
leftUrl='"ocean_3_left.jpg"
"http://www.web3d.org/WorkingGroups/media/textures/
  panoramas/ocean_3_left.jpg"'
```

```
rightUrl='"ocean_3_right.jpg"
"http://www.web3d.org/WorkingGroups/media/textures/
  panoramas/ocean_3_right.jpg"'
topUrl='"ocean_3_top.jpg"
"http://www.web3d.org/WorkingGroups/media/textures/
  panoramas/ocean_3_top.jpg"'
/>
3) <TimeSensor DEF='SharkClock' cycleInterval='5'/>
<PositionInterpolator DEF='SharkPositionInterpolator'
  key='0 .5 1' keyValue='0 -1 0, 0 1 0, 0 -1 0'/>
<OrientationInterpolator DEF='SharkOrientation
  Interpolator' key='0 .25 .75 1' keyValue='0 1 0 0,
  0 1 0 .57, 0 1 0 -.57, 0 1 0 0'/>
<Transform DEF='SharkTransform'>
<Transform rotation='0 1 0 -1.57'>
<Inline url='"Shark2.wrl"
"http://www.web3d.org/TaskGroups/x3d/translation/
  examples/KelpForestExhibit/Shark2.wrl"'/>
</Transform>
1) <TouchSensor DEF='SharkTouchSensor'/>
</Transform>
<ROUTE fromNode='SharkClock' fromField=
'fraction_changed' toNode='SharkPositionInterpolator'
toField='set_fraction'/>
<ROUTE fromNode='SharkPositionInterpolator' fromField=
'value_changed' toNode='SharkTransform' toField=
'set_translation'/>
<ROUTE fromNode='SharkClock' fromField=
'fraction_changed' toNode=
'SharkOrientationInterpolator' toField='set_fraction'/>
<ROUTE fromNode='SharkOrientationInterpolator'
fromField='value_changed' toNode='SharkTransform'
toField='set_rotation'/>
2) <ROUTE fromNode='SharkTouchSensor' fromField=
'touchTime' toNode='SharkClock' toField=
'set_startTime'/>
</Scene>
</X3D>
```

This example is similar to the earlier Dolphin scene; however, we have replaced our dolphin with a shark. At first one might think this would be quite involved, but one of the strengths of using a component-based language such as X3D is that we can replace similar pieces very easily. In this case we reused a shark model from the Monterey Bay Aquarium Kelp Forest scene online at http://www.web3d.org/x3d/content/examples/KelpForestExhibit/shark2.x3d by replacing the dolphin inline url with the shark model url. We also renamed nodes to document better the scene graph as a shark scene, and modified our scene viewpoint.

We added a TouchSensor (1) which we identified with a DEF name of SharkTouchSensor. The role of DEF and USE in X3D is identical to usage in

VRML97. In order to ROUTE to or from a node, it needs a unique name that can be referenced by the X3D runtime environment. We might also reuse geometry defined in a scene by referencing the DEF name in a USE clause. After adding the TouchSensor, we needed to add a new ROUTE (2) sending the *touchTime* from this sensor to our TimeSensor, which will in turn drive our behaviours after the user clicks on the shark geometry. The final modification was to ensure the TimeSensor was not active when the scene was loaded, but must receive an explicit *startTime* from the TouchSensor to initiate the desired behaviours.

3.6 Viewing Our Content – The Power of XSLT and XML

You may have noticed while reading through our examples that you are actually seeing a VRML97 depiction of the X3D content described. Do not worry, nothing is wrong. What you are seeing is an example of the power of XML. We are using the Extensible Stylesheet Language for Transformations (XSLT) to transform the scene graphs written in the X3D language to the same scene graph expressed in VRML97. Moreover, the X3D examples have been transformed through XSLT for formatted display in HTML. Transformations with XSLT might even be written to create Scalable Vector Graphics (SVG) formats for an X3D scene! Currently existing XSLT files for converting X3D to VRML97 and to HTML are provided in Open Source by the Web3D Consortium and can be found online at http://www.web3d.org/x3d/. With alternative rendering formats becoming increasingly available for the content developer to rely on, the use of server side delivery of content based on the context of the end user or different derivations of client side manipulation become increasingly more interesting.

For those desiring a direct XML rendering of the X3D content, the Web3D Consortium's Open Source project Xj3D is available for download. Xj3D is being developed concurrently with the specification. Current information on this effort can found at http://www.xj3d.org.

3.7 The Road Ahead

As the X3D specification documents all become an international standard and support expands through the commercial world for this standard, greater opportunities for the language will emerge. Application as a composite part of MPEG-4, binary encodings and other extensions will enable content creators to make more and more interesting content at higher levels of complexity. Other areas of developing interest include the CAD 3D working group, Binary compression, shader languages, PDA rendering contexts and others.

3.8 Conclusion

In this chapter, we have exposed the reader to many of the fundamentals of the emerging standard for 3D graphics on the Web, X3D. From basic scene construction to incorporation of simple behaviours, we have attempted to walk you through enough of the syntactical requirements while keeping a high-level overview perspective on the underlying infrastructure support that makes X3D possible. In Chapter 5 we will review the use of ECMAScript and the Java programming language to do more interesting scene manipulation and for dynamic scene delivery based on client needs.

3.9 Acknowledgments

Screenshots are VRML views of the result X3D scenes through Xj3D, the Web3D Consortium-sponsored Open Source implementation for an X3D/VRML97 Browser, and the ParallelGraphics Cortona browser. X3D examples were written and validated using X3D-Edit 2.4. Thanks are due to the X3D Specification team and contributors to Xj3D for their continued dedication and hard work in these areas.

References

Ames AL, Nadeau DR and Moreland JL (1997) *VRML Sourcebook*, 2nd edn New York: Wiley.
Blais CL, Brutzman D, Horner DP and Nicklaus S (2001) Web-based 3D technology for education – the AVAGE project. In *Proceedings, 2001 Interservice/Industry Training, Simulation, and Education Conference*, Orlando, FL, 26–29 November 2001.
Blais CL, Brutzman D, Harney JW and Weekley J (2002a) Emerging Web-based 3D graphics for education and experimentation. In *Proceedings, 2002 Interservice/Industry Training, Simulation, and Education Conference*, Orlando, FL, 2–5 December 2002.
Blais CL, Brutzman D, Harney JW and Weekley J (2002b) Web-based 3D reconstruction of scenarios for limited objective experiments. In *Proceedings of the 2002 Summer Computer Simulation Conference*, San Diego, CA, 17–19 July 2002.
Nicklaus S (2001) *Scenario Authoring and Visualization for Advanced Graphical Environments*. Master's Thesis, Naval Postgraduate School.

The Web3D Consortium
Specifications:
Extensible 3D (X3D- ISO/IEC 19775:200x), Virtual Reality Modelling Language (VRML- ISO/IEC 14772:1997): http://www.web3d.org/x3d/specifications
X3D TaskGroup and X3DEdit: http://www.web3d.org/x3d.html
Software Development Kit: http://sdk.web3d.org
Xj3D Developer's Website: http://www.xj3d.org
Xj3D Open Source X3D/VRML toolkit: http://www.web3d.org/x3d/applications/xj3d

The World Wide Web Consortium
Specifications:
Extensible Markup Language (XML): http://www.w3.org/XML
Extensible Stylesheet Transformations (XSLT): http://www.w3.org/TR/xslt11

Chapter 4
SVG as the Visual Interface to Web Services

Shane Aulenback

4.1 Introduction

As XML becomes more important to business and consumers alike, data is being stored in more ways than in the historical document-centric days. Access to data is becoming timelier and more complicated. Therefore, the delivery and presentation required for that data must evolve at the same pace.

The introduction of Web Services is the latest method to address the delivery side of the equation. XML-authored content is replacing compound documents of days gone by. Web Services offer XML-based standard interfaces for accessing and querying data. However, this is creating a gap in the publication of this data, specifically when rich graphical visualization and interactivity are required. The technology gap is not as big as it first appears, however.

SVG is emerging as the technology of choice for Web-based graphics publications. As it is an XML language, it is the natural choice for representing other XML-based data. Containing rich effects, SMIL animation capabilities for creative presentations and full DOM access via ECMAScript, SVG is more than just a static graphics language. Unlike other proprietary formats available on the Web, SVG is a W3C open standard.

By adopting SVG, enterprises need not fear of being locked into contracts with specific vendors or technology. As it is completely human readable and standards compliant, the burden falls on vendors to offer compelling tools to their customers and not on the customers to work within the restrictions imposed by the vendor.

This chapter will describe the relationship between XML data, Web Services and SVG as a visual interface. First we will provide the definition of a Web Service. Next we will identify the core components of a Web Service and the workflow of a typical Web-based visualization or application. We will then move on to describing SVG and how these connections can be made. Finally, we will point out the technological gaps in providing a solution today and showcase the tools being provided from vendors such as Corel Corporation that will close the gap and make this a viable solution.

4.2 Web Services

An XML-based Web Service is a standards-based approach to delivering self-contained applications over the network (i.e., the Web). Web Services can be as simple as delivering data such as a stock quote or as complicated as delivering full application-like usability with relevance to the end user (such as an interactive stock chart covering a personal portfolio).

It can be argued that today's Web pages for many online applications such as banking are already, in substance, Web Services of a proprietary nature. Some standards do exist for creating and communicating between Web Services. However, a Web Service can be any Web-based mechanism for reading or writing data. As such, unless standards are created and implemented for the visual interface to Web Services, the change from any content contributor would result in a new design-to-development cycle for the mechanism exposing or consuming the resulting data.

XML-based Web Services provide two compelling characteristics that are attracting developers. First is their ability to easily reveal components. At design time or runtime, an application based on XML Web Services is able to discover existing components and expose them to the user. The second characteristic of Web Services is their ability to integrate with other applications. In essence, a Web Service is at its core made up of XML and can therefore reside anywhere, abstract any data source and yet integrate seamlessly with any other Web Service or host application.

The current missing item in Web Services is the visual interface. As eluded to above, currently XML-based Web Services are forced to integrate inside closed, proprietary applications. This not only diminishes the attraction of Web Services, it also increases the cost to maintain such applications, thereby defeating the value proposition Web Services offer to today's developers. Without an XML-based visual interface that can dynamically alter its appearance and functionality, developers are forced to make their decisions at design time, which does not allow their application to respond at runtime. Furthermore, changes to the data or functionality of the Web Service results in new application development requirements.

In an XML-based visual interface, a developer is able to use existing open standards techniques and languages such as SVG and XSLT to transform one XML document to another. A change to any of the XML assets requires at most, a change to one transformation, which reduces the cost of maintenance and increases the accuracy of the data exposed to the end user.

The key to this successful deployment is XML from end to end, including the ultimate visual interface that is exposed to the end user. Without it, the links in the chain are broken and the value proposition quickly lost.

4.2.1 The Technical Underpinnings of a Web Service

XML forms the foundation for the delivery of Web Services. XML by itself, however, cannot be considered a Web Service. For a Web Service to extend beyond the simplistic definition of information delivery, a common framework is needed (see Figure 4.1).

SOAP (Simple Object Access Protocol) is the industry standard for exchanging structured data between applications running on a network. It is made up of a framework describing what is in the message, a set of rules for expressing the data and a method for representing remote procedure calls. It can be used by service aggregators for accessing services provided over a network represented by the BIND designation in Figure 4.1.

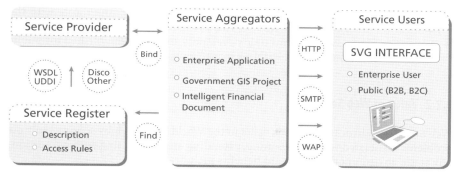

Figure 4.1 Web Services architecture outlining the importance of standards in every layer. The term "register" is used generically to describe any method for making the service known to its intended aggregator (public or private).

The programmatic interface is described in XML form using WSDL (Web Services Description Language). This enables a developer to build the usable application. Finally, UDDI (Universal Description, Discovery and Integration) is a registry for developers to quickly find and use publicly available Web Services. Using UDDI, or other technologies used to locate applications not intended for public consumption, such as Microsoft and IBM's Web Service Inspection documents (currently used in the .NET Framework), a service aggregator is able to search for services that meet his or her needs. Once found, the WSDL provides the programmatic description the aggregator would use to access the service in his visual interface.

Because all of these technologies are structured and standards based, they can be readily incorporated into a RAD (Rapid Application Development) tool to expose the functionality of the service without needing to understand the underlying technology, much like WYSIWYG HTML editors of today. These tools exist today, and one such example is Corel® Smart Graphics Studio™, from Corel Corporation (www.corel.com).

One advantage of a standards-based communication layer is that application code can be separated from the result. By providing a communication layer, a Web Service is independent of the underlying code and data that it represents. Combining multiple Web Services into multiple client applications does not require reinventing each application, but rather the recombining of assets.

According to a Giga Information Group, Inc. report, Web Services, XML and Java/J2XX continue to dominate the ever-evolving scene of technology standards: "As companies strive to move away from proprietary development platforms and tools, standards become the essential ingredient that makes that possible. Standards, whether in hardware, software or networks, provide the mechanisms that allow different types of applications and devices to interoperate" (Meyer, 2001).

The Web Service communicates to the client through standard Internet communication protocols such as HTTP or WAP. In very simple Web applications, the information is typically static HTML delivered to a browser. When full client-side application is required, the client is responsible for getting that data into an application.

The core requirements of a Web Service are outlined as follows:

- A Web Service delivers new and legacy application intelligence via a standard communication layer.

- A Web Service can be used in any application that can communicate with the connection described by the Web Service's WSDL.
- A Web Service is usable by multiple developers and can be published for public consumption or maintained within a private enterprise network.

4.2.2 Value of Web Services

Web Services deliver tremendous value to the World Wide Web by solving multiple problems associated with distributing, extending and interacting with a traditionally static environment. Significant benefits include:

- Delivering application intelligence to a medium that has only consumed static data.
- Delivering timely and relevant information, accelerating decision-making.
- Improving communication between disparate business units, improving productivity.
- Allowing combination of systems, reducing development costs.
- Allowing the separation of the interface and the logic, significantly reducing development and system maintenance costs.
- Extensibility allows services created today to meet the demands of tomorrow.
- Scalability allows each Web Service to run (and be reused) in multiple locations.
- Ability to host in an asynchronous environment, making the overall application more fault tolerant.

Web Services provide a new method of interacting with data and logic deemed critical for business operations. No longer are expensive and lengthy development cycles needed to create the necessary data or functionality for delivery. However, the design and delivery are not conducive to richer functionality. A more powerful visual interface layer is required to deliver applications effectively. To most end users, the interface is the application and, coding efficiencies aside, the end user is the primary recipient of the value of Web Services. Figure 4.2 shows an example of this framework that combines a rich graphical interface with dynamic data to display any type of application to the user.

It demonstrates the typical architecture of a Web Service-based application. The application intelligence, the data and the relationships between them are each a type of Web Service. At runtime, the Web Services are accessed and their results are combined to deliver a timely view of the relevant information via a rich, interactive visual interface to multiple devices.

4.2.3 What's Missing?

It is clear that Web Services open the door for a new way of developing Web-based applications. The gap occurs at the final stage. How does one create a compelling visual interface to represent and interact with their Web Services? Current Web-based technologies provide great interfaces for static visualizations and form-based queries. Other technologies offer rich interfaces but are proprietary and not well suited to accessing XML data, Web Services or programmatic interfaces. There is also a gap in the tools available for creating dynamic Web Interfaces.

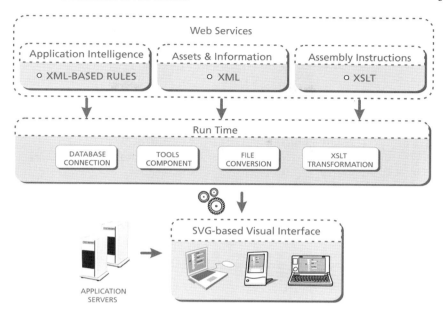

Figure 4.2   Dynamic component Web Service-based framework.

New technologies such as SVG are beginning to emerge and show themselves to be capable of filling the gap, specifically with the introduction of such products as Corel Smart Graphics Studio from Corel Corporation (www.corel.com/ smartgraphics). Corel has combined the power of SVG with XML and Web Services to offer a WYSIWYG environment for visualizing and interacting with your data.

4.3 SVG – the Right Choice

SVG offers an excellent framework with which to build rich, interactive and extensible visual interfaces. One can go so far as to say that a vector graphic format is the logical way to deliver information both at the present time and in the future. Vector formats provide quality, scalability and extensibility that cannot be obtained in a raster image. Although this chapter is focused on the Web Application as the output medium, it is not a stretch to imagine the same needs for delivering a rich visual representation of dynamic data to print or other, less powerful, Web-based devices such as cell phones.

This is not to suggest that bitmaps will not continue to play an important role in the delivery of information, however, just that the data-driven and interactive components are best delivered using vectors. In fact, SVG offers the ability to embed or link to raster images, and so can serve as a host environment for the portions of the interface that is required in raster format. Take the following example application, shown in Figure 4.3.

This interface requires bitmap and vector images and rich interactive GUI (Graphical User Interface) controls. However, what is not obvious from looking at

Figure 4.3   An SVG-based visual interface (Example 1).

Figure 4.4   An SVG-based visual interface (Example 2).

the visual interface is the supporting Web Services. The data that represents the district boundary lines in the left pane is actually stored as XML and offered through an external Web Service. Similarly, Figure 4.4 shows the same application, but with a visualization on the location of water wells provided through a Web Service from a different organization.

The following code shows a portion of the WSDL associated with the service exposing the well-water locations. What this demonstrates is that the vector graphics do not actually exist, but rather are created at runtime and are based on data available from multiple sources exposed through a Web Service infrastructure. This holds true for the items represented in the comboboxes, which also require an efficient runtime model with client–server interactions.

```xml
<?XML version="1.0" encoding = "utf-8"?>
<definitions xmlns:http="http://schemas.xmlsoap.org/
  wsdl/http/"
  xmlns:soap="http://schemas.xmlsoap.org/wsdl/soap/"
  xmlns:s="http://www.w3.org/2001/XMLSchema"
  xmlns:s0="http://tempuri.org/"
  xmlns:soapenc="http://schemas.xmlsoap.org/soap/
    encoding/"
  xmlns:tm="http://microsoft.com/wsdl/mime/textMatching/"
  xmlns:mime="http://schemas.xmlsoap.org/wsdl/mime/"
  targetNamespace="http://tempuri.org/"
  xmlns="http://schemas.xmlsoap.org/wsdl/">
    <types>
      <s:schema elementFormDefault="qualified"
        targetNamespace="http://tempuri.org/">
      <s:element name="SetWellData">
        <s:complexType>
          <s:sequence>
            <s:element minOccurs="0" maxOccurs="1"
              name="wellNumber" type="s:string" />
            <s:element minOccurs="0" maxOccurs="1"
              name="easting" type="s:string" />
            <s:element minOccurs="0" maxOccurs="1"
              name="northing" type="s:string" />
            <s:element minOccurs="0" maxOccurs="1"
              name="zone" type="s:string" />
            <s:element minOccurs="0" maxOccurs="1"
              name="depth" type="s:string" />
          </s:sequence>
        </s:complexType>
      </s:element>
      <s:element name="SetWellDataResponse">
        <s:complexType>
          <s:sequence>
            <s:element minOccurs="1" maxOccurs="1"
name="SetWellDataResult" type="s:int" />
          </s:sequence>
        </s:complexType>
      </s:element>
      <s:element name = "GetWellData">
        <s:complexType>
          <s:sequence>
            <s:element minOccurs="0" maxOccurs="1"
              name="wellNumber" type="s:string" />
```

```
          </s:sequence>
        </s:complexType>
      </s:element>
      <s:element name="GetWellDataResponse">
        <s:complexType>
          <s:sequence>
            <s:element minOccurs="0" maxOccurs="1"
              name="GetWellDataResult"
              type="s0:welldata" />
          </s:sequence>
        </s:complexType>
      </s:element>
      <s:complexType name="welldata">
        <s:sequence>
          <s:element minOccurs="0" maxOccurs="1"
            name="WellNumber" type="s:string" />
          <s:element minOccurs="0" maxOccurs="1"
            name="Northing" type="s:string" />
          <s:element minOccurs="0" maxOccurs="1"
            name="Easting" type="s:string" />
          <s:element minOccurs="0" maxOccurs="1"
            name="Zone" type="s:string" />
          <s:element minOccurs="0" maxOccurs="1"
            name="Depth" type="s:string" />
        </s:sequence>
      </s:complexType>
      <s:element name="GetAllWellData">
        <s:complexType />
      </s:element>
. . .
```

There are multiple technologies designed to interface with information published over the Internet, each having its own strengths and weaknesses. However,
SVG is the most appropriate technology to provide the solution above in that it
provides richness (see Figure 4.5), yet has the same key values of openness, extensibility and scalability inherent in Web Services.

Enterprise systems need to maintain extensibility, scalability, legacy format
compatibility and cross-platform support to ensure that technology created today
remains usable tomorrow. This can only truly be accomplished by abstracting
data using Web Services and offering open standards-based visual interfaces using
SVG. Because SVG is data aware, it enables the client–server architecture to support dynamically loading SVG fragments at runtime as portions of the graphic
change. SVG is by definition XML, so it supports namespaces and metadata;
this allows portions of an otherwise static graphic to be externally processed and
modified. Full event handler supports offer user event-driven behaviours. Finally,
because SVG is an open standard, it is distributable across many platforms and
media using any one of several SVG viewers such as the Corel SVG Viewer
(www.corel.com/svgviewer).

Taking advantage of all of the features of SVG and combining them with Web
Services and server-side technologies, one can create very compelling visual
interfaces. This technology combination is known as Smart Graphics and is the

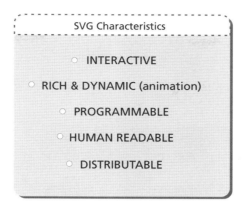

Figure 4.5   Value characteristics of SVG.

technology that will allow developers to build and maintain rich applications in a way that they never could in the past.

4.3.1 SVG-based Smart Graphics

Today's Web Services are very data-centric. Their programmatic interfaces allow a developer to abstract the data away from the application that is destined to consume it. As long as the programmatic interface is maintained, both the data that it represents and its visual representation can remain separate. This is the core architecture of Smart Graphics. By maintaining a separation of the data, logic and presentation layer, the resulting visual interface is very efficient to build and inexpensive to maintain. It allows data experts to worry about data, graphic designers to worry about presentation and developers to concentrate on the logic that ties it all together. Each person can work independently in the workflow and avoid such redundancies as depicted in Figure 4.6.

Smart Graphics enable graphically based visual interfaces to link with data and systems. Intelligence within the graphic can lie either completely on the server side, completely within the client or in some subset in between. Intelligence in this case is defined by the ability of the graphic to present relevant information based on the underlying data. For example, the axis in a simple bar chart can have the intelligence to scale according to the data that is being presented. A change to the data that describes the bar in the chart does not require a designer to create and maintain a new graphical representation or the developer to modify the logic in the application to visualize the new scale. The data is changed independently. Similarly, if the presentation of the bar chart needs to be changed, it is only a small job for a graphic designer to do so. Using a product such as Corel Smart Graphics Studio, all three stakeholders can use the same tool, create independent but reusable assets and worry only about their field of expertise.

4.3.2 The SVG Solution

Smart Graphics technology, although based on SVG, goes beyond what SVG is capable of on its own. SVG is viewed in a viewer on the client. Because Web Services

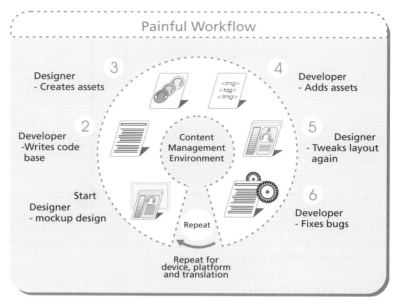

Figure 4.6   The painful workflow.

are server based, there is a breakdown in SVG's ability to consume them. Let us look at an example.

SVG provides a <use> element in its definition. An example SVG file with this tag is as follows:

```
<?xml version="1.0"?>
<!DOCTYPE svg PUBLIC "-//W3C//DTD SVG 1.0//EN"
  "http://www.w3.org/TR/2001/REC-SVG-20010904/DTD/
  svg10.dtd">
<svg xmlns="http://www.w3.org/2000/svg" viewBox="0 0
  1000 1000"
  xmlns:xlink="http://www.w3.org/1999/xlink">
    <use x="100" y="100" width="400" height="400"
      xlink:href="http://localhost/WebService1/
      Service1.asmx/getSymbol?
      nPercent=30#MySymbol"/>
    <use x="500" y="500" width="400" height="400"
      xlink:href="http://localhost/WebService1/
      Service1.asmx/getSymbol?
      nPercent=0#MySymbol"/>
</svg>
```

The external <use> tag allows an otherwise static SVG file to change fragments (dynamically) within itself based on server-side data. The syntax is fairly basic. Within the <use> tag, a size and position for the inserted fragment are specified. The remainder is an xlink to a Web Service that will return the SVG and the

"#MySymbol" represents the element ID that one wishes extracted. However, it is up to the Web Service to provide the SVG fragments. A typical Web Service for this would then contain a code fragment similar to the following:

```
public XmlDocument getSymbol( int nPercent )
{
    string str1="<svg><symbol id=\"MySymbol\" viewBox=\"0
        0 100 100\"><rect x=\"0.5\" y=\"0.5\" width=\"99\"
        height=\"99\" fill=\"none\" stroke=\"black\"
        stroke-width=\".2\" /><text x=\"";
    string str2="%\" y=\"15\" font-size=\"10\">From a web
        service</text><line x1=\"0\" y1=\"0\" x2=\"100\"
        y2=\"100\" stroke=\"red\" stroke-width=\".2\"/>
        <line x1=\"100\" y1=\"0\" x2=\"0\" y2=\"100\"
        stroke=\"red\" stroke-width=\".2\"/></symbol></svg>";
    string str = str1 + nPercent.ToString() + str2;
    XmlDocument myDoc = new XmlDocument();
    myDoc.LoadXml(str);

    return myDoc;
}
```

Immediately, the limitation of SVG by itself is obvious. The presentation layer for the graphic is now completely encased within the code fragment. The data that was required to create the graphic and the graphic itself are now completely embedded in the business logic. If a designer wants to change the presentation of the "MySymbol" graphic, a developer is required. If the data dictating the content of the graphic itself changes, once again the developer is required to implement the Web Service.

The alternative would be for the Web Service simply to provide the data that describes the graphic as was depicted in Figure 4.4. However, one then moves the accountability for processing the data to the client. SVG poses a few limitations to that approach. First, it would require the presentation layer to contain the logic for interpreting the data. Hence any change to the data structure would require a change to the presentation. It would also require a very thick client. This increases both the demand on the processing power of the client machine and the demand on bandwidth.

Finally, the <use> tag is for inserting SVG fragments. One would need to implement ECMAScript handlers to talk to a Web Service, load the XML data structure and then modify the SVG using the DOM APIs. This requires a developer that is very familiar with ECMAScript to be involved in the process. It also introduces the risk of viewer incompatibility as not all viewers implement the same subset of DOM. Hence one wants to minimize the processing logic on the client to the interactivity needs of the Web application, not the data-driven needs of the presentation layer.

You can now see why SVG by itself cannot take full advantage of a data-logic-presentation separation of Web Service application development. While you may be able to create rich visual interfaces, the painful workflow depicted in Figure 4.6 is repeated, hence development and maintenance costs are higher than they need to be.

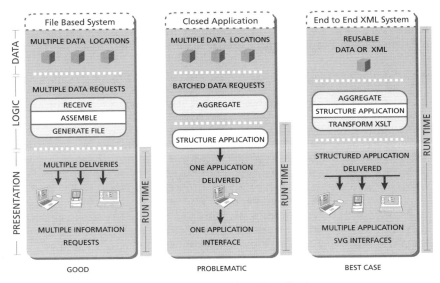

Figure 4.7   Three systems for Web applications.

4.3.3 The Smart Graphics Solution

Smart Graphics takes the best of SVG and solves the problems that were identified above. Separation of data, logic and presentation is the key to a successful Web Services-based application. Smart Graphics solves this with the introduction of another open standard-based technology to the workflow, XSLT. XSLT (eXtensible Stylesheet Language Transformations) is used to transform one XML document into another XML document. When used with the XML data returned from Web Services and applied to an SVG-based visual interface, we can completely transform a typical closed system into an end-to-end XML-based solution that completely separates data, logic and presentation and solves the painful workflow depicted in Figure 4.6. Figure 4.7 shows the transformation between these three systems with Smart Graphics represented by the end-to-end XML system.

By creating a Smart Graphics-based system, the three entities of data, logic and presentation are completely separated from each other. The data can now be stored in any system the enterprise chooses. Whether this is a database, a CMS or returned real-time from a hardware device, the enterprise need only ensure they have a programmatic interface via a Web Service available to query the data independently of the data structure. Using standards such as WSDL, this task is simple and can be implemented by a developer in a relatively short period. Both the data content and the data structure can change. So long as the programmatic interface remains constant, any system deployed need not be altered.

A designer can author the presentation layer in SVG. Many well-known vector authoring packages on the market today, such as CorelDRAW®, are capable of producing SVG graphics. Being a completely human-readable XML language, SVG can also be authored in any text-authoring program. Using ECMAScript within the presentation layer, a designer can also add client-side interactivity.

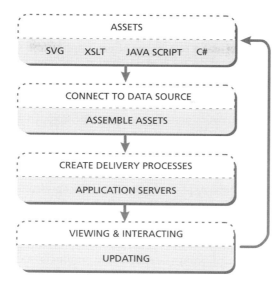

Figure 4.8   Framework stack outlining four key groupings of activities in delivering Web Services to a visual interface layer.

Finally, XSLT is used to code the logic for combining the programmatic data interfaces to the rich SVG presentation layer. By having the Web Service return the data in a structured XML format – which may be different from the underlying data model – we are able to introduce XSLT to transform one XML format (the data) into another (the presentation). In essence, this technology changes the static graphic created by the designer into a data-driven graphic.

As XSLT is an open standard, a developer can learn this language and an enterprise is not tied to any specific vendor. However, the XSLT can be put in the hands of the designer using products such as Corel Smart Graphics Studio. This tool allows the designer to consume their SVG assets for the presentation, see the structured XML data returned from the Web Service and visually implement the logic using a WYSIWYG environment which generates XSLT. The entire system can then be deployed on a server as a Web Service and delivered on the client side using any one of a number of SVG viewers such as Corel SVG Viewer. Figure 4.8 demonstrates the application stack for a Smart Graphics deployed application.

4.4 Summary

With the World Wide Web, we have seen a dramatic change in the way information is exposed and visualized. Typical desktop application paradigms are shifting towards a more Web-based deployment infrastructure and, as such, technology for creating, consuming and visualizing our data must change with it. This chapter has shown how Web Services are a step in that direction, but by themselves are not capable of completing the shift. It has also shown that technologies such as SVG are opening the possibilities for rich visualizations and interactivity with that data, but by themselves are offering an expensive application deployment strategy.

It is obvious that to build SVG applications effectively requires a combination of technologies that are currently available, although not in one usable environment. Appropriate tools are needed to reduce the effort, improve the workflow between development and design and decrease maintenance. Although some tools exist on the market today, joining them together in order to make a working application is difficult and reduces the core value of Web Services. Tools are also required that make it easier to solve the needs of both server and client.

Web Services as a framework alone is a very compelling distributed application delivery system. The fact that the major development tools vendors support environments for building applications only furthers the scope of the opportunity for the designer, the developer and the enterprise. SVG represents a compelling technology for interfacing with Web Services because it provides richness and interactivity while ensuring that the application logic and the application interface layers remain separated. To deliver application interfaces requires the addition of other technologies such as Java, ECMAScript, C#, and XSLT. However, the appropriate tools allowing design-development workflow integration and open-standard output make the development of the next generation of applications possible.

With the introduction of Smart Graphics and products such as Corel Smart Graphics Studio, the two technologies are being bridged and offer a rich experience for users at a low cost to enterprise. For more information about this breakthrough technology and tools to help with deployment, visit Corel Corporation at www.corel.com/smartgraphics.

4.5 Acknowledgments

The author would like to thank many of his colleagues for their help and support in the creation of Smart Graphics, which has allowed him the opportunity to tell others of this great innovation. Also, he would like to thank many colleagues for their assistance in the preparation of this chapter, specifically Rob for the background material, Sean for the wonderful edits and James for the great images. Finally, he would like to thank the management at Corel for the allowing him the time to prepare this work.

Reference

Meyer J (2001) *Web Services, XML and Java/J2XX Continue to Dominate the Ever-Evolving Scene of Technology Standards.* Giga Information Group, Inc.

Chapter 5
X3D Graphics, Java and the Semantic Web

James Harney, Curt Blais, Alan Hudson and Don Brutzman

5.1 Introduction

This chapter will show the reader how to use the Java™ programming language to manipulate X3D graphics scenes. Although familiarity with Java is not a prerequisite for understanding the material presented, familiarity with ECMAScript, Java or other object-oriented programming language will aid the reader's understanding. First, we will review the X3D Object model and the concept of fields and nodes that compose the building blocks we use to create an X3D scene. We then will examine how we can utilize more advanced manipulation of an X3D with Java and ECMAScript to make more interesting content. Finally, we look at how X3D can be leveraged in the framework of an XML-based Web for dynamic representation and interaction of information in a Web Services context.

5.2 The X3D Object Model

The X3D system model explained in Chapter 3 is based on the idea of various abstract individual entities referred to as objects. There we saw that an X3D graphics scene was arranged through declarative placement of various objects with behaviours added through specification of routes. The X3D description contains two primary types of objects: fields and nodes. Fields can be thought of as lightweight components derived from a base X3DField Object. Nodes are more complex objects that are composites of various other objects. These are derived from the base X3DNode Object. Nodes consist of one or more fields that send and/or receive events or store data for the respective node. Interestingly, nodes can also be fields of other nodes. Additionally, X3D nodes can implement further functionality through the use of programmatic interfaces representing common functionality such as grouping nodes and bounding boxes.

In the X3D Object model, there are some basic rules for all objects:

1. They must have a type name.
2. They must have an implementation.

There are additional rules for objects derived from the X3DNode Object:

1. They have zero or more field values.
2. They have zero or more events that they can send or receive.
3. They must have a name.

5.3 X3D Fields

Fields define the state of nodes in our X3D scene. Node state is persistent but dynamic through values sent or received in the form of events. Fields can contain a single value of a given type or an array of values of a certain type. In X3D, the characters SF prefixed to a type name means that the field contains a single value of this type. Multivalued (array) fields have a type designated with the prefix MF. For example, if field ABC is of type SFVec3f, then it contains one value of type Vec3f. On the other hand, the type MFNode designates an array of Node type values.

X3D supports four means of access to a node's fields:

1. initializeOnly: allows an initial value to be supplied for the field but no further changes can be made to this value after the scene is loaded.
2. inputOnly: allows an event to be received to change the value of the field, but does not permit read access.
3. outputOnly: allows an event to be sent to indicate the change in value of the field, but does not allow data to be passed to the node to set the value of the field.
4. inputOutput: permits full access to the field such as supplying an initial value, receiving dynamic input for changing the value of the field, and sending events when the value of the field changes.

Now, since a field with inputOutput access can receive routed events just like an inputOnly field, can generate events similar to an outputOnly field, and can contain state such as an initializeOnly field within an X3D file, certain rules apply to its use. Say our inputOutput field is called myField. If we want to treat it as an inputOnly field, then we can refer to it as set_myField. To refer to it as an outputOnly field type, we can reference the output event as myField_changed. When the inputOutput field receives an event, it must generate an event that contains the same value and time-stamp of that received. The X3D Specification lists the following rules for determining the initial value of an inputOutput field (in order of precedence):

1. the defined value in the X3D file.
2. the default value for the field according to the respective node.

There are also naming conventions for the types of fields we have covered so far:

1. All names which contain multiple words should start with a lower-case letter and successive words should be capitalized with no spaces between words (so-called Camel case). The two exceptions are use of the prefix set_ and the suffix _changed described below.
2. All inputOnly fields should have the prefix set_, with exceptions for adding and removing children.
3. Fields with access type inputOnly and outputOnly that are of type SFTime do not utilize the set_ prefix or _changed suffix for these fields.
4. All other X3D outputOnly fields should have the suffix _changed appended except for the outputOnly fields of type SFBool. Boolean outputOnly fields should begin with the word "is" (e.g., isMyClockStarted).

Now that we have reviewed some of the syntactical rules and guidance concerning the building blocks of the fundamental components comprising our X3D system, namely nodes and fields, we will review the X3D specific field types from the VRML 2.0 specification. As we mentioned previously, a field type can be defined as containing a single value (prefixed with the characters SF) or multiple value (prefixed with the characters MF), giving us two general classes of field types. Within each of these general classes, there are currently 15 field types that we will quickly review in order to aid in understanding the remainder of the chapter.

SFBool and MFBool. The SFBool field type represents a single Boolean value of either TRUE or FALSE. The MFBool field specifies an ordered listing of multiple Boolean values. Since programming languages can implement the Boolean data type differently, X3D leaves the implementation details to the programming API being utilized. For the SFBool field, if it is uninitialized, its initial value is defined to be FALSE. However, the initial value of an uninitialized MFBool field is an empty list.

SFColor and MFColor. SFColor is a single 3-tuple consisting of three floating point values representing red, green and blue (RGB) components of a colour. An MFColor field contains zero or more SFColor values. The value or each component of the triplet can be in the range from 0.0 to 1.0 inclusive. The initial value of an SFColor field, if not initialized, is the triplet (0 0 0); i.e., black. As before, an uninitialized MFColor field is an empty list.

SFColorRGBA and MFColorRGBA. These are similar to the SFColor and MFColor fields except that they also provide an alpha channel value with the red–green–blue values to support transparency. The SFColorRGBA field type contains one RGBA (red–green–blue–alpha) 4-tuple; MFColorRGBA contains zero or more RGBA 4-tuples and is an empty list when uninitialized. The colour and alpha values have the same 0.0–1.0 range as the SFColor and MFColor field types. The Alpha channel values are in the fourth position, with 0.0 being fully transparent and 1.0 being fully opaque or solid. The SFColorRGBA uninitialized value is (0 0 0 0).

SFDouble and MFDouble. The SFDouble and MFDouble field types were not included in the X3D's predecessor, VRML 2.0. The SFDouble field comprises a single double-precision floating point number whereas the MFDouble type contains zero or more of these values. These types are not considered to be a "Level 1" component in X3D since they were not in the original VRML specification but represent X3D specific types. Also, although the implementation of these types is intended to leverage processing capabilities for double-precision floating point values, they are permitted to be implemented using fixed-point numbering that has at least 14 decimal digits of precision and exponents in the range $[-12, 12]$. Similarly to the other field types, the uninitialized value is 0.0 for the SFDouble field and the empty list for the MFDouble field.

SFFloat and MFFloat. The SFFloat field type contains one single-precision floating point number. The MFFloat type contains an ordered array of these types. There is an allowable encoding for implementing this field using fixed point numbers that provides at least six decimal digits of precision with the same range for the exponents as for SFDouble and MFDouble. SFFloat has an uninitialized value of 0.0 and the uninitialized value for MFDouble is the empty list.

SFImage and MFImage. The SFImage field contains a single uncompressed 2D pixel image. The SFImage field starts with three integers giving the width, height and number of components contained within the image, followed by width times height hexadecimal or integer values representing the pixels in the image. MFImage fields contain zero or more SFImage fields. There is further information regarding the encoding of pixel and alpha channel values for these field types in the X3D Specification, but that is beyond the scope of this chapter. The default value of an SFImage field is (0 0 0). The MFImage field is an empty list if it has not been initialized.

SFInt32 and MFInt33. SFInt32 contains one 32-bit integer; MFInt32 contains zero or more of these values. Each value is a signed integer. The uninitialized value of an SFInt32 field is 0 and the uninitialized value of an MFInt32 field is an empty list.

SFNode and MFNode. The SFNode field contains a single X3D Node. An MFNode contains zero or more X3D nodes. Since all X3D Nodes inherit from a base type of X3DNode, they may all be assigned to this field type (within the syntactical rules of X3D, of course). Unlike the other single-value field types, an uninitialized SFNode field's value is NULL. As usual, an uninitialized MFNode field is an empty list.

SFRotation and MFRotation. The SFRotation field contains three floating point values denoting a normalized axis of rotation (xyz vector) and the desired angle of rotation about this axis in radians. An MFRotation field contains zero or more rotations. The uninitialized value of a SFRotation field type is (0 0 1 0); i.e., a rotation of 0 radians about the Z-axis. The value of an uninitialized MFRotation type is the empty list. From the X3D specification, the 3×3 matrix representation of a SFRotation value (x y z a) is

```
[tx²+c     txy+sz   txz-sy
 txy-sz   ty²+c     tyz+sx
 txz+sy   tyz-sx   tz²+c ]
where c=cos(a),  s = sin(a),  and t = 1-c.
```

SFString and MFString. We also have string field types available in X3D. SFString and MFString contain strings encoded with the UTF-8 character set. The SFString field type contains a single string value and the MFString type contains zero or more strings. Any characters can appear in a string. The initial value of an uninitialized SFString field type is the empty string and the initial value of an uninitialized MFString field is the empty list.

SFTime and MFTime. SFTime and MFTime represent values of time. SFTime field specifies a single time value and the MFTime field contains zero or more time values. These values are represented by a double-precision floating point number. Time values represent the total number of seconds since some time origin, and are normally indicated by the number of seconds since 1 January 1970, midnight, Greenwich Mean Time. The initial value of an SFTime field is -1 and the MFTime uninitialized value is the empty list.

SFVec2d and MFVec2d. The SFVec2d and MFVec2d field types represent two-dimensional vectors, where each component of the vector is a double-precision floating point value. SFVec2d contains one vector and MFVec2d has zero or more vectors. The initial value of an uninitialized SFVec2d field is (0 0) and the value of an uninitialized MFVec2d field is the empty list.

SFVec2f and MFVec2f. SFVec2f and MFVec2f are analogous to SFVec2d and MFVec2d but contain two-dimensional vectors consisting of single-precision floating point values. The uninitialized default values remain the same at (0 0) and the empty list, respectfully.

SFVec3d and MFVec3d, SFVec3f and MFVec3f. Finally, there are three-dimensional vector data types represented by 3-tuples of double-precision floating point values (SFVec3d and MFVec3d) and 3-tuples of single-precision floating point values (SFVec3f and MFVec3f).

5.4 X3D Nodes and Object Hierarchy

In Chapter 3, we reviewed most of the core components of X3D graphics and also many of the nodes in those components. These can be thought of as "built-in" nodes which are available to the content creator within the selected profile. The X3D architecture was based on a hierarchy that we can refer to as the X3D object hierarchy. Closely related to the Component ideal, the hierarchy defines nodes that consist of common attributes from a common base node.

5.5 Modifying Objects via Programmatic Access

We saw in the Chapter 3 that we can modify field values via the ROUTING mechanism, providing a way to create simple to complex behaviours within our X3D scene. In order to provide greater flexibility for content creators, some of the X3D profiles permit programmatic access to objects within our X3D system. In this manner, we can read and write field values, call functions or methods, expose our world to networking or even create new geometry on the fly. There are three types of programmatic access defined for X3D: (1) external access from a Web page or embedded byte code from Java/native applications, (2) scripting contained within the scene from a supported scripting language such as ECMAScript or Java and (3) creation of extension nodes (for example nodes written in Java, C++, or another language that are declared to the X3D system through the X3D declaration).

We will look at how we can leverage some of these capabilities through the use of Java in the X3D script node and further apply some of these ideals to demonstrate aspects of Semantic Web and Web Services concepts.

5.5.1 Application Programming Interfaces (APIs)

In the upcoming example, the interface between our X3D scene and Java code will be handled by the Script node, part of the X3D Scripting Component. For dynamic response to user inputs and external events, we use the Scene Authoring Interface (SAI) from the Script node. The scripting environment contained within the scene (in our case a Java application) can receive, process and send new events while maintaining state information. The X3D Specification team has designated the Script node for backwards compatibility with VRML97 Scripting, with the exception of cases where the VRML specification was occasionally vague or ambiguous (leaving implementation details to the browser manufacturer in a few cases). This variability in interpretation was not desired for X3D. Therefore, X3D-compliant implementations will default to the similar but more carefully defined X3D event model behaviour.

5.5.2 Script Node Activation and Execution

When the scene loads, a Script node is activated and may execute an optional initialization method. It later can execute when it receives a run-time event or during shutdown. The browser running our X3D code executes the inline script or program referenced by the Script node's URL field. Below is a simple scene that triggers a Java class identified in a Script node when the user clicks on the Sphere geometry:

```
<Scene>
<Script DEF='MyScript' 4) url="'MyExample.class'">
3) <field name='myInput' type='SFFloat'
  accessType='inputOnly'/>
</Script>
<Transform DEF='MyButton'>
<Shape>
<Appearance>
<Material diffuseColor='0 0 1'/>
</Appearance>
<Sphere/>
</Shape>
2) <TouchSensor DEF='MySensor'/>
</Transform>
1) <ROUTE fromNode='MySensor' fromField='touchTime'
toNode='MyScript' toField='myInput'/>
</Scene>
```

In this X3D snippet, we route (1) the touchTime event from the TouchSensor (2), triggered when the Blue Sphere is clicked on by the user, to the myInput field (3) in our Script node. This field is declared to be of type SFFloat and accessType inputOnly (i.e., only receives incoming events). Receipt of the event triggers the processEvent() method in our Java class MyExample.class defined in the url field of the Script node (4). When the scene is loaded, this class executes its initialize() method which prints out a statement to the Java console to indicate that it has been invoked. Note that the initialize() method is not required to be defined, we just choose to do so in this case.

The Script node is executed at initialization and shutdown of the X3D scene containing the node. We can make use of the programming concept of threading if we need to create processes that are going to do work separately from the event model triggering of the Script node (such as receiving network packets to influence objects in our virtual world). Script nodes receive all events in timestamp order. Therefore, conceptually, it takes no time for a Script node to receive and process an event since the timestamps correspond to the triggering event, but it will take some amount of time to execute the Script. Also, if the set_url field of our Script node is changed at runtime, the shutdown() method of the script will be called and the replacement script will then have its initialize() method invoked.

Below is a Java code snippet for the scene shown in Figure 5.1. The print statement in the initialize() method causes output of "Initialize called" to the console window with the scene is loaded (Figure 5.2). "Hello Scripting" is printed to the console window when the touch action in Figure 5.1 is performed.

```
import java.util.Map;
import org.web3d.x3d.sai.*;
public class MyExample
    implements X3DScriptImplementation,
X3DFieldEventListener {
```

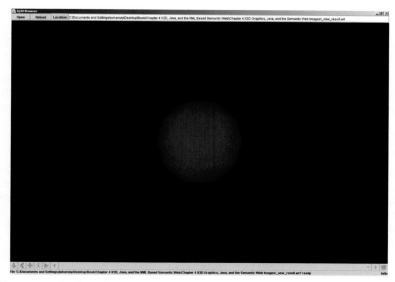

Figure 5.1   A simple world with a touch sensor that triggers execution of our HelloScripting Java program.

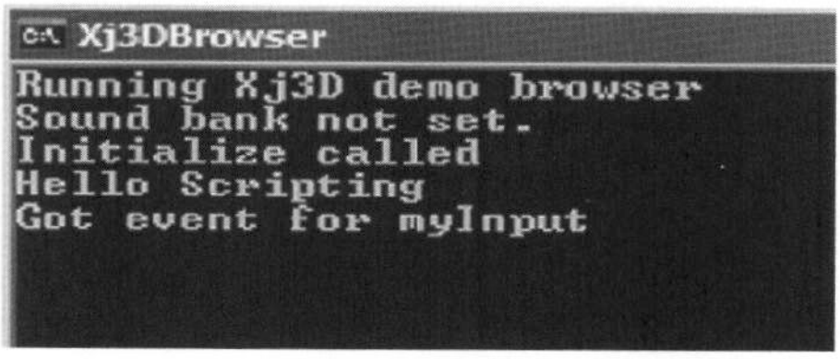

Figure 5.2   Console output from our HelloWorld program.

```
    public void setBrowser(Browser browser) {     }
    public void setFields(X3DScriptNode externalView,
Map fields) {
        X3DField inputField =
(X3DField)fields.get("myInput");
        inputField.addX3DEventListener(this);
    }
    public void initialize() {
        System.out.println("Initialize called.");
    }
    public void eventsProcessed() {     }
    public void shutdown() {     }
    public void readableFieldChanged(X3DFieldEvent evt)
{
        System.out.println("Hello Scripting");
        SFTime field = (SFTime) evt.getSource();
        System.out.println("Got event for " +
field.getDefinition().getName());
```

```
            System.out.println("value: " +
field.getValue());
    }
} // end MyExample.java
```

As shown, the Script node may implement an eventsProcessed() method, which is called after receiving one or more events. The events that we generate with this method are given the timestamp of the last event processed by the X3D system.

5.5.3 X3D Node Manipulation with Java

We can also gain access to other nodes within our X3D system with the Script node. We first have to set the directOutput field of the Script node to TRUE and give the script a USE handle to an already defined node within our scene graph, as the initialization reference for an SFNode/MFNode field. Once this has been done, we can then directly manipulate the node's fields or dynamically add and subtract children to that node. We will see an example of this later in the chapter.

Let us consider a few other aspects of Script node fields. If the mustEvaluate field of our Script node is set to FALSE, the X3D browser can delay sending any input events to the scripts until it detects that its outputs are needed by the browser itself. If we set it to TRUE, however, the browser is forced to send the input events to the script as soon as it can, whether or not it thinks the script needs them. We would typically use this technique if the Script node is going to contain effects not known to the browser beforehand, such as networking or other unpredictable feedback from inputs, in order to avoid detrimental impact on scene rendering performance.

Once we have access to an X3D Node (as described earlier), we are able to read the contents of that particular node's fields. Furthermore, if we set the Script node's directOutput field to TRUE, we can also send events to any node the Script node can access and dynamically make or delete scene graph routes. If, conversely, we set directOutput to FALSE (which is also the default value), we can only use the script to affect our X3D system through fields defined as outputOnly. The resulting behaviour of the scene is at the discretion of the browser implementation when we try to modify directly a node while directOutput is set to FALSE.

We can also obtain information directly from our X3D browser within the Script node; for example, the current time, display frame rate, current URL of the loaded world and other values are defined by the API for the scripting language being utilized (in our case, Java). Additionally, where we place Script nodes in our X3D scene graph has no effect on the operation of the scripting, when it receives events or when it sends them.

Hence, consider the following Script node snippet comprising a portion of a larger example we will be examining through the remainder of this chapter:

```
<Script DEF='WedgewoodScript' 3) mustEvaluate='true'
   directOutput='true'
url='"WedgewoodController.class"'>
4) <field name='nextInput' type='SFFloat'
   accessType='inputOnly'/>
5) <field name='backInput' type='SFFloat'
   accessType='inputOnly'/>
```

```
6) <field name='listInput' type='SFFloat'
   accessType='inputOnly'/>
1) <field name='WedgewoodGroup' type='SFNode'
   accessType='initializeOnly'>
2) <Transform USE='ContentPane'/>
</field>
</Script>
<ROUTE fromNode='BackSensor' fromField='touchTime'
   toNode='WedgewoodScript' toField='backInput'/>
<ROUTE fromNode='NextSensor' fromField='touchTime'
   toNode='WedgewoodScript' toField='nextInput'/>
<ROUTE fromNode='MiddleSensor' fromField='touchTime'
   toNode='WedgewoodScript' toField='listInput'/>
```

In this snippet we show the setup for our larger example coming up later in this chapter. We define a Script node with a field of type SFNode that is of accessType initializeOnly (1). As a child of the node, we define a Transform node (2) that has a "by-reference" handle to an empty transform node defined earlier in our scene named "ContentPane". We have defined directOutput and mustEvaluate (3) to be TRUE so that we can directly affect the contents of the TransformNode ("ContentPane") and respond immediately to user-driven events within our scene that will affect values of inputOnly field's nextInput (4), backInput (5) and listInput (6).

With the ability to manipulate the scene through routes or direct modification of nodes and fields, we have the tools needed to create complex dynamic scenes, as will be shown as we extend our example in the following sections.

5.6 Applicability to Emerging Semantic Web Concepts

Before proceeding, we need to define the context of this example a little further. We will be considering a situation in which objects with common characteristics or attributes are grouped together in a coherent fashion using information represented in XML. Actions can apply to the objects as a collective or individually, and the objects can initiate their own actions as needed. Information about the objects can be organized in a hierarchical fashion to provide greater meaning (semantics) for establishment and accessibility as services. Encoding information about Web-based resources in a manner that can be readily read and understood by human and software agents alike is the basis of the Semantic Web. Such resources include Web Services, loosely coupled software components made available over the Internet through an XML-based protocol stack comprising description, discovery, and invocation. This section shows some simple exploratory examples of these new Web concepts.

Since X3D is an XML encoding, we can leverage the content of the X3D file in several ways in the context of the Semantic Web. First, X3D can define a 3D view for user interactions with a Web Service (since it is a Web-based 3D graphics language for describing scene graphs). With profiles supporting varying levels of service, we can utilize XML stylesheets (XSL) to offer different forms of the same content based on the user device we detect querying our Web site or connecting with our Web Service. For example, a user accessing a service through a mobile phone browser may only be interested in viewing a scene containing 2D components, whereas a desktop user would have capacity for more complex scene generation, interaction, feedback and immersion.

In X3D, we can also include data describing our scenes in several ways. One approach is through the use of XML metadata tags. We are limited only by our imagination as to what information we put in metadata tags, but normally try to provide information that may be of interest to others (including software agents) who will employ the service. As an example, consider the following use of meta tags in the X3D header:

```
<meta name='filename' content='AntiqueViewer.x3d'/>
<meta name='description' content='Simple Antique Viewer
  for collectible plates.'/>
<meta name='author' content='James Harney'/>
<meta name='created' content='2 January 2003'/>
<meta name='revised' content='7 January 2003'/>
<meta name='generator' content='X3D-Edit,
http://www.web3d.org/TaskGroups/x3d/translation/README.
X3D-Edit.html'/>
</head>
```

Here, we only include descriptive information about the AntiqueViewer file such as filename, description, author and date modified, but in our payload data or scenes that comprise building blocks we can describe dimensions, references and other potentially useful information about the content of the file.

Another way in which we can include descriptive data within our X3D scene is through the use of the X3D WorldInfo node:

```
<WorldInfo info='"Allows dynamic viewing of and infor-
mation about collectible antique Christmas plates"'
title='"Antique Viewer"'/>
```

This node differs from the meta node in that it is actually a part of the scene graph. Unlike an XML comment, the WorldInfo node has well-defined attributes which can be queried by other programs trying to determine how to use the X3D file within a service.

5.6.1 The AntiqueViewer Example

Let us now put these various pieces together. Imagine that we are trying to establish a large clearing house for Web-based antique viewing or resale. Perhaps there will be different antique Web Services available for us to access to support our business. In this example we will show a subset of a collectible Christmas plate catalog. Specifically, we will see how the Java programming language can be used to create a user-driven X3D scene for viewing and interacting with our mini-catalog.

In Figure 5.3, we see that our catalog of antique collectible plates for viewing consists of Christmas plates. Every plate has a year and a name of what it is depicting, in addition to 2D and 3D depictions. We are going to use our X3D scene for communicating this information to the user, in this case on a desktop PC. The same scene is shown in Figure 5.4 from a different viewing perspective.

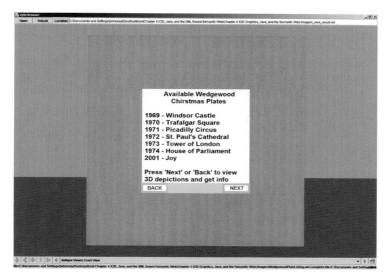

Figure 5.3   AntiqueViewer.X3D rendered in the Xj3D X3D/VRML97 browser.

Before getting into the details of the X3D file, when creating this scene we had to decide how we wanted to frame or best convey the information to the user in a visual context. In our case, we decided that this portion of the scene would be comprised of a "mini-cabinet" framed by a small room. We also decided to follow the standard convention of representing length measurements in our scenes in metres, i.e., one unit of distance in the 3D space being equivalent to 1 metre in the real world. For collectible plates, this meant that we were working in units of less than 1 metre, but if someone wanted to reuse the scene in another world then they

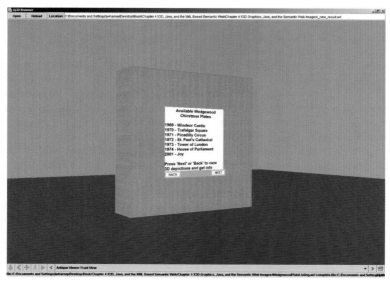

Figure 5.4   The AntiqueViewer.X3D from a different perspective.

would not have to worry about what scale we authored in and how to convert our scale to the standard conventions. Following established authoring conventions promotes reuse.

The room and cabinet can be created with a modelling tool such as Blender (http://www.blender.org), but in our case we used X3D-Edit (primarily the IndexedFaceSet X3D node) to piece together the cabinet and corresponding room. A portion of the X3D file is as follows:

```
1) <Transform DEF='ContentPane' translation='0 0-.02'/>
2) <Group DEF='ContainerGroup'>
<Transform DEF='TopSideOfViewer'>
<Shape>
<Appearance>
<Material/>
<TextureTransform scale='5 5'/>
<ImageTexture DEF='WoodTexture'
url='"WoodTexture.jpg"'/>
</Appearance>
<IndexedFaceSet solid='false' coordIndex='0 3 2 1 0 -
1'>
<Coordinate point='-.4 .2 0, -.4 .4 0, .4 .4 0, .4
.20'/>
</IndexedFaceSet>
</Shape>
. . .
```

We will refer to the Transform node (1) by its DEF name of "ContentPane". We will dynamically add and remove children to it for rendering in our AntiqueViewer through the use of Java in the X3D Script node.

This scene graph excerpt shows a standard geometry pattern (2) that we simply repeat with slight variation for creation of the viewing frame. In this case, we depict a mock-up of a small room with the wooden antique cabinet for providing information and rendering 2D and 3D views of our collectible plate catalog.

We want interaction with our world to be user centric, allowing the client to decide what information he or she wants to have delivered. In this example we will dynamically add information to the scene, but all information will be known to our Java application beforehand. We can easily interface the Java code to a database service or peer-to-peer content provider to provide dynamically the same information and scenes for on-the-fly delivery and rendering to the client application.

We will render the collectible item when the next, back or middle button is selected by the user. When the action is performed, the touchTime field of the applicable TouchSensor node in the scene is routed to the corresponding Script field. The X3D nodes for this action are as follows:

```
<Transform DEF='RightLowerUIButton'>
<Shape>
<Appearance>
<Material diffuseColor='0 0 1'/>
<ImageTexture url='"NextTexture.jpg"'/>
</Appearance>
```

```
<IndexedFaceSet solid='false' coordIndex='0 1 2 3 0 -1'
texCoordIndex='2 3 0 1 2 -1'>
<Coordinate point='.2 -.16 0, .1 -.16 0, .1 -.2 0, .2 -
.2 0'/>
<TextureCoordinate point='0 0, 1 0, 1 1, 0 1'/>
</IndexedFaceSet>
</Shape>
<TouchSensor DEF='NextSensor'/>
</Transform>
```

When the applicable button is selected by the user with the pointing device, the software triggers the processEvent method within our Java class. This method dynamically removes any previous children of our empty TransformNode (DEF="ContentPane") and then adds the applicable scene as a child of the same node.

Let us look at the Java setup required:

```
import java.util.Map;
import org.web3d.x3d.sai.*;

public class WedgewoodController
    implements X3DScriptImplementation,
X3DFieldEventListener {
    public static final String topLevelPage =
"TopLevelWedgewoodPage.x3d";
    public static final String[] plates =
{"1969WedgewoodChristmasPlate.x3d",
        "1970WedgewoodChristmasPlate.x3d",
"1971WedgewoodChristmasPlate.x3d"};

    public static final int NEXT_INPUT = 0;
    public static final int BACK_INPUT = 1;
    public static final int LIST_INPUT = 2;
    private Browser browser;
    private SFNode wedgewoodGroupField;
    private X3DScene scene;
    //indicator for which scene to dynamically render
    int choice;
    //indicator for rendering a listing of available
    boolean list;
    public WedgewoodController() {
        choice = 1;
        list = false;
    }
    public void setBrowser(Browser browser) {
        this.browser = browser;
    }

    public void setFields(X3DScriptNode externalView,
Map fields) {
```

```
        wedgewoodGroupField = (SFNode)
fields.get("WedgewoodGroup");
        X3DField nextInput = (X3DField)
fields.get("nextInput");
        nextInput.addX3DEventListener(this);
        nextInput.setUserData(new Integer(NEXT_INPUT));
    }
    public void initialize() {
        scene =
(X3DScene)browser.getExecutionContext();
        createPlate(topLevelPage);
    }
    public void eventsProcessed() {
    }
    public void shutdown() {
    }
    public void createPlate(String url) {
        X3DNode inlineNode =
scene.createNode("Inline");
        MFString urlField = (MFString)
inlineNode.getField("url");
        urlField.setValue(1,new String[] {url});
        X3DNode wgrp = wedgewoodGroupField.getValue();
        MFNode grp = (MFNode) wgrp.getField("set_chil-
dren");
        grp.setValue(1, new X3DNode {inlineNode});
    }
        . . .
```

The import statement provides access to a standard collection of well-known
interfaces that are implemented by the browser developers:

```
import org.web3d.x3d.sai.*;
```

Normally we utilize a set of stubbed interfaces provided by Web3D Consortium
which we compile against without relying on any particular browser implementation.

In the code excerpt above, we left out a series of declarations for URLs identifying our collectible plate catalog. These declarations can appear as follows:

//We're totally self contained on this one, so we list all components that can be
added here

```
        public static final String topLevelPage = "Inline
        {url [\"TopLevelWedgewoodPage.wrl\"]}";
        public static final String plate1969 = "Inline
{url [\"1969WedgewoodChristmasPlate.wrl\"] }";
        public static final String plate1970 = "Inline
{url [\"1970WedgewoodChristmasPlate.wrl\"] }";
        public static final String plate1971 = "Inline
{url [\"1971WedgewoodChristmasPlate.wrl\"] }";
```

As we said, one can receive this sort of information via a networked client setup in the Script node, whether from a Web Service or via some communications protocol such as the Distributed Interactive Simulation (DIS) Component. These string declarations will provide the basis for our dynamic content creation.

Data members of our class include a handle to our X3D browser, a Node reference, and a handle to the X3D scene object, as well as two class variables that help keep track of the scene state so that we can tell what content needs to be dynamically rendered:

```
private Browser browser;
private SFNode wedgewoodGroupField;
private X3DScene scene;
//indicator for which scene to dynamically render
  int choice;
//indicator for rendering a listing of available plates
  boolean list;
```

When the browser initializes a script, it calls methods setBrowser(), setFields(), and initialize(). Implementation of these methods was shown in the code excerpt earlier. The setBrowser() method obtains the handle to the X3D browser. The setFields() method obtains a handle to the Wedgewood grouping node and sets event listeners for each of the fields corresponding to user selection actions. As we will see later, occurrence of these events causes invocation of the readableFieldChanged() method to take appropriate action based on the user selection.

In the initialize() method, we read the reference to the empty TransformNode from our X3D scene, place a default scene there, render the scene, and update the internal state of our system (Figure 5.5). The following descriptions step through the initialize() code statements, including the method createPlate() that accesses

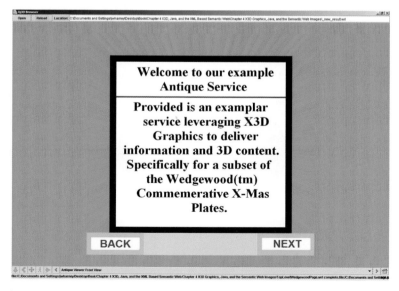

Figure 5.5   AntiqueViewer.X3D after scene loading and call to initialize() have completed.

and displays the selected item. Note that createPlate() will also be called when processing events in readableFieldChanged().

- We first get a handle to the X3D browser that our scene is being run by:
1) **scene** = (X3DScene)**browser.getExecutionContext()**;

- We call method createPlate() passing the X3D node holding the initial scene for our application:
2) **createPlate(topLevelPage)**;

- In the createPlate() method, we create an Inline node to load the top-level content:
3) **X3DNode inlineNode** = scene.create**Node("Inline")**;

- Next, we get the URL field for the Inline node:
4) **MFString urlField** = (MFString) inlineNode.getField("url");

- We set the URL field to the location of the content:
5) **urlField**.setValue(1, new String[] {topLevelPage});

- We get the base node of our Wedgewood group:
6) **X3DNode wgrp** = wedgewoodGroupField.getValue();

- We then get the set_children field of the Wedgewood group:
7) **MFNode grp** = (MFNode) wgrp.getField("set_children");

- We display the Inline node geometry by changing the children of the node in the scene graph:
8) grp.setValue(1, new X3DNode[] {inlineNode});

We have set the scene so that our Script node will be triggered by the user clicking

Figure 5.6 Display of the 1969 WedgewoodPlateInformation.X3D scene dynamically loaded upon user selection of the item.

the back, next or middle buttons in our scene. We need to be able to tell what triggered the event and render the applicable scene dynamically. To do so, we need to
implement the readableFieldChanged() method in the WedgewoodController.java
file. Code is provided below:

```
public void readableFieldChanged(X3DFieldEvent evt) {
    int eventId = ((Integer)evt.getData()).intValue();
    switch(eventId) {
        case NEXT_INPUT:
            ++choice;
            list = false;
            break;
        case BACK_INPUT:
            —choice;
            list = false;
            break;
        case LIST_INPUT:
            ++choice;
            list = true;
            break;
    }
    if (choice > plates.length - 1)
        choice = 0;
    else if (choice < 0)
        choice = plates.length - 1;

    createPlate(plates[choice]);
}
```

The logic simply determines the event that occurred and sets choice accordingly
(with some added logic to ensure the value stays in range). The createPlate()
method is called to display the selected item as discussed previously (Figures 5.6,
5.7 and 5.8).

5.6.2 Scene Authoring Interface (SAI)

The majority of what we have shown so far in this chapter has dealt with concepts
familiar to users of the VRML97 Scripting interface definition. A new area of development that we have mentioned for X3D is providing a core set of interface classes
on top of the VRML Scripting API, referred to as the SAI. Although not mature
enough at the time of this writing to provide a detailed example, the reader is
referred to http://www.web3d.org for more information. When completed, a scene
author will more easily be able effect changes within an X3D scene through either
Java or ECMAScript. The syntax for SAI Java calls is similar to what we have seen
using the traditional VRML libraries, but one will have to verify the API and applicable packages to import for this emerging capability.

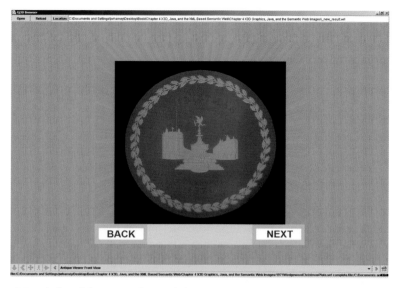

Figure 5.7   Display of the 1970 WedgewoodChristmasPlate.X3D scene after selection by the user.

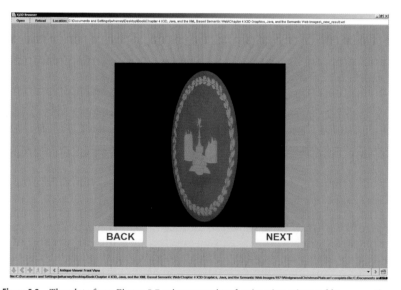

Figure 5.8   The plate from Figure 5.7 using prescripted animation triggered by user action.

5.6.3 ECMAScript in the Script Node

We can also do similar programming logic with ECMAScript in the Script node for X3D. Perhaps the biggest items of note, however, are the following: (1) for a small amount of functionality, inline scripting can be preferred to producing Java byte

code to run in our script nodes, mainly for authoring ease; (2) interpreted scripting code can run much slower when one has added a lot of programmatic functionality; and (3) the ECMAScript API calls are different from the Java API calls, so
it is generally best to have the scripting API references available for the first few
scenes authored with these techniques.

Although we will not go into the syntactical differences here, one can reference
ECMAScript saved as a .js file externally to the X3D scene much as we did with the
Java class in the Script Node url field. In fact we can list a Java class, followed by an
ECMAScript file, followed by an inline script with the first available URL being the
one loaded and used by our Script node.

The following is a short example of the use of inline ECMAScript in an
X3D file. Refer to the many resources listed at the Web3D Consortium's home
page for additional and more advanced information on its use than what we
show here.

In this example, we simply want to print to the Browser console some of the
accessible browser information (follows the example of the parse test from the
Xj3D project for ECMAScript).

```
<Script>
<![CDATA[
ecmascript:
     function initialize() {
     Browser.println('Name: ' + Browser.getName());
     Browser.println('Version: ' +
Browser.getVersion());
     Browser.println('URL: ' + Browser.getWorldURL());
  }
     ]]>
</Script>
```

Visually, this renders nothing to our X3D browser, but when we look at the console
window, we see that it has in fact printed the information we have requested
(Figure 5.9).

Figure 5.9   Xj3D browser console window with the expected output from our simple ECMAScript
example.

5.7 Conclusions

In this chapter, the reader has been exposed to programmatic access to X3D scenes through the X3D Scripting Component and primarily through the use of the Java programming language.

5.8 Acknowledgments

Screenshots are VRML views of the result X3D scenes through the Web3D Consortium-sponsored Open Source implementation for an X3D/Vrml 97 Browser, Xj3D and the ParallelGraphics Cortona browser. X3D editing was written and validated within X3D-Edit 2.4. Thanks are due to the X3D Specification team and contributors to Xj3D for their continued dedication and hard work in these areas.

References

Ames AL, Nadeau DR and Moreland JL (1997) *VRML Sourcebook*, 2nd edn. New York: Wiley.
Berners-Lee T, Hendler J and Lassila O. The Semantic Web. *Scientific American*, May 2001.
Blais CL, Brutzman D, Horner DP and Nicklaus S (2001) Web-based 3D technology for education – the SAVAGE project. In *Proceedings, 2001 Interservice/Industry Training, Simulation, and Education Conference*, Orlando, FL, 26–29 November 2001.
Blais CL, Brutzman D, Harney JW and Weekley J (2002a) Emerging Web-based 3D graphics for education and experimentation. In *Proceedings, 2002 Interservice/Industry Training, Simulation, and Education Conference*, Orlando, FL, 2–5 December 2002.
Blais CL, Brutzman D, Harney JW and Weekley J (2002b) Web-based 3D reconstruction of scenarios for limited objective experiments. In *Proceedings of the 2002 Summer Computer Simulation Conference*, San Diego, CA, 17–19 July, 2002.
Brutzman D (1998). The virtual reality modeling language and java. *Communications of the ACM*, **41**:(6), 57–64.
ECMAScript Language Specification. Available: http://www.ecma-international.org/publications/files/ecma-st/Ecma-262.pdf
Fensel D (2001) *Ontologies: a Silver Bullet for Knowledge Management and Electronic Commerce*. Berlin: Springer.
Nicklaus S (2001) *Scenario Authoring and Visualization for Advanced Graphical Environments*. Master's Thesis, Naval Postgraduate School.

The Web3D Consortium

Specifications:
Extensible 3D (X3D- ISO/IEC 19775:200x), Virtual Reality Modeling Language (VRML- ISO/IEC 14772:1997): http://www.web3d.org/fs_specifications.htm
X3D TaskGroup and X3DEdit: http://www.web3d.org/x3d.html
Software Development Kit: http://sdk.web3d.org
Xj3D Developer's Website: http://www.xj3d.org
Xj3D Open Source X3D/VRML toolkit: http://www.web3d.org/TaskGroups/source

The World Wide Web Consortium

Specifications:
Extensible Markup Language (XML): http://www.w3.org/XML
Extensible Stylesheet Transformations (XSLT): http://www.w3.org/TR/xslt11

Chapter 6
Distributed User Interfaces: Toward SVG 1.2

Kurt Cagle

The SVG specification first published in 2000 was designed with the intent to provide a graphical framework for vector-based imagery on the Internet. For a number of reasons – some technical, some political – the recommendation contained a number of limitations that have slowed the advent of the language. In the latter part of 2003, the Graphics/SVG Working Group of the W3C published the working draft of the next version of SVG, which significantly improves the proposed capabilities of the language as a vehicle for both graphics rendering and more generalized user interface deployment (W3C, 2003).

This chapter looks more specifically at some of the changes implicit within the SVG 1.2 working draft that will hopefully provide a meaningful answer to how such applications can and will be written.

6.1 Referential SVG

The use of Scalable Vector Graphics has been growing dramatically, although the adoption was not exactly what the working group members or SVG experts had suspected. Part of the reason for this has to do with the fact that for a great number of applications, vector graphics are generally superior to their bitmapped equivalents. Vector graphics can obviously be transformed more efficiently (and with better fidelity) than bitmapped graphics, occupy far fewer bytes and can be modified dynamically. However, the real advantage of vector graphics comes from the fact that any such graphic is semantically modular – you can designate a piece of the graphic to have its own identity, and this graphic can consequently be modified independently of any other part of the graphic, can contain metadata and can be referenced and used outside of the context of the larger containing graphic. Once again, it is the referential capabilities of SVG as XML that give it a major edge.

Up to SVG 1.1, however, this referential quality was very limited in scope – you could effectively only reference content that was created within the document itself. Admittedly, even this is a significant advantage over other coding environments. For instance, if you wanted to change the fill of a rectangular button from a red to a blue gradient on a roll-over of the graphic, all that was needed was to change the reference to the gradient object itself with a <set> element, as illustrated in Listing 6.1:

Listing 6.1. GradientTest.svg

```
<svg xmlns="http://www.w3.org/2000/svg"
  xmlns:xlink="http://www.w3.org/1999/xlink"
```

119

```
viewBox="0 0 1000 750">
<linearGradient id="normalBackground">
  <stop offset="0%" stop-color="maroon"/>
  <stop offset="100%" stop-color="red"/>
</linearGradient>
<linearGradient id="highlightedBackground">
  <stop offset="0%" stop-color="navy"/>
  <stop offset="100%" stop-color="blue"/>
</linearGradient>
<g transform="translate(400,275)" id="main">
  <rect x="0" y="0" width="200" height="200"
    fill="url(#normalBackground)">
    <set attributeName="fill" attributeType="CSS"
         to="url(#highlightedBackground)"
         begin="mouseover" end="mouseout"
         fill="remove"/>
  </rect>
</g>
</svg>
```

Beyond the elimination of scripting for at least the simple applications, one of the more significant aspects of even this level of referential indirection is the fact that you have created an abstraction layer. Rather than specifically manipulating the colour values associated with the gradients directly, the code above defines two states, a #normalBackground state and a #highlightedBackground state, and sets up an animation such that when a mouse-over occurs, the fill is directed to move to the #highlightedBackground state until such time as the mouse moves back out.

One effect of this is that the specific implementations of the background states consequently become largely irrelevant. For instance, suppose that you wanted to have a situation where the default state for the rectangle is a pattern of red circles, and when you roll over the rectangle, these became blue diamonds (as shown in Listing 6.2):

Listing 6.2. PatternTest.svg

```
<svg xmlns="http://www.w3.org/2000/svg"
  xmlns:xlink="http://www.w3.org/1999/xlink"
    viewBox="0 0 1000 750">
    <defs>
      <circle r="5" cx="0" cy="0" id="circlePattern"/>
      <g transform="rotate(45)" id="diamondPattern">
        <rect x="-5" y="-5" width="10" height="10"/>
      </g>
      <pattern id="normalBackground" width="20"
        height="20"
        patternContentUnits="userSpaceOnUse"
          patternUnits="userSpaceOnUse">
        <use xlink:href="#circlePattern" x="10"
          y="10" fill="red"/>
      </pattern>
      <pattern id="highlightedBackground" width="20"
        height="20" patternContentUnits="userSpaceOnUse"
```

```
                patternUnits="userSpaceOnUse">
        <use xlink:href="#diamondPattern" x="10"
          y="10" fill="blue"/>
    </pattern>
  </defs>
  <g transform="translate(400,275)" id="main">
      <rect x="0" y="0" width="200" height="200"
            fill="url(#normalBackground)" stroke="black">
            <set attributeName="fill" attributeType="CSS"
                 to="url(#highlightedBackground)"
                 begin="mouseover" end="mouseout"
                 fill="remove"/>
      </rect>
  </g>
</svg>
```

What is perhaps most important here that, despite the fact that the implementation has become a much more complex background, the displayed code (within the <g> attribute with id = "main") remains the same in both cases:

```
<g transform="translate(400,275)" id="main">
  <rect x="0" y="0" width="200" height="200"
    fill="url(#normalBackground)" stroke="black">
    <set attributeName="fill" attributeType="CSS"
         to="url(#highlightedBackground)"
         begin="mouseover" end="mouseout"
         fill="remove"/>
  </rect>
</g>
```

This referential aspect becomes much more fully manifest in SVG 1.2 because this standard explicitly opens up the connection with other external resources. In essence, you can specify an SVG graphic by its URL with an associated XPointer id (denoted by the # character) in order to reference specific items within that resource (Listing 6.3):

Listing 6.3. ReferencedPatternTest.svg

```
<svg xmlns="http://www.w3.org/2000/svg"
  xmlns:xlink="http://www.w3.org/1999/xlink"
    viewBox="0 0 1000 750">
    <g transform="translate(400,275)" id="main">
      <rect x="0" y="0" width="200" height="200"
        fill="url(wacky.svg#normalBackground)"
      stroke="black">
        <set attributeName="fill" attributeType="CSS"
             to="url(wacky.svg#highlightedBackground)"
             begin="mouseover" end="mouseout"
             fill="remove"/>
      </rect>
    </g>
</svg>
```

where the file wacky.svg acts as a library of individually defined sub-graphics, in
this case patterns (Listing 6.4):

Listing 6.4.   Wacky.svg

```
<svg xmlns="http://www.w3.org/2000/svg"
  xmlns:xlink="http://www.w3.org/1999/xlink"
  viewBox="0 0 1000 750">
    <defs>
      <circle r="5" cx="0" cy="0" id="circlePattern"/>
      <g transform="rotate(45)" id="diamondPattern">
      <rect x="-5" y="-5" width="10" height="10"/>
    </g>
    <pattern id="normalBackground" width="20"
      height="20"
      patternContentUnits="userSpaceOnUse"
            patternUnits="userSpaceOnUse">
        <use xlink:href="#circlePattern" x="10" y="10"
        fill="red"/>
    </pattern>
    <pattern id="highlightedBackground" width="20"
      height="20"
      patternContentUnits="userSpaceOnUse"
            patternUnits="userSpaceOnUse">
        <use xlink:href="#diamondPattern" x="10" y="10"
        fill="blue"/>
    </pattern>
  </defs>
</svg>
```

One implication of the ability to reference external resources as if they were local to
the SVG file is that it now makes it possible to create a repository of specialized SVG
"images" that can be referenced. These certainly include other graphical images, but
as the above example illustrates, these can also include patterns, masks, gradients
and complex filters, in addition to animations and interactive effects acting upon
these. For instance, if the diamond pattern in Listing 6.4 was changed from

```
<g transform="rotate(45)" id="diamondPattern">
  <rect x="-5" y="-5" width="10" height="10"/>
</g>
```

to

```
<g transform="rotate(45)" id="diamondPattern">
  <rect x="-5" y="-5" width="10" height="10">
    <animateTransform attributeName="transform"
        attributeType="XML" type="rotate"
        values="0;360" repeatCount="indefinite"/>
  </rect>
</g>
```

then when a mouseover occurs on the rectangle, the diamonds within the pattern
will appear to rotate.

A second consequence of this new linkage is the fact that it becomes possible to create Level of Detail (LOD) graphics. LOD is a term that originally arose in 3D contexts – objects in the distance generally do not need to be rendered to the level that nearby objects do, so simpler shapes can be used to approximate these objects until a certain proximity is reached (or some event is triggered). The same principle works in two dimensions, except that the proxy can be a simplified graphic (such as an outline) or a simple abstract of text, but when the event is triggered (a mouse click, for instance) the graphic is replaced with a more detailed rendering of the same (or a more complex text passage).

This linking mechanism works fairly well for representing deeper levels of information of a graphical nature, but as many of the applications where this kind of linking architecture involved formatted text, there is definitely a need for better text handling and manipulation. Fortunately, this is the second primary area of improvement in the SVG 1.2 working draft.

6.2 Bringing HTML into SVG

One of the primary problems that SVG 1.0/1.1 has had in gaining significant adoption comes from its limited ability to handle flowing text. That you can draw text in SVG is undeniable – it includes the ability to build inline fonts and handles kerning and other text related concepts fairly well – but the text that is created needs to be placed into the graphic one page at a time.

This has been rectified in SVG 1.2. There are in fact now two different ways to work with flowing blocks of text, depending on your requirements. The first involves inserting XHTML code within a foreign object in the SVG code itself and the second the creation of a set of flow regions that blocks of text can be flowed into. Taken together, these options go a long way towards adding the dimension of textual content into graphics.

XML languages, being essentially descriptions, can have the intriguing property of mixing well with other XML languages. Although the idea of incorporating SVG within HTML is reasonably well known (and is covered elsewhere in this book), you can also go the other route of inserting HTML content (or more properly XHTML content) within SVG through the use of the <foreignObject> element. Significantly, because of the difficulties of making this work, however, the foreignobject approach was generally not implemented in earlier versions and the general recommendation within the SVG 1.1 specification was that the foreignObject content be considered just a repository for working code.

However, in the Adobe SVG 6.0 viewer (ASV 6.0) [and presumably in other SVG 1.2 compliant viewers such as the Corel SVG Viewer (CSV)], a foreignObject tag with embedded XHTML will actually display that content as formatted HTML, wrapping content and all.

For instance, the initial quote in this chapter could be rendered into SVG as shown in Listing 6.5:

Listing 6.5.   AmayaOnTheTrain.svg

```
<?xml version="1.0"?>
<svg xmlns="http://www.w3.org/2000/svg"
   xmlns:xlink="http://www.w3.org/1999/xlink"
   xmlns:h="http://www.w3.org/1999/xhtml"
```

```
    width="100%" height="100%" viewBox="0 0 1000 750"
    x="0" y="0">
  <foreignObject width="400" x="10" y="10" height="750">
    <h:body>
        <h:p>Amaya stared through the train's rain-
streaked window, only vaguely seeing Seattle's bejeweled
skyscrapers faintly against the pervasive gloom of the
wintry night sky. She missed the clackety-clackety-clack
of the older trains that had gone on this route, replaced
now with the maglev line that rode smooth and quiet and
utterly, totally dull, only the faintest of accelerations
giving lie to the illusion that she wasn't in one of
those very buildings.</h:p>
        <h:p>She needed to know more, but that was to be
expected. Knowledge was like that. There was always more.
Fifty years before, the Cyberians, people such as Marvin
Minsky, had played with the first glimmerings of
artificial intelligence, feeling at the time that if
they could simply build up a large enough knowledge base
then they could create computer systems that would be
able to correlate that information and somehow become
sentient - "I know, therefore I am." Yet the more they
built, their students built, then those students'
students built on this edifice the more they realized
that knowledge itself was a lot harder to capture.</h:p>
        <h:p>Knowledge was fractal, she had realized, as
they had - a distributed multi-dimensional gossamer web
that permeated the human experience. This implicit
concept became explicit with the coming of the web in the
1990s. The web wasn't a static database of information,
but was instead a highly interactive explosion of
activity that crossed modalities - e-mail and mailing
lists and interactive adventures and web portals and
syndication feeds, an entire fauna of creatures within
its own exotic ecosystem. Knowledge by itself wasn't
enough - it was the fractal, distributed way that the
knowledge moved, the process. Old Rene Descartes had got
it right. She wondered, as the monorail shot over Lake
Washington, if the Earth was beginning to awaken and say
to herself, "I think, therefore I am."</h:p>
        <h:p> -- from Midnight Rain, 2004, Kurt
        Cagle</h:p>
      </h:body>
    </foreignObject>
</svg>
```

This illustrates a number of basic concepts about using <foreignObject>:

- The foreign object can be bounded. Here, for instance, the width and height of the object are set to "400" and "750" user units, respectively. This is especially crucial for word wrap behaviour, as the word will wrap at or before the width boundary.

Figure 6.1 "Amaya On The Train".

- The HTML is defined using the XHTML namespace – xmlns:h = "http://www.w3.org/1999/xhtml".
- The "root" element in this case is not the <html> tag, but the <body> tag. One interesting implication of this is that you can in fact have multiple HTML documents resident in the same SVG document.

However, this illustrates only a small portion of what *can* be done with HTML within SVG. A foreign object is not kept isolated in the document object model. Instead, it is retained as part of the SVG, which means that it shares the same style-sheets, event handling space and DOM manipulation, can receive animation events and so forth. In essence, it becomes part of the SVG document, which is usually made possible by the SVG engine mapping the HTML elements to some combination of SVG.

The same HTML content, but this time taking advantage of style-sheet properties, is shown in Listing 6.6 and Figure 6.1.

Listing 6.6.   AmayaOnTheTrain2.svg

```
<svg xmlns="http://www.w3.org/2000/svg"
xmlns:xlink="http://www.w3.org/1999/xlink"
  xmlns:h="http://www.w3.org/1999/xhtml" width="100%"
height="100%" viewBox="0 0 1000 750"
  x="0" y="0" preserveAspectRatio="none">
 <linearGradient id="nightSky" gradientTransform=
  "rotate(90)">
  <stop stop-color="black" offset="0%"/>
  <stop stop-color="#404080" offset="50%"/>
```

```
        <stop stop-color="black" offset="50.1%"/>
        <stop stop-color="#804020" offset="100%"/>
      </linearGradient>
      <linearGradient id="fire" gradientTransform
        ="rotate(90)">
        <stop stop-color="yellow" offset="0%"/>
        <stop stop-color="red" offset="100%"/>
      </linearGradient>
      <linearGradient id="textGlow" gradientTransform
        ="rotate(90)">
        <stop stop-color="white" offset="0%"/>
        <stop stop-color="#FFC000" offset="99%"/>
      </linearGradient>
      <style type="text/css">
 body {font-family:Garamond;fill:white}
 h1 {font-size:36;font-weight:bold;fill:url(#fire)}
 p {font-size:14;fill:url(#textGlow)}
 p.attribution {text-align:right;font-style:italic;}
      </style>
      <defs>
        <svg viewBox="-6000 0 8000 2000" width="800"
          height="150" id="skyline">
              <path class="fill str0" d="M-5761 1767c409,
-65 704,-71 704,-711 -12 -664 886 -21 0 456 437 0 0 -235
255 -259 362 211 0 138 482 -14 48 -1044 -320 -55 -111
-60 264 -155 674 0 201 118 -41 89 -352 66 142 855 1079
-28 0 -664 412 0 0 -629 201 -36 2 -171 576 0 17 162 261
1 0 341 171 0 0 -221 732 0 0 97 650 0 0 249c0,0 -48,280
0,320 47,39 438,194 457,154 18,-41 -30,247 -30,247l529
0 355 -307 174 -27 0 401 325 142 812 3 48 372 983 12 525
287 -2035 12 -9863 -72z"/>
        </svg>
        <rect x="0" y="0" width=".01" height=".04" fill=
"yellow" id="window"/>
        <pattern patternUnits="objectBoundingBox"
patternContentUnits="objectBoundingBox"
        width="1" height="1" id="windowLight"
patternTransform="scale(0.2,0.3)">
      <rect x="0" y="0" width="1" height="1" fill="black"/>
      <use xlink:href="#window" x=".200" y=".200"/>
      <use xlink:href="#window" x=".500" y=".250"/>
      <use xlink:href="#window" x=".700" y=".150"/>
      <use xlink:href="#window" x=".250" y=".420"/>
      <use xlink:href="#window" x=".850" y=".550"/>
      <use xlink:href="#window" x=".100" y=".600"/>
      <use xlink:href="#window" x=".290" y=".640"/>
      <use xlink:href="#window" x=".420" y=".500"/>
      <use xlink:href="#window" x=".420" y=".900"/>
      <use xlink:href="#window" x=".800" y=".720"/>
      <use xlink:href="#window" x=".250" y=".10"/>
```

```
    <use xlink:href="#window" x=".90" y=".80"/>
    <use xlink:href="#window" x=".70" y=".150"/>
    <use xlink:href="#window" x=".50" y=".670"/>
  </pattern>
</defs>
<rect x="0" y="0" width="1000" height="750"
fill="url(#nightSky)"/>
<use xlink:href="#skyline" x="200" y="250"
fill="url(#windowLight)"/>
<foreignObject width="400" x="10" y="10" height="750">
    <h:body>
      <h:h1 id="title">A Night Trip Into Seattle</h:h1>
      <h:hr/>
```

<h:p>Amaya stared through the train's rain-streaked window, only vaguely seeing Seattle's bejeweled skyscrapers faintly against the pervasive gloom of the wintry night sky. She missed the clackety-clackety-clack of the older trains that had gone on this route, replaced now with the maglev line that rode smooth and quiet and utterly, totally dull, only the faintest of accelerations giving lie to the illusion that she wasn't in one of those very buildings.</h:p>

<h:p>She needed to know more, but that was to be expected. Knowledge was like that. There was always more. Fifty years before, the Cyberians, people such as Marvin Minsky, had played with the first glimmerings of artificial intelligence, feeling at the time that if they could simply build up a large enough knowledge base then they could create computer systems that would be able to correlate that information and somehow become sentient - "I know, therefore I am." Yet the more they built, their students built, then those students' students built on this edifice the more they realized that knowledge itself was a lot harder to capture.</h:p>

<h:p>Knowledge was fractal, she had realized, as they had - a distributed multi-dimensional gossamer web that permeated the human experience. This implicit concept became explicit with the coming of the web in the 1990s. The web wasn't a static database of information, but was instead a highly interactive explosion of activity that crossed modalities - e-mail and mailing lists and interactive adventures and web portals and syndication feeds, an entire fauna of creatures within its own exotic ecosystem. Knowledge by itself wasn't enough - it was the fractal, distributed way that the knowledge moved, the process. Old Rene Descartes had got it right. She wondered, as the monorail shot over Lake

```
Washington, if the Earth was beginning to awaken and say
to herself, "I think, therefore I am."</h:p>

    <h:p class="attribution"> -- from Midnight Rain,
       2004, Kurt Cagle</h:p>
    </h:body>
   </foreignObject>
</svg>
```

The CSS involved with this foreign object content should be familiar to anyone who has worked with CSS in HTML, although there are also some subtle differences. For instance, within the <style> block:

```
<style type="text/css">
body {font-family:Garamond;fill:white}
h1 {font-size:36;font-weight:bold;fill:url(#fire)}
p {font-size:14;fill:url(#textGlow)}
p.attribution {text-align:right;font-style:italic;}
</style>
```

The <style> *must* be identified as being of type "text/css" or the matching will not work. Although not yet implemented, it is entirely likely that XSLT transformations via "text/xsl" will also be accepted as legitimate transformations, especially in conjunction with RCC and the Live Templates proposals discussed later in this chapter.

Although not to be covered here, you can also access the various HTML elements through the SVG DOM, both with the getElementById() function and with the getElementsByTagName() function, can assign content into the nodes (in a manner similar to that discussed in the next section) and can create new HTML elements with the standard SVG DOM functions.

6.3 Flowing Text Into the Web

HTML is an interim language. It started out as a language for describing physics abstracts, and although it has become much more multi-purpose since then, it is a language with enough limitations that in time (over the course of the next decade) it will eventually fade out of existence.

One reason for this has to do with the fact that HTML occupies a curious precarious existence between being a language for describing content and a language for describing presentation. As CSS has moved into the mainstream, HTML has increasingly become more generic and less focused on semantics, with CSS classes taking over the role of denoting meaning from <h1>, <ol> and <p> tags.

A second problem that HTML faces is the fact that its "flow-model" is essentially geared towards the notion of a single Web page. It is possible with CSS to position content into columns, and it is similarly possible to use tables to do the same thing, but the disadvantage of both is that there is no concept of flowing from one page to another, from one column to another on the same page, or from a column to a related column on some other page. In other words, HTML presents a different presentation interface than most print publications.

Why is this interface issue a problem? In part, this has to do with the physical characteristics of reading. It turns out that when reading, the muscles of the eye can move only so far in a line from left to right before tiring, a distance of 6 inches for most people. However, computer screens, especially with larger screens even on laptops, can often have Web text that extends for 10–12 inches horizontally, making it difficult to read. Print publications solve this problem by breaking content into separate columns that are short enough to be read without tiring out the eyes, but HTML has no real provisions for doing this.

A second problem comes from scroll bars. A Web page is more properly a Web "scroll"; at any given time you can only see a potentially small window into it, and to retrieve the rest, you have to break the page metaphor, move the mouse to the scroll bar, then reposition the content to find the information that you were seeking. This paradigm has become especially abused in recent years as designers have sought to use scroll-bar regions contained within other scroll bar regions, which inevitably results in the user having to guess the plane on which the relevant content is located.

The ability to flow text into multiple pages and multiple columns over those pages would make the Web act more like a newspaper or a magazine except that it is one that spans an infinitely complex document. The Adobe PDF format uses this metaphor to good effect to create laid-out pages that can be readily be searched, selected and expanded/contracted to all sorts of different devices. To a certain extent this is one of the reasons why the PDF format has retained its popularity even in the face of the capabilities offered by HTML – it represents a different metaphor, one that is more familiar to most people and that more readily handles the task of printing (which HTML does not do at all well).

PDF faces two limitations of its own, however. First, once a document is encoded within PDF, that document's format is largely immutable – you cannot arbitrarily change the number of columns or resize the content without also scaling the text, rather than reorienting the text to fit a more reasonable arrangement. The second, perhaps more significant, fact is that the text is not contained within an XML representation, and as such is much more difficult either to modify or query in an XML setting – not impossible, but requiring a deep enough knowledge of the Acrobat API to write the requisite code.

The solution to this particular conundrum was to have been XSL-Formatting Objects (XSL-FO). This particular standard was designed as a vehicle for laying out text in complex formats, using multi-column flow regions for defining everything from marginalia (such as a page number, title or date in a header or footer) to specific page content broken up by columns and paragraphs.

XSL-FO, unfortunately, never really took off in a big way. As a page markup language it was too heavily tied to the ideas of book publishers rather than magazine publishers. It did not employ CSS classes even though it supported CSS properties, making it difficult to group such properties as named styles. It was only marginally better at flowing content than HTML was, and it was extraordinarily complex to boot.

Given the failure of XSL-FO, despite the fact that some kind of XML-based page formatting language obviously has a certain innate utility, it is worth stepping back and examining the problem of laying out a publication (as a use case, assume a magazine of some sort) in a way that can be readily handled in XML. Such an application would need to do the following:

- **Pagination.** It should be possible to designate specific pages that are viewable at the appropriate times.

- **Shaped Flows.** It should be possible to specify given columns, or even non-rectangle regions, through which text can flow. This includes the possibility of knockout regions.
- **Graphics Support.** It should be possible to create rules and other compositional elements and position them easily.
- **Styles.** It should be possible to associate a particular block of text (or some span of that text) with an arbitrary style made up of presentation properties.
- **Master Elements.** It should be possible to define presentation properties, graphics, etc., that are common for all pages (to handle things such as page numbers and page count numbers in marginalia, for instance).

One solution, far from immediately obvious but nonetheless an echo of how such things are done with applications such as FrameMaker or Quark, is to create a template that defines the regions that text gets poured into, along with some way of associating each block of regions with some external text. This is the approach that SVG 1.2 uses for its new page layout capabilities. The working draft defines two new major constructs to make this happen, the <page> element and the <flow> element.

The purpose of the <page> element is to define multiple pages within an SVG document. This is an element that the language has needed for some time, because many of the most compelling applications for SVG are not so much in the creation of static graphics, but rather in the creation of dynamic pages for everything from slide-shows to magazines to animation scenes. Although it is certainly possible to do this with individual SVG files, the difficulty faced here comes in the fact that cohesion between files (such things as graphical backgrounds, common symbols or fonts and data resources) must be supplied by the developer, often resulting in a great deal of duplication. By using pages within an SVG document, publications, rich slide-shows and application wizards become much more feasible.

As it stands now, a <page> element is a child of a <pageSet> element, which is in turn a child of an <svg> document. A <pageSet> plays a number of roles – it makes it possible to create elements that are common to all of the pages in a given section, acts as a boundary for navigational elements (such as page numbers) and may also play a role in creating default layouts.

The following is a tentative example of a page document:

```
<svg xmlns="http://www.w3.org/2000/svg" version="1.2"
   streamable="true">

 <defs>
   <!-- definitions here are always available -->
 </defs>

 <g>
   <!-- graphics here are always visible -->
 </g>

 <pageSet id="notebook">
    <page id="introduction">
     <!-- graphics for page 1 go here -->
    </page>

    <page id="basicPrinciples">
     <!-- graphics for page 2 go here -->
    </page>
```

```
  <page id="newContent">
   <!-- graphics for page 3 go here -->
  </page>
 </pageSet>
</svg>
```

The flow text capability, on the other hand, is beginning to come together nicely. The <flow> element acts as a binding agent – it binds a selection of text to a flow region, a combination of one or more shape elements (such as <rect>, <circle>, <ellipse>, <polyline> or <path>) that are defined elsewhere within the SVG document. For instance, in Listing 6.7, the text fragment pulled from the novel is now distributed across four columns – one rectangular one for the title, two for the text body and one (a circle) for text to flow into what appears as a moon:

Listing 6.7.   AmayaOnTheTrain3.svg

```
<svg xmlns="http://www.w3.org/2000/svg"
   xmlns:xlink="http://www.w3.org/1999/xlink"
    xmlns:h="http://www.w3.org/1999/xhtml" width="100%"
   height="100%" viewBox="0 0 1000 750"
    x="0" y="0" preserveAspectRatio="none">
  <linearGradient id="nightSky"
    gradientTransform="rotate(90)">
     <stop stop-color="black" offset="0%"/>
     <stop stop-color="#404080" offset="50%"/>
     <stop stop-color="black" offset="50.1%"/>
     <stop stop-color="#804020" offset="100%"/>
  </linearGradient>
  <linearGradient id="fire"
    gradientTransform="rotate(90)">
     <stop stop-color="yellow" offset="0%"/>
     <stop stop-color="red" offset="100%"/>
  </linearGradient>
  <linearGradient id="textGlow" gradientTransform
    ="rotate(90)">
     <stop stop-color="white" offset="0%"/>
     <stop stop-color="#FFC000" offset="99%"/>
  </linearGradient>
  <style type="text/css">
.title {font-size:36;font-weight:bold;fill:url(#fire)}
.para {font-size:13.5;fill:url(#textGlow);font-
  family:Garamond;}
.moonText {font-size:13;fill:black;font-
  family:Verdana;text-align:center;}
.moonTextHighlight {font-weight:bold;}
.attribution {text-align:right;font-
  style:italic;}</style>
  <defs>
     <svg viewBox="-6000 0 8000 2000" width="800"
       height="150" id="skyline">
```

```
        <path class="fill str0" d="M-5761 1767c409,-65
704,-71 704, -711-12 -664 886 -21 0 456 437 0 0 -235
255 -259 362 211 0 138 482 -14 48 -1044 -320 -55 -111
-60 264 -155 674 0 201 118 -41 89 -352 66 142 855 1079
-28 0 -664 412 0 0 -629 201 -36 2 -171 576 0 17 162 261
1 0 341 171 0 0 -221 732 0 0 97 650 0 0 249c0,0 -48,280
0,320 47,39 438,194 457,154 18,-41 -30,247 -30,247l529
0 355 -307 174 -27 0 401 325 142 812 3 48 372 983 12
525 287 -2035 12 -9863 -72z"/>

    </svg>
    <rect x="0" y="0" width=".01" height=".04"
      fill="yellow" id="window"/>
    <pattern patternUnits="objectBoundingBox"
  patternContentUnits="objectBoundingBox"
      width="1" height="1" id="windowLight"
  patternTransform="scale(0.2,0.3)">
      <rect x="0" y="0" width="1" height="1"
        fill="black"/>
      <use xlink:href="#window" x=".200" y=".200"/>
      <use xlink:href="#window" x=".500" y=".250"/>
      <use xlink:href="#window" x=".700" y=".150"/>
      <use xlink:href="#window" x=".250" y=".420"/>
      <use xlink:href="#window" x=".850" y=".550"/>
      <use xlink:href="#window" x=".100" y=".600"/>
      <use xlink:href="#window" x=".290" y=".640"/>
      <use xlink:href="#window" x=".420" y=".500"/>
      <use xlink:href="#window" x=".420" y=".900"/>
      <use xlink:href="#window" x=".800" y=".720"/>
      <use xlink:href="#window" x=".250" y=".10"/>
      <use xlink:href="#window" x=".90" y=".80"/>
      <use xlink:href="#window" x=".70" y=".150"/>
      <use xlink:href="#window" x=".50" y=".670"/>
    </pattern>
  </defs>
  <rect x="0" y="0" width="1000" height="750"
   fill="url(#nightSky)"/>
  <circle cx="650" cy="200" r="100" id="moon"
    opacity="0.4" fill="white"/>
  <use xlink:href="#skyline" x="200" y="250"
   fill="url(#windowLight)"/>
  <rect x="10" y="10" width="400" height="40"
    id="column1" fill="none"/>
  <rect x="10" y="50" width="200" height="420"
    id="column2" opacity="0.4"/>
  <rect x="250" y="50" width="200" height="420"
    id="column3" opacity="0.4"/>
  <flow class="para">
  <flowRegion>
      <region xlink:href="#column1"/>
      <region xlink:href="#column2"/>
```

```
            <region xlink:href="#column3"/>
            <region xlink:href="#moon"/>
    </flowRegion>
    <flowDiv>
            <flowPara class="title">A Night Trip Into
Seattle</flowPara>
            <flowRegionBreak/>
            <flowPara>Amaya stared through the train's
rain-streaked window, only vaguely seeing Seattle's
bejeweled skyscrapers faintly against the pervasive
gloom of the wintry night sky. She missed the clackety-
clackety-clack of the older trains that had gone on
this route, replaced now with the maglev line that rode
smooth and quiet and utterly, totally dull, only the
faintest of accelerations giving lie to the illusion
that she wasn't in one of those very buildings.
</flowPara>
            <flowPara>She needed to know more, but that was
to be expected. Knowledge was like that. There was
always more. Fifty years before, the Cyberians, people
such as Marvin Minsky, had played with the first
glimmerings of artificial intelligence, feeling at the
time that if they could simply build up a large enough
knowledge base then they could create computer systems
that would be able to correlate that information and
somehow become sentient - "I know, therefore I am." Yet
the more they built, their students built, then those
students' students built on this edifice the more they
realized that knowledge itself was a lot harder to
capture.</flowPara>
            <flowPara>Knowledge was fractal, she had
realized, as they had - a distributed multi-dimensional
gossamer web that permeated the human experience. This
implicit concept became explicit with the coming of the
web in the 1990s. The web wasn't a static database of
information, but was instead a highly interactive
explosion of activity that crossed modalities - e-mail
and mailing lists and interactive adventures and web
portals and syndication feeds, an entire fauna of
creatures within its own exotic ecosystem. Knowledge by
itself wasn't enough - it was the fractal, distributed
way that the knowledge moved, the process. Old Rene
Descartes had got it right. </flowPara>
            <flowRegionBreak/>
            <flowPara class="moonText">She wondered, as the
monorail shot over the lake, if the Earth herself was
beginning to awaken, to say to herself, "<flowSpan
class="moonTextHighlight">I think, therefore I am.
</flowSpan>"</flowPara>
    </flow>
</svg>
```

The <flowRegion> element here contains four <region> references, pointing to the three rectangles and the circle defined earlier in the document. Each region must be a shape – you cannot point to a <g> element or a <use> tag. Notice the process of abstraction going on here – the <flowRegion> as defined points to four distinct abstract entities: #column1, #column2, column3 and #moon, without having any idea about the specific implementations of these particular entities, other than knowing that each region consists of a single path.

The <flowDiv> element contains the content to flow into the flow region, broken up into specific flow paragraphs called <flowPara> elements. Unlike the HTML example given in the previous section, a flow paragraph is simply a block of copy with no defined semantics. You can apply CSS classes to the <flowPara> elements, giving you control over presentation down to the block level.

Note that in the "moonText" <flowPara> element you can also get even more granular, using the <flowSpan> element to apply highlighting over a short text segment. The <flowSpan> element is analogous to the HTML <span> element:

```
<flowPara class="moonText">She wondered, as the monorail
shot over the lake, if the Earth herself was beginning
to awaken, to say to herself, "<flowSpan
class="moonTextHighlight">I think, therefore I
am.</flowSpan>"</flowPara>
```

The <flowRegionBreak> element serves to force text into the next shape in the region (or out of the region entirely if in the last element. Note that the text itself is retained in a buffer in memory, it is just not displayed because there are no containers to display it to. In the above example there are two <flowRegionBreak> elements – the first separates the title from the body text, whereas the second (after the text has already flowed from the second to the third column) separates the body text from the text within the circle of the moon.

Even with the current capabilities, there is more than enough to expand significantly what SVG can do with text layout, and there are enough hints of what SVG will be able to do once it reaches full Recommendation stage that it is worth rethinking the role of SVG strictly as a graphics tool.

6.4 Rendering Custom Content

So far, while the sections in this chapter have focused on referential SVG and the use of both XHTML and the SVG flow elements, there seems to be little here that moves the discussion to the concept of building a universal browser, one that can effectively take any XML, no matter how complex, and provide some kind of rendering mechanism. Yet with the advent of the topics covered here along with the existing capabilities, it should be possible to generate most two-dimensional content with SVG. The question then becomes one of figuring out an effective mechanism for doing so.

This question ties together two very distinct problems – how to create a generalized, principally declarative engine for displaying arbitrary XML and how to build "components" within XML that can emulate similar binary components. Although there are a number of candidates being considered, the one with the largest degree of current support is RCC – *Rendering Custom Content*.

In SVG 1.1, the <use> element is an example of a referential cloning element – the SVG engine establishes a reference to the original object, then allows the user the option of setting new attributes that override attributes that are not otherwise fixed, which normally occurs with an element within a <defs> element where a given attribute on that element is specified. Although this is actually fairly useful in a large number of cases, it means that <use> elements cannot contain text, a major limitation when it comes to building simple things such as buttons or other components.

As one of SVG's principle goals was precisely to create simple (and not so simple) components, this restriction has been at least partially responsible for the limited adoption of this particular technology. Not surprisingly, one of the major demands on the SVG 1.2 specification has been the development of a more robust, preferably XML-based, solution to creating richer functionality. To that end, the RCC module has been proposed to help facili-tate this.

The idea behind RCC is actually very ingenious. Rather than trying to build a complex method of specifying data-binding, RCC takes another approach altogether – a user can define their own custom namespace as a local XML exten-sion to SVG. For instance, suppose that you wanted to implement a presentation "language" for doing simple slide show applications. It would be broken up into different "pages" of content, which in turn would contain both section and page titles, sub-paragraphs and bulleted text. An example of that is contained in SimplifiedComplexity1.svg, a presentation given at a conference on SVG (part of which is displayed in Listing 6.8):

Listing 6.8. SimplifiedComplexity1.svg (detail)

```
<svg width="100%" height="100%" viewBox="0 0 1000 750"
xmlns="http://www.w3.org/2000/svg" version="1.2"
preserveAspectRatio="none">
 <desc>
   <title>Simplified Complexity, Complex
     Simplicity</title>
</desc>
 <!-- XPointer reference to the location for the
   flowchart extensions -->
   <extensionDefs xlink:href="presentations.
     svg#presentation"/>

   <p:presentation
   xmlns:p="http://www.metaphoricalweb.com/
   ns/presentation">
   <p:section>
       <p:title>Simplified Complexity and Chaotic
Simplicity</p:title>
        <p:page>
          <p:title></p:title>
          <p:quoteBlock>
            <p:para>
"There is always so much interest in doing," Symbol
Girl said softly, shaking her head with a hint of
sadness. As she did so the young woman placed
```

a small silver coin in the air, taking her hand away to
let the coin float unsupported.

```
      </p:para>
      <p:para>
```
"Even titles, those things that reflect roles, are
simply a statement of the actions that we are purported
to do -- an executive executes ... makes things happen.
A manager manages, a writer writes, a programmer
programs, a preacher preaches. We are the actions that
we perform."</p:para>
```
      <p:para>
```
A second coin joined the first, and Amaya saw that both
had acquired a slight spin, lazily orbiting around
Symbol Girl as the coins flipped over, heads, tails,
heads, tails. "It is a terrible thing to be known for
what you do, not who you are. Such titles create
expectations, and place the people who perform these
actions into a very narrow and stratified caste that is
more binding than any prison."</p:para>
```
      <p:para>
```
A third coin followed, then a fourth, each spinning in
its own chaotic orbits, until in time she stood within
a constellation of coins.</p:para>
```
      <p:para>"The world is. Life is, and then is
```
not."</p:para>
```
      <p:para>Symbol Girl raised one hand
```
slightly, and the glittering constellation froze in
place. "I suspect that life would have far more meaning
for people if they spent less time doing
and more time simply being."</p:para>
```
      </p:quoteBlock>
      </p:page>
      <p:page>
       <p:title>Imperative Languages: I Do</p:title>
       <p:listBlock>
         <p:para>For the last fifty years, the
```
dominant form of programming
```
         has been imperative, with most of that
```
based upon descendents of
```
         Algol (SmallTalk, C, C++, C#, Java, etc.).
```
Imperative languages have
```
         a number of basic characteristics:</p:para>
         <p:item>Operations take place by commanding
```
devices to perform
```
         specific actions</p:item>
         <p:item>Phrased another way: Functions are
```
performed on devices.</p:item>
```
         <p:item>State is maintained by independent
```
variables, and

```
                variables can be changed repeatedly.</p:item>
                <p:item>Functions can induce side
effects.</p:item>
                <p:item>Type is intrinsic to the language and
platform.</p:item>
                </p:listBlock>
                </p:page>
                <!-- more pages -->
            </p:section>
        <!-- more sections -->
</p:presentation>
```

Note from the namespace that this is not a "standard" language namespace – it was designed solely for my own use, although I am also quite sure there are a number of such presentation schemas already in existence. The point here is the fact that this information has no implied presentation layer – it is, strictly, tags and text. It is up to me to create that presentation layer, and in this case it does so by taking an XSLT-type approach to working with the elements via templates in order to create shadow trees.

In this particular case, the source XML document's root node is compared with a set of templates that are defined within the SVG RCC document. If the root node finds a match in the set of templates, then the SVG elements of that template are assigned to the "shadow tree" of that particular node (the green set of elements within the topmost yellow). Normally, the processor will stop at this point, unless the template contains a <refContent/> element within it. The <refContent> indicates that the children (or some other subset) of the current element matched by the template must themselves be applied to the sets of templates, with the same effects.

Should an element be passed by a <refContent> node and there is no template to match that element, then the element will be passed into the shadow tree of the object unchanged, attached as appropriate children. Text, attributes, comments and so forth will automatically pass through in this manner, which means that you can use your namespace and still embed SVG tags in the markup.

The significance here is that the term "shadow tree" is slightly deceptive. There are in fact a number of small trees that basically come into existence when the object is processed, and although they can (in the right context) be accessed from the central document, they are attached to the source XML tree.

The presentations.svg document (Listing 6.9) shows this principle in action. As the name suggests, the purpose of this particular SVG document is to provide the templates to make presentation slide shows possible, along with the code to wire them together.

Listing 6.9.   Presentations.svg makes possible a simple SVG slideshow application

```
<svg xmlns="http://www.w3.org/2000/svg" version="1.2"
xmlns:ev="http://www.w3.org/2001/xml-events"
xmlns:xlink="http://www.w3.org/1999/xlink" viewBox="0 0
    1000 750">
        <desc>Class file for presentation</desc>
        <style type="text/css">
```

```
.head {font-size:40;}
.body {font-size:20; font-family:Times New Roman;}
  </style>
      <script type="text/javascript">var page;
var oldPage
var presentationElt=null;
var pages=null;
  </script>
      <rect x="0" y="0" width="1000" height="750"
        fill="yellow" id="descriptor"/>
  <flow class="body">
      <flowRegion>
         <region xlink:href="#descriptor"/>
      </flowRegion>
      <flowDiv>
         <flowPara class="head">Presentation
           Widget</flowPara>
         <flowPara>This widget creates the control
           structures necessary to make
      a simple-slide-show presentation possible. I'll
be adding documentation to this
      as I get it going. Right click on this pane to
see the source code.</flowPara>
      </flowDiv>
  </flow>
  <extensionDefs id="presentation"
    namespace="http://www.metaphoricalweb.com/
      ns/presentation">
      <!-- Example needs to be upgraded to show
handling of mutation events -->
      <defs>
       <font id="FontID0" fullFontName="Symbols"
fontVariant="normal" fontWeight="400">
      <font-face
        font-family="Symbols">
      </font-face>
    <missing-glyph><path d="M0 0z"/></missing-glyph>
    <glyph unicode="°" horiz-adv-x="293"><circle cx="0"
cy="250" r="150"/><!--<path d="M276 591c0, -51 -15,
-90 -39, -120 -24,-27 -54, -42 -87,-42 -33,0 -63,15
-87,45 -27,30 -42,72 -42,120 0,48 12,90 36,120 24,30
54,48 93,48 33,0 63,-18 87,-51 27, -33 39,-72 39,
-120z"/>--></glyph>
        </font>
         <g id="rightArrowGraphic">
            <path stroke="black" stroke-width="2" d="M
0,0 L 0,-10 40,-10 40,-20 50,0 40,20 40,10 0,10z">
               <set attributeName="stroke"
attributeType="CSS" to="white" begin="mousemove"
  dur="0.5s" fill="remove"/>
```

```
            </path>
          </g>
          <g id="leftArrowGraphic">
            <path stroke="black" stroke-width="2" d="M 0,0
L 0, -10 -40,-10 -40,-20 -50,0 -40,20 -40,10 0,10z">
                <set attributeName="stroke"
attributeType="CSS" to="white" begin="mousemove"
  dur="0.5s" fill="remove"/>
            </path>
        </g>
        <symbol id="connectorline">
            <path transform="translate(0,50)"
stroke="black" stroke-width="3" fill="black" d="M 0,0 L
90,0 L 90,-10 L 100,0 L 90,10 L 90,0"/>
        </symbol>
        <linearGradient id="bannerGradient">
            <stop offset="0%" stop-color="blue"/>
            <stop offset="100%" stop-color="blue" stop-
opacity="0.2"/>
        </linearGradient>
        <linearGradient id="blueGradient1"
gradientTransform="rotate(90)">
            <stop offset="0%" stop-color="navy"/>
            <stop offset="100%" stop-color="black"/>
        </linearGradient>
        <style type="text/css">
.nodeText {font-size:20;text-anchor:middle;}
.terminalNode {fill:lightBlue;stroke:navy;
              stroke-width:5;}
.processNode {fill:lightGreen;stroke:green;
              stroke-width:5;}
.conditionalNode {fill:yellow;stroke:brown;
                  stroke-width:5;}
.presentation {fill:url(#blueGradient1);}
.sectionText {fill:white;font-size:30;
              font-family:Verdana;}
.quoteBlock {font:white;font-size:21;
             font-family:Verdana;}
.listBlock {font:white;font-size:21;
            font-family:Verdana;}
.listItem {font:white;font-size:18;
           font-family:Verdana;}
@font-face {font-family:"Symbols";src:url("#FontID0")
            format(svg)}
.fnt0 {font-weight:normal;font-size:24;
       font-family:Symbols}

        </style>
          <linearGradient id="bannerGradient">
            <stop offset="0%" stop-color="yellow"/>
```

```
          <stop offset="100%" stop-color="black"
stop-opacity="0"/>
        </linearGradient>
        <circle cx="-5" cy="-5" fill="yellow" r="10"
id="bullet"/>
      </defs>

      <elementDef name="presentation">
      <prototype>
        <g>
          <rect class="presentation" x="0" y="0"
width="1000" height="750" id="presentationBackground"/>
          <refContent select="section"/>
        </g>
        <g transform="translate(900,700)">
          <use xlink:href="#leftArrowGraphic" x="0"
y="0" opacity="1" id="leftArrow" onclick="change Page
(0)">
          </use>
          <use xlink:href="#rightArrowGraphic"
x="0" y="0" opacity="1" id="rightArrow" onclick="change
Page(0)">
          </use>
        </g>
      </prototype>
      <script ev:event="SVGBindBegin"
type="text/javascript"><![CDATA[
    re=/page=(.*)/
    re.exec(url);
    pageStr=RegExp.$1;
    if (pageStr==""){
        page=0;
        }
    else {
        page=parseInt(pageStr);
        }
    presentationElt=evt.target;

presentationNS="http://www.metaphoricalweb. com/ns/
presentation";
      pages = presentationElt.getElementsByTagNameNS
(presentationNS,"page");

    ]]>
      </script>
      <script ev:event="SVGBindEnd"
type="text/    javascript"><![CDATA[
      notifyButtons();

    ]]>
        </script>
```

```
            <script type="text/javascript"><![CDATA[
        function changePage(delta){
          var currentPage=pages.item(page);
currentPage.shadowTree.childNodes.item(1).setAttribute
("display","none");
        page += delta;
        currentPage = pages.item(page);
currentPage.shadowTree.childNodes.item(1).setAttribute
("display","block");
        notifyButtons();
        }
    function goToPage(pageName){
        var currentPage=pages.item(page);
currentPage.shadowTree.childNodes.item(1).setAttribute
("display","none");
        for (var i=0;i!=pages.length;i++){
          var queryPage=pages.item(i);
          if (queryPage.getAttribute("id")==pageName){
              page=i;
              break;
              }
        }
        currentPage = pages.item(page);
currentPage.shadowTree.childNodes.item(1).set
Attribute("display","block");
        notifyButtons();
        }
    function notifyButtons(){
presentationNS="http://www.metaphoricalweb.com/
              ns/presentation";
        var leftArrow = presentationElt.
                        shadowTree.get
                        ElementById("leftArrow");
        var rightArrow = presentationElt.
                        shadowTree.get
                        ElementById("rightArrow");
        url=window.parent.document.URL;
        re=/(page=.*)/
        urlPrev=url.replace(re,"page="+(page - 1));
        urlNext=url.replace(re,"page="+(page + 1));
      if (page==0){
        leftArrow.setAttribute("fill","navy");
        rightArrow.setAttribute("fill","yellow");

        leftArrow.setAttribute("onclick","change
          Page(0)");
        rightArrow.setAttribute("onclick","change
          Page(1)");
```

```
        rightArrow.setAttribute("onclick","change
Page(1)");
        }
    else {
      if (page == pages.length - 1){
            rightArrow.setAttribute("fill","navy");
            leftArrow.setAttribute("fill","yellow");
            leftArrow.setAttribute("onclick","change
              Page( - 1)");
rightArrow.setAttribute("onclick","changePage(0)");
            }
        else {
            rightArrow.setAttribute("fill","yellow");
            leftArrow.setAttribute("fill","yellow");
            leftArrow.setAttribute("onclick","change
Page( - 1)");

rightArrow.setAttribute("onclick","change Page(1)");

        }
    }
    var currentPage = pages.item(page);
    currentPageShadow = currentPage.shadowTree.
childNodes.item(1);
    currentPageShadow.setAttribute("display",
  "block");
    var listItems=currentPage.getElementsByTagNameNS
(presentationNS,"item");
    for (var index=0;index<listItems.length;
        index++){
      var listItem=listItems.item(index);
      }

    }
//]]>
      </script>
    </elementDef>
    <elementDef name="section">
        <prototype>
          <g transform="translate(10,10)">
            <rect class="banner" x="0" y="0"
width="990" height="40" fill="url(#bannerGradient)"/>
                    <g class="sectionText"
transform="translate(10,30)">
                        <refContent/>
                    </g>
          </g>
        </prototype>
    </elementDef>
    <elementDef name="title">
```

```
            <prototype>
                <text>
                            <refContent/>
                </text>
            </prototype>
        </elementDef>
        <elementDef name="page">
            <prototype>
                <g transform="translate(0,50)"
display="none" class="page">
                    <refContent/>
                </g>
            </prototype>
        </elementDef>
        <elementDef name="quoteBlock">
            <prototype>
                <flow class="quoteBlock">
                  <flowRegion>
                    <region xlink:href="#quoteBlock"/>
                  </flowRegion>
                  <flowDiv>
                      <refContent/>
                  </flowDiv>
                </flow>
            </prototype>
        </elementDef>
        <elementDef name="listBlock">
            <prototype>
                <flow class="listBlock">
                 <flowRegion>
                    <region xlink:href="#quoteBlock"/>
                 </flowRegion>
                  <flowDiv>
                      <refContent/>
                  </flowDiv>
                </flow>
            </prototype>
            <script ev:event="SVGBindEnd"
type="text/javascript"><![CDATA[
      lbElt=evt.target;
      lbShadow = itemElt.shadowTree;
      for (var i=0;i !=lbShadow.attributes.length;i++){
          var attr=lbShadow.attributes.item(i);
          alert(attr.nodeName);
          }

      ]]>
            </script>
        </elementDef>
        <elementDef name="para">
```

```
            <prototype>
                <flowPara>
                    <refContent/>
                </flowPara>
            </prototype>
        </elementDef>
        <elementDef name="item">
            <prototype>
                <flowPara>
                <flowSpan class="listItem"><flowSpan
class="fnt0">°</flowSpan> <refContent/></flowSpan>
                </flowPara>
            </prototype>
        </elementDef>
        <elementDef name="linkItem">
            <prototype>
                <flowPara>
                    <flowSpan class="listItem">°
[<refContent/>]</flowSpan>
                </flowPara>
            </prototype>
            <script ev:event="SVGBindEnd"
type="text/javascript"><![CDATA[
        itemElt=evt.target;
        flowPara=itemElt.shadowTree.childNodes.item(1);
        flowSpan=flowPara.childNodes.item(1)
        if (itemElt.getAttribute("xlink:href")!=''){
            var ref=itemElt.getAttribute("xlink:href");
            if (ref.substring(0,1)=="#"){
            ref=ref.substring(1);

flowSpan.setAttribute("onclick""goTo Page ('"+ref+"')");
            //flowSpan.setAttribute("f","underline");
            flowSpan.setAttribute("cursor","pointer");
            }
        }
        for (var i=0;i !=flowPara.attributes.length;i++){
            var attr=flowPara.attributes.item(i);
            }
        ]]>
                </script>
        </elementDef>
        <elementDef name="a">
            <prototype>
                <a xlink:href="#" target="new">
[<refContent/>]</a>
                </prototype>
            <script ev:event="SVGBindEnd"
type="text/javascript"><![CDATA[
        itemElt=evt.target;
```

```
            a = itemElt.shadowTree.childNodes.item(1);
            var ref=itemElt.getAttribute("xlink:href");
            a.setAttribute("xlink:href",ref);
        ]]>
            </script>
    </elementDef>
    <elementDef name="tag">
            <prototype>
            <flowSpan>&lt;<refContent/>&gt;</flowSpan>
            </prototype>
    </elementDef>
    <elementDef name="attribute">
    <prototype>
            <flowSpan style="font-style:italic;font-
weight:bold;">
                    <refContent/>
            </flowSpan>
        </prototype>
    </elementDef>

    <elementDef name="quotePara">
        <prototype>
            <flowPara>
                <refContent/>
            </flowPara>
        </prototype>
    </elementDef>
    </extensionDefs>
</svg>
```

There is, admittedly, a lot of code here. However, this application is not all that hard to understand when broken down. First, it is necessary to associate a particular source namespace with the presentation layer, through the <extension-Defs> element:

```
<extensionDefs id="presentation"
namespace="http://www.metaphoricalweb.com/ns/
presentation">
```

Notice how this differs from the <extensionDefs> element in the calling document:

```
<extensionDefs xlink:href="presentations.svg#
presentation"/>
```

The RCC document associates an id with this particular set of extension defini-tion elements (note that this is an open tag) and associates with the id a namespace, here "http://www.metaphoricalweb.com/ns/presentation". On the other hand, in the calling document, you have a referent to the RCC document (presentations.svg) along with an XPointer to the element with id #presentation, that is, to the <extensionDefs> element just discussed.

What this does is to create a binding in the calling document, so that any time an element of the namespace in question is found, the SVG engine will run it up against the templates (in this case <elementDef> elements), to see if the items match. This can only occur once for any given element in the source document, by the way – the SVG engine keeps track of which elements are processed through recursion to keep them from being processed again.

In general, you can think of an RCC element as being a closed global space – any elements that are defined outside of the <extensionDefs> block are essentially treated as globals (at least over the scope of this particular transformation). This is a good place to put <defs> type elements that are used at any scope within the application in question, for example, bullet glyph characters and banner backgrounds (in addition to script variables that need to be accessed by all libraries within the file). You can also create <defs> and <script> blocks within the <extensionDefs> block of an RCC document, but these will exist only in the scope of the particular namespace. This is handy when a single RCC document contains four or five different widgets, though this is not always the best programming practice, of course.

The first element that the SVG processor will encounter in the Simplified Complexity example will be the <presentation> element:

```
<elementDef name="presentation">
   <prototype>
      <g>
         <rect class="presentation" x="0" y="0"
width="1000" height="750" id="presentationBackground"/>
         <refContent select="section"/>
      </g>
      <g transform="translate(900,700)">
         <use xlink:href="#leftArrowGraphic" x="0"
y="0" opacity="1" id="leftArrow" onclick="changePage(0)">
         </use>
         <use xlink:href="#rightArrowGraphic" x="0"
y="0" opacity="1" id="rightArrow"
onclick="changePage(0)">
         </use>
      </g>
   </prototype>
   <!-- multiple script blocks here -->
</elementDef>
```

An <elementDef> object has a name attribute that contains the name of the node to be matched within the defining namespace. It also has one <prototype> element that contains the shadow tree definition. Here this creates a rectangle which serves as the text display area (#presentationBackground) corresponding to the size of the SVG document, and passes on a <refContent> element (which we shall come back to shortly). The <use> elements place left and right arrows on the screen in the lower right-hand corner, and bind them with a script which will change pages, but only to the current page (a null operation, in essence). The <prototype> element is necessary, as it identifies that code which gets transferred into the shadow tree (including, potentially, <script> elements).

That <refContent> element is the glue that holds this whole process together. The <refContent> element passes all child elements, their attendant attributes and text and CDATA nodes on to the RCC templates to be processed in turn (although not their link to the templated element). The *select* attribute on this particular refContent indicates that only section elements should be passed (along with their child nodes), and is in essence a very limited XPath implementation that allows only named nodes (e.g., section), bracketed numbers (the expression [2] for the second child node) or named nodes with bracketed indexes (section[2] would indicate the second section element found, for instance).

Two new events have also been defined for RCC, SVGBindBegin and SVGBindEnd, which can be defined within script blocks with the associated XML events-based attribute *ev:event*, as follows:

```
<script ev:event="SVGBindBegin" type="text/javascript">
  <![CDATA[
// This is called before the SVG is bound to the custom
control
]]></script>
```

```
<script ev:event="SVGBindBegin" type="text/javascript">
<![CDATA[
// This is called after the SVG is bound to the custom
control, but before the SVG is rendered.
]]></script>
```

These two events serve fairly different purposes. SVGBindBegin performs any initialization that is needed, and is occasionally called upon to perform any preprocessing on the custom elements being defined. It is not actually likely to be invoked by the developer very often. SVGBindEnd, on the other hand, can be a major workhorse. One of the biggest reasons for this is because there currently exists no clean way (using RCC) to pass attributes from a custom tag to some internal representation except through script.

As a very simple example of this, suppose that you wanted to create an element called <centreRect> that generated a rectangle centred on the bounding rect of the document. The calling document (Listing 6.10) would declare the namespace point to the source, then invoke the component:

Listing 6.10.   RCC_AttributeTester.svg

```
<svg width="100%" height="100%" viewBox="0 0 1000 750"
  xmlns="http://www.w3.org/2000/svg"
  xmlns:xlink="http://www.w3.org/1999/xlink"
  xmlns:test="http://www.metaphoricalweb.com/ns/test"
  version="1.2">
  <extensionDefsxlink:href="RCC_AttributeTest.svg#
   attributeTest"/>
  <test:centerRect width="400" height="340"/>
</svg>
```

The RCC document itself is about as simple, but because attributes cannot be assigned in RCC except through script, the SVGBindEnd binding has to handle this:

```
<svg xmlns="http://www.w3.org/2000/svg" version="1.2"
 xmlns:ev="http://www.w3.org/2001/xml-events"
  xmlns:xlink="http://www.w3.org/1999/xlink" viewBox="0
  0 1000 750">
```

```
<extensionDefs id="attributeTest"
namespace="http://www.metaphoricalweb.com/ns/test">
    <elementDef name="centerRect">
       <prototype><rect x="0" y="0" width="200"
          height="0" fill="red"/></prototype>
       <script ev:event="SVGBindEnd"
type="text/javascript"><![CDATA[
var centerRect = evt.target;
var shadowRect = centerRect.shadowTree.firstChild;
width=centerRect.getAttribute("width");
height=centerRect.getAttribute("height");
cx=500; // half of viewBox width;
cy=375 // half of viewBox height;
x=cx-(width/2);
y=cy-(height/2);
shadowRect.setAttribute("width",width);
shadowRect.setAttribute("height",height);
shadowRect.setAttribute("x",x);
shadowRect.setAttribute("y",y);
    ]]>
    </script>
  </elementDef>
  </extensionDefs>
</svg>
```

Notice that most of this information consists of either acquiring or setting attributes based upon other attributes. The current description, as given above, is wholly inadequate for long-term declarative development, and it is actually likely that in the next version, a formal expression evaluator syntax will be included, one which I am pushing to be based upon XPath. If it were (assuming an XSLT-like syntax), then the above template may very well be written as shown in Listing 6.11:

Listing 6.11.   RCC_AttributeHypothetical.svg

```
<svg xmlns="http://www.w3.org/2000/svg" version="1.2"
 xmlns:ev="http://www.w3.org/2001/xml-events"
 xmlns:xlink="http://www.w3.org/1999/xlink" viewBox=
 "0 0 1000 750">
  <extensionDefs id="attributeTest"
namespace="http://www.metaphoricalweb.com/ns/test">
    <elementDef name="centerRect">
       <prototype>
          <rect x="{viewBox(document)/@width-(@x/2)}"
             y="{viewBox(document)/@height-(@y/2)}"
             width="{./@width}"
             height="{./@height}"
             fill="red"/>
       </prototype>
      </elementDef>
     </extensionDefs>
</svg>
```

This would not completely eliminate the need for pre- and postbinding code, but it would dramatically reduce it. Note that the syntax is just a hypothetical guess as to how such an attribute-based syntax would be given, but it is consistent with other W3C notations.

One final aspect of this should be brought up. Obviously, the goal in creating such an RCC tree is to permit more sophisticated interactions with the "model," the custom namespace content that is bound to the controls. It should be possible to set up event listeners on specific elements that will in turn invoke the rebinding mechanisms. These events are described within the SVG 1.2 working draft as "mutation events," and in most cases they already exist within the model. However, the specific syntax for invoking SVGBindX from these events has not yet been clearly spelled out.

6.5 Live Templates, dSVG and XForms

Recursive programming using templates, inline code for assigning attributes, path-based access and the use of a set of namespace associations may sound vaguely familiar – these characteristics all describe XSLT. While the similarity did not escape the W3C SVG working group, they wanted to build a simple binding mechanism (RCC) for testing purposes first, then see how the SVG and XSLT specifications could merge. The current favourite in this regard is a proposal called Live Templates.

One of the problems with the RCC model as given above is the fact that it requires the XML in the namespace to be wrapped in an <svg> tag and associated with a specific <extensionDefs> file. However, it is far more likely that this option may prove problematic in a Web Services environment where wrapping the results of an XML query in an <svg> "envelope" could add considerably to the amount of processing.

Live Templates works on different assumptions. Specifically, Live Templates treats the problem space as follows:

- The data source is an XML resource that can be retrieved from an HTTP GET query against a URL, which works for both Web content and Web Services content.
- The transformation is (in most cases) a secondary file that can be loaded in and applied against the source object.
- The SVG file would contain a <generateContent> element, which would transform the first against the second in response either on load or in response to some external events.

In general, this would require three files (or, more accurately, URL reference-able resources): an XML data source, an XSLT transformation file and the SVG file that would merge the two. The W3C SVG Working Draft proposes a number of examples, of which one will be considered here. In this particular case, you have a button that is added into the SVG using the <generateContent> element. This acts as something like a super <use> statement, letting SVG developers locate where the object should be and the specified width and height of the object as appropriate. The SVG document is fairly straightforward (Listing 6.12):

Listing 6.12. GenerateContent

```
<svg width="10 cm" height="3 cm" viewBox="0 0 100 30"
    version="1.2"
```

```
    xmlns="http://www.w3.org/2000/svg"
xmlns:xlink="http://www.w3.org/1999/xlink">

<style type="text/css"<>![CDATA[
  .pushButton {
    fill: green;
    stroke: black;
    stroke-width: 3
    }
 ]]<>/style>
<script type="text/ecmascript"< <![CDATA[

var angle = 0;

function myCallback(evt) {

  var document = evt.target.ownerDocument;
  var elem = document.getElementById( "message" )

  // set rotation transform attribute on text.
  angle = angle + 10;
  var transform = "rotate("+ angle +" 100,20 )";
  elem.setAttribute( "transform", transform );
  }

 ]]> </script>
<text id="message" x="20" y="20" font-size="10">
  Below is a button, please press it</text>

  <generateContent
     x="10" y="10" width="30" height="30"
     transformer="buttons.xsl"
     type="text/xsl"
     input="buttonInstance.xml" />
</svg>
```

The referenced template file:

```
<pushButton xmlns="http://bar.example.org/buttons"
action="myCallback(evt)"/>
```

The referenced XML transformer file:

```
<xsl:stylesheet version="1.1"
   xmlns="http://www.w3.org/2000/svg"
   xmlns:bar="http://bar.example.org/buttons"
   xmlns:xsl="http://www.w3.org/1999/XSL/Transform">

    <xsl:template match="bar:pushButton">

    <xsl:variable name="action" select="./@action"/>

    <g class="pushButton" fill="blue"
      onclick="{$action}" >

    <rect width="100%" height="100%"/>
        <svg x="10%" y="10%" width="80%" height="80%">
```

```
                    <xsl:apply-templates select="./*"/>
                </svg>

        </g>
    </xsl:template>
</xsl:stylesheet>
```

When invoked, this would generate the following:

```
<svg width="10 cm" height="3 cm" viewBox="0 0 100 30"
    version="1.2"
    xmlns="http://www.w3.org/2000/svg"
xmlns:xlink="http://www.w3.org/1999/xlink">

<style type="text/css"<>![CDATA[
    .pushButton {
        fill: green;
        stroke: black;
        stroke-width: 3
    }
    ]]<>/style>

<script type="text/ecmascript"< <![CDATA[
    var angle = 0;

    function myCallback(evt) {

        var document = evt.target.ownerDocument;
        var elem = document.getElementById( "message" )

        // set rotation transform attribute on text.
        angle = angle + 10;
        var transform = "rotate(" + angle + " 100,20 )";
        elem.setAttribute( "transform", transform );
    }

    ]]> </script>

<text id="message" x="20" y="20" font-size="10">Below
    is a button, please press it</text>

    <g transform="translate(10,10)">
        <svg width="30" height="30" >

            <g class="pushButton" fill="blue"
onclick="myCallback(evt)" >

            <rect width="100%" height="100%"/>
                <svg x="10%" y="10%" width="80%"
                    height="80%"/>

            </g>
        </svg >
    </g >

</svg>
```

This is one of those instances where the use cases are very simple but the implementations are not; the code here actually works very effectively in the RCC context. A <generateContent> approach can work in those situations where the resulting SVG is likely to be much more complex (as will actually typically be the case), but again here you need to have the ability to reapply the transformation at various levels to keep the performance from being hideous.

The specification also addresses the Dynamic SVG proposal as offered by Corel, along with XForms. In both cases, the assumption is basically the same – these are treated as custom content namespaces that can be manipulated via the RCC or Live Templates architecture, an appraisal with which I am personally in agreement.

6.6 A Future of Distributed User Interfaces

The SVG 1.2 Working Draft (W3C, 2003), although still incomplete, offers a number of very compelling pieces that will have a direct impact on the way in which we build large-scale, distributed applications. To put this into perspective, consider that until relatively recently, applications were designed on the premise that the presentation of that application was very tightly coupled with the schema of the data being used, and changes to that schema would have a deleterious, if not downright disastrous, effect on the application (although this was also a model that a number of vendors have used to push sales of new operating systems or office suites).

In the context of the expanded capabilities inherent within SVG for such things as pagination and page flow, what emerges instead is a model where the very presentation layer can effectively reconfigure itself in response to XML data from a given namespace, and because of the referential nature of SVG, it should be possible to retrieve this new configuration by creating a key against the namespace to retrieve an RCC document from a certain location, or even by placing the link to the RCC document within the XML structure itself.

Note that this system is not completely autonomous. A given XML structure may very well have a number of different configurations that it could take depending on the specific requirements of the interface in question. For instance, a content management system will generate a very different interface for laying out the content presentation than it will in editing the stories contained within the CMS, displaying the content to an audience or sending the content to a printer-friendly format. In essence, the one factor that cannot be encoded specifically is *intent*.

This is where the development of RDF and other meta-language tools may most strongly intersect with SVG. RDF is a useful vehicle for creating requisite condition associations between intent and implementation – when this condition occurs, display this presentation layer for this namespace XML instance, and so forth. By being able to quantify intent better, it makes it easier for presentation systems to configure themselves in response to incoming, transient data.

Reference

W3C (2003) *Scalable Vector Graphics (SVG) 1.2. W3C Working Draft 13 November 2003*. Available: http://www.w3.org/TR/SVG12/

Chapter 7
Publishing Paradigms for X3D

Nicholas F. Polys

7.1 Introduction: Publishing Paradigms

As the demands of data and user tasks evolve and expand, the field of Information Visualization presents many challenges for designers and systems developers. Of primary concern is the mapping of data records and attributes to a visual presentation that enables the user to detect patterns and relationships within the data. The goal of this mapping is to minimize the user's cognitive requirements for understanding and insight into the nature of the data that may not be apparent from viewing it in its raw form. The mapping of data to a visualization must take into account the data's volume and types and this chapter will discuss some approaches to this display problem. However, static presentations are limiting in their power to inform because the data and mappings cannot be interactively explored or rearranged. Computer-based visualizations can address this problem because users can now have control over the selection of data records, the encoding of those records as visual markers and the presentation of those markers in a 2D screen or a 3D world. In this chapter, we will examine how data may be mapped to interactive 3D worlds that may be published and distributed over the World Wide Web (WWW).

In the early days of Web publishing, repurposing data content for multiple formats and platforms was expensive and, as a result, a majority of useful information was locked into technology "silos" for a particular delivery format, method and platform. International standards organizations serve the computing community by developing and specifying open platforms for digital data exchange. By adhering to industry standards, organizations can lower their software and data integration costs and maximize their data re-use while guaranteeing reliability and user access beyond market and political vagaries. Extensible Markup Language (XML) and Extensible 3D (X3D) are two examples of such standards and are covered in this volume. This chapter provides an overview of issues, strategies and technologies used for publishing information visualizations with XML and X3D.

7.1.1 File Formats and the Identity Paradigm

Initially, the majority of published information on the World Wide Web was in a format called HyperText Markup Language (HTML). HTML was revolutionary in

153

that it specified a declarative language for sharing documents (Web pages) across a network. The resulting boom to now multiple millions of Web pages is largely due to the simplicity and portability of this language. Information and images can be easily layed out, linked and accessed from all over the globe. If the author knows the HTML content header and tags, a basic document can be produced with a text editor and an image editing program. A document's headings, layouts, images, links, colours and fonts are all described with HTML tags. More complex or innovative layouts require the use of <table> tags, which are difficult to manage without authoring software.

One major drawback of HTML is that its tags are strictly specified and overloaded. Tags in an HTML document represent both the informational content *and* the presentation of that content, that is, the data and the display information are included in the same file, often in the same tags. This limitation makes HTML tags less attractive as a data storage medium since it is difficult to repurpose data to other formats and applications. For example, if a customer's name and order number are enclosed by separate header tags, such as <h1>, there is no way to distinguish which information is the name and which information is the number from the tags in the file alone. Cascading Stylesheets (CSS) attempts to separate content and presentation in HTML by allowing the author to specify classes of tags with defined display attributes such as font, colour, fill and border. CSS provides flexibility by allowing definitions to reside within document files or as remote resources. CSS is useful for presenting the same page with different styles. However, this flexibility is not really a qualitative improvement in the language because the tagset is mostly unchanged and still finite in its descriptive power for data.

Virtual Reality Modelling Language (VRML) is an international standard (ISO/IEC 14772-1:1997 and ISO/IEC 14772-2:2002), but was designed as a portable format for describing and delivering interactive 3D worlds. The VRML standard is similar to HTML in that it is declarative, strictly specified and carries both data and display information. In contrast to an HTML page, the VRML scene contains spatial viewpoint and navigation information, 3D geometry with colours, transparency and textures, text, fonts, links, backgrounds and temporal information such as object animations and behaviours (defined in Interpolators, Sensors and Scripts). Also, in contrast to HTML, VRML authors have the ability to define their own node types through the PROTO(type) node. The PROTO definitions can reside within the document file or as remote resources.

In VRML and X3D, nodes are analogous to element tags and fields are analogous to element attributes. Nodes are instantiated in a directed, acyclic graph called the scenegraph. A VRML file describes a scenegraph of interactive objects in space which the user can see and navigate through. Coloured and textured objects are manifested in the world (the scene), animated and visualized from a viewpoint or camera. When discussing Web3D media, the "viewpoint" will be referred to as the Viewpoint node itself and the "camera" as the rendered result of the Viewpoint via any superseding transformations. Similarly, "navigation" refers to the scale and nature of the user's control over their Viewpoint (by way of the values bound in the active NavigationInfo node).

Early ease of authoring was complicated by lack of browser compliance with the standards and scripting support for JavaScript (now officially "ECMAScript") varied widely. In some cases, Web publishers were forced to maintain multiple, browser-specific copies of their content in order to guarantee the widest possible accessibility. This amount of redundancy is expensive, even to percolate a small change across multiple Web site versions. Yet as the standards, client software and server technologies have matured, HTML, VRML or ECMAScript compliance is less the reason for maintaining multiple Web sites. Now, the motivation for permutable content is founded on the goal of customizing information for an audience or partner with a range of capabilities and interests. Although HTML enabled the exponential growth of the Web, it also required organizations to grapple with content management and personalization issues. The result was the design and deployment of Web "application servers" and Web "portals". We shall examine how these architectures currently apply to Web publishing and then to Web3D content, specifically X3D and VRML.

Hypertext Markup Language was originally designed to describe and deliver hypertext documents over the Web. Virtual Reality Modelling Language was originally designed to describe and deliver interactive 3D worlds over the Web. They are consequently unable to describe much else. Each is really only suitable as a Web publishing format, not as the formats for content storage, archiving and exchange. If pages are authored and maintained in a specific format (such as HTML or VRML) and the content is also delivered in that format (HTML or VRML), we can characterize the architecture as conforming to the "Identity Paradigm" – the source is identical with the deliverable. As mentioned above, this presents some problems both with maintaining a large set of documents and with re-using the documents' information in other contexts. Due to the limitations and expenses of this methodology, there was an immediate demand for other solutions. XML and X3D were designed to meet this demand.

7.1.2 Server Technologies and the Composition Paradigm

In recent years, a number of alternatives have been provided by Web server technologies and scripting languages to address these issues of maintaining static Identity Paradigm archives. Some well-known technologies include Server Side Includes (SSI), Perl, Hypertext Preprocessor (PHP) and Java Server Pages (JSP). These technologies do have significant differences, but the common denominator is that they permit the composition and delivery of a document "on-the-fly" in response to a user request. For example, when a user requests a page through the Hypertext Transfer Protocol (HTTP), SSI can get the current date and time from the Web server and display it in the delivered page. SSI can also insert markup fragments into a document. This allows different documents to include consistent display objects [such as headers, menus, tables and footers in 2D HTML and Heads-Up-Displays (HUDs) in 3D], reducing redundant content across multiple documents.

Scripting languages add another level of capability since they can connect and query online databases to recover information for display. For example, the user requests an online data set and the server script queries a database and writes it into the delivered (result) document. These solutions can all be classified as supporting the "Composition Paradigm", where documents are dynamically generated from one or more data sources. The Composition Paradigm brings more flexibility to Web publishing as developers can define common elements in a single location, pull data from multiple sources and combine them according to a user's request. As a result, dynamic Web sites are now commonplace.

A crucial issue in Web publishing that relates to the Composition Paradigm is the notion of content-type headers, or MIME types. MIME stands for Multipart Internet Mail Extension and was originally designed to distinguish files in Email attachments. The MIME type tells the client what kind of data is contained in the file so that the client can decode and handle it appropriately. For files on a local machine, this delegation can be accomplished simply by the file extension. In a Web server context, however, the MIME type is sent first as a single line and does not appear in the document source. Each Web server is configured to associate a document MIME type with a file extension and deliver it to the client. Web browsers or client operating systems also maintain such a list, which determines what plug-in or application will display the content. Hence every file on the Web has a content header that declares what kind of file it is.

Table 7.1 shows the relevant content types treated in this chapter. X3D (VRML V3.0) is a new standard for creating real-time 3D content. The specification of X3D's Architecture and API follows ISO/IEC FCD 19775:200x. Using the VRML97 specification as its starting point, X3D is cross-platform and hardware independent. It adds a number of new features, such as XML integration, multi-texturing, NURBS and a new scripting API. The X3D "Classic" encoding is a brace-and-bracket utf8 file encoding that looks like VRML97. The X3D "XML" encoding uses XML tags and attributes. At the time of writing, the X3D "Binary" encoding is still under development, but suffice it to say that a given scenegraph may be equivalently expressed in any encoding. The encoding specification for X3D is ISO/IEC FCD 19776:200x.

In practice, composability is generally accomplished with three ingredients: a structured template(s) for the delivered document, an accessible data source and a server technology such as SSI, PHP, JSP or Perl to compose the template with the appropriate data. Document templates basically structure the delivered document. As we shall see in Section 7.3.2, they are the skeletal form of the file, either implicit or explicit. Accessible data sources include both databases (i.e., SQL) and/or documents or fragments of documents. Server-side scripts manage the data sources and populate the template before it is sent to the user. The composed content is then delivered to the user with the appropriate MIME type.

On an Apache Web server, you might want to compose an X3D or VRML scene with PHP, Perl or some other server-side scripting language, but still have user's 3D plug-ins recognize it when it is received. In the case of composing VRML

Table 7.1   Principle filename extensions and MIME content types discussed in this chapter

File format	Content type/filename extension
Text	text/plain
HTML	text/html
VRML V2.0	model/vrml
XML	text/xml
VRML V3.0:	
X3D (Classic encoding)	model/x3d + vrml
	.x3dv and .x3dvz
X3D (XML encoding)	model/x3d + xml
	.x3d and .x3dz
X3D (Binary encoding)	model/x3d + binary
	.x3db and .x3dbz

or X3D Classic files, you could specify MIME types for a given folder by adding the line

```
AddType application/x-httpd-php .php .wrl .x3dv
```

or analogous definition to the .htaccess file in the directory on the Web server. This line configures the Web server to treat .wrl and .x3dv files and .php file requests as PHP files. This way, the Hypertext Preprocessor (PHP) engine is invoked when it serves both types of files and downstream applications such as browser plug-ins will recognize VRML and X3D content composed from PHP scripts in that directory.

The Composition Paradigm introduced a new level of capability for publishing dynamic Web content. In enabled Web "Portals", which refer to a single site that links and includes relevant information for a particular audience or domain. Portals are usually dynamic and customizable per individual user. Users can specify what information is included in what part of the layout, and what look and feel they prefer. In most cases, this kind of personalization system requires the user either to log in to the site or grant permission to set a cookie on their machine. Once the user is identified by the system, personalized content can be dynamically generated and delivered. This includes delivering customized information content to a user who is logged in from a workstation, a VR system or a mobile device, such as a PDA.

7.1.3 XML and the Pipeline Paradigm

The World Wide Web Consortium's (W3C) meta-language codification of XML has opened new and powerful opportunities for information visualization, as a host of structured data can now be transformed and/or repurposed for multiple presentation formats and interaction venues. XML is a textual format for the interchange of structured data between applications (W3C, 1998–2002; Kay, 2001; White, 2002). The great advantage of XML is that it provides a structured data representation built for the purpose of separating content from presentation. This allows the advantage of manipulating and transforming content independently of its display. It also dramatically reduces development and maintenance costs by allowing easy integration of legacy data to a *single data representation which can be presented in multiple contexts or forms,* depending on the needs of the viewer (i.e., the client). Publishers reduce the ratio of maintained source files to presentation venues as source data tends toward semantic markup (Apache Foundation, 2002).

Data becomes portable as multiple formats may be generated downstream according to application or user needs. Another important aspect of XML is the tools that it provides: the DTD and the Schema. The Document Type Definitions (DTD) define "valid" or "legal" document structure according to the syntax and hierarchy of the language elements. The Schema specifies data types and allowable expressions for the language elements and their attributes – it is a primitive ontology describing the document language's semantics. Using any combination of these, "high-level markup tags" may be defined by application developers and integration managers. This allows customized and compliant content to be built by authors and domain specialists. These tags could describe prototyped user-interface elements, humanoid taxonomies or geospatial representations. Developers describe the valid datamodel for their application using the DTD and Schema, share it over the Web and standardize it amongst their community.

XML can be as strict or as open as needed. Content, or fragments of content, can be "well-formed" and still processed with most XML tools. Typically, data validation is at author time, but it can be done at serving, loading or runtime if needed. Publishing advances using XML technologies can be characterized as the "Pipeline Paradigm" – information is stored in an XML format and transformed into a document or parts of a document for delivery. From an XML-compliant source document (or fragment), logical transformations [Extensible Style Sheet Transformations (XSLT)] can be applied to convert the XML data and structure to another XML document or fragment. A series of such transformations may be applied ending with a presentation-layer transformation for a final delivery-target style, content-type integration and display.

Numerous developer resources exist for the W3C's XSLT specification (Kay, 2001; White, 2002). However, a review of the typical XSL Transformation process is in order:

1. An XSLT engine parses the source XML document into a tree structure of elements.
2. The XSLT engine transforms the XML document using pattern matching and template rules in the .xsl style-sheet.
3. Template elements and attribute values replace matched element/attribute patterns in the source document to the result document.

The Web3D Consortium's next-generation successor to VRML is X3D. Like XML, which moves beyond just specifying a file format or a language like VRML or HTML, it is a set of objects and interfaces for interactive 3D Virtual Environments with defined bindings for multiple profiles and encodings collected under a standard API (Walsh and Sévenier, 2001; Web3D, 2002). Like VRML, the X3D specification describes the abstract performance of a directed, acyclic scenegraph for interactive 3D worlds. In addition, it takes advantage of recent graphics advancements such as MultiTexturing and information technology advancements such as XML. X3D can be encoded with an XML binding using DTDs and Schema (Web3D, 2002). The X3D Task Group has provided a DTD, Schema, an interactive editor and a set of XSLT and conversion tools for working with X3D and VRML97. Using the XML encoding of X3D, authors can leverage all the benefits of XML and XML tools such as user-defined markup tags, XSLT, authoring environments and server systems.

Additionally, rather than defining a monolithic standard, the X3D specification is modularized into components which make up "Profiles". Profiles are specific sets of functionality designed to address different applications – from simple geometry interchange or interaction for mobile devices and thin clients to the more full-blown capabilities of graphical workstations and immersive computing platforms. The notion of X3D Profiles is important for publishing visualizations and we will examine them in more detail in subsequent sections. X3D may be presented in a native X3D browser such as Xj3D (Web3D, 2002), or transformed again and delivered to a VRML97 viewer.

7.1.4 Hybrid Paradigm

The last publishing paradigm we will describe is the "Hybrid Paradigm". The Hybrid Paradigm combines the Pipeline and Composition paradigms. Data from

Publishing Paradigms

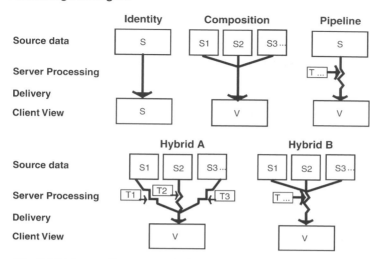

Figure 7.1   Publishing paradigms summarized: S = source; V = view; T = transformation.

various sources and transformational pipelines can be dynamically composed into a scene and delivered to the client machine. Apache Cocoon and Perl with the Gnome XML libraries are two well-known examples of technologies that permit such a flexible scheme. Figure 7.1 shows the principal differences between the paradigms described in this section.

7.2 Visualizing Information

Card et al. (1999) have defined Information Visualization as "The use of computer-supported, interactive, visual representations of abstract data to amplify cognition" (p. 7). This definition provides us with a clear starting point to describe visualization techniques for X3D as it distinguishes abstract data from other types of data that directly describe physical reality or are inherently spatial (e.g., anatomy or molecular structure). Abstract data includes things such as financial reports, collections of documents and Web traffic records. Abstract data does not have obvious spatial mappings or visible forms, hence the challenge is to determine effective visual representations and interaction schemes for human analysis, decision-making and discovery. Therefore, information visualization concerns presenting the user with the perceptual substrates for comprehension and insight. It must account for the nature, scope and amount of data and also human cognitive factors in the building of mental models.

7.2.1 Graphical Information Design

The nature of visual perception is obviously a crucial factor in the design of effective graphics. The challenge is to understand human perceptual dimensions and map data to its display in order that dependent variables can be instantly perceived and processed preconsciously and in parallel (Friedhoff and Peercy, 2000). Such properties of the visual system have been described (i.e., sensitivity to texture, colour, motion, depth) and graphical presentation models have been formulated to exploit these properties, such as preattentive processing (Pickett et al., 1996) and visual cues and perception (Keller, 1993).

Primary factors in visualization design concern both the data (its dimensionality, type, scale, range and attributes of interest) and human factors (the user's purpose and expertise). Different data types and tasks require different representation and interaction techniques. How users construct knowledge about what a graphic "means" is also of inherent interest to visualization applications. For users to understand and interpret images, higher level cognitive processes are usually needed. A number of authors have enumerated design strategies and representation parameters for rendering signifieds in graphics (Bertin, 1981; Tufte, 1990) and there are effects from both the kind of data and the kind of task (Schneiderman, 1996). Card et al. (1999) examined a variety of graphical forms and critically compared visual cues in scatter-plots, cone-trees, hyperbolic trees, tree maps, points-of-interest and perspective wall renderings. As we shall see, their work is important since any of these 2D visualizations may be embedded inside, or manifested as, a virtual environment.

Interactive computer graphics present another level of complication for determining meaning as they are responsive, dynamic and may take diverse forms. There are challenges both on the input medium for the user and the action medium for the user. These are known as the Gulf of Evaluation and the Gulf of Execution, respectively (Norman, 1986). Typically in the literature, visualizations are described and categorized per user task such as exploring, finding, comparing, and recognizing (patterns). These tasks are also common in interactive 3D worlds. Information objects may need to be depicted with affordances for such actions. Here we shall examine how interactive visual markers can be designed and delivered with X3D.

7.2.2 Visual Markers

General types of data can be described as quantitative (numerical), ordinal and nominal (or categorical). Visualization design requires the mapping of data attributes to "visual markers" (the graphical representations of those attributes). Mappings must be computable (they must be able to be generated by a computer) and they must be comprehensible by the user (the user must understand the rules that govern the mapping in order to interpret the visualization). The employment of various visual markers can be defined by the visualization designer or defined by the user. Tools such as Spotfire (Ahlberg and Wistrand, 1995) and Snap (North and Schneiderman, 2000) are good examples of this interactive user control over the display process. This functionality can also be accomplished with X3D. In addition, a set of "modes" of interaction have been proposed for exploratory data visualizations which attempt to account for user feedback and control in a runtime display (Hibbard et al., 1995a). Table 7.2 summarizes the ordering of visual markers by accuracy for the general data types. These rankings lay a foundation for identifying parameters that increase the information bandwidth between visual stimuli and user.

Table 7.2   Accuracy rankings for visual markers by general data type

Data type	Quantitative	Ordinal	Nominal
Graphical representation	Position Length Angle/slope Area Volume Colour/density (Cleveland and McGill, 1984)	Position Density Colour Texture Connection Containment Length Angle Slope Area Volume (Mackinlay, 1986)	Position Colour Texture Connection Containment Density Shape Length Angle Slope Area Volume (Mackinlay, 1986)

Schneiderman (1996) outlined a task and data type taxonomy for information visualizations which is also useful for our description of techniques for X3D. Top-level tasks are enumerated as Overview, Zoom, Filter, Detail-on-demand, Relate, History and Extract. Overview refers to a top-level or global view of the information space. Zoom, Filter and Details-on-demand refer to the capability to "drill down" to items of interest and inspect more details (of their attributes). History refers to the "undo" capability (i.e., returning to a previous state or view) and Extract is visualizing sub-sets of the data. Enumerated data types are One-dimensional, Two-dimensional, Three-dimensional, Multidimensional, Temporal, Tree and Network. Since each of these can be implemented with X3D, these distinctions will be referred to throughout the remainder of the chapter.

Card et al. (1999) and Hibbard et al. (1995b) have described a reference model for mapping data to visual forms that we can apply to our discussion. Beginning with raw data, which may be highly dimensional and heterogeneous, data transformations are applied to produce a "Data Table" that encapsulates the records and attributes of interest. The data table also includes metadata which describes the respective axis of the data values. Visual mappings such as those shown in Table 7.2 are then applied to the data table to produce the visual structures of the visualization. The final transformation stage involves defining the user views and navigational mechanisms to these visual structures. As the user interactively explores the data, this process is repeated. Ideally, the user has interactive control (feedback) on any step in the process (the data transformation, visual mappings and view transformations).

7.3 Design Principles and Interactive Strategies

Many challenges exist in the design of interactive 3D worlds and interfaces when integrating symbolic and perceptual information (Bolter et al., 1995). Similarly to efforts for 2D Visualization, researchers have experimented with the mapping of attributes to various visualization metaphors including the cone-tree, the city and the building metaphor (Dos Santos et al., 2000). They have shown that accurate characterization of the data is crucial to a successful 3D visualization, especially when the scenegraph is auto-generated. Bowman et al. (1998, 1999, 2003) have implemented and evaluated "Information-Rich Virtual Environments" (IRVEs) with a number of features that are common to most Web3D information spaces. Information-rich virtual environments "... consist not only of three-dimensional graphics and other spatial data, but also include information of an abstract or symbolic nature that is related to the space", and IRVEs "embed symbolic information within a realistic 3D environment" (Bowman et al., 1999). This symbolic information could be attributes such as text and numbers, images, audio clips and hyperlinks that are related to the space or the objects in the space. In this section, we will attempt to formalize an approach that is consistent with the capabilities of X3D.

Delivering arbitrary XML data to information visualizations with the Pipeline Paradigm requires both design and implementation considerations. As mentioned above, the generation of a data table is the first step in the delivery of a visualization. The transformation of raw data to the data table may be accomplished by XSLT or extracted by an XPath query or a query to a database. For the second phase of mapping – the data table to visual structures – we should remember from our definition that the abstract data in the table does not contain any inherently spatial information; it requires that the author determine the visual markers that will be employed. We shall examine this step in more detail in Section 7.4 especially as it relates to XSLT and X3D.

When designing 3D scenes for any purpose, a crucial step is that of "Storyboarding", which helps authors specify what objects the scene contains and their appearance, from what points of view it can be perceived and what kinds of interaction are appropriate at various points in time and space. When designing a usable visualization, Schneiderman's (1996) mantra of information design should ring in your head: "Overview first, zoom and filter, then details-on-demand".

7.3.1 Scene Production Process

Beginning with user requirements, a typical scene production process will follow these steps:

1. Define environment and locations.
2. Define user interface and viewpoints.
3. Define interactions.
4. Organize declarative scenegraph.
5. Model objects.
6. Build prototypes.
7. Transform data and compose visual markers.
8. Deliver to user.

Steps 1–4 can be accomplished from the storyboard. Step 5 is typically done with a 3D modelling package that can export X3D or VRML. Steps 4 and 6 require at minimum a text editor and a developer familiar with the scenegraph capabilities of X3D or VRML. Steps 7 and 8 use server technologies and scripts to manifest the scene and deliver its final presentation form to the user.

7.3.2 Scene Structure

Structured design in the case of X3D means dividing a scene into blocks which account for the various functional parts of the world. Using a modular structure to build a scene means that it may be built (composed) and managed from any number of applications or databases to the final target presentation. The result of this approach should be an implicitly structured X3D document template describing scenes in the form of:

Served Content type

1. Header.
2. Scenegraph root:
   - Custom node declarations: PROTO definitions and/or EXTERNPROTO references.
   - Universe set (Backgrounds, global ProximitySensors).
   - HUD and User Interface.
   - Scripts.
   - World and Inhabitants set (lighting, geometry and objects).
   - ROUTEs.

The X3D specification defines a set of standard nodes that can be instantiated in the scenegraph, what kinds of events they can send and receive and where they can live in the scenegraph. The "transformation hierarchy" of a scenegraph describes the spatial relationship of renderable objects. The "behaviour graph" of a scenegraph describes the connections between fields and the flow of events through the system. Events in the X3D scenegraph are called ROUTEs and exist between nodes. If nodes are uniquely named (DEFed), data events can be programmatically addressed and routed to that node. Custom logic and behaviours can be built into a scene with Script nodes which use ECMAScipt and/or Java to execute data type conversion, computation and logic with events.

Designing scenes in modular blocks has additional benefits. For example, if the universe and HUD are kept consistent while the user navigates an information space, this helps to maintain the notion of presence when the world and its inhabitants change. Such runtime swapping of scenegraph branches (blocks) is possible with Browser API method calls in a Script node (see Section 7.4.4).

A primary consideration in mapping data to a visual form is the range of values in the data. For quantitative and ordinal data, designers should examine the highest and lowest values in order to scale coordinates properly. For categorical data, the number of categories will determine the colours that can be employed. Since visual mappings must be comprehensible, axes, labels and colour legends should be instantiated. Designers may choose to put axes and labels in the universe block or the world block, depending on the design and compositional resources of their visualization application.

7.3.2.1 Custom Nodes

Authors can aggregate nodes and field interfaces into "Prototype" nodes (PROTOs), which can be easily instantiated and reused in other scenegraphs and negraph locations. Prototypes allow the efficient definition, encapsulation and use of interactive 3D objects. As we shall see, Prototypes are especially suited to ᵤₑsigning visual markers and interactive widgets. In the interest of promoting the re-use of code without redundancy, Prototypes can also be defined in external files (EXTERNPROTOs). This prototype definition is a separate, singular resource that can be instantiated into multiple scenes.

One caveat to this abstract document structure is important: the ability to use Prototypes (e.g., PROTOs and EXTERNPROTOs) to create user-defined objects and to use Scripts to define special behaviours (e.g., world or interaction logic) exist only in the "Immersive Profile" (and higher) of X3D, which is analogous to (but not identical with) the functionality enabled by VRML97. As we mentioned above, Profiles are specific sets of functionality designed to address different application domains (Web3D, 2003). The "Interchange Profile" contains a node-set to describe simple geometries, materials and textures for sharing between applications such as modelling tools. The "Interactive Profile" adds interpolator nodes for animation, sensors and event utilities for interactive behaviours and a more capable lighting model. Additionally, on top of the Immersive Profile, other software components may be defined and implemented. Currently specified components include Humanoid Animation (H-Anim), Geospatial 3D graphics (Geo-VRML) and Distributed Interactive Simulation (DIS). The "Full Profile" refers to full support for all components currently defined in the X3D specification. Authors should design to Profiles as they define what capabilities the client has – what nodes it can read and render.

7.3.2.2 Viewpoints and Navigation

An X3D scene defines objects in Euclidean coordinates, and animation interpolators generally proceed along linear time (although programmatic generation and manipulation of time values are possible with the Script node). Virtual environment X3D scenes would not be visible or explorable without a way to describe user viewpoints and navigation. A key to understanding how this is accomplished with X3D (or VRML) is the idea of a runtime "binding stack". A binding stack is basically a list of "bindable" children nodes in the scene where the top node is active or "bound". The first Viewpoint and NavigationInfo nodes defined in a file are the first to be actively bound. Other Viewpoint and NavigationInfo nodes are made active by ROUTEing a Boolean event of TRUE to their set_bind field. When this happens, the user's view and navigation function according to the field values of the newly bound node. Alternatively, events routed to the active node change the observed behaviour of that node. For example, the Viewpoint node has fields for position, orientation, fieldOfView and jump. The fieldOfView defines the user's viewing frustum and can therefore be modulated to create fish-eye or telescoping effects. It is recommended that a FALSE value be used for the jump field, as the user's view is then smoothly animated to that Viewpoint when it is bound, reducing disorientation (Bowman et al., 1997).

Similarly, the NavigationInfo node carries fields that have a direct impact on the user's perception, including avatarSize, speed and type. For example, as a user navigates into smaller and smaller scales the avatarSize and speed fields should also be proportionally scaled down. Specified X3D navigation types are "WALK", "FLY", "EXAMINE", "LOOKAT", "ANY", and "NONE". While the first five types give the user different ways of controlling their movement within the scene, in some cases it may be preferable to use "NONE" in order to constrain their movement. Such a value would be desirable in the case of a "guided tour." If developers have access to mouse or wand data in their runtime engine, they can build their own navigation types using prototypes, scripts and other scenegraph nodes.

7.3.2.3 Example Scenegraph: a Heads-Up-Display

ProximitySensor nodes output events called position_changed and orientation_changed. By placing a ProximitySensor at the origin, we have access to constant updates of the user's location and direction in the 3D world. If appropriate, we can then place a Heads-Up-Display (HUD) in front of the user and within their field-of-view. ROUTEing the output of the ProximitySensor to the HUD's parent transform allows the HUD to travel continually with the user. The following code fragments illustrated this basic design:

```
<Scene>
<ProtoDeclare name="markerP">
  <ProtoInterface> ...
  </ProtoInterface>
    <ProtoBody> ...
    </ProtoBody>
</ProtoDeclare>
  . . .
<Group DEF="universe_context">
  <ProximitySensor DEF="universe_origin" center=
  "0 0 0" size="1000 1000 1000"/>
    <NavigationInfo type="EXAMINE ANY"/>
<Background/>
</Group>
  <Group DEF="HUD_UI">
    <Transform DEF="HUD">
      <Transform translation="-0.05 0.03 -0.2">
        <!-- some hud scenegraph translated by an offset
          to user's point of view -->
        <Shape DEF="hud_geometry">
          <Box size=".1 .1 .1"/>
          <Appearance>
            <Material diffuseColor="1 1 1"/>
          </Appearance>
        </Shape>
      </Transform>
    </Transform>
</Group>
. . .
<Group DEF="worldGroup">...
</Group>
  . . .
```

```
<ROUTE fromField="position_changed" fromNode=
  "universe_origin" toField="set_translation"
  toNode="HUD"/>
<ROUTE fromField="orientation_changed" fromNode=
  "universe_origin" toField="set_rotation"
  toNode="HUD"/>
</Scene>
```

7.4 X3D and XSLT Techniques

Kim and Fishwick (2002) demonstrated the power of the content/presentation distinction when they used XML, Schemas and XSLT to render their XML descriptions of dynamic, physical systems to different 3D visual and system metaphors that they call "rubes". Dachselt et al. (2002) have demonstrated an abstracted, declarative XML and Schema to model Web3D scene components and especially interfaces. More recently, Dachselt et al. (2003) leveraged object-oriented concepts and XML Schema to componentize scenegraph node sets in the definition of user interface "Behaviour Graphs", which can be applied to arbitrary geometries or widgets. Finally, XSLT data transformations for audience-specific interactive visualizations have been shown for the delivery of Chemical Markup Language (CML) using X3D and VRML (Polys, 2003).

Applying the power of XSLT to the delivery of interactive 3D scenes is relatively new, and much more research is required in this area. As mentioned in Section 7.1.3, the representation of an XML document is by a tree data model. The nodes of the source graph can be selected and their attributes operated on in XSLT by the definition of `<xsl:templates match=""/>` that use XPath expressions and the `<xsl:variable name=""/>` element. XPath provides 13 axes by which the data tree may be navigated: child, descendant, parent, ancestor, following-sibling, preceding-sibling, following, preceding, attribute, namespace, self, descendant-or-self and ancestor-or-self. The target X3D tree (scenegraph) can be composed with the DOCTYPE

```
<!DOCTYPE X3D PUBLIC "ISO//Web3D//DTD X3D 3.0//EN"
  "http://www.web3d.org/specifications/x3d-3.0.dtd">
```

There is a content model in X3D (expressed in the DTD and Schema) that constrains the target output and lets tools validate scene. While more formal theories including graph transformation principles are still forthcoming, we can begin to describe techniques for mapping data to visual structures (X3D nodes) for information visualization.

Including the X3D and VRML specifications, a number of resources exist (Ames et al., 1997; Walsh and Sévenier, 2001) that describe the syntax and behaviour of nodes in the scenegraph. Therefore, we will not cover all nodes in detail in this chapter, but rather show how particular nodes may be used to manifest visual markers for information visualizations. We will consider the X3D Immersive Profile as the target platform, although position, orientation, size, colour and shape can be mapped to the Interchange and Interactive profiles. All that is required to deliver content to these platforms is an alternative set of XSLT stylesheets that map the data to the supported target nodes and fields (attributes).

7.4.1 Target Nodes – Geometry

The Transform node manifests its children in the scene and provides fields such as translation, rotation and scale that account for position, orientation and size respectively. The Transform node's translation field takes an SFVec3f (a 3 float tuple) to define coordinates in 3-space where the children are located. Rotation is an SFRotation field where the first three values define a vector which serves as the rotation axis and the last value is an angle in radians which is the amount of rotation around that axis. The scale field is also a SFVec3f which defines a scaling factor for the node's children between 0 and 1 along each dimension (x, y and z).

Shape is obviously a crucial X3DChildNode. The Shape node describes both geometry and its appearance, such as colour and texture. The X3D colour model is defined in RGB space and specified in the Material node. In X3D, colour is specified by RGB values. The specularColor and emissiveColors modulate the diffuse colour by lighting, shape and point-of-view. In the literature on information visualization, there is a distinction between hue and saturation as visual markers in display mappings (Mackinlay, 1986). When colours are interpolated, the VRML Sourcebook (Ames et al., 1997) notes that colours are converted to HSV space (which does have a saturation factor) and then converted back to RGB. For readers interested in specifying saturation factors or converting between these colour spaces, the book by Foley et al. (1995) can be recommended. When mapping data to colour as a visual marker, it is important to use distinctive or contrasting colour scales so that users can differentiate the rendered values.

Three-dimensional geometry in an X3D scene may be built with any number of nodes, including the geometric "primitives" (Box, Cylinder, Sphere) and others such as PointSet, IndexedLineSet, IndexedFaceSet, Extrusion, the Triangle* family and Text. Each of these nodes has its own field signature and, depending on the designer's goal or user's task, the same data may be mapped to these different markers. Some brief notes about these shapes are in order. The PointSet node may be used for a scatter-plot, for example, but as a point does not have any volume, their specific values may be difficult to perceive in the rendering. Owing to the way in which some primitives' dimensions (e.g., the Cylinder's height and the Box's size) are defined, they usually need to be Transformed (offset) by half of this dimension. IndexedFaceSet and IndexedLineSet geometries require a coordIndex field to specify the order in which the Coordinate points are connected.

In addition, X3D has extended VRML geometries by adding the Geometry2D component. Arc2D, ArcClose2D, Circle2D, Disk2D, Polyline2D, Polypoint2D and Triangleset2D are defined with this component. Similar 2D primitives are defined in SVG (W3C, 2002; this volume). The shapes in this component are new to Web3D worlds, and we expect them to be very useful in future visualization and interface designs. Currently, the Geometry2D component is only supported in the Immersive Profile.

7.4.2 Target Nodes – Hyperlinks and Direct Manipulation

The Anchor node is a grouping node that provides the ability for the user to click on its children and load an external resource. This is analogous to the hyperlinking

<a> tag in HTML and the default behaviour is for the resource to replace totally the currently loaded scene. The url field is of MFString type that lists the location of one or more resources. The browser attempts to find the first resource and load it; if it is not accessible, it tries the next one. Similarly to the HTML hyperlink, the Anchor's parameter field can specify a frame or window target where the resource is to be loaded. When X3D or VRML files are specified as the resource, the link may also include a Viewpoint which is to be bound. This is done simply by appending #DEFedViewpointName to the url. The specified resource may also be a CGI script on the server and variable values may be passed to it, for example:

```
url
http://www.somedomain.org/sample/vistransformer.pl?
marker=markerP&data=autos
```

In this case, the CGI script is responsible for delivering the content header and composing the scene.

Direct manipulation (such as clicking on an object and dragging it) in X3D can be accomplished through the use of DragSensors such as the PlaneSensor, CylinderSensor and SphereSensor. These nodes are activated when the user clicks on any of its sibling nodes and the output values are typically ROUTEd to a Transform node to effect a translation or rotation. A TouchSensor generates events such as isOver, and touchTime events (among others) that can be ROUTEd to other nodes in the scenegraph such as Scripts to process user actions. Again, depending on the application and inter-activity requirements, these may also be included in a Prototype definition.

7.4.3 Examples

Using the knowledge we have outlined above, let us have a look at some examples (Figures 7.2–7.4) of using XSLT to transform some abstract data into X3D scenes. Here is some sample XML data :

```
<Vehicles>
  <Auto name="SUV2001" MPG="8" Cylinders="8"
    Price="40,000"/>
  <Auto name="SUV2000" MPG="12" Cylinders="8"
    Price="35,000"/>
  <Auto name="Van2000" MPG="16" Cylinders="6"
    Price="30,000"/>
  <Auto name="Pickup1990" MPG="23" Cylinders="4"
    Price="21,000"/>
  <Auto name="Sedan1999" MPG="30" Cylinders="4"
    Price="18,000"/>
  <Auto name="Compact2002" MPG="38" Cylinders="4"
    Price="14,000"/>
</Vehicles>
```

In order to transform this data to an X3D visualization with XSLT, we define a tem-plate (or set of templates) that extract the source elements and attribute values in which we are interested. The templates in an XSLT stylesheet provide a mapping

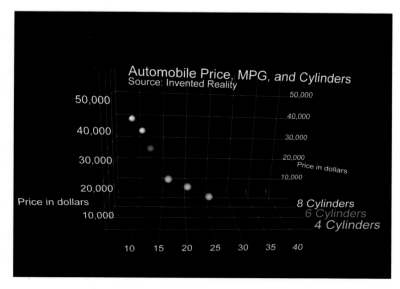

Figure 7.2   X3D scatter-plot geometry using positioned, colour-coded Spheres as the visual markers.

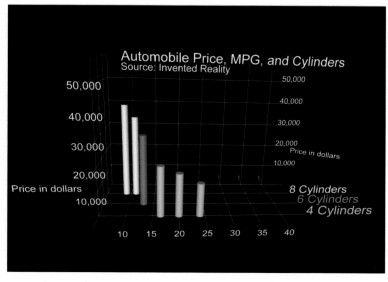

Figure 7.3   X3D bar graph (or histogram) geometry using positioned, colour-coded Cylinders and markers. Box primitives could also be used in this way.

from XML data to X3D informational objects. Common XSLT design patterns have been described, such as fill-in-the-blank, navigational, rule-based and computational (Kay, 2001). Based on this mapping, the XSL Transformation engine writes the data values into the template X3D tags and writes the result to the network or to

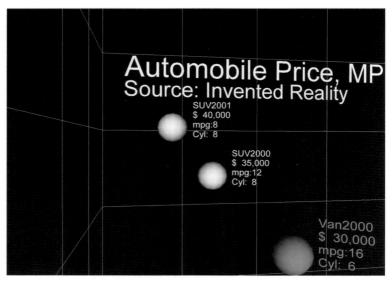

Figure 7.4 A zoomed-in view of Prototyped visual markers encapsulating perceptual and abstract information. The user has navigated into the higher price range.

a file (as in Section 7.5). For this example source data, we might write our XSLT as follows:

```
<?xml version="1.0"?>
<xsl:stylesheet version="1.0"
  xmlns:xsl="http://www.w3.org/1999/XSL/Transform">
<xsl:output method="xml" encoding="UTF-8" media-type=
  "model/x3d+xml" indent="yes" cdata-section-elements=
  "Script" doctype-system="http://www.web3D.org/
  TaskGroups/x3d/translation/x3d-compact.dtd"/>

    <xsl:template match="/">
      <X3D profile="Immersive">&#10; <head>&#10;
        <meta content="translatedVehicleData.x3d"
          name="filename"/>
        <meta content="XSLT translation 1"
          name="description"/>
        <meta content="n_polys" name="author"/>
        </head>
        <Scene>
          <!-- Insert EXTERN / PROTO declarations,
            universe set, UI,

            and Scripts as needed -->
              <xsl:apply-templates/>
          </Scene>
      </X3D>
</xsl:template>
<xsl:template match="Vehicles">
```

```
        <Group DEF="worldGroup">
          <xsl:for-each select="Auto">
<xsl:variable name="name" select="@name"/>
<xsl:variable name="mpg" select="@MPG"/>
<xsl:variable name="cyl" select="@Cylinders"/>
<xsl:variable name="price" select="@Price"/>
                   <Transform>
                      <!-- Manipulate the variables as
                         necessary and instantiate X3D visual
                         markers (target geometry) -->
                   </Transform>
          </xsl:for-each>
        </Group>
     </xsl:template>

</xsl:stylesheet>
```

Let us take a look at how some visual markers may be instantiated in an X3D scene. The following code fragment (shown in Figure 7.2) generates a scatter-plot view of the automobile dataset using an XSLT stylesheet to map quantitative data to a Transform node's translation field and categorical values to Material:

```
<Group DEF="worldGroup">
  <Transform translation=".8 4 1">
    <Shape DEF="marker1">
    <Appearance>
      <Material diffuseColor="1.0 1.0 1.0"/>
    </Appearance>
      <Sphere radius=".15"/>
    </Shape>
  </Transform>
  <Transform translation="1.2 3.5 1">
    <Shape>
    <Appearance>
      <Material diffuseColor="1.0 1.0 1.0"/>
    </Appearance>
      <Sphere radius=".15"/>
    </Shape>
  </Transform>
  <Transform translation="1.6 3 2">
    <Shape>
    <Appearance>
      <Material diffuseColor="0.31 0.3 0.61" />
    </Appearance>
      <Sphere radius=".15"/>
    </Shape>
  </Transform>
  <Transform translation="2.3 2.1 3">
    <Shape>
    <Appearance>
      <Material diffuseColor="0.89 0.44 0.89" />
```

```
      </Appearance>
        <Sphere radius=".15"/>
      </Shape>
    </Transform>
  ...
  </Group>
```

The second example (Figure 7.3) implements quantitative values mapped to
Cylinder height (which are Transformed vertically by half their height
value) and categorical values mapped to Material. The target X3D code for this
example would be as follows:

```
<Group DEF="worldGroup">
  <Transform translation=".8 2 1">
    <Shape DEF="marker2">
    <Appearance>
      <Material diffuseColor="1.0 1.0 1.0"/>
    </Appearance>
      <Cylinder height="4" radius=".15"/>
    </Shape>
  </Transform>
  <Transform translation="1.2 1.75 1">
    <Shape>
    <Appearance>
      <Material diffuseColor="1.0 1.0 1.0"/>
    </Appearance>
      <Cylinder height="3.5" radius=".15"/>
    </Shape>
  </Transform>
  <Transform translation="1.6 1.5 2">
    <Shape>
    <Appearance>
      <Material diffuseColor="0.31 0.3 0.61" />
    </Apearance>
      <Cylinder height="3" radius=".15"/>
    </Shape>
  </Transform>
  <Transform translation="2.3 1.05 3">
    <Shape>
    <Appearance>
      <Material diffuseColor="0.89 0.44 0.89" />
    </Appearance>
      <Cylinder height="2.1" radius=".15"/>
    </Shape>
  </Transform>
  ...
</Group>
```

Prototypes' definitions can add another level of efficiency to the definition of
data objects where multiple nodes can be encapsulated and re-used. In the first
two examples, the initial overview Viewpoint gives us a rough idea about the

distribution of automobiles across the three variables. However, we would probably
want to find out more detailed information about an automobile that met our criteria. To accomplish this without cluttering the visual space, we can define our visual
markers with an LOD (Level-of-Detail) functionality, which renders different children based on the user's proximity. One such design would show the detailed view
(a Text node reading the name, miles per gallon and price) when the user zooms
in closer to an item of interest. In addition, Text could be placed on a Billboard
node that rotates its children around their y-axis to always face the user.

Our third example populates a Prototype instance with values and has the high
LOD containing Billboarded Text and the low level containing the geometry
from the first example. The Prototype declaration is named "markerP". The code
for these visual markers using the automobile dataset is as follows:

```
<Group DEF="worldGroup">
  <ProtoInstance name="markerP">
    <fieldValue name="position" value=".8 4 1"/>
    <fieldValue name="cost" value="40,000"/>
    <fieldValue name="name" value="SUV2001"/>
    <fieldValue name="numcyl" value="8"/>
    <fieldValue name="miles" value="8"/>
    <fieldValue name="color" value="1.0 1.0 1.0"/>
  </ProtoInstance>
  <ProtoInstance name="markerP">
    <fieldValue name="position" value="1.2 3.5 1"/>
    <fieldValue name="cost" value="35,000"/>
    <fieldValue name="name" value="SUV2000"/>
    <fieldValue name="numcyl" value="8"/>
    <fieldValue name="miles" value="12"/>
    <fieldValue name="color" value="1.0 1.0 1.0"/>
  </ProtoInstance>
  <ProtoInstance name="markerP">
    <fieldValue name="position" value="1.6 3 2"/>
    <fieldValue name="cost" value="30,000"/>
    <fieldValue name="name" value="Van2000"/>
    <fieldValue name="numcyl" value="6"/>
    <fieldValue name="miles" value="16"/>
    <fieldValue name="color" value="0.31 0.3
      0.61"/>
  </ProtoInstance>
  <ProtoInstance name="markerP">
    <fieldValue name="position" value="2.3 2.1 3"/>
    <fieldValue name="cost" value="21,000"/>
    <fieldValue name="name" value="Pickup1990"/>
    <fieldValue name="numcyl" value="4"/>
    <fieldValue name="miles" value="23"/>
    <fieldValue name="color" value="0.89 0.44
      0.89"/>
  </ProtoInstance>
...
</Group>
```

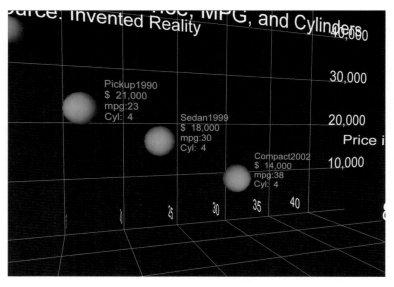

Figure 7.5 A zoomed-in view of Prototyped markers encapsulating perceptual and abstract information. The user has navigated into the lower price range.

Figures 7.4 and 7.5 show a sample visual marker PROTO that includes LOD,
Billboard and Text features. From outside the detail LOD range, the scene
would look exactly as in Figure 7.2.

XSLT can, of course, also be used to transform and compose X3D from data that
has inherent spatial meaning such as locations, sizes and connectivity. For example,
Figures 7.6 and 7.7 show the results of two different stylesheets that process a
Chemical Markup Language (CML) file of the cholesterol molecule to X3D. The
first version (Figure 7.6) builds geometry from atom and bond elements and text
from abstract attributes and other meta-information.

The second transformed version (Figure 7.7) shows that the XSLT can add control widgets to the resulting X3D scene; in this case, a slider controls the transparency of every atom. In addition, the transformation in Figure 7.7 shows a new
text style and also movable measuring axis instantiated in the "universe block" of
the scene.

Figures 7.8 and 7.9 illustrate the XML to X3D transformation results of a finite-
difference mesh of tissue used for in silico biological simulation.

7.4.4 Scene Management and Runtimes

Another important consideration in the composition and maintenance of world
content is the use of the Inline node. In VRML, Inlines were opaque in that
events could not be ROUTEd between the inlined and the inlining scenes. This event
opacity is also a limitation of the Browser.createX3DFromURL method since
nodes in the new world are not programmatically addressable. If authors wanted
dynamically to replace a world block and connect it with event ROUTEs, the

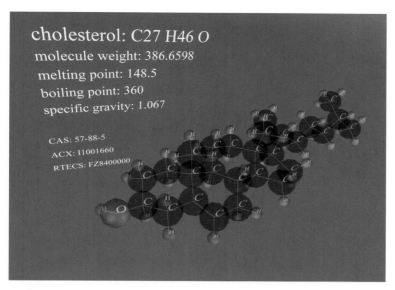

Figure 7.6 The results of an XSLT transformations of a CML file for cholesterol.

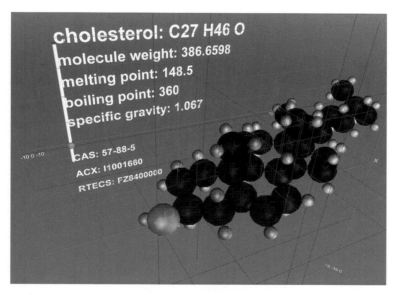

Figure 7.7 The results of an XSLT transformation of a CML file for cholesterol. A new FontStyle has been used and a slider widget has been added during the transformation and ROUTEd to visual markers in the scene.

not-so-obvious solution in VRML has been to define the entire replacement scene as a Prototype and then use the `Browser.createX3DfromString` method to add the new node and the `Browser.addRoute` method to connect events to it.

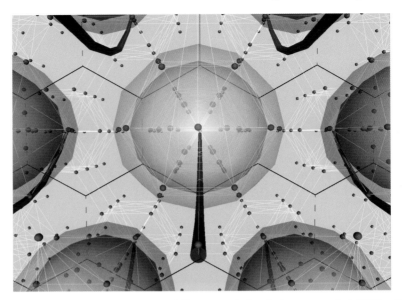

Figure 7.8 Underside view of an XML finite-difference mesh description generated via XSLT to X3D in order to visualize the spatial locations and connectivity of mesh points.

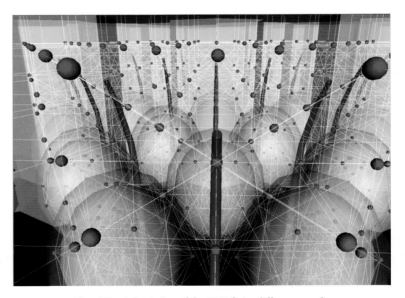

Figure 7.9 A front view of the XML finite-difference mesh.

The new X3D API is called the Scene Access Interface (SAI) and unifies the object definitions for both internal and external scripting. The SAI is a much more rich and rigorous programming specification than VRML supported and it introduces a number of new objects and functions. The bindings for the Java and ECMAScript languages are described in ISO/IEC FCD 19777:200x.

The Browser object interface, for example, has a number of useful methods for managing content dynamically, such the Browser.createX3DFromURL or Browser.createX3DFromString methods that can be invoked from a Script. These methods (whose analogues were specified in VRML97) allow scene content to be swapped during runtime. The content is added to a specific part of the scenegraph by specifying a DEFed node which the new content replaces. If the world has been designed in a modular way as we described above, this can be a very powerful technique.

Other important functionality newly introduced in X3D is the use of IMPORT and EXPORT keywords with Inlines. The IMPORT statement provides ROUTEing access to all the fields of an externally defined node with a single statement and without a PROTO interface wrapper and Scripts building String objects. The EXPORT statement is used within an X3D file to specify nodes that may be imported into other scenes when inlining the file. Only names exported with an EXPORT statement are eligible to be imported into another file (Web3D, 2002). In this way, entire X3D files can declare event communication routes for embedding and embedded files. This is a significant improvement in the composability and re-use of X3D worlds themelves.

7.5 Publishing Technologies

We have examined some techniques for transforming XML data to X3D with the use of XSLT stylesheets. The X3D Task Group has provided a number of XSLT stylesheets for the transformation of X3D to VRML97 and also X3D to HTML. Also, courtesy of the National Institute of Standards and Technology, a translator application for VRML97 → X3D data migration has been made freely available and been integrated into a number of Web3D editing tools including the structured editor X3D Edit (Web3D, 2003) and others. Within the Pipeline and Hybrid paradigms, there are two general ways we shall consider in publishing XML content to X3D (or other): the back-end production of a file archive, and the serving of a transformed and presented source document in response to a "live" (networked) visualization request. Thus we distinguish between the auto-generation of content archives and the serving of dynamic content for on-the-fly service.

Given server overhead, bandwidth and delivery constraints, periodically auto-generating content archives may be appropriate. These approaches use X3D source files and directories with naming conventions and scripted XSLT to produce framed HTML, VRML and X3D document trees complete with linked with chapters, titles and embedded views of the source file. The generated document trees can be organized and hyperlinked for navigation with a Web browser, for example. The X3D Task Group's Web collection of X3D content examples is an ideal showcase of this technique (Web3D, 2002). The auto-generation can be done with straightforward batched XSLT Java (Kay, 2001; McLaughlin, 2001; White, 2002) or Perl (Brown, 2002; Polys, 2003) scripts. These content publications can then be served over the Web or distributed on CD or DVD as in the Identity Paradigm.

The second approach is to use XSL Transformations "on-the-fly" using common Web server software such as Apache Cocoon, Perl and the XML Gnome libraries, or PHP (Brown, 2002). This approach can provide custom presentations of the source data with a proportionate server and network overhead. Either of these delivery approaches may be classified as conforming to the Pipeline, Composition or Hybrid paradigms depending on how the data is transformed and composed.

7.6 Summary

In this chapter, we have reviewed the literature on interactive 3D visualizations and enumerated criteria to design successful and comprehensible visualizations. We looked at modular approaches to X3D scene design and production and examined how XSLT can be used to transform and deliver XML data to X3D visualizations within current publishing paradigms. The separation of content from presentation in XML gives organizations a great deal of flexibility in how developers re-purpose and publish their data. The XML encoding of X3D allows developers to leverage the power of XML to transform the same data to multiple forms and interactive contexts. As XML databases and server technologies improve, we can expect further refinements to the techniques we have outlined.

The investigation of human computer interaction for information-rich 3D worlds and visualizations is still in its infancy. We expect that by enumerating effective data mappings, the combinations of coordinated information and media types and interaction strategies for information-rich virtual environments, we can work toward advantageous computational, compositional and convivial systems for real-time exploration, analysis and action. This work will have a direct impact on the usability and design of such heterogeneous 3D worlds. With such mappings, coordinations and strategies in hand, effective displays and user interfaces may be automatically generated or constructed by users depending on the expertise level and the task. The coming years hold great potential to amplify the bandwidth between interactive computer graphics technologies and human understanding.

7.7 Acknowledgments

Screenshots are VRML views of the result X3D scenes through the ParallelGraphics Cortona browser. X3D syntax was validated within X3DEdit 2.4. Thanks are due to Dr Doug Bowman, Dr Christopher North, Scott Preddy and the Virginia Tech Visualization and Animation Research (UVAG) Laboratory for their continued support and review of this chapter.

Most thanks are due to my dear friend, advocate and wife, Kat Mills.

References

Ahlberg C and Wistrand E (1995) IVEE: an Information Visualization and Exploration Environment. In *Proceedings of IEEE InfoVis*, 66–73, 142–143. Spotfire: www.spotfire.com

Ames AL, Nadeau DR and Moreland JL (1997) *VRML Sourcebook*, 2nd edn. New York: Wiley.

Apache Foundation (2002) Apache Web server: http://www.apache.org. Cocoon: http://xml.apache.org / cocoon/. Hypertext Preprocessor: http://www.php.net. Tomcat: http://jakarta.apache.org/tomcat/ index.html.

Bertin (1981) *Graphics and Graphic Information Processing* (transl. Berg W and Scott P). Berlin: Walter de Gruyter.

Bolter J, Hodges LF, Meyer T and Nichols A (1995) Integrating perceptual and symbolic information in VR. *IEEE*, July.

Bowman D, Koller D and Hodges L (1997) Travel in immersive virtual environments: an evaluation of viewpoint motion control techniques. In *Proceedings of the Virtual Reality Annual International Symposium (VRAIS)*, pp. 45–52.

Bowman D, Hodges L and Bolter J (1998) The virtual venue: user–computer interaction in information-rich virtual environments. *Presence: Teleoperators and Virtual Environments*, 7(5)8, 478–493.

Bowman D, Wineman J, Hodges L and Allison D (1999) The educational value of an information-rich virtual environment. *Presence: Teleoperators and Virtual Environments*, 8(3), 317–331.

Bowman D, North C, Chen J, Polys N, Pyla P and Yilmaz U (2003) Information-rich virtual environments: theory, tools, and research agenda. In *ACM Symposium on Virtual Reality Software and Technology (VRST)*.

Brown M (2002) *XML Processing with Perl, Python, and PHP*. San Francisco: Sybex.

Card S, Mackinlay J and Schneiderman B (1999) *Information Visualization: Using Vision to Think*. San Francisco: Morgan Kaufmann.

Cleveland W (1993) *Visualizing Data*. Summit, NJ: Hobart Press.

Cleveland WS and McGill R (1994) Graphical perception: theory, experimentation and application to the development of graphical methods. *Journal of the American Statistical Association* 79, 387.

Dachselt R and Rukzio E (2003) Behavior3D: an XML-based framework for 3D graphics behavior. In *Proceeding of the Web3D 2003 Symposium*, ACM SIGGRAPH.

Dachselt R, Hinz M and Meissner K (2002) CONTIGRA: an XML-based architecture for component-oriented 3D applications. In *Proceedings of the Web3D 2002 Symposium*, ACM SIGGRAPH.

Dos Santos CR, Gros P, Abel P, Loisel D, Trichaud N and Paris JP (2000) Mapping information onto 3D virtual worlds. In *Proceedings of IEEE International Conference on Information Visualization*, London, 19–21 July 2000.

Foley JD, van Dam A, Feiner SK and Hughes JF (1995) *Computer Graphics: Principles and Practice in C*, 2nd edn. Boston: Addison-Wesley.

Friedhoff R and Peercy M (2000) *Visual Computing*. New York: Scientific American Library.

Gnome XML and XSLT Libraries for Perl. Available: http://www.gnome.org

Hibbard W, Levkowitz H, Haswell J, Rheingans P and Schoeder F (1995a) Interaction in perceptually-based visualization. In Grinstein G and Levkoitz H (eds), *Perceptual Issues in Visualization*. New York: Springer, pp. 23–32.

Hibbard W, Dyer CR, Paul BE (1995b) Interactivity and the dimensionality of data displays. In Grinstein G and Levkoitz H (eds), *Perceptual Issues in Visualization*. New York: Springer, pp. 75–82.

Kay M (2001) *XSLT*, 2nd edn. Birmingham: Wrox Press.

Keller PR (1993) *Visual Cues: Practical Data Visualization*. Piscataway, NJ: IEEE Computer Society Press.

Kim T and Fishwick P (2002) A 3D XML-based customized framework for dynamic models. In *Proceedings of the Web3D 2002 Symposium*, ACM SIGGRAPH.

Mackinlay J (1986) Automating the design of graphical presentations of relational information. *ACM Transactions on Graphics*, 5, 111–141.

McLaughlin B (2001) *Java and XML*, 2nd edn. Cambridge: O'Reilly.

Norman DA (1986) Cognitive engineering. In Norman DA and Draper SD (eds), *User Centered System Design*. Hillsdale, NJ: Lawrence Erlbaum Associates, pp. 31–61.

North C and Schneiderman B (2000) Snap-together visualization: can users construct and operate coordinated views? *International Journal of Human – Computer Studies*, 53, 715–739.

Perl Mongers: http://www.perl.org

Pickett RM, Grinstein G, Levkowitz H, Smith S (1995) Harnessing preattentive perceptual processes in visualization. In Grinstein G and Levkoitz H (eds), *Perceptual Issues in Visualization*. New York: Springer.

Polys NF (2003) Stylesheet transformations for interactive visualization: towards a Web3D chemistry curricula. In *Proceedings of the Web3D 2003 Symposium*. ACM SIGGRAPH.

Schneiderman B (1996) The eyes have it: a task by data type taxonomy for information visualizations. *Proceedings of IEEE Visual Languages*, 336–343.

Sun Microsystems Java and Java Server Pages. Available: http://java.sun.com/products/jsp/

Tufte E (1990) *Envisioning Information*. Cheshire, CT: Graphics Press.

Walsh A and Sévenier M (2001) *Core Web3D*. Upper Saddle River, NJ: Prentice-Hall.

White C (2002) *Mastering XSLT*. San Francisco: Sybex.

The Web3D Consortium (2002)
Specifications:
Extensible 3D (X3D-ISO/IEC 19775:200x), Virtual Reality Modelling Language (VRML- ISO/IEC 14772:1997): http://www.web3d.org/fs_specifications.htm

X3D TaskGroup and X3DEdit: http://www.web3d.org/x3d.html
Software Development Kit: http://sdk.web3d.org
Xj3D Open Source X3D/VRML toolkit: http://www.web3d.org/TaskGroups/source

The World Wide Web Consortium (2002)
Specifications:
Extensible Markup Language (XML): http://www.w3.org/XML
Extensible Stylesheet Transformations (XSLT): http://www.w3.org/TR/xslt11

PART 2
Applying SVG and X3D to Specific Problems

Chapter 8
Visualizing Complex Networks

Chaomei Chen and Natasha Lobo

8.1 Introduction

Theoretical foundations of network analysis have traditionally been studied in graph theory. Numerous graph-theoretical algorithms have been developed and used in solving a variety of problems. Recently, networks have become a central topic of research in theoretical physics, especially statistical physics. A number of concepts have played key roles in the latest proliferation of such studies, including small-world networks and scale-free networks.

Many underlying phenomena studied by physicists are known as non-linear systems because a linear relationship between the input and the output, or between a cause and its effect, does not exist. Mathematically, a power law is one of the most commonly used methods to describe such relationships. Researchers are particularly interested in two types of dynamics in complex networks: (1) event-driven processes, a dynamic process is apparently caused by external interferences, for instance, a snow avalanche caused by a storm; (2) self-organized criticality, a system in which dramatic changes may take place in the absence of major causes at the macroscopic level. Many of the studies in the current complex network theory have not yet reached a level that one can specifically identify the cause–effect relations associated with the dynamics observed over a complex network. There is considerable evidence, however, to believe that the ability to distinguish the two types of dynamic processes in the near future will lead to much more insights into complex networks.

Chen and Börner (2002) identified the top 10 problems for visual interfaces to digital libraries. Among these top 10 problems, three are particularly relevant to the subject of this chapter. First, what are the common elements that have been found in every successful example of visual interfaces of digital libraries? Which features have worked well in some cases, but not others? Which features so far have shown no conclusive benefits? Examples in areas such as visual information retrieval, visual information exploration and empirical studies of information visualization (Chen and Czerwinski, 2000) are likely to provide valuable clues. Second, how should we build on the success of visual interfaces and explore promising areas of applications? Some exciting candidates include bibliometrics, scientometrics, knowledge tracking and knowledge discovery. These areas have special requirements and special tasks. Many of these areas have indeed developed their own approaches to handle complex information visually. Insights, experiences and lessons learned from these fields are valuable sources of inspiration. Third, to what extent will the algorithms and solutions that have been tried and worked on small-scale networks scale? Researchers in information visualization are striking for faster responses, incremental updates and a scale-proof layout performance. The fourth problem is about labelling in visual interfaces. There are two aspects of this problem. One is to display readable labels and the other is to select meaningful labels. When numerous objects are displayed in a visual interface, one has to be selective in objects that get labelled. Some objects should be labelled prominently, some should be labelled moderately and some should not be labelled at all. Making meaningful labels is equally challenging if not more challenging than making readable labels.

Currently, there is still a huge conceptual gap between statistical mechanics of large-scale networks and the comprehensive study of networks in particular application domains in terms of theoretical foundations, methodologies and empirical verifications. Much of the work has been conducted by researchers in their own disciplines, using methodologies established in their own fields and focusing on issues concerning their own disciplines the most. For instance, statistical physicists focus on topological abstractions of underlying phenomena, whereas domain analysts in information science focus on citation networks in scientific publications as a surrogate to understand the structure of scientific knowledge and the dynamics of scientific communities. Findings in each field have great potential to become mutually beneficial to other fields.

In this chapter, we shall focus on the advances in complex network theory over the last few years, especially in relation to research in small-world networks and scale-free networks. Researchers have studied the topology of such networks and the mechanics that can replicate topological properties. Such studies provide necessary theoretical foundations for network visualization.

The rest of the chapter is organized as follows. First, we outline the latest advances in complex network theory, with special focus on studies in relation to citation networks. Second, we describe the methodologies used for analysing citation networks. In particular, we examine the key challenging issues concerning the visualization of complex citation networks. Then we identify the questions that are particularly relevant to the development of the new generation of applications in X3D.

8.2 Complex Networks

8.2.1 Classes of Networks and their Characteristics

Three classes of networks have attracted intensive attention over the recent years: random networks, small-world networks and scale-free networks. Many phenomena are traditionally analysed as a random network. Small-world networks contain effective short-cut links and more clustered nodes. Research shows that rewiring links in a random network can lead to a small-world network. It was found that the World Wide Web is a small-world network (Barabási et al., 2000). Scientific collaboration in terms of co-authorship forms small-world networks (Newman, 2001). Scale-free networks are networks where degree distributions follow power laws. Scale-free networks contain extremely well-connected nodes, known as hubs. The Web is also a scale-free network. Small-world networks (Watts and Strogatz, 1998) and scale-free networks (Barabási et al., 2000) have been intensively studied over the last few years, for instance, in relation to the topology of the Internet, movie actor networks and scientific collaboration networks (Barabási et al., 2000, 2002; Girvan and Newman, 2001; Albert and Barabasi, 2002; Dorogovtsev and Mendes, 2002).

Recent research has focused on the topology and connectivity of these networks, in particular to identify highly connected hubs, the extent of the impact of their failure and alternative optimal designs for ensuring security, maintainability and evolution. For instance, the knowledge of the topology of social networks can be used to prevent the spread of diseases and the study of the structure of power grid networks can facilitate stability of power transmissions.

A scale-free network can be explained by its "degree distribution" definition in comparison with that for regular and random networks. The degree of a node is the number of links to that node. The frequency of distribution of nodes by degree is called degree distribution. In a regular network, all the nodes have the same degree so the degree distribution will show the frequency of nodes having a certain degree value equal to the number of nodes in the network. In a random graph, the degree distribution follows a Poisson bell-shaped curve. In scale-free networks, however, the distribution follows a power law, where the curve is highly skewed and decays much more slowly that a Poisson (Strogatz, 2001). This means that there are a large number of nodes with fewer links and few nodes with a large number of links. In other words, no single characteristic scale can be defined for the node degrees and hence they are called scale-free.

A scale-free network can be characterized by a degree distribution that decays as a power law (Amaral et al., 2000). This power law distribution is in the form $P(k) \sim k^{-\gamma}$, where k is the node degree, which implies that the probability of finding a node with k links to other nodes is proportional to $k^{-\gamma}$. The size of the exponent γ varies from one network to another but normally falls into the range $2 < \gamma \leqslant 3$. Researchers have identified a number of scale-free networks, including the Internet, the World Wide Web, international airports and metabolic networks. For example, it is 2.2 for a co-authorship network, between 2.0 and 2.4 for metabolic networks and 2.1–2.45 for the World Wide Web (Goh et al., 2002). These networks all have an uneven degree distribution: some nodes are "very well connected hubs" and some are hardly connected. Hubs have an important role in the dynamic process of a network. For instance, hubs would be the prime targets for cyber attacks with malicious intent. When these nodes with higher degrees are removed, the system rapidly experiences network fragmentation. These well-connected hubs are also the funnels for the quick spread of diseases in the case of human networks. To stop such contagious diseases or computer viruses from spreading, one has to focus on protecting the hubs.

Scale-free networks can also have small-world properties where it may take only a few hops for a node to make a connection with another node. There is a good chance, though, that in a scale-free network, many transmissions would be carried en route one of the well-connected hub nodes, such as Google.com in the World Wide Web.

The topologies and dynamic properties of complex networks were studied by scientists to understand the reasons behind the evolution of a rich range of possible scale-free structures. It has been discovered that new nodes are added continuously and attach themselves preferentially to existing nodes with probability proportional to the degree of the target node (Strogatz, 2001). This behaviour is called "preferential attachment" (PA). PA states that the vertices with more edges are preferentially selected for the connection to the new vertex with the probability linearly proportional to the degree of that vertex (Kahng et al., 2002). Preferential attachment can be hindered by two factors:

1. **Ageing of the vertices.** This effect can be observed for the network of actors: in time, every actress or actor will stop acting. Here, therefore, a highly connected vertex will, eventually, stop receiving new links. The vertex will still be part of the network with previous links, but it no longer receives new links. The ageing of the vertices thus limits the preferential attachment preventing a scale-free distribution of connections.
2. **Cost of adding links to the vertices or the limited capacity of a vertex.** This effect is observed in the network of world airports: for reasons of efficiency, commercial airlines prefer to have a small number of hubs where all routes would connect. To a first approximation, this is indeed what happens for individual airlines, but when we consider all airlines together, it becomes physically impossible for an airport to become a hub to all airlines. Due to space and time constraints, each airport will limit the number of landings/departures per hour and the number of passengers in transit. Hence physical costs of adding links and limited capacity of a vertex will limit the number of possible links attaching to a given vertex (Amaral et al., 2000).

8.2.2 The Growth of Networks

The Internet is a good example of a continuously growing complex network interconnecting large numbers of computers around the world. Growing networks go through a great deal of topological changes during their dynamical evolution (Vazquez et al., 2002). Their topological properties are used to test and optimize future evolution processes; for example, a better understanding of the Internet structure is required to design routing and searching algorithms and to protect the spreading of viruses. Studies have been performed on another complex evolving network, the co-authorship network of scientists to determine the dynamics processes leading to the structure and topology of such networks and the factors that play a major role in their evolution (Barabási et al., 2002). The World Wide Web is also a complex evolving network, where nodes and links are added or removed frequently. The evolution of the Web and the Internet depends largely on the "preferential attachment" of new nodes to the already existing ones and the ageing property of nodes.

Newman recently studied collaboration networks in several fields derived from large databases over a 5-year interval (Newman, 2001). He found that collaboration networks have all the general properties of small-world networks: short paths and a large clustering coefficient in comparison with Erdös-Rényi's random networks of similar size. He also found a power law degree distribution in these net-works.

Barabási et al. (2002) analysed co-authorship networks in the field of mathematics and neuroscience. They uncovered that these networks also have power law degree distributions with exponents of 2.4 for mathematics and 2.1 for neuroscience. The main results are as follows: (1) these networks are scale-free and the degree distribution follows a power law and decays steadily; (2) the average of the shortest paths over the studied networks decreases over time, suggesting a potential explanation of the formation of a small-world network; (3) the clustering coefficient decays over time, indicating scientists might increasingly collaborate with one another; (4) the relative size of the largest cluster increases, which suggests that there were percolations or the emergence of the giant components in random networks; (5) the number of nodes in co-authorship networks increased owing to the arrival of new authors; and (6) node selection is governed by preferential attachment.

Steyvers and Tenenbaum (2001) studied a growth model similar to preferential attachment in three semantic networks: associative networks, WordNet and Roget's Thesaurus. These networks have small-world properties: sparse, short average pathlengths between words and strong local clustering. The distributions of the number of connections in these semantic networks follow power laws. They use two evolution heuristics in their model: (1) preferentially choose large neighbourhoods and (2) preferentially make connections to nodes with high utility. When new concepts are added to well-connected concepts or the neighbours of such concepts in the network, their model replicates small-world properties and the power-law distributions in the number of connections.

Nevertheless, a new mechanism that can produce scale-free networks is proposed to show that the power-law degree distribution is not related either to dynamical properties or to preferential attachment (Caldarelli et al., 2002). Instead, without increasing the number of vertices in time and without resorting to the rich-get-richer principle, researchers managed to generate networks whose statistical properties are scale-free. Assigning a quenched fitness value to every vertex and drawing links among vertices with a probability depending on the fitness of the two involved sites give rise to a good-get-richer mechanism, in which sites with larger fitness are more likely to become hubs (i.e., to be highly connected).

Scale-free networks are vulnerable to attacks on hubs, although they are robust to attacks on other types of nodes. A limited capacity of especially these nodes and edges can pose a serious limitation on the evolution of a growing network. Avalanche of breakdowns through the network can occur when nodes are sensitive to overloading. If a node is overloaded, it breaks down by becoming disconnected from its neighbours. A recent example is the blackout of 11 US States and two Canadian Provinces on 10 August 1996. Holme and Kim (2002) proved that for the network to be connected, the capacity of the nodes to relay connections has to increase with the size of the network. Holme (2002) proved that this is also the case for edges. Other research topics in the evolution of complex networks include weighted evolving networks (Yook et al., 2001), bipartite graphs (Strogatz, 2001) and directed relationships in networks (Kahng et al., 2002).

A number of methods have been routinely used in computer science and information science to reduce the complexity of a given network so that one can use existing algorithms to analyse, model, and visualize them. Pathfinder network scaling is the most representative one in the third category (Schvaneveldt, 1990). Pathfinder networks have been increasingly used in studies of citation networks (Chen, 1999; Chen and Paul, 2001; Chen et al., 2001).

In order to integrate findings in statistical mechanics, we must first re-examine these methods and address a number of theoretical and practical questions. What are the implications of imposing a selection threshold on a dataset? If the link degree of a large network follows a power law distribution, will the top slice of the dataset still manifest the property? To what degree does a link reduction algorithm alter the scale-free property? In this chapter, we raise the awareness of these issues in the context of requirements for VRML and the new generation of X3D applications so as to foster further studies in related areas.

8.2.3 Strong Ties and Weak Ties

Network analysis traditionally focuses on strong ties rather than weak ties in networks. Algorithms are devised to detect the strongest links and extract the shortest

paths in networks. Link reduction algorithms typically remove weak links and preserve strong ones.

The practical significance of weak ties in social networks was established by
sociologist Granovetter (1973) in his argument for the strength of weak ties. He
argued that we obtain substantial new information through weak ties such as
casual acquaintances rather than through strong ties such as close personal
friends. Burt (1992) indicated that it was not so much the strength or weakness of
a tie that determined its information potential, but rather whether there was a
structural hole between someone's social network. A structural hole can be seen as
a person who has strong between-cluster connections but weak within-cluster
connections in a social network. Burt showed that the number of connections in a
social network is important, but the value of each connection depends on how
important it is for maintaining the connectivity of a social network (Burt, 2001).

In some networks, ties are not only weak in strength, but also difficult to
observe. Sparrow (1991) described three problems of criminal network analysis:

1. Incompleteness – the inevitability of missing nodes and links that the investi-
   gators will not uncover. By sharing information and knowledge, a more complete picture of possible danger can be drawn.
2. Fuzzy boundaries – the difficulty in deciding who to include and who not to
   include.
3. Dynamic – these networks are not static, they are always changing. Instead of
   looking at the presence or absence of a tie between two individuals, Sparrow
   suggested looking at the waxing and waning strength of a tie depending on the
   time and the task at hand.

Krebs (2002) studied a portion of the network centred on the 19 hijackers of
9.11 as a social network. The social network of the 19 hijackers was constructed
based on trusted ties. Many were school chums from many years ago, some had
lived together for years and others were related by kinship ties. Deep, trusted ties,
that were not easily visible to outsiders, wove this terror network together.

Few studies of statistical mechanics have focused on the role of weak ties in networks (White and Houseman, 2002), in contrast to the rapidly increasing number
of strong-tie studies. It is particularly important to understand phenomena such as
knowledge diffusion. Currently, neither statistical mechanics nor citation analysis
has paid sufficient attention to weak ties in terms of theoretical models, methodologies and empirical studies.

8.3 Citation Networks

Citation analysts often face three major challenges in analysing complex citation
networks: scalability, clarity and dynamics.

As the size or the density of a network increases, the complexity associated with
its topology increases at a much faster rate. Algorithms that work perfectly well
with a small-scale network may not be able to scale up – they may break down in
front of a large-scale network. One example is multidimensional scaling (MDS).
Most MDS algorithms do not scale well, with the exception of some recent break-
throughs (Roweis and Saul, 2000; Tenenbaum et al., 2000; Morrison et al., 2002).

Reducing the complexity of a given network is one of the most commonly used
strategies in network analysis. A variety of network transformation algorithms

have been developed for reducing the complexity of a network. Two major categories of such algorithms are link reduction and clustering. Link reduction focuses on reducing the number of links that one must take into account. In general, the fewer links a network has, the easier it can be analysed. Let a graph $G = (V, E)$ denote our underlying network, where V is the set of vertices, or nodes, and E is the set of edges, or links. Link reduction algorithms aim to reduce the size of E, $\aleph E$, whereas V remains intact. For example, a minimum spanning tree $G_{MST} = (V, E_{MST})$, $\aleph E_{MST}$ becomes $\aleph V - 1$; in a Pathfinder network $G_{PF} = (V, E_{PF})$, $\aleph E_{PF} = \aleph(\cup E_{MST})$ (Schvaneveldt, 1990). In contrast, clustering algorithms aim to divide the set V into smaller ones $\{V_i\}, i = 1, 2, \ldots, k$, such that $V = V_1 \oplus V_2 \oplus V_3 \oplus \cdots V_k$ and $\aleph V_i < \aleph V$.

A major problem inherited from a large-scale network is the loss of clarity, especially in terms of the clarity of graphical representations. A large amount of links may cross each other and clutter the display. Even worse, the presence of too many links can severely reduce the power of visual communication as important patterns may be buried in the seemingly unstructured spaghetti of links.

A common way to deal with the loss of clarity is to control the number of links to be displayed at a given moment, either by hiding certain links from the display or by bringing certain links into the display.

The dynamics of an evolving network is by far the most fundamental challenge among the three discussed here. So far, modelling network evolution is still in its early stages, especially in the context of network visualization. Research on scale-free networks has revived the interest in network evolution. Visualizing evolving networks will become one of the hottest research topics between statistical mechanics and information visualization. VRML, X3D and SVG will provide crucial techniques.

In a recent study, we examined citation and co-citation networks of superstring theory in physics and compared both citation and co-citation degree distributions with particular reference to two superstring revolutions. Further studies in more depth and breadth are recommended so as to establish a sound theoretical and practical basis for a new generation of citation analysis.

Redner (1998) studied the citation distribution of two large data sets from the citation databases of the Institute for Scientific Information (ISI). One contains 783 339 papers published in 1981 along with 6 716 198 citations made between 1981 and June 1997. The other contains 24 296 papers published in volumes 11–50 of *Physical Review D*, which are cited at least once between 1975 and 1994. The second dataset contains 351 872 citations. Render found that the asymptotic tail of the citation distribution follows a power law, $N(x) \sim x^{-\alpha}$, with an exponent $\alpha \approx 3$. The distribution of citations is a rapidly decreasing function of citation count but is not described by a single function over the entire range of citation degree. He suggested that the citation distribution provides an appealing venue for theoretical modelling.

An et al. (2001) studied the graph theoretical properties of the citation networks for three different areas within computer science: neural networks, automata and software engineering. They found that the in-degree citation distribution follows a power law. They also extracted weakly connected components, strongly connected components, biconnected components and minimum cuts between authority papers in different areas and shortest paths between pairs of papers. They attempted to extract research communities with standard graph theoretic algorithms, but the citation network retained a large, well-connected component. They recommended the use of more sophisticated algorithms such as balanced graph partition algorithms to deal with such large, well-connected components. The balanced graph partition problem is NP-hard, but local search strategies are available (Charles and Mattheyses,

1982; Kernighan and Lin, 1970). Their study also suggests that the temporal evolution of the local link structure of citation networks is a good candidate for predicting research trends or for studying the life span of specialties and communities.

Co-citation networks are networks in which links are determined by co-citation counts between a pair of papers, a pair of authors or a pair of journals. When a pair of such items is referenced together by a scientific publication, the instance is called a co-citation. Co-citation networks have play a fundamental role in citation analysis (Small, 1973; White and Griffith, 1981; Chen, 1999, 2003; Chen and Paul, 2001).

Unlike citation distributions, studies of co-citation distributions are rare, except for the work of van Rann (1990, 1991, 2000), in which the focus was on the size of co-citation clusters, rather than co-citation link degrees. To be co-cited, a reference must appear at least twice in the dataset. The co-citation degree of a node is calculated as the number of times it was co-cited with others, which is the same as the co-citation counts we used in our previous studies of co-citation networks (Chen and Paul, 2001).

Available studies in complex networks indicate that citation networks in general follow power law distributions. Given that network scaling algorithms are commonly used in the study of citation networks, it is essential to clarify the impact of these algorithms on power law distributions: to what extent do they alter a power law distribution?

8.4 Large-scale Network Visualization

Visualizing large-scale complex networks poses not only technical challenges but also challenges in terms of overall visual–spatial metaphors, organization principles and interpretation models. Problems such as display clutter, node positioning and perceptual tension can reduce the quality of the picture and hinder accurate interpretation (Eick, 1996; Wills, 1999). Display clutter occurs when the picture is overwhelmed with information leading to visual confusion. Perceptual tension occurs when the displays are contrary to general human tendencies of interpreting visuals. For example, nodes close to each other can be interpreted as related whereas those away from each other can be considered as unrelated. Three-dimensional layouts with strategies for handling these problems have been used in the majority of network visualization tools. Three–dimensional layouts solve the problem of lines crossing over each other, thus depicting a more navigable and less confusing model. Wills (1999) analysed the available layout algorithms designed for large-scale networks and designed NicheWorks specifically for visualizing large-scale networks. He used NicheWorks in analysing Web sites and detecting international telephone fraud. Cichlid[1] is a visualization tool that provides high-quality 3-D, animated visualizations of a wide range of networks and related information. In a recent example, the evolution of the biotechnology industry was analysed and visualized as a network of collaborative ties among organizations (Powell et al., 2002)

The Internet Mapping Project[2] was started at Bell Laboratories in the summer of 1998. Its long-term goal is to acquire and save Internet topological data over a long period of time. Branigan and Cheswick (1999) provided an example of using the

---

[1] http://moat.nlanr.net/Papers/cichlid-pam2k.pdf
[2] http://research.lumeta.com/ches/map/

Internet map to show the effects of war on the Yugoslavian network. They mapped the Yugoslavian network every day since the end of March and focused on the accessibility of the network. They noticed that the network was stable until about 3 May 1999, then, it changed drastically. As shown in single-day snapshots of the network map between 1 and 10 May, a fair amount of the Yugoslavian network disappeared and subsequently reappeared on a daily basis. They also mapped Bosnia's Internet during the same period of time. Although their traces showed no common communication routes, part of Bosnia vanished at the same time, probably because the two countries share power grid connections.

Network Simulator (NS)[3] is a discrete event simulator targeted at networking researches. NS provides many important protocols and attractive features in the networking world. Network Animator (Nam[4]) is a Tcl/TK-based animation tool for viewing network simulation traces and real-world packet traces. It supports topology layout, packet level animation and various data inspection tools. Nam's major goal is to show simulation trace files graphically. It takes a simulation trace file from the NS and then presents each line of the trace file graphically. NS's users can use some appropriate NS commands to create a Nam trace file corresponding to a simulation's results. Nam can show many situations in the networking world, for example, topology layout, queuing packets, dropped packets, control packets using in routing algorithms and mobility of a node.

Java Network Visualiser (Javis) is the re-implementation of Nam in Java. Javis and Nam share the same objective: showing Nam trace files created by the NS graphically. Javis is designed to understand networking principles through visualization, simulation, emulation and application.

8.5 Network Visualization in VRML and X3D

Visualization is essentially a mapping process from physical representations to perceptual representations, choosing encoding techniques to maximize human understanding and communication. It has been used in maps, scientific drawings and data plots for thousands of years. Today we have various computer-aided processes and tools by means of which information can be explored to gain insight into the data, observe trends and patterns and permit decision-making. The human brain has the ability to understand and retain visuals faster than that for the written text. It is this ability along with the power of visuals to trigger immediate recognition for patterns and the continually increasing need to generate and study data of various size and complexity that has made information visualization a very important aspect of data representation.

The tools and techniques of visualization have been used to analyse and display large volumes of, often time-varying, multidimensional data in such a way as to allow the user to extract significant features and results quickly and easily. Advanced tools for 3D modelling are available for visualizing information. Virtual reality techniques are being used to view and manipulate data in a true three-dimensional environment.

---

[3] http://www-mash.cs.berkeley.edu/ns/
[4] http://www.isi.edu/nsnam/nam/index.html

8.5.1 Conversions between VRML and X3D

The primarily organizing structure in VRML is a scene graph. A scene graph determines exactly how individual objects are interconnected to each other. To view a
VRML world, the user needs to have a VRML viewer program installed. A VRML
viewer can be a stand-alone program, a helper application or a plug-in for the Web
browser. Microsoft and Netscape each include a VRML browser plug-in in their
standard Web browser distributions. A VRML browser typically provides a variety
of navigation controls for the user to walk through the virtual world, interact with
its content, trigger animations and listen to 3D sound effects (Nadeau, 1999). Some
of the most widely used VRML browsers are CosmoPlayer, blaxxun's Contact,
ParallelGraphics' Cortona and Intervista's WorldView. X3D extends the geometry
and behaviour capabilities of VRML97 using the XML syntax. X3D is designed to
provide 100% backward compatibility to VRML97. X3D browsers are available
from commercial companies such as Nexternet's Piveron X3D browser, Open-
Worlds' Horizon X3D browser and ParallelGraphics's Cortona X3D.

Given the number of VRML models accumulated over the last several years on the
Web, considerable efforts have been made to ensure a smooth and efficient conversion
between VRML and X3D. A number of comprehensive tools have been developed to
facilitate such conversion tasks. For instance, the Institute for Information Processing
and Computer Supported New Media (IICM), Graz University of Technology, Austria,
developed a VRML parser called *pw*. This VRML parser has been incorporated into a
number of popular tools that provide the capability of converting from VRML to X3D
models. Converting X3D models to VRML models can be done by utilizing existing
tools such as the XML parser Xerces and XSLT processor Xalan.

A conversion package for VRML97 and X3D models was developed in Java by
the Visualization and Usability Group in the Information Technology Laboratory
at NIST[5]. The NIST converter is based on the *pw* VRML parser developed by the
IICM and the specification of "x3d-compact.dtd" and "X3dToVrml97.xsl", both
available at www.web3d.org.

X3D-Edit[6] is a useful tool that allows editing, authoring and validation of X3D
or VRML scene-graph files. It uses the XML tag set defined by the X3D Compact
Document Type Definition (DTD) in combination with Sun's Java and IBM's Xeena
XML editor. X3D-Edit embeds the NIST Translator. There are also a number of
lightweight converters such as VRML2X3D/X3D2VRML, which is downloadable
from the Web[7].

We tested the NIST's converter by converting a VRML97 model to X3D. The
VRML model contains an animated visualization sequence of a citation network
on anthrax research. The citation network contains 358 nodes and 360 links; in
fact, this is a Pathfinder network ($q = N-1$ and $r = \infty$). The animation sequence
visualizes the evolution of the citation network between 1945 and 2002. It depicts
the transformation of citation and co-citation events associated with the network
using a variety of rendering and animation techniques such as colour mapping,
varying the level of transparency and changing visual–spatial attributes.

In the following examples, we illustrate the key features of our model in both
VRML and X3D. The VRML file contains 168 585 lines of text, whereas the X3D file
is slightly shorter, containing 127 000 lines of one million words. If we open the

[5] http://ovrt.nist.gov/v2_x3d.html
[6] http://www.web3d.org/TaskGroups/x3d/translation/README.X3D-Edit.html
[7] http://www.cybergarage.org/vrml/cv97/cv97java/sample/x3dvrml.zip

X3D file in a word processor such as MS Word, it can be as long as 2239 pages. The length is largely due to the animation feature, which relies on interpolated values of transparency to depict the evolution of the citation events in a chronological order. Table 8.1 shows excerpts from the VRML file and their counterparts in the X3D file.

Table 8.1   Examples of how objects in VRML are converted to X3D

VRML format	X3D format
#VRML V2.0 utf8	<?**xml** version="1.0" encoding="UTF-8"?> <!DOCTYPE X3D PUBLIC "http://www.web3D.org/TaskGroups/x3d/ translation/x3d-compact.dtd" "/www.web3D.org/TaskGroups/x3d/ translation/x3d-compact.dtd">

DEF Clock **TimeSensor** {
  cycleInterval 30
  loop TRUE
}
	<**TimeSensor** DEF="Clock" loop="true" cycleInterval="30.0"/>

DEF EntryPoint **Viewpoint** {
  position 0 −250 150
  orientation 1 0 0 1.00
  fieldOfView 1.149
  description "Landscape"
}
	<**Viewpoint** DEF="EntryPoint" position= "0.0 −250.0 150.0" orientation="1.0 0.0 0.0 1.0" description="Landscape" fieldOfView="1.149"/>

Anchor {
  url "network.html#ArticleID"
  parameter "target=details"
  description "ArticleID, PY, Cited Work"
  children [......]
}
	<**Anchor** url="'network.html#ArticleID'" description="ArticleID, PY, Cited Work" parameter="'target=details'">

Transform {
  translation 93.8 33.4 0
}
	<**Transform** translation="93.8 33.4 0.0">

material DEF NODE1956 **Material** {
  ambientIntensity 0.27
  diffuseColour 0.23 0.81 0.44
  specularColour 0.99 0.94 0.81
  shininess 0.45
}
	<**Material** DEF 5 "NODE1956" ambientIntensity="0.27" shininess="0.45" diffuseColour="0.23 0.81 0.44" specularColour="0.99 0.94 0.81"/>

geometry **Sphere** {
  radius 3
}
	<**Sphere** radius="3.0"/>

DEF NODEXPath **ScalarInterpolator** {
  key [0.00, 0.10, 0.20, 0.30, 0.40, 0.50,
  0.60, 0.70, 0.80, 0.90, 1.00]
  keyValue [0.90, 0.90, 0.90, 0.90, 0.50,
  0.50, 0.50, 0.50, 0.0, 0.0, 0.0]
}
	<**ScalarInterpolator** DEF="NODEXPath" key=" 0.00, 0.10, 0.20, 0.30, 0.40, 0.50, 0.60, 0.70, 0.80, 0.90, 1.00" keyValue=" 0.90, 0.90, 0.90, 0.90, 0.50, 0.50, 0.50, 0.50, 0.0, 0.0, 0.0"/>

geometry **Cylinder** {
  radius 1.200
  height 6.000
}
	<**Cylinder** radius="1.2" height 5 "6.0"/>

ROUTE Clock.fraction_changed TO BARXPath.set_fraction	<**ROUTE** fromNode="Clock" fromField="fraction_changed" toNode="BARXPath" toField="set_fraction"/>
ROUTE BAR1999Path.value_changed TO BARX.set_transparency	<**ROUTE** fromNode="BAR1999Path" fromField="value_changed" toNode="BARX" toField="set_transparency"/>

8.5.2   Other 3D Technologies

In addition to VRML/X3D, there are other 3D technologies, notably OpenGL, Java3D, Shout 3D, WildTangent, XGL and Active Worlds. Java3D is worthy of particular attention owing to the popularity of Java. Java3D provides a Java API for composing and displaying 3D geometry in Java applets. It is not part of the Java core APIs. The Java 3D API also introduces some concepts not commonly considered part of the graphics environment, such as 3D spatial sound to provide a more immersive experience for the user.[8] The XGL file format is designed to represent 3D information and capture all of the 3D information that can be rendered by SGI's OpenGL rendering library. It uses XML 1.0 syntax. Active Worlds, one of the oldest interactive 3D chat worlds, is a multi-user 3D format used to build objects and collaborative worlds. Blaxxun, Cosmo Software, Macromedia, Parallel-Graphics, Superscape and WildTangent are major players in 3D and animation.[9] In terms of authoring tools, there are a variety of Web3D authoring tools. Some support multiple formats from VRML, Java3D, to X3D, such as 3D World Shaper. Some support only a single format.

8.6   Visualizing the Evolution of Citation Networks

Researchers have documented two superstring revolutions in the last two decades: the first was in 1984 and the second in 1995. We have reported a domain analysis of string theory in a special topic issue of the *Journal of the American Society for Information Science and Technology* on visualizing scientific revolutions (Chen & Kuljis, 2003), but it was conducted without direct reference to statistical mechanics: we did not examine the citation distribution and the co-citation distribution.

The String Theory data was extracted from the Web of Science (1981–2001) using top-level terms as topical queries. The dataset contains 3708 citing articles on string theory or superstring. Between these articles, they cited a total of 137 655 unique bibliographic references.

8.6.1   Citation and Co-citation Degree Distributions

We model the citation distribution over the dataset in several slightly different ways, including the citation distribution over the entire dataset and the citation distribution over a top-sliced subset selected by a citation threshold we used in modelling and visualizing the domain structure. The threshold we studied here is 35 citations, which leads to a subset of 395 references. Four bibliographic references in the subset are regarded as outliers – they represent only one instance of each level of excessive citations at 150, 327, 331 and 339.

In addition, we compare each year's citation distribution between 1991 and 2000. Our hypothesis is that given the second superstring revolution took place in 1995, if the revolution indeed alters the topology of the citation network, then we

---

[8] http://java.sun.com/products/java-media/3D/collateral/j3d_api/j3d_api_2.html
[9] http://wp.netscape.com/plugins/3d_and_animation.html?cp=pi1

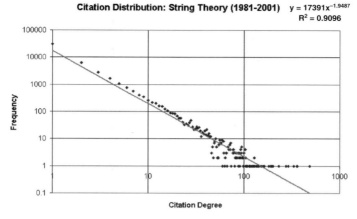

Figure 8.1   The citation distribution of the entire dataset on String Theory (1981–2001). The distribution follows a power-law model with an exponent of 1.95.

want to know whether such changes can be reflected at a macroscopic level in the time series of distributions.

Similarly to citation distributions, we inspect the co-citation distributions on the entire dataset and the top-sliced subset. The subset is visualized in a three-dimensional model, consisting of a base map using a geodesic Pathfinder network and a thematic map depicting the annual growth of citations.

The use of Pearson coefficients was originally introduced to author co-citation analysis (ACA) (White and McCain, 1998; Chen, 1999). Recently, researchers have independently studied the implications of using Pearson coefficients versus using more straightforward co-citation counts (Noel et al., 2002; White, 2003). We address the question from a co-citation degree distribution point of view.

Pathfinder network scaling extracts shortest paths from a network. Pathfinder networks have generated meaningful and promising results in knowledge domain visualization. We need to understand further the theoretical and practical implications of the scaling process. For example, to what extent can we preserve the scale-free property in the original network? Similarly, when we apply link reduction algorithms such as minimum spanning tree algorithms, are we altering the fundamental topological properties of an original network in some significant way? What factors do we need to take into account in the practice of network visualization in general?

The citation distribution of the entire String Theory dataset follows a power law, with the exponent of 1.9 (see Figure 8.1). The time series of 10 annual citation degree distributions reveals a significant jump from 1996 to 1997 and a drop from 1997 to 1998; the magnitude of both changes is greater than two standard deviations of the exponents over the 10-year period (see Figure 8.2). Given that the second superstring revolution took place in 1995, this would be a particular interesting point of departure for more in-depth studies to clarify potential connections between the revolution and the global changes in topological properties.

The distribution of co-citation counts follows a power law, with an exponent of 2.24, which explains 90% of variance. The plot in Figure 8.3 shows some references off the straight line of the power law model, suggesting that the number of highly co-cited references may not be as many as the power law model might expect.

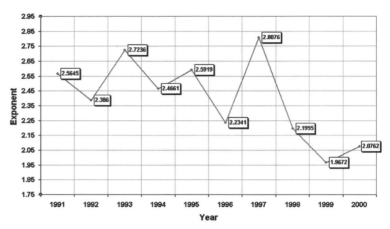

Figure 8.2 The citation distributions over a 10-year period (1991–2001). The most severe changes are between 1996 and 1998, when the exponents changed more than two standard deviations: 2.1 standard deviations up from 1996 to 1997 and 2.2 down from 1997 to 1998.

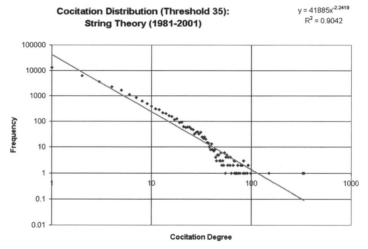

Figure 8.3 The co-citation distribution of a top-sliced co-citation network in String Theory (1981–2001). The entry threshold is 35 citations. A power-law model with an exponent of 2.24 accounts for 90% of variance.

8.6.2 A Visualization Model

Figure 8.4 is a screenshot of the network visualization in VRML97. Users can explore the structure of the network, the detailed attributes associated with each individual node and the temporal changes of the growing network. These facilities enable them to address questions at the system level or at the subject domain level. For instance, it displays not only the article that has the most citations in the past, but also its neighbouring nodes and their citation history. Furthermore, the animated

Figure 8.4   A three-dimensional visualization of the top-sliced String Theory dataset.

visualization of the citation growth rate of a cluster of articles makes it possible for domain analysts to detect potentially significant advances in the field.

One of the implications of the latest advances in complex network theory is that one may usefully incorporate the knowledge of scale-free properties, or small-world properties, into the study of the evolution of networks. For instance, a progressive visualization of the growth of a network can be devised such that if the addition of new links is consistent with an expectation of a theoretical model, the visualization of the updates of relevant metrics will highlight such a relationship. In other words, by combining with theoretical works of networks, network visualization can be used in a wider range of activities, especially in understanding the dynamics of an evolving network.

There are many challenges to be resolved before we can achieve our goals. In terms of the development of VRML and X3D, more powerful modelling capabilities are needed for dealing with the complexity of real-world networks. As the interest in large-scale networks continues to rise, the demand for a substantial amount of built-in modelling blocks for network visualization will certainly increase. An increased network modelling and visualization capability of the new generation of cross-platform 3D graphics standards, browsers and authoring tools will fundamentally expand the scope of X3D. In return, an expanded scope will attract more and more users and developers.

At a more pragmatic level, accessing 3D models should be made more seamlessly across different platforms and as an integral part of the user's computing environment at the operating system level. Currently, from time to time the user has to go through the tedious process of installing and even uninstalling 3D browsers. The

Figure 8.5 The evolution of a knowledge domain structure over time. The green sphere in the centre of each frame depicts a scientific article. The horizontal links are co-citation relationships. The vertical bar rising from the sphere represents the accumulative citations that this particular article received.

Figure 8.6 An early stage of the evolution. The network already has two notable clusters of articles. On the other hand, the network also has many articles that are not published until later years.

expected ISO standard status in as early as 2004 should profoundly improve the situation.

We shall complete the chapter with a few screenshots from our animated visualization originally written in VRML 2.0 and converted to X3D recently using NIST's converter package. Figure 8.5 shows a sequence of snapshots from the animated visualization sequence. A TimeSensor is used to control the animation. Each tick of the clock corresponds to one calendar year in the scientific literature world. In frames prior to its year of publication, the sphere is rendered semi-transparently. It becomes increasingly opaque when it is published, when it is first cited and when it is co-cited with its neighbouring nodes. Users can easily tell which articles were published first and in which year the citations grew fast.

In addition, the animation also represents the formation of the underlying network by showing the emergence of co-citation links in synchronization to the historical chronology. Figure 8.6 shows the earliest of three snapshots of a knowledge domain visualization model, in which many articles are not yet published in the literature. However, the semi-transparent rendering of such articles provides a useful hint to the user – a lot more has been going on after that particular year. The user can easily identify articles that formed clusters at that particular time. Figure 8.7 shows the scene a few years later. Clusters grew larger and citation bars grew taller. Clusters were consolidated by more articles in similar colours. New articles appear like mushrooms, indicating the emergent of research fronts. Figure 8.8 shows the

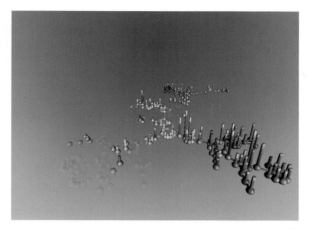

Figure 8.7   A few years later. The network grows larger with new articles and new links, whereas existing articles have gathered more and more citations. The nature of newly found "continents" in the network indicates the direction of the field.

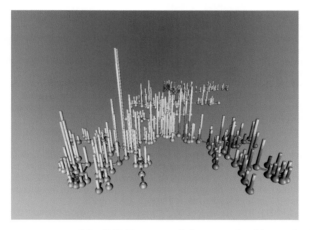

Figure 8.8   A more recent scene of the field. New research fronts escalated in previously unpopulated areas in snapshots of the scene.

most recent snapshot of the scene. The most striking feature of the visualization is the rapid growth of clusters of articles in previously unpopulated areas, implying the emergence of completely new research fronts. Furthermore, these new articles have attracted citations far more quickly than articles of previous generations. Their citations have been accumulated at an escalating rate, and such fast growth of a field is captured by our animated visualization.

8.7 Concluding Remarks

In this chapter, we started with the latest advances in complex network theory in statistical physics and discussed the implications of the new discoveries on network visualization, especially scientific networks such as citation and co-citation networks. We emphasized that the emergent field of visualizing the evolution of networks provides not only a promising domain of applications for 3D technologies such as VRML and X3D, but also a number of challenges that the designers must meet. The push and pull from complex network theory and visualizing the evolution of large-scale complex networks should be taken into account by the designers and vendors of X3D in the near future so that X3D techniques can reach a much wider user population than its predecessors such as VRML97 and Java3D.

References

Albert R and Barabasi A (2002) Statistical mechanics of complex networks. *Reviews of Modern Physics*, **74**, 47–97.

Amaral LAN, Scala A, Barthelemy M and Stanley HE (2000) *Classes of Small-world Networks*, **97**, No. 21.

An Y, Janssen J and Milios E (2001) *Characterizing and Mining the Citation Graph of the Computer Science Literature (CS-2001-02)*. Halifax, Nova Scotia: Dalhousie University.

Barabási A-L, Albert R and Jeong H (2000) Scale-free characteristics of random networks: the topology of the World-Wide Web. *Physica A*, **281**, 69–77.

Barabási A-L, Jeong H, Neda Z, Ravasz E, Schubert A and Vicsek T (2002) Evolution of the social network of scientific collaborations. *Physica A*, **311**, 590–614.

Branigan S and Cheswick B (1999) *The Effects of War on the Yugoslavian Network*. Lumeta. Available: http://research.lumeta.com/ches/map/yu/index.html

Burt RS (1992) *Structural Holes: the Social Structure of Competition*. Cambridge, MA: Harvard University Press.

Burt RS (2001) The social capital of structural holes. In Meyer M (ed.), *New Directions in Economic Sociology*. New York: Russell Sage Foundation.

Caldarelli G, Capocci A, Rios PDL and Munoz MA (2002) Scale-free networks without growth or preferential attachment: good get richer. Available: http://arxiv.org/pdf/cond-mat/0207366

Charles MF and Mattheyses RM (1982) A linear-time heuristic for improving network partitions. Paper presented at the 19th IEEE Design Automation Conference.

Chen C (1999) Visualising semantic spaces and author co-citation networks in digital libraries. *Information Processing and Management*, **35**, 401–420.

Chen C (2003) *Mapping Scientific Frontiers: the Quest for Knowledge Visualization*. London: Springer.

Chen C and Börner K (2002) Top-ten problems in visual interfaces of digital libraries. In Börner K and Chen C (eds), *Visual Interfaces to Digital Libraries*, Berlin: Springer, pp. 227–232.

Chen C and Czerwinski M (2000) Empirical evaluation of information visualizations. *International Journal of Human–Computer Studies*, **35**, 631–635.

Chen C and Kuljis J (2003) The rising landscape: a visual exploration of superstring revolutions in physics. *Journal of the American Society for Information Science and Technology*, **54**(5).

Chen C and Paul RJ (2001) Visualizing a knowledge domain's intellectual structure. *Computer*, **34**(3), 65–71.

Chen C, Kuljis J and Paul RJ (2001) Visualizing latent domain knowledge. *IEEE Transactions on Systems, Man, and Cybernetics*, **31**, 518–529.

Dorogovtsev SN and Mendes JFF (2002) Evolution of networks. *Advances in Physics*, **51**, 1079–1187.

Eick SG (1996) Aspects of network visualization. *IEEE Computer Graphics and Applications*, **16**(2), 69–72.

Girvan M and Newman MEJ (2001) *Community Structure in Social and Biological Networks*. Available: arXiv:cond-mat/0112110

Goh KI, Oh E, Jeong H, Kahng B and Kim D (2002) Classification of scale-free networks. *Proceedings of the National Academy of Sciences of the United States of America*, **99**, 12583–12588.

Granovetter M (1973) The strength of weak ties. *American Journal of Sociology*, **78**, 1360–1380.

Holme P (2002) Edge overload breakdown in evolving networks. *Physical Review E*, **66**, 036119. 036111–036119.036117.

Holme P and Kim BJ (2002) Vertex overload breakdown in evolving networks. *Physical Review E*, **65**, 066109.066101–066109.066108.

Kahng B, Park Y and Jeong H (2002) Robustness of the in-degree exponent for the World-Wide Web. *Physical Review E*, **66**, 046107.046101–046107.046106.

Kernighan BW and Lin S (1970) An efficient heuristic procedure for partitioning graphs. *The Bell System Technical Journal*, **29**, 291–307.

Krebs VE (2002) Mapping networks of terrorist cells. *Connections*, **24**(3), 43–52.

Morrison A, Ross G and Chalmers M (2002) A hybrid layout algorithm for sub-quadratic multidimensional scaling. Paper presented at the IEEE Symposium on Information Visualization, Boston, MA.

Nadeau DR (1999) Building virtual worlds with VRML. *IEEE Computer Graphics and Applications*, **19**(2), 18–29.

Newman MEJ (2001) *Proceedings of the National Academy of Sciences of the United States of America*, **98**, 404.

Noel S, Chu CH and Raghavan V (2002) Visualization of document co-citation counts. Paper presented at the 6th International Conference on Information Visualisation, London.

Powell WW, White DR, Koput KW and Owen-Smith J (2002) The evolution of a science-based industry: dynamic analyses and network visualization of biotechnology (www.fek.umu.se/dpcc/powell.pdf).

Redner S (1998) How popular is your paper? An empirical study of the citation distribution. *European Journal B*, **4**, 131–134.

Roweis ST and Saul LK (2000) Nonlinear dimensionality reduction by locally linear embedding. *Science*, **290**, 2323–2326.

Schvaneveldt RW (ed.) (1990) *Pathfinder Associative Networks: Studies in Knowledge Organization*. Norwood, NJ: Ablex.

Small H (1973) Co-citation in the scientific literature: a new measure of the relationship between two documents. *Journal of the American Society for Information Science*, **24**, 265–269.

Sparrow M (1991) The application of network analysis to criminal intelligence: an assessment of the prospects. *Social Networks*, **13**, 251–274.

Steyvers M and Tenenbaum J (2001) *Small worlds in semantic networks*. Available: http://www.psych.stanford.edu/~msteyver/small_worlds.htm

Strogatz SH (2001) Exploring complex networks. *Nature*, **410**, 268–276.

Tenenbaum JB, de Silva V and Langford JC (2000) A global geometric framework for nonlinear dimensionality reduction. *Science*, **290**, 2319–2323.

van Raan A (1990) Fractal dimensions of co-citations. *Nature*, **347**, 626.

van Raan A (1991) Fractal geometry of information space as represented by co-citation clustering. *Scientometrics*, **20**, 439–449.

van Raan A (2000) On growth, ageing, and fractal differentiation of science. *Scientometrics*, **47**, 347–362.

Vazquez A, Pastor-Satorras R and Vespignani A (2002) Large-scale topological and dynamical properties of the Internet. *Physical Review E*, **65**, 066130.066131–066130.066112.

Watts DJ and Strogatz SJ (1998) Collective dynamics of "small-world" networks. *Nature*, **393**, 440–442.

White D and Houseman M (2002) The navigability of strong ties: small worlds, tie strength and network topology. *Complexity*. Available: http://eclectic.ss.uci.edu/~drwhite/Complexity/SpecialIssue.htm

White H (2003) Pathfinder networks and author cocitation analysis: a remapping of paradigmatic information scientists. *Journal of the American Society for Information Science and Technology*, **54**(5), 72–81.

White HD and Griffith BC (1981) Author co-citation: a literature measure of intellectual structure. *Journal of the American Society for Information Science*, **32**, 163–172.

White HD and McCain KW (1998) Visualizing a discipline: an author co-citation analysis of information science, 1972–1995. *Journal of the American Society for Information Science*, **49**, 327–356.

Wills GJ (1999) NicheWorks: interactive visualization of very large graphs. *Journal of Computational and Graphical Statistics*, **8**, 190–212.

Yook SH, Jeong H, Barábasi, AL and Tu Y (2001) Weighted evolving networks. *Physical Review Letters*, **86**, 5835–5838.

Chapter 9
Applying SVG to Visualization of Chemical Structures and Reactions

John Leaver

9.1 Introduction

9.1.1 SVG in Chemistry Educational Resource Development

This chapter is concerned with making use of SVG in the development of educational resources for teaching organic chemistry. For a general introduction to SVG, see Eisenberg (2002). It is hoped that it will be of interest to those involved in the delivery of introductory organic chemistry courses and also to non-chemists as an example of applying SVG to a "real-world" educational situation. For those involved in chemical education, it will also highlight some possibilities for the inclusion of IT/computing and mathematical material in the context of a science learning activity. A brief chemical introduction for non-chemists will be found in Section 9.2; this is intended solely to familiarize non-chemists with some aspects of the "shorthand" way in which organic chemists represent molecules.

9.1.2 Why Use SVG to Represent Chemical Structures?

It is becoming relatively common these days for educationalists to develop Web content to act as learning resources. Many physical science educators will have dabbled with HTML to produce resources for their students. The possibilities offered by hyperlinked documents with assorted content are immediately obvious and appealing. The inclusion of graphical content is a clear requirement to extend the functionality and attractiveness of these learning materials. Much is possible using conventionally produced graphics, included as GIFs, JPEGs and PNGs, and even animated content is possible with animated GIFs and the use of commercial software such as Macromedia Flash. SVG is just another tool for the educational resource developer to add to her or his toolkit. There are, of course, also the advantages of file size and portability highlighted elsewhere in this book. In the context of representing organic chemical structures, however, there are features of SVG that make it particularly suitable. Many of the simple shapes that may be used to represent complex organic molecules are created with relative ease using just a few lines of SVG code. The creation of such structures also provides opportunities for the employment of some fairly straightforward programming and the application of some basic mathematics, thereby enhancing the possibilities for the development of learning activities that integrate chemical, computing and mathematical skills.

9.1.3 Web Site

This chapter contains examples that involve the development of SVG code and also some HTML and JavaScript. There are also references to on-line materials and resources. The most convenient way to provide up-to-date access to these various resources is, of course, via the Web. To facilitate this, a Web site has been set up with the address http://www.chem-svg.org.uk. All the examples mentioned in the chapter will be found on the Web site, together with links to other resources such as the home pages for software highlighted in the chapter. It is also hoped that others who develop chemistry teaching resources that make use of SVG may want to provide links to these for inclusion on the site, or provide the resources themselves for inclusion on the site if they are not available elsewhere on the Web. The author may be contacted at john@chem-svg.org.uk to discuss either of these possibilities.

9.1.4 Outline of Chapter

The remainder of this chapter is divided up as follows. Section 9.2 is a brief introduction to representing organic chemical structures and reaction mechanisms for non-chemists. Section 9.3 considers ways of creating chemical structures in SVG. The first part is an example of hand coding to highlight some of the relevant features available in SVG and to provide ideas for possible student projects involving chemical, computing and mathematical skills. It examines the modest aim of depicting the structure of cholesterol using SVG. The remainder of Section 9.3 looks at a variety of possibilities for drawing chemical structures using available software, with the proviso that the resulting output is an SVG file. Section 9.4 briefly examines some possibilities with respect to using SVG to represent reaction mechanisms, where animation is a requirement.

9.2 Chemical Introduction for Non-chemists

9.2.1 Representing Molecules

Open a textbook on organic chemistry and you will find pages of diagrams representing the structures of organic (carbon-containing) molecules, reaction schemes representing transformations of one molecule into another and reaction mechanisms showing how the transformations happen. For typical examples, see Hornby and Peach (1993) and March and Smith (2001). Organic molecules all contain one or more carbon atoms and it is an important property of carbon atoms that they are able to form molecules involving linking into chains and rings. Each carbon atom can have four bonds to other atoms and the majority of "spare" bonds are taken up by hydrogen atoms, while some will be to so-called "functional groups", for example the alcohol group —OH. So, if we represent carbon atoms with a C, hydrogen atoms with an H, oxygen atoms with an O and so on, and use straight lines to represent bonds between atoms, we may represent organic chemical structures as in Figure 9.1a. It will immediately be obvious that this is a rather cluttered way of representing the molecules concerned. We may simplify the representation considerably by using the following rules. Carbon atoms are represented by the end of a line or the point at which two or more lines meet. Hydrogen atoms are left out altogether, we just remember that each carbon can have four bonds and assume that any "spare" bonds are taken up by hydrogen atoms. Functional groups are represented using conventional abbreviations. Applying these rules to the structures in Figure 9.1a, we arrive at the representations depicted in Figure 9.1b. These are clearly much easier to draw while still conveying all the information of the more cluttered structures. These fairly simple collections of lines allow complex chemical structures to be depicted with relative ease, as shown in Figure 9.3.

9.2.2 Reaction Mechanisms

A reaction mechanism is an attempt to depict the stages involved when one molecule is transformed into another, particularly in the context of how electrons flow within and between molecules. Exhaustive information on reaction mechanisms can be found in March and Smith (2001). Conventionally, these movements of electrons are represented using "curly arrows". Electrons have moved from the site indicated by the tail of the arrow to the site indicated by the head of the arrow. Reaction mechanisms may involve a sequence of such movements and are usually represented in books by a sequence of stages involving electron movement. Figure 9.2 provides an example of a reaction mechanism, an "electrophilic aromatic substitution", which merely means that the reagent is attracted to a site of high electron density (electrophilic), the molecule concerned contains a benzene ring structure (aromatic) and, as a consequence of the reaction, one thing is replaced by another (substitution). SVG offers the possibility of presenting such processes in an animated form, and Section 9.4 will examine the representation of electrophilic aromatic substitution in such a way.

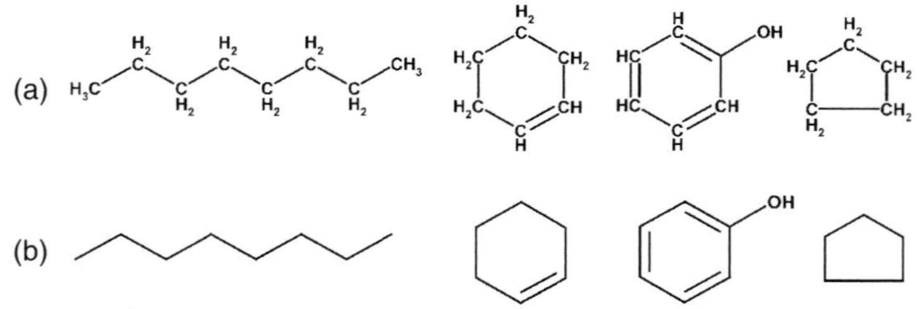

Figure 9.1   Comparison of representations of organic structures.

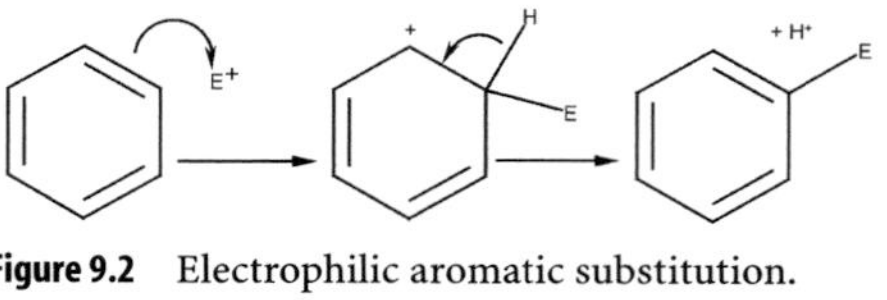

Figure 9.2   Electrophilic aromatic substitution.

9.3 Creating Chemical Structures in SVG

9.3.1 An Exercise in Creating Structures Using SVG

In this section, we shall take a look at how we might create some simple structural building blocks for constructing organic molecular skeletal structures in SVG. This process will be somewhat laborious, but has the advantages that it will highlight some aspects of the SVG language useful for chemical structure drawing, will hopefully encourage chemical educators to experiment further and requires only a simple text editor and an SVG-enabled browser to carry out. The subsequent sections all require various software downloads or use of commercial packages.

As indicated in Section 9.2.1, it is possible to represent a variety of organic molecules using chains and rings drawn with straight lines and the occasional letter to represent an atom other than carbon or hydrogen. Many structures may therefore be depicted using a collection of suitably placed lines and polygons.

It is usually helpful to have something to aim for, so our fairly modest aim in this section will be to represent the cholesterol molecule using "hand-written" SVG! The structure of cholesterol is shown in Figure 9.3.

Clearly, one important thing that we shall need to be able to do is draw and position hexagons on an SVG page. Those who have not thought about trigonometry recently might enjoy referring to Maor (2002). SVG uses a coordinate system in which there are two perpendicular axes in the plane of the screen or paper. The origin $(0, 0)$ is positioned at the top left of the display area and the x and y coordinates increase from left to right and from top to bottom, respectively. It would be useful to be able to create hexagons of a particular size and position them within the display area and with respect to one another. Two obvious parameters to use when describing the position and size of a hexagon are the coordinates of its centre and the length of its side (as we are considering regular hexagons, all sides are the same length). SVG has a polygon element with the following syntax:

```
<polygon points="x1,y1 x2,y2 x3,y3 x4,y4 x5,y5
   x6,y6"/>
```

This will draw a six-sided polygon (fewer or more pairs of coordinates may be used, but we want to draw hexagons). The hexagon will be constructed from lines joining each successive pair of coordinates and will be closed by drawing a line from the last pair of coordinates back to the first. Therefore, to use the polygon element we need to be able to convert centre coordinates and side length for the hexagon to a set of six pairs of coordinates corresponding to the positions of the vertices of the hexagon.

Using the notation of Figure 9.4, it should be clear that the line GA or v is equal in length to the hexagonal side length, s (ABG being an equilateral triangle). The

Figure 9.3 The structure of cholesterol (simplified).

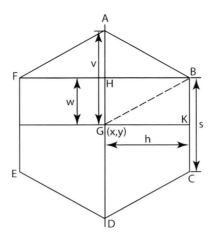

Figure 9.4   A hexagon labelled for use in the following discussion.

Table 9.1   Determination of coordinates for
constructing a hexagon

Vertex	x-Coordinate	y-Coordinate
A	x	$y - s$
B	$x + h$	$y - (s/2)$
C	$x + h$	$y + (s/2)$
D	x	$y + s$
E	$x - h$	$y + (s/2)$
F	$x - h$	$y - (s/2)$

y-coordinates for the vertices A and D will therefore be $y - s$ and $y + s$, respectively (the x-coordinate is obviously x for both of these vertices). It should also be clear that w, the vertical displacements of vertices B, C, E and F from the centre, is equal to $-s/2$ for B and F and $+s/2$ for C and E. If we apply Pythagoras's theorem to triangle BKG (or BHG), then $(s/2)^2 + h^2 = s^2$, which rearranges to $h = \sqrt{(3/4)S^2}$ or, again considering triangle BKG, in which angle BGK is 30°, $\tan 30 = (s/2)/h$, i.e., $h = s/(2\tan 30)$. We may now represent the desired coordinates of the six vertices, in terms of the centre (x, y) and side length as shown in Table 9.1 [where $h = s/(2\tan 30)$ or $\sqrt{(3/4)s^2}$].

It is now a straightforward process to convert x, y and s to coordinates for vertices A–F. It is sensible to automate the process to some extent as we are likely to want to do the calculation for several hexagons. Two possible options would be a simple spreadsheet or a brief program in any available language. We shall use the latter as it will provide greater flexibility. To maintain the possibility of carrying out this exercise using just a text editor and a Web browser, we shall use a JavaScript tool to help generate the SVG required to draw the cholesterol structure. It is not intended to develop a fully working JavaScript molecule drawing application – this tool is only required to allow us to complete the following tasks:

● Draw hexagons of a particular side length at a particular position.
● Indicate the coordinates of possible adjacent hexagons.

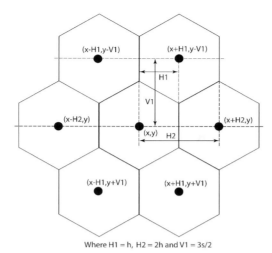

Where H1 = h, H2 = 2h and V1 = 3s/2

Figure 9.5 Coordinates of adjacent hexagons.

The coordinates of possible adjacent hexagons may be determined fairly easily. Figure 9.5 shows how the displacement of the centres of adjacent hexagons may be determined.

The horizontal ($H1$ and $H2$) and vertical ($V1$) displacements are therefore easily determined from a knowledge of the side length of the original hexagon.

The following JavaScript listing may be typed into a text editor and saved with a suitable file name ("cyclohexane.html", for example). The JavaScript should be fairly easy to follow. For a useful text on JavaScript, see Flanagan (2001). The side length and x- and y-coordinates of the hexagon are collected via an HTML form (see Figure 9.6). These values are then used to calculate the coordinates of the six corners of the required hexagon. The calculated values are incorporated into the SVG code required to draw the hexagon. Additionally, the coordinates of possible adjacent hexagons are calculated. The SVG code and adjacent hexagon coordinates are then placed in form fields on the Web page. The SVG code may easily be copied and pasted into an SVG document in a text editor. The adjacent coordinate values may be used to generate SVG code for the next hexagon in a polycyclic structure, such as cholesterol.

Listing 9.1.   A cyclohexane ring SVG generator

```
<!DOCTYPE HTML PUBLIC "-//W3C//DTD HTML 4.0
  Transitional//EN">

<html>
<head>
<title>Generating Cyclohexane Ring SVG Code</title>
<style type = "text/css">
<!--
h1 {font-family: comic sans ms, sans-serif; font-size:
  16pt; color: #996666; }
.text {font-family: comic sans ms, sans-serif; font-size:
  12pt; color: black; background-color:    transparent; }
```

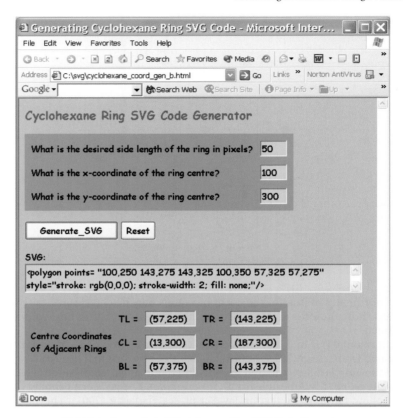

Figure 9.6 Screenshot of Cyclohexane Ring SVG Code Generator.

```
.field {font-family: comic sans ms, sans-serif; font-
  size: 12pt; color: black; background-color: yellow; }
.butt {font-family: comic sans ms, sans-serif; font-
  size: 12pt; color: black; }
body {background-color: #99ccff;}
-->
</style>
<script language=javascript>
<!--
function hex_coord_gen(){

$side_length = eval(document.hexacalc.side_length.value);
$x_coord = eval(document.hexacalc.x_coord.value);
$y_coord = eval(document.hexacalc.y_coord.value);
$horiz_disp = Math.sqrt(0.75*Math.pow($side_length, 2));
$vertex_a_x = Math.round($x_coord);
$vertex_a_y = Math.round($y_coord - $side_length);
$vertex_b_x = Math.round($x_coord + $horiz_disp);
$vertex_b_y = Math.round($y_coord - $side_length/2);
$vertex_c_x = Math.round($x_coord + $horiz_disp);
```

```
$vertex_c_y = Math.round($y_coord + $side_length/2);
$vertex_d_x = Math.round($x_coord);
$vertex_d_y = Math.round($y_coord + $side_length);
$vertex_e_x = Math.round($x_coord - $horiz_disp);
$vertex_e_y = Math.round($y_coord + $side_length/2);
$vertex_f_x = Math.round($x_coord - $horiz_disp);
$vertex_f_y = Math.round($y_coord - $side_length/2);

$h1 = Math.round($horiz_disp);
$h2 = Math.round(2*$horiz_disp);
$v1 = Math.round(3*$side_length/2);
document.hexacalc.tl.value =' (' + eval($x_coord -
   $h1) + ',' + eval($y_coord - $v1) + ')';
document.hexacalc.tr.value = ' (' + eval($x_coord +
$h1) + ',' + eval($y_coord - $v1) + ')';
document.hexacalc.cl.value = ' (' + eval($x_coord -
   $h2) + ',' + eval($y_coord) + ')';
document.hexacalc.cr.value = ' (' + eval($x_coord +
   $h2) + ',' + eval($y_coord) + ')';
document.hexacalc.bl.value = ' (' + eval($x_coord -
   $h1) + ',' + eval($y_coord + $v1) + ')';
document.hexacalc.br.value = ' (' + eval($x_coord +
   $h1) + ',' + eval($y_coord + $v1) + ')';
return '<polygon points = "' + $vertex_a_x + ',' +
   $vertex_a_y + '' + $vertex_b_x + ',' + $vertex_b_y +
   ' ' + $vertex_c_x+',' + $vertex_c_y + ' ' +
   $vertex_d_x + ',' + $vertex_d_y + '' + $vertex_e_x +
   ',' + $vertex_e_y + ' ' + $vertex_f_x + ',' +
   $vertex_f_y + '" style = "stroke: rgb(0,0,0);
   stroke-width: 2; fill: none;"/>';
}
-->
</script>
</head>

<body>
<h1>Cyclohexane Ring SVG Code Generator</h1>
<form name=hexacalc>

<table cellspacing=10 bgcolour=#00cccc>
<tr><td><span class=text>What is the desired side
   length of the ring in pixels? </span></td><td><input
   class=field type=text name=side_length size=4></td></tr>
   <tr><td><span class=text>What is the x-coordinate of
   the ring centre? </span></td><td><input class=field
   type=text name=x_coord size=4 ></td></tr>
   <tr><td><span class=text>What is the y-coordinate of
   the ring centre? </span></td><td><input class=field
   type=text name=y_coord size=4 ></td></tr>
   </table>
```

```
<br>
<input class=butt type=button value=Generate_SVG
  name=converter
onclick="document.hexacalc.vertices.value=
  ( hex_coord_gen())">

<input class=butt type=reset value=Reset>
<br><br>
<span class=text>SVG: </span><br><textarea class=field
  type=text name=vertices rows=2
  cols=80></textarea><br><br>
<table cellspacing=10 bgcolour=#00cccc>
<tr><td rowspan=3><span class=text>Centre
  Coordinates<br> of Adjacent Rings</span></td><td><span
  class=text>TL = </span></td><td><input class=field
  type=text name=tl size=10></td><td><span
  class=text>TR = </span></td><td><input class=field
  type=text name=tr size=10></td></tr>
<tr><td><span class=text>CL = </span></td><td><input
  class=field type=text name=cl
  size=10></span></td><td><span
  class=text>CR = </span></td><td><input class=field
  type=text name = cr size=10></td></tr>
<tr><td><span class=text>BL = </span></td><td><input
  class=field type=text name=bl size=10></td><td><span
  class=text>BR = </span></td><td><input class=field
  type=text name=br size=10></td></tr>
</table>

</form>
</body>
</html>
```

If loaded into a JavaScript-enabled Web browser, the code in Listing 9.1 will produce a page looking like Figure 9.6.

This rudimentary program allows us to build up polycyclic structures in SVG with reasonable ease. The cholesterol structure, for example, may be constructed as follows. First, in a suitable text editor, create an empty SVG document like that in Listing 9.2.

Listing 9.2.   Empty SVG document

```
<?xml version="1.0" standalone="no"?>

<!DOCTYPE svg PUBLIC "-//W3C//DTD SVG 1.0//EN"
"http://www.w3.org/TR/2001/REC-SVG-
  20010904/DTD/svg10.dtd">
<svg width="600px" height="400px">

</svg>
```

All the code that we generate can now be placed between the <svg></svg> tags. We have given ourselves a 600 × 400 pixel space in which to draw our cholesterol structure, so we shall start by drawing the bottom-left ring of the structure with a side length of 50 pixels and centred at 100,300 (as in Figure 9.6). Clicking the "Generate_SVG" button generates the relevant SVG code to draw the hexagon. This may be copied from the text box and pasted into our SVG, as in Listing 9.3.

Listing 9.3.   Adding a polygon

```
<svg width="600px" height="400px">
        <polygon points= "100,250 143,275 143,325 100,350
          57,325 57,275"
          style="stroke: rgb(0,0,0); stroke-width: 1;
          fill: none;"
              />
</svg>
```

The JavaScript program also tells us that the next hexagon in the structure for cholesterol will be centred at 187,300. These coordinates may therefore be used to generate the code for the adjacent ring and by repeating the process the code for two more rings may be generated, as in Listing 9.4.

Listing 9.4.   Adding adjacent polygons

```
<svg width="600px" height="400px">
<polygon points="100,250 143,275 143,325 100,350 57,325
  57,275"
        style="stroke: rgb(0,0,0); stroke-width: 1; fill:
          none;"
              />
<polygon points="187,250 230,275 230,325 187,350 144,325
  144,275"
        style="stroke: rgb(0,0,0); stroke-width: 1; fill:
          none;"
              />
<polygon points="230,175 273,200 273,250 230,275 187,
  250 187,200"
        style="stroke: rgb(0,0,0); stroke-width: 1; fill:
          none;"
              />
<polygon points="317,175 360,200 360,250 317,275 274,
  250 274,200"
        style="stroke: rgb(0,0,0); stroke-width: 1; fill:
          none;"
              />
</svg>
```

This, when previewed in an SVG-enabled browser, appears as in Figure 9.7.
The top-right ring should be a pentagon. This is easily achieved by editing the code for the fourth polygon to remove the fourth angle, as in Listing 9.5.

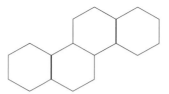

Figure 9.7   Preview of Listing 9.4.

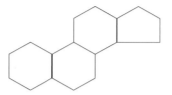

Figure 9.8   Preview of Listing 9.5.

Listing 9.5.   Modification of fourth polygon

```
<polygon points= "317,175 360,200 360,250 274,250 274,
   200"
     style="stroke: rgb(0,0,0); stroke-width: 1;
       fill: none;"
             />
```

The chains at the top right of the structure may be created by generating the code as though a sequence of four hexagons were required but then modifying the polygons to polylines and editing out the unwanted lines, as in Listing 9.6.

Listing 9.6.   Editing polygons to polylines

```
<svg width="600px" height="400px">
<polygon points= "100,250 143,275 143,325 100,350 57,325
   57,275"
     style="stroke: rgb(0,0,0); stroke-width: 1; fill:
       none;"
             />
<polygon points= "187,250 230,275 230,325 187,350 144,325
   144,275"
     style="stroke: rgb(0,0,0); stroke-width: 1; fill:
       none;"
             />
<polygon points= "230,175 273,200 273,250 230,275
   187,250 187,200"
     style="stroke: rgb(0,0,0); stroke-width: 1; fill:
       none;"
             />
<polygon points= "317,175 360,200 360,250 274,250 274,
   200"
```

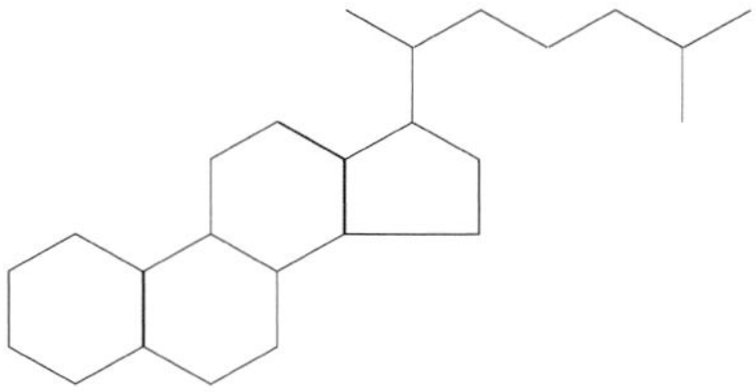

Figure 9.9   Preview of Listing 9.6. Polygons edited to polylines.

```
      style="stroke: rgb(0,0,0); stroke-width: 1; fill:
        none;"
             />
<polyline points= "274,100 317,125 317,175 274,200 231,
  175"
      style="stroke: rgb(0,0,0); stroke-width: 1; fill:
        none;"
             />
<polyline points= "318,125 361,100 404,125"
      style="stroke: rgb(0,0,0); stroke-width: 1; fill:
        none;"
             />
<polyline points= "405,125 448,100 491,125 491,175"
      style="stroke: rgb(0,0,0); stroke-width: 1; fill:
        none;"
             />
<polyline points= "492,125 535,100"
      style="stroke: rgb(0,0,0); stroke-width: 1; fill:
        none;"
             />
</svg>
```

This, when previewed, looks as in Figure 9.9.

We have now nearly created the cholesterol structure in SVG. The two vertical bonds can easily be added by hand coding, as can the OH group and its bond with some trial and error. This just leaves the double bond in the bottom-right ring. This can be hand coded, or generated using a version of the cyclohexane ring generator adapted to produce the code for benzene rings. This modified JavaScript program will be found on the Web site (and is not listed here to save space). The final version of the SVG code for the cholesterol structure is given in Listing 9.7 and the structure is visualized in Figure 9.10.

Listing 9.7.   SVG code for cholesterol structure

```
<?xml version="1.0" standalone="no"?>

<!DOCTYPE svg PUBLIC "-//W3C//DTD SVG 1.0//EN"
"http://www.w3.org/TR/2001/REC-SVG-20010904/DTD/
  svg10.dtd">
<svg width="600px" height="400px">
```

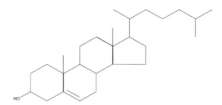

Figure 9.10 Preview of Listing 9.7 – cholesterol.

```
<polygon points="100,250 143,275 143,325 100,350 57,325
  57,275"
      style="stroke: rgb(0,0,0); stroke-width: 1; fill:
        none;"
            />
<polyline points="31,340 57,325"
      style="stroke: rgb(0,0,0); stroke-width: 1; fill:
        none;"
            />
<text x="12" y="348">HO</text>
<line x1="143" y1="275" x2="143" y2="225" style="stroke:
  rgb(0,0,0); stroke-width: 1;" />
<polygon points="187,250 230,275 230,325 187,350 144,
  325 144,275"
      style="stroke: rgb(0,0,0); stroke-width: 1; fill:
        none;"
            />
<polyline points="187,340 152,320"
      style="stroke: rgb(0,0,0); stroke-width: 1; fill:
        none;"
            />
<polygon points="230,175 273,200 273,250 230,275 187,
  250 187,200"
      style="stroke: rgb(0,0,0); stroke-width: 1; fill:
        none;"
            />
<line x1="273" y1="200" x2="273" y2="150" style="stroke:
  rgb(0,0,0); stroke-width: 1;" />
<polygon points="317,175 360,200 360,250 274,250 274,200"
      style="stroke: rgb(0,0,0); stroke-width: 1; fill:
        none;"
            />
<polyline points="274,100 317,125 317,175 274,200 231,
  175"
      style="stroke: rgb(0,0,0); stroke-width: 1; fill:
        none;"
            />
```

```
<polyline points="318,125 361,100 404,125"
        style="stroke: rgb(0,0,0); stroke-width: 1; fill:
          none;"
             />
<polyline points="405,125 448,100 491,125 491,175"
        style="stroke: rgb(0,0,0); stroke-width: 1; fill:
          none;"
             />
<polyline points="492,125 535,100"
        style="stroke: rgb(0,0,0); stroke-width: 1; fill:
          none;"
             />
</svg>
```

With knowledge of simple geometry and some basic programming, it is possible to generate SVG code to depict structures of complex molecules fairly easily. However, to create a wide range of structures in SVG using the methods that we have been looking at would be laborious, although an interesting exercise (especially in the context of a student project). It is more likely that for the general-purpose production of Web-based chemistry resources, educators will want to employ more sophisticated tools. The following sections look at some possibilities that may be of interest. There are four categories of software that might be considered: drawing packages without chemical enhancements and with no capacity to save in SVG format, drawing packages without chemical enhancements but with the capacity to save in SVG format, chemical drawing packages without the capacity to save in SVG format and chemical drawing packages with an SVG file option. As we are concerned particularly with creating SVG chemical structures for use in educational resources, we shall only consider the second, third and fourth of the possibilities. There will be a rudimentary attempt at comparing ease of use of the various packages in terms of obtaining a useable chemical structure in SVG format. In each case the experience of using the package to create an SVG drawing of a molecule of "porphyrillic acid" (randomly selected by opening a copy of the Merck Index) will be described. This comparison is summarized in a table.

9.3.2 SVG-enabled Non-chemical Drawing Packages

There are several drawing packages available that are able to save drawings as SVG files but that do not have any drawing tools aimed specifically at chemists. How effectively these may be used to produce chemical structures is therefore related to the level of sophistication of the drawing package and the complication of the intended structure. In this category, we shall look briefly at just two packages that may be used to some effect: Adobe Illustrator and Jasc WebDraw. The first is included because it is the "industry standard" drawing package and the second because it is aimed specifically at producing SVG.

9.3.2.1 Adobe Illustrator

Adobe Illustrator is a very versatile drawing package and, despite it not being aimed specifically at chemical drawing, it took only 12 minutes to produce an adequate

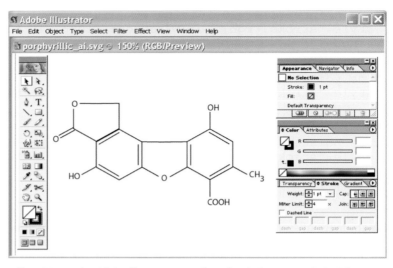

Figure 9.11   Using Adobe Illustrator to produce chemical structures in SVG format.

depiction of porphyrillic acid and save it as an SVG file. A screenshot is shown in Figure 9.11.

The process was very straightforward. An initial hexagon was drawn; this was then copied, pasted and edited to a pentagon; the hexagon and pentagon were duplicated again and positioned to form the overall skeleton. A 30° line was drawn, suitable for use where double bonds were needed, and then duplicated, reflected and positioned as required. The various functional groups were then added as text with opaque white rectangles being used to mask out the rings for the heterocyclic oxygen atoms (possibly not the most elegant way to do this). Creating the structure was a remarkably painless process and an indication of how easy Illustrator is to use.

9.3.2.2   Jasc WebDraw

WebDraw is unusual in that it is aimed specifically at creating Scalable Vector Graphics. In this exercise, a pre-release version was used. It has an excellent set of drawing tools for basic shapes but seemed slightly more "fiddly" to use than Illustrator. It took just under 20 minutes to produce a reasonable depiction of the target molecule in SVG format; see Figure 9.12.

An important feature of WebDraw is the facility to edit the SVG source code, which will make it a particularly attractive option to those interested in producing reusable "snippets" of chemical structural SVG code.

9.3.3 Non-SVG Chemical Drawing Packages

There are several commercial and freeware packages available for drawing organic chemical structures. Some examples are ChemDraw, Isis Draw and ChemSketch. All provide an easy route to the drawing of chemical structures. In some cases the

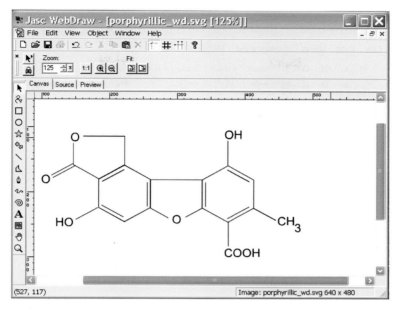

Figure 9.12 Using Jasc WebDraw to produce chemical structures in SVG format.

file formats used may lend themselves to easy conversion to SVG. Particularly attractive from an educational point of view are those packages that are free for educational use. Isis Draw is easy to use and will allow for the rapid production of complex organic molecules (porphyrillic acid in under 2 minutes, for example). An easy way to convert the drawing to SVG is to select all of the drawing in Isis Draw and to copy and paste into Adobe Illustrator, from which it may be saved as an SVG file. This considerably speeds up the drawing process compared with using Illustrator alone and also produces a neater structure. Chem Sketch is an alternative to Isis Draw but it has a slightly less friendly interface and takes rather longer to obtain similar results (6 minutes for the porphyrillic acid structure, although this may reduce with greater familiarity). If Illustrator is available, either of these packages will speed up the production of chemical structures in SVG format.

9.3.4 SVG-enabled Chemical Drawing Packages

Two freely available packages will be looked at: WinDrawChem and MarvinSketch.

9.3.4.1 WinDrawChem

This is a basic chemical drawing package, but with the advantage of being able to save directly in SVG format. The porphyrillic acid structure was created in about 5 minutes. The GUI has some peculiarities of behaviour: a dragged object lags behind the pointer but then overshoots when the mouse button is released; rings

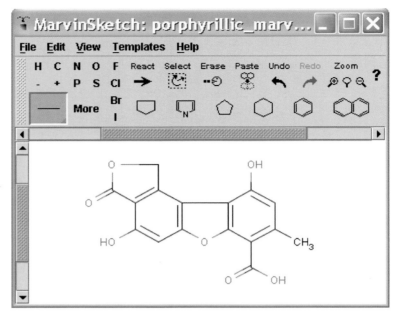

Figure 9.13   Using MarvinSketch to produce chemical structures in SVG format.

need to be drawn and then attached to adjacent rings by careful positioning. These problems make this program less efficient to use than it could have been.

9.3.4.2 MarvinSketch

This is an excellent tool, but it is a Java program so you will need install a Java Virtual Machine if you do not already have one. The installation process is very straightforward. The xml-Batik SVG generator is also required. Further details of these, with up-to-date links, will be found on the chem-svg Web site.

MarvinSketch (named after the paranoid android from "The Hitchhiker's Guide to the Galaxy") is very easy to use and has some excellent aids to drawing, such as atoms that indicate when the mouse pointer is in range. This removes the need for careful positioning as the bonds and rings just snap into the correct position. Another nice touch is atom colouring (oxygen red, nitrogen blue, etc.), which can be turned off if a black and white drawing is required.

The porphyrillic acid structure took only 90 seconds to draw in MarvinSketch and could then be saved directly as SVG. This is such a nice tool to use that it is worth going to the trouble of installing a JVM and xml-Batik to have it available. A screenshot of MarvinSketch is shown in Figure 9.13.

The various methods used to create SVG drawings of the porphyrillic acid molecule are summarized in Table 9.2.

The best tool for easy and rapid structure drawing combined with the generation of small SVG files is MarvinSketch; it is also free!

Table 9.2   Comparison of tools for creating chemical structures as SVG graphics

Software	Time taken (minutes)	File size (kb)	Comments
Adobe Illustrator	12	226	Excellent range of drawing tools allows chemical structures to be drawn well, but not quickly
Jasc WebDraw	18	4	Very useful if modification of the SVG code is required
Isis Draw	2	237	Excellent chemical drawing tool but file must be converted to SVG externally
ChemSketch	6	236	Very good for some other uses, such as viewing 3D molecules
WinDrawChem	5	5	Slightly awkward interface, but good SVG generation
MarvinSketch	1.5	6	Excellent, easy to use, small SVG file generated, but requires JVM and xml-Batik to run

9.4 Visualizing a Reaction Mechanism

9.4.1 Outline of the Problem

In the previous section, we were interested in creating static representations of organic chemical structures for use within Web-based learning materials. In printed materials, reaction mechanisms must, of course, be represented as a sequence of static images. On a Web page, however, it is possible to use animation to display the course of a reaction mechanism. Before the advent of SVG, this could have been achieved by using a GIF animation or, rather more sophisticatedly, by using the Macromedia Flash route. SVG raises the possibility of producing animated reaction mechanisms without having to buy any expensive software (an attractive idea to those who work in education). The remainder of this section briefly explores this possibility, looking particularly at the electrophilic substitution mechanism mentioned before. Once again, this is a possible starting point for a student project that would allow for the development of both chemical knowledge and IT skills.

9.4.2 Animating an Electrophilic Substitution Mechanism

A fairly basic animation of an electrophilic substitution is created by the SVG code provided in Listing 9.8. Some numbered comments, indicating the elements involved in the animation, have been added to the code. These are referred to in the brief discussion that follows the listing.

A screenshot of the animation in its final state is provided in Figure 9.14. However, being an animation, it should really be viewed in its animated form and it is suggested that you view the file on the chem-svg website before reading the following comments.

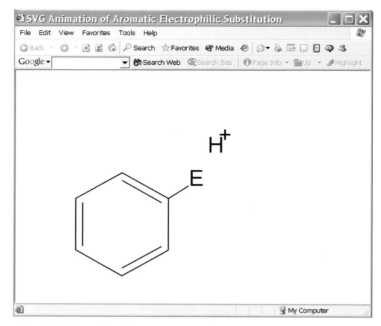

Figure 9.14   Screenshot of SVG animation of aromatic electrophilic substitution.

Listing 9.8.   SVG to create a simple animation of an aromatic electrophilic substitution

```
<?xml version="1.0" standalone="no"?>
<!DOCTYPE svg PUBLIC "-//W3C//DTD SVG 1.0//EN"
  http://www.w3.org/TR/2001/REC-SVG-20010904/DTD/
  svg10.dtd>

<svg width="500" height="500">

<title>SVG Animation of Aromatic Electrophilic
  Substitution</title>

<!--1: THE HEXAGON FOR THE AROMATIC RING -->
<polygon points="200,200 287,250 287,350 200,400
  113,350 113,250"
style="stroke:#000000; stroke-width:2; fill:none"/>

<!--2: THE BOND THAT IS ATTRACTED TO THE ELECTROPHILE-->
<line x1="200px" y1="215px" x2="274px" y2="258px"
style="stroke: #000000; stroke-width:2; fill:none">
<animate attributeName="x1" begin="3s" dur="2s"
  fill="freeze" calcMode="linear" to="340px"></animate>
<animate attributeName="y1" begin="3s" dur="2s"
  fill="freeze" calcMode="linear" to="245px"></animate>
<animate attributeName="x2" begin="3s" dur="2s"
  fill="freeze" calcMode="linear" to="287px"></animate>
```

```
<animate attributeName="y2" begin="3s" dur="2s"
  fill="freeze" calcMode="linear" to="250px"></animate>
<animate attributeName="x1" begin="5s" dur="2s"
  fill="freeze" calcMode="linear" to="325px"></animate>
<animate attributeName="y1" begin="5s" dur="2s"
  fill="freeze" calcMode="linear" to="225px"></animate>
</line>

<!-- 3: THE BOND TO THE VISIBLE HYDROGEN -->
<line x1="287px" y1="250px" x2="325px" y2="225px"
style="stroke: #000000; stroke-width: 2; fill:none">
<animate attributeName="x2" begin="3s" dur="2s"
  fill="freeze" calcMode="linear" to="325px"></animate>
<animate attributeName="y2" begin="3s" dur="2s"
  fill="freeze" calcMode="linear" to="210px"></animate>
<animate attributeName="x1" begin="5s" dur="2s"
  fill="freeze" calcMode="linear" to="200px"></animate>
<animate attributeName="y1" begin="5s" dur="2s"
  fill="freeze" calcMode="linear" to="215px"></animate>
<animate attributeName="x2" begin="5s" dur="2s"
  fill="freeze" calcMode="linear" to="274px"></animate>
<animate attributeName="y2" begin="5s" dur="2s"
  fill="freeze" calcMode="linear" to="258px"></animate>
</line>

<!-- 4: THE TWO OTHER DOUBLE BONDS IN THE RING -->
<line x1="274" y1="343" x2="200" y2="385"
style="stroke: #000000; stroke-width: 2;fill:none">
</line>
<line x1="126" y1="343" x2="126" y2="258"
style="stroke: #000000; stroke-width: 2; fill:none">
</line>

<!-- 5: THE VISIBLE HYDROGEN ATOM -->
<text style="fill: #000000; fill-opacity: 1.0;
  font-size: 32pt; font-family: Arial, sans-serif;"
  x="325px" y="225px">H
<animate attributeName="x" begin="3s" dur="2s"
  fill="freeze" calcMode="linear" to="325px"></animate>
<animate attributeName="y" begin="3s" dur="2s"
  fill="freeze" calcMode="linear" to="210px"></animate>
<animate attributeName="x" begin="5s" dur="2s"
  fill="freeze" calcMode="linear" to="360px"></animate>
<animate attributeName="y" begin="5s" dur="2s"
  fill="freeze" calcMode="linear" to="160px"></animate>
</text>

<!-- 6: THE ELECTROPHILE -->
<text style="fill: #000000; fill-opacity: 1.0; font-
  size: 32pt; font-family: Arial, sans-serif;"
  x="220px" y="50px">E
```

```
<animate attributeName="x" begin="0s" dur="5s"
  fill="freeze" calcMode="linear" to="340px"></animate>
<animate attributeName="y" begin="0s" dur="5s"
  fill="freeze" calcMode="linear" to="255px"></animate>
<animate attributeName="x" begin="5s" dur="2s"
  fill="freeze" calcMode="linear" to="325px"></animate>
<animate attributeName="y" begin="5s" dur="2s"
  fill="freeze" calcMode="linear" to="225px"></animate>
</text>

<!--7: THE POSITIVE CHARGE ON THE ELECTROPHILE -->
<text style="fill: #000000; fill-opacity: 1.0;
  font-size: 32pt; font-family: Arial, sans-serif;"
  x="240px" y="30px">+
<animate attributeName="x" begin="0s" dur="5s"
  fill="freeze" calcMode="linear" to="360px"></animate>
<animate attributeName="y" begin="0s" dur="5s"
  fill="freeze" calcMode="linear" to="235px"></animate>
<animate attributeName="fill-opacity"
  attributeType="CSS" begin="0s" dur="5s"
  from="1.0" to="0.0" fill="freeze"></animate>
</text>

<!-- 8: THE POSITIVE CHARGE THAT LEAVES WITH THE
  HYDROGEN -->
<text style="fill: #000000; fill-opacity: 1.0;
  font-size: 32pt; font-family: Arial, sans-serif;"
  x="345px" y="205px">+
<animate attributeName="x" begin="3s" dur="2s"
  fill="freeze" calcMode="linear" to="345px"></animate>
<animate attributeName="y" begin="3s" dur="2s"
  fill="freeze" calcMode="linear" to="190px"></animate>
<animate attributeName="x" begin="5s" dur="2s"
  fill="freeze" calcMode="linear" to="380px"></animate>
<animate attributeName="y" begin="5s" dur="2s"
  fill="freeze" calcMode="linear" to="140px"></animate>
<animate attributeName="fill-opacity"
  attributeType="CSS" begin="0s" dur="5s" from="0.0"
  to="0.0" fill="freeze"></animate>
<animate attributeName="fill-opacity"
  attributeType="CSS" begin="5s" dur="2s" from="0.0"
  to="1.0" fill="freeze"></animate>
</text>

<!-- 9: THE POSITIVE CHARGE TEMPORARILY ON THE RING -->
<text style="fill: #000000; fill-opacity: 1.0;
  font-size: 32pt; font-family: Arial, sans-serif;"
  x="190px" y="190px">+
<animate attributeName="fill-opacity"
  attributeType="CSS" begin="0s" dur="4s" from="0.0"
  to="0.0" fill="freeze"></animate>
```

```
<animate attributeName="fill-opacity"
  attributeType="CSS" begin="4s" dur="1s" from="0.0"
  to="1.0" fill="freeze"></animate>
<animate attributeName="fill-opacity"
  attributeType="CSS" begin="5s" dur="2s" from="1.0"
  to="0.0" fill="freeze"></animate>
</text>
</svg>
```

It is hoped that the SVG code is reasonably easy to follow. However, some brief comments on specific features may be helpful to those who would like to develop this idea as a learning resource, and some features of the SVG that may be of particular interest are outlined below.

The positions of lines, text and other objects may be changed with time; for example, the bond indicated by comment 2 is initially defined by the x-and y-coordinates of its ends ($x1, y1$ and $x2, y2$). Both ends of the line are moved to new positions using <animate attributeName=" "> to modify the $x1, y1, x2$ and $y2$ values. All movements of this sort may easily be planned by storyboarding the animation on graph paper.

It is also possible to make things appear and disappear by fading in or out (such as the various positive charges; see comments 7–9). If the original appearance is defined using a CSS style to indicate the opacity of an object, this may then be altered using <animate attributeName="fill-opacity">.

SVG provides an easy and effective way to animate reaction mechanisms and there is considerable scope for producing more sophisticated animations than that provided here. This could easily form the basis of a student project or collective assignment in which individual students (or small groups) are provided with basic information on SVG and given the task of producing animated reaction mechanisms. No expensive software is required and the project could provide evidence for the development of chemical knowledge, the use of IT for the presentation of information and a variety of computing and numerical skills depending on the exact requirements of the assignment.

9.5 Conclusion

It is hoped that this brief outline has whetted the appetite of those involved in the delivery of chemical education to experiment with SVG as a method of visualizing molecules and reactions. There are many ways in which these visualizations might be enhanced. For example, a reaction mechanism might be accompanied by an energy profile synchronized to the progress of the reaction. A certain amount of control might be added by employing a suitable scripting language. More sophisticated results might be obtained using server-side scripting using Perl and PHP. These and other developments will be featured on the chem-svg Web site. Another important development, outside the scope of this chapter, is chemical markup language (CML). Those wishing to explore this topic should consult Murray-Rust et al. (2000, 2001).

The author would be very interested to hear of any chemical visualizations using SVG that may be developed as a consequence of reading this chapter and would be happy to place interesting examples on the chem-svg Web site.

References

Most material relevant to the chemical drawing software reviewed is Web-based and hence to a certain extent ephemeral. The Web site associated with this chapter will maintain up-to-date links to the software, where possible, and can be found at http://www.chem-svg.org.uk.

Eisenberg JD (2002) *SVG Essentials*. Sebastopol, CA: O'Reilly.

Flanagan D (2001) *JavaScript: the Definitive Guide*. Sebastopol, CA: O'Reilly.

Hornby M and Peach J (1993) *Foundations of Organic Chemistry*. Oxford: Oxford University Press.

Maor I (2002) *Trigonometric Delights*. Princeton: Princeton University Press.

March J and Smith M (2001) *March's Advanced Organic Chemistry: Reactions, Mechanisms and Structure*. New York: Wiley.

Murray-Rust P, Rzepa H, Wright M and Zara S (2000) A universal approach to web-based chemistry using XML and CML. *Chemical Communications*, 1471–1472.

Murray-Rust P, Rzepa H and Wright M (2001) Development of chemical markup language (CML) as a system for handling complex chemical content, *New Journal of Chemistry*, 618–634.

Chapter 10
Using Metadata-based SVG and X3D Graphics in Interactive TV

Artur Lugmayr and Seppo Kalli

10.1 Introduction

Why do people spend hours sitting in front of their TV sets? To be mesmerized by soap operas? Do they simply want to relax from a hard working day? Or is it a medium chosen for retrieving information from news broadcasts? The answer is simple: TV is highly narrative and tells stories with a certain structure, shows famous actors, brings breaking news from far distant places and presents dissimilar opinions and viewpoints – just like fairytale storytellers a few centuries ago at a bonfire. Digitalization and new technologies allow "interacting with content" (Ryan, 2001). Analogue television provided very limited opportunities for getting involved in the story space as the audio and video were a monolithic structure.

Digital, interactive TV (digiTV) provides new technological methodologies to interact with the consumer in an immersive fictive story space. Choosing actors and scene constellations, influencing the story flow and providing new interaction devices move the consumers themselves on-stage. The technological challenges are enormous and require the convergence of multimedia home equipment and substantial convergence of multiple multimedia standards. The development of digitized audio and video streaming solutions by the Motion Picture Experts Group (MPEG) opened standards for the deployment of digiTV as defined by the Digital Video Broadcasting (DVB) project, and new visual representation modalities in the form of advanced 2D and 3D graphics opened up much greater potential for creating illusions.

The scope of this chapter evolves with the presentation of digiTV's essentials and its convergence with the third generation of Web-based multimedia. New audiovisual content models are presented and software architecture for consumer devices is shown. Content in the form of graphics is not an isolated aspect. Television tells narratives in a virtual story space, with which the consumer can interact. A narration cube underlines a more contextual approach and unifies interactive, narrative and content aspects. This approach leads to new service types and application scenarios of graphics in digiTV.

10.2 The Fascinating World of DigiTV

What will it be – the home device, which plays DVDs, CDs and radio, shows TV programmes and controls the refrigerator? The mainstream consumers will be

offered a variety of means for organizing their private multimedia items in a personalized manner anytime, anywhere, to any consumer device. Computer systems
will disappear, and processors, bus systems and software programs are invisible
and transparent. Currently industry competes for the home-multimedia centre:
TV equipment producers push their digital equipment, PC and operating systems
promote the PC as a home gateway, and HiFi equipment may also be used to gain
access to consumer home markets. No one knows what will become the multimedia home centre, which will play multimedia home content and interface with
consumer gadgets such as mobile phones, digital cameras and mobile computers
(Wallich, 2002). Nor does anyone yet know what the multimedia home gateway will
look like.

However, independently of how the home device will look, high interconnection
of devices in a larger context requires abstract data structures for their description. Metadata enables integration and embedding into a metadata-based network
of services, as e.g., the XML enable Web does. The Web provides network infrastructure for device interconnection and XML permits platform-independent,
adaptable and profiled service design. A very basic interactive service is the
Electronic Program Guide (EPG), which shows and guides through TV content and
helps to personalize, visualize and select different programme channels. A news
ticker helps it keep up-to-date with breaking news. Figure 10.1 shows an example of
an EPG.

One point should be clear, that digital interactive TV (digiTV) with its set-top
boxes (STBs) offers a downsized computer system with advanced multimedia capabilities and full Internet access. Thus, an STB is more than just a simple box decoding encrypted digital TV content. It could become the mainstream consumer home
device covering the above features. By adding graphic capabilities, as provided by
SVG and X3D, one can have advanced visual representations of multimedia content
and new service scenarios operating behind advanced user interfaces. The task of

Figure 10.1   The Electronic Program Guide (EPG) is one basic application included as software on every
set-top box.

SVG and X3D is to increase content perception, visualization and interaction facilities on this platform.

One existing applicable scenario is a simple Web-browser system on-box, for viewing SVG content on a Web-browser system implemented on an STB. A more advanced TV of the future could be seen as a broadcast video game, consisting of a virtual scene, where content elements are influenced and altered by the consumer's desires. A comprehensive virtual scene would be broadcast, in which the content elements would be altered by the consumer's desires. Thus, the consumer could exchange the actor's face with his or her own scanned face or – more generally – replace whole scene sets as if it were a computer game. Would it be everyone's desire to spice up a boring soap opera by changing the story elements according to one's own imagination? Narrative systems with multiple story flows and content elements could be altered by the consumer's desires. The TV shows could end as the consumer wishes.

We do not yet know which innovative services will find a market breakthrough, or how the new applications might appear. New technologies need to be explored and require experimenting. At the end of this chapter we attempt to pinpoint new service scenarios enabled by SVG and X3D. Before we explore the key digiTV standard as provided by DVB, we shall show how this standard can be converged with emerging metadata standards and then focus on the convergence of SVG, X3D and digiTV.

We propose the following assumptions and statements to be valid in this study:

- Our viewpoint is focused on the convergence of multimedia home equipment "under the hood" of digiTV devices such as the home multimedia hub for accessing interactive multimedia services.
- Convergence of multimedia standards, as developed by digiTV standardization bodies, MPEG (e.g., MPEG-7, MPEG-21) and the W3C (e.g., XML, XML-Schema, SVG, X3D).
- Metadata is an enabler of third-generation Web Services deployed on digiTV facilities, by adding resource adaptation, semantic and platform-independent paradigms.
- The Web as such expands to a networked environment providing space for semi-broadcast, broadcast and Internet services such as third-generation multimedia services.
- TV in its current form is a highly narrative medium. Digitalization processes provide more tools and techniques for telling stories. A heterogeneous model, as provided by the narrative cube introduced within the scope of this chapter, groups the different technical facilities.
- Layering multimedia assets is a solution for representing multimedia assets on different layers with its atomic processable units.

10.3 DigiTV – The Essentials

On a very abstract level, the generic digiTV infrastructure consists of five key partners in a value-added service chain, as shown in Figure 10.2. The broadcast service provider (BSP) packages and delivers (enhanced broadcasting profile) digital TV content in the form of audio/video services with applications over a broadband broadcast channel to the consumers and their consumer multimedia home network

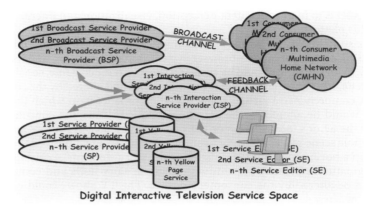

Figure 10.2   Abstract digiTV infrastructure.

(CMHN). Local home digiTV equipment acts as the first access point to services and permits user interactivity. A feedback channel capability, the channel between local digiTV equipment and the Internet, is connected via an interaction service provider (ISP) over wired or wireless transport networks (interactive broadcast profile and Internet access profile). Convergence of broadcast channels and inter-action channels leads to a hybrid communication environment for full interactive services over multiple communication channels.

Current TV content is mainly delivered by BSP in-house production or large video production firms. The service editor (SE) is responsible for creating services, implementing applications, producing advertisements and video material, etc. In a digitized environment service providers (SPs) may create a common Web content, reacting to consumer interactions. For example, a travel agency would put inter-active advertisements into the broadcast stream. After the consumer clicks on to the advertisement, a feedback channel to the travel agency is opened, and flight tickets could be purchased.

10.3.1 DVB: European Initiative for Deploying DigiTV

The European initiative for delivering digiTV is based on the opened standard families of the Digital Video Broadcasting (DVB) (European Telecommunications Standards Institute, 2002a) project. The initiative was founded by significant key partners in the field of broadcasting and its standards are defined by the European Telecommunication Standards Institute (ETSI). DVB standards define audio, video, conditional access, interfacing, measurement, application environment, multiplexing, subtitling and transmission of digiTV.

DVB specifies MPEG-2 (International Organization for Standardization, 1994) as a delivery medium for high bit rate audio, video and data content to consumer devices in the range from 4 (PAL quality) up to 9 Mbit/s (CCIR-601 studio quality). Different profiles, such as High Definition Television (HDTV) or Standard Definition Television (SDTV) at frame rates of 30 or 25 Hz, aspect ranges of 4:3, 16:9 and 2.21:1 and luminance resolutions of $720 \times 576, 544 \times 576, 480 \times 576, 352 \times 576$ or 352×288 are defined.

10.3.2 MHP as an Application Platform

Part of the DVB standard family is dedicated to defining implementation guidelines for platform-independent modular hardware and software design. The Multimedia Home Platform (MHP) (European Telecommunications Standards Institute, 2002b) supports a lightweight version of the Java programming environment (DVB-J) as based on SUN's JDK 1.1 (SUN Microsystems, 2002), with additional libraries specially designed for broadcasting and extensions defined by MHP. Java permits platform-independent service design and deployment for converging Internet network and digiTV services. Specifications cover the functionality of hardware resources, system software for an abstract resource description, operating system software, middleware software and an application environment to deploy platform-independent interactive software. Software layers guarantee platform-independent service deployment and the convergence of Internet network and digiTV services. MHP therefore defines several required components for the experience of digital, interactive television: application programming interfaces, development guidelines, broadcast profiles, security mechanism, content formats, transmission protocol types, etc.

DVB-J is a subset of Java, especially designed for embedded digiTV systems. Applications running on this platform are so-called "Xlets", comparable to lightweight versions of applets running on a Web browser. Where several profiles, such as an enhanced broadcast profile, interactive broadcast profile and Internet access profile are supported by DVB-J applications, DVB-HTML only supports the latter two. DVB-HTML is designed to make HTML usable on digiTV equipment.

10.3.3 Converging Lightweight Graphics Towards the Third Generation of Multimedia

Multimedia assets are the content with which the consumer interacts. Multimedia assets are of any type: video, audio, metadata, 3D graphics, etc. Their compilation to one unified and meaningful collection of different service sub-elements is obviously required. This requires a more contemporary and top-down approach for the creation of broadcast shows. Technical and user perceptive requirements have to be covered. To them belong synchronization of multimedia assets, invoking SVG and X3G as an extension of current digiTV standards, multi-channel networks for interaction and delivery of content, provision of a model for grouping multimedia assets and their atomic units and considering the limitations of low-performance digiTV equipment.

10.4 Reference System Architecture for MHP Devices

The STB as a generic home multimedia hub is a dedicated computer system for processing multimedia content. An I/O system provides interconnection with peripherals such as PDAs, remote controls and video camera based input devices. It is responsible for obtaining a high bit rate MPEG-2 TS over a broadcast protocol stack from either a broadcast or feedback network channel. A small personal computer system is the heart of the overall STB and controls the tuner system, conditional access system and decoder hardware. The architecture is shown in Figure 10.3.

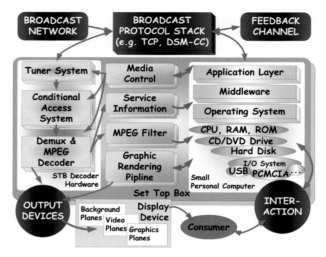

Figure 10.3   Basic architecture for digiTV STBs as a home multimedia hub.

10.4.1 Providing Services on MHP Platforms

The consumer sees complete services presented as a compound of multiple multimedia assets on a digiTV platform. Services are uniquely identified and composed of audio streams, video streams, service-related information, additional data and applications. Each services signals by a flag, executed explicitly either by the consumer with Navigator of EPG systems, or implicitly by auto-start mechanisms. The runtime environment provides service-specific life-cycle execution models, resource management, a specific service context, execution of simultaneous applications, persistence of services and their related data and manages signalling flags.

Services are listed in tables multiplexed into the broadcast stream or updated via the feedback channel. The resident Navigator decodes and presents the content of the table to the end-user or starts services automatically branded with auto-start flags. Services might also start other services or applications. Signalling flags help to control the service states.

Currently two different execution models and application life-cycles are supported by MHP: the DVB-J model and the DVB-HTML model. The DVB-J model is more related to actual Java-based applications, which are loaded, executed, paused and then destroyed. The DVB-HTML model provides a similar life-cycle, but its purpose is more related to display a set of documents and their related lightweight applications as content format.

10.4.2 Graphic Capabilities of MHP Devices

A common MHP-defined reference model for its graphical facilities optimizes multimedia asset presentation for displaying common TV components. This includes features for positioning video and graphic elements, layering of elements, user interface elements, subtitles and raw graphical primitives. Four application-controllable pipelines are responsible for composing subtitles, background elements, video and graphics on to a display device. Depending on the underlying hardware and software platform, each processing function and operation can be application controlled. This includes scaling, positioning, clipping, pan-scan, decoding and composition. Essential components in a digiTV system are subtitles as graphic capability or content format, which will not be further explained in this section.

10.4.2.1 Display Planes

The separate rendering of background, video and graphics elements on to three different display planes is essential to visualize the characteristics of different multi-media asset types. Each application can place background graphics on to a rectangular region on the background planes. Video can be similarly placed on the background planes overlaying video planes. User interface components and graphical primitives are displayed on the topmost graphic planes. Porter Duff rules apply and define the graphics composition behaviour between several planes.

10.4.2.2 Coordinate Systems

Optimized pixel-oriented coordinate systems for position elements on its planes are defined by MHP. The device space considers variations between different display devices by providing a device space coordinate system. Each of the following coordinate spaces is embedded within this logical coordinate system. Specific requirements for presenting MPEG video in a coordinate system are determined by the input video coordinate system, which includes scaling, clipping and up-sampling. Application providers use a device screen abstraction for placing objects of the subtitle screen, video screen and graphic screen within a normalized coordinate system, with the top-left corner as $[0, 0]$ and the bottom-right corner as $[1, 1]$. A root container, containing more complex graphic elements such as user interface components, is added to the abstract screen device. This container defines the user coordinate system for placing additional graphical objects. Common transformation rules between coordinate systems apply, considering different pixel aspect ratios. Relating the pixel oriented coordinate systems to 4:3 or 16:9 displays with a pixel resolution of 768×576 leads, e.g., to pixel aspect ratios of 1:1 or 46:36.

10.4.2.3 Java and Graphics in MHP

MHP utilizes the Java JDK 1.1 reference model for rendering lightweight components. Graphics capability is thus limited to minor 2D graphic shapes such as lines, rectangles, arcs, ovals and polygons rendered by container elements. Additional content formats such as different image types promise additional graphical enhancement. A larger set of lightweight user interface components defined for broadcast use have been defined and specified.

Several graphical components are placed in a transparent root container, the concept of which is similar to a frame or window. Repainting is done as added last, repainted first until the root container is reached. Porter Duff decomposition rules also apply. Due to the different characteristics of PC- and digiTV-based systems,

MHP extends basic Java functionality by alpha colour composition, support for transparent images with off-screen buffers and extended colour capability.

10.4.3 Broadcast Protocol Stack

In principle, the broadcast protocol stack, as presented in Figure 10.4, can be divided into Interworking protocols, broadcast protocols and feedback protocols. Figure 10.4 shows the protocol suites part of a broadcast protocol stack. Several Internet protocol suites (e.g., TCP, HTTP) belong to the Interworking protocols encapsulated into an all-IP layer. Interworking protocols also package application and presentation layer protocol types as binary or textual XML. Point to multipoint broadcast protocols as based on an MPEG-2 Transport Stream (TS) addresses the transmission of streams to the consumer terminal. An MPEG-2 TS encapsulates services, provides validation and error recovery, provides multi-protocol encapsulation facilities to encapsulate generic protocols carried in the payload of IP packages, provides service information about the stream structure and its content and provides object and data carousels. The carousel mechanism is very specific for broadcast content. Different multimedia assets are packaged to a virtual file system and encapsulated in an MPEG-2 TS. This guarantees a reliable mechanism for updating files relating to services on the consumer terminal.

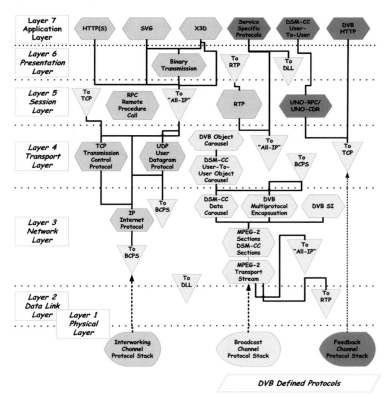

Figure 10.4   ISO/OSI reference model as a broadcast protocol stack.

10.4.4 Delivering SVG and X3D

The delivery of graphics content can be categorized by DVB profiles, transmission modes, content encoding or synchronization models. As previously stated, three deployment profiles are defined by DVB standards, which should be the major categorization criterion for the delivery of textual or binary content encoded graphic metadata:

* The enhanced broadcast profile does not provide a feedback channel and hence does not consider interactivity over an IP network, but supports local interactivity. Asynchronous and synchronous transmission modes enabled by this and any other DVB profile are streaming, incremental update, and complete data updates. Streaming is supported by encapsulating graphics content into MPEG-2 TS packets. Incremental updates focus on the transmission of graphic content step by step. A complete metadata file is delivered as one by the complete data update mode. Synchronization to video content is supported by a time stamp mechanism.
* More interesting is the interactive broadcasting profile, supporting interaction facilities over a feedback network. In contrast to the enhanced broadcast profile, synchronization mechanisms are also related to network interactions.
* The Internet access profile offers facilities similar to any graphic content deployed on the Internet. Its only restriction is due to platform performance capabilities, limiting complex content types. Multi-channel synchronization models are required to handle content over several channels.

The DVB features include incremental updates and complete data updates which can be provided by the object/data carousel mechanisms or event mechanisms. If either of those update mechanisms is applied, a broadcast environment requires continuous transmission of content acting as a base for consequent updates.

10.5 The Narration Cube: A Novel Approach to DigiTV Converge Services

For centuries, stories and narration were the medium for communicating news. Viewpoints, happenings, metaphors and scenes were packed into a common and easily understood language. Dances, drawings, mimics and the style of narration supported the entertainment value. In the information age we retrieve content and service offers from myriads of sources and have the technology to categorize, reference, collect and further distribute it. We know how to handle and manage content in the form of bookmarks and a hard disk full of multimedia content. Efforts concentrate on managing content, rather than simply enjoying the flow of the presentation and getting involved into it. Difficult tools to handle and process content are present and technical support is difficult to obtain.

Digitalization of TV means channel multiplication, with more content from more sources to handle. Even though content is presented well, and more choices are offered, this does not mean that the consumer has the ability to perceive and process the flow and knowledge adequately. Emphasizing narratives as a basic content element shown on digiTV requires more than seeing content as a large piece of compressed information. Three dimensions support the consumer in maintaining

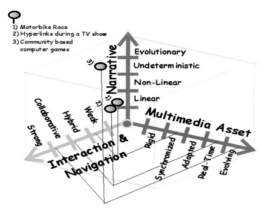

Figure 10.5   The Narrative Cube.

the flow of knowledge in an adequate manner. The narration cube, presented in Figure 10.5, is the basic model for interrelating narrative elements, interaction and multimedia assets. As an example, news broadcasts multiply in the world of digiTV.

10.5.1 Multimedia Asset Axis

The multimedia axis is categorized according to static or rigid assets, synchronized assets, adapted assets, real-time manipulated assets and evolving assets. Static or rigid content is simply one monolithic stream composed of video and audio, as currently present in analogue television. Other examples are movies, news broadcasts and advertisements, etc. Most of the pure broadcast services such as EPGs also belong to this category.

Synchronized assets add new content-related features to streamed content. This might be in the form of add-ons or triggered events such as advertisement banners fitting to the currently presented movie content. An advertisement banner pops up during a news broadcast about the Tyrolean Alps, offering a one-way trip to a nicely located valley. "Atmospheric" effects enhancing the thriller aspects of a movie belong to this category of assets. Additional horrifying sound effects enhance the perception of a horror scene. To remove thrill from a movie as displayed for children, some nice relaxing music smooths the frightening scenes. Adaptation of assets is required to provide the ability to stream to different consumer end devices over different bandwidth requirements. Additional information sources fitting to the current broadcast also belong to this category. A use scenario for synchronized assets is shown in Figure 10.6.

Adapted assets relate more to available resources for services and transcoding processes. Bandwidth limitations might reduce video quality. High-performance user terminals provide applications to render complex virtual scenes on the graphics planes. Owing to the highly diverse landscape of consumer terminals, adaptation of multimedia assets is the key issue in delivering content anytime, anywhere and in any way.

Real-time manipulated assets require high hardware performance as they directly alter the content of multimedia assets. Examples are metadata extractors

Figure 10.6   Use scenario 1: utilization of the screen overlaying panel to visualize additional information about a motorbike race.

describing content. Their catalysis and usage are related to creating services utilizing extracted data.

Evolving assets relate more to the fact that consumers themselves can create content and deploy it on the digiTV platform. The broadcast has more the role of providing a visual content framework, where the consumers can add their own objects and content creations. This can be in form of movie pieces, items and other type of multimedia assets.

10.5.2 Interaction and Navigation Axis

The definition and categorization of interaction and navigation facilities distinguishes the level of communality and local interaction devices.

Weak interactivity relates to simple input devices such as the remote control, joystick, keyboard or mouse equipment, which require no further explanation. Simple interactive services such as Web browsers or clickable content elements belong to this type of interaction.

A more interesting subject is hybrid interactivity, which allows the interconnection and networking of any type of electric equipment. Communication models between different computer systems, home server solutions, PDAs, mobile phones and virtual reality equipment belong to this category. Other examples are touchless mouse pointers or Web-cam based input devices reacting to the consumer's body language by tracking gestures. Figure 10.7 shows hyperlinks inserted into a running broadcast show. The virtual mouse pointer is controlled via a Web-cam, which helps to position the pointer.

Whereas the last two interaction models focus more on technical equipment, collaborative interactivity relies on the fact that communities interact with each other. Communities form interest groups, discussion groups, exchange messages, meet and form a certain kind of virtual society. These moments of interaction are best categorized within collaborative interactivity. Examples are computer games, where multiple consumers perform a battle, which is broadcast live.

Figure 10.7   Use scenario 2: hyperlinks inserted into a running broadcast show.

Strong interactivity consists of elements of each interaction and narrative facility described above. Communities interacting in a real, ubiquitous environment surrounded by electronic interaction equipment also belong to this category. Interaction is intuitive and provided by transparent computer systems, rather than visible electric equipment. Simple examples are mobile phones with augmented reality glasses, where the consumer plays interactive games within a small village. Broadcast data functions as an update or data casting factor.

10.5.3 Narrative Axis

Everything deployed on a digital television is a narrative! But, what is a narrative on a digiTV platform and which characteristics does it have? To develop measurements for story evolvement is a difficult task. To develop a technical solution, a reference model is required. Basically, a narrative has a certain theme, participants (e.g., antagonists, protagonist), evolves within certain borders limiting the story flow and is mostly based on the ideas of a creative digital multimedia author. Examples are political discussions covering breaking news and stories for children. A very basic categorization of the narration flow is part of one axis of the narrative cube. It is an abstraction of narrative ideas presented by Samsel and Wimberly (1998) and Ryan (2001).

A linear narration is the typical narration as commonly known in analogue TV. The consumer obtains one piece of non-interactive content, where he or she has to prefigure the overall story by himself. No ability to change the story flow and configure the narrative space itself is given.

Non-linear narratives evolve by providing different alternatives and decision points. The consumer can select either explicitly or implicitly different story paths. This allows the creation of tree-like decision paths along which the narrative proceeds. Personalized automatic systems might select the most appropriate choices for the consumer.

Undeterministic narratives ease the restriction of simple story trees along which the narrative can evolve to more complex story spaces. The consumer controls not only the story evolvement, but also the space in which it takes place. Examples are computer games merged with broadcast content, where the consumer moves in a virtual 3D computer scene. New objects can be inserted and the outlook of scenes altered. Communities with certain interests might participate in the evolving process. Undeterministic narratives can be seen as open, non-linear narratives, with a common shared space, rules and guidelines stated by the story director, and provide a set of story pieces and items altered by a user community. Existing examples are collaborative computer games, where on solving puzzles of one level, a common story background is broadcast to the game community.

Evolutionary narratives soften topical restrictions and offer a much higher degree of freedom. Communities create their own narration flow, topics are not limited and predictions of where the story will be at a certain point in time can not be made. An existing example is a chat server providing infrastructure for the creation of different discussion groups and 3D object-equipped private rooms. Topics are created by consumers, and it is not predictable with which virtual objects they are equipping their 3D private rooms or what they are chatting about. The mixture of real worlds with an intelligent virtual universe is already obsolete. Virtual actors in the form of intelligent computer software might insert a certain structure and limitations into the evolving processes.

10.5.4 Interaction Models and Multimedia Asset Support Narratives

Interrelating axes is a great challenge. The multimedia asset axis provides the space within which narratives are told and 3D models support the creation of the visual environment with which a consumer can interact. Interaction and navigation allow story space exploration and altering. Multimedia assets and interaction and navigation support the evolving narrative. It is clearly stated that the outcome should be a consistent, intelligently presented and semantically challenging told story.

SVG and X3D belong to the multimedia asset axis and interaction and navigation axis. Both standards provide technical facilities to visualize content objects and support different types of interaction models. They cover many issues for porting a broadcast environment to the third generation of multimedia systems by integrating graphics aspects capable of being executed in a lightweight environment. SVG and X3D provide a temporary solution for presenting supervised or non-supervised narratives in a more sophisticating and narrative way, which is especially applicable to the third generation of multimedia systems requiring intelligence and semantics.

Interactive graphic visualizations as add-on content in the form of vector graphics of chemical objects during a scientific broadcast support the consumer in e-Learning. Navigation through multimedia databases with rich visual graphics elements enhances consumer perception and navigation through multimedia content. Semantic models, bringing a meaning to data, would come from the narrative axis. Extracted data about content has to be catalysed in a certain form. This means that extracted data provides the basis for services utilizing it. For an example, a metadata extractor provides information about the position and orientation of scene objects. X3D utilizes this data to replace those with consumer-defined ones. Consumers would equip their own story space with their chosen objects. Another use scenario of SVG is the utilization of browser systems for more complex graphic elements on on-screen displays.

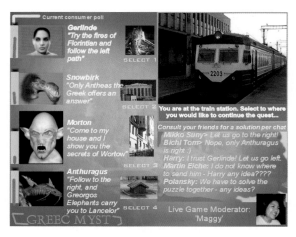

Figure 10.8 Use scenario 3: scenario for a community based solution for solving a node in a narrative.

Figure 10.8 shows an example of a non-linear narrative, evolving according con-sumer's desires, based on collaborative interactive models and synchronized mul-timedia asset features. In this case the narrative style would be non-linear, as only decision points are inserted.

10.6 Content Is King: DigiTV's Rich Multimedia Assets and Its Deployment

Multimedia assets are the content with which the consumer interacts. Their com-pilation to one unified and meaningful collection of different service sub-elements is required and guaranteed by the narrative cube. The narrative cube is only one approach for categorizing and interrelating services. It provides a novel unified approach for service integration within a narrative concept.

The technical solution still requires more refinement for the creation of broad-cast shows. Four concepts support a technical solution towards the implemen-tation of the narrative cube and thus the development of an advanced graphics platform on digiTV: (1) a layered model for multimedia content unifying multi-media assets types; (2) the third-generation of web-based services as an approach for increasing the narratives and semantics of multimedia content; (3) DVB's con-tent formats that restrict advanced graphics types; (4) a software architecture for deploying graphics content.

10.6.1 Layering Multimedia Content

We modified the concept of movie maps as conceptualized by Muller and Tan (1999) for our more advanced graphics deployment scenarios. This model relates to the narrative cube as support for describing the multimedia asset axis. It refines the cube in terms of atomic units processed, adaptability, involving existing content

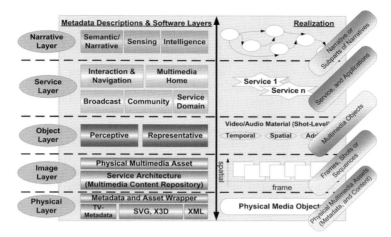

Figure 10.9   Layering digiTV's multimedia assets. Metadata structures and components relevant for the deployment of related services are shown.

models and deeper decomposition of multimedia content. Its layers are presented in Figure 10.9.

The lowest layer is the physical layer as given by transmission modes or content storage models, where entire broadcast shows are the atomic unit of processing (e.g., video stream).

On one layer higher, the image layer, audiovisual features are described. Frames, shots or sequences of them act as atomic units upon which image processing methods are applied (e.g., colour enhancement of a shot). Both layers are relevant for multimedia assets categorization in terms of its rigid, synchronized or adapted categories.

Relevant for the deployment of additional graphics objects and their visualization, synchronization and metadata description is the object layer. The object layer provides contextual information for the hierarchical decomposition of broadcast shows. Multiple scenarios are enabled: spatial decomposition in the form of movement, animation or behaviour, temporal decomposition in the form of story timelines, content inserts, information of timeline decomposition of broadcast show objects, etc. A special feature of broadcasting is add-on content not rigidly synchronized to the broadcast show, but fitting topically. The atomic unit is an object itself.

The service layer combines multiple objects to give an entity which is useful for the consumer. It is formed by programming source code and provides tool sets for different application scenarios, such as for interaction, community services, multimedia home or specific service domains.

Special interest is given to the narrative layer describing lower-layer atomic units in terms of their meaningful mapping on the plot timeline. In the narrative cube this layer interrelates more tightly with the narrative axis. The atomic units are complete narratives or sub-elements of them.

10.6.2   Towards the Third Generation of TV-based Multimedia

Van Ossenbruggen et al. (2001) carefully described the requirements and features of second- and third-generation Web-based multimedia systems. The second generation of TV-based multimedia services relies on knowing the multimedia content structure itself in the form of metadata definitions and document presentation abstractions. Content and its descriptions are strictly separate entities, and visual appearance is based on descriptions which are known beforehand. Third-generation TV-based multimedia involves semantic structure integration and embeds descriptions directly to multimedia assets.

Both generations fit the concept of the narrative cube in providing more narrative and semantic structures and relate several axes of the narrative cube in terms of intelligent broadcast show presentation, pure machine-processable content, reuse of multimedia assets and enhancing semantic meaning of content. A simple example is SVG's capability of adding embedded annotations for further processing to content. Even though the technical base platform is enabled, the narrative cube provides a more unified approach to adding narratives regarding story evolvement and community processes as based on the interaction axis. It supports community, and interacting with content in more advanced terms the cube could define the basis for the fourth generation of Web-based TV.

10.6.3 Content Formats on DVB-compliant Consumer Devices

As shown in Table 10.1, a DVB-compliant environment supports a rich environment as content types. Special features of a digiTV environment are MPEG-2 I frames, providing a representative frame of continuous video stream. Teletext is a very broadcast-specific content type, such as the sRGB colour model. Other content types relate to MPEG-2 video drips, which are short video sequences. Application-specific presentation elements are rigidly defined by Java or Java extensions.

10.6.4 Reference Software Architecture for Implementing the Narrative Cube

Figure 10.9 shows, in addition to the layered components of a broadcast show, also the software modules required for processing each atomic unit at. Each metadata

Table 10.1 Sample content formats on DVB-compliant consumer devices defined by MHP

Content type	Description
Image formats and bitmap pictures	JPEG, PNG, GIF, MPEG-2 I Frames
Audio formats	MPEG-1 audio (layer 1, 2)
Video formats	MPEG-2 video drips
MIME types	Definition of filename extensions of several DVB compliant content types (e.g., ".jpg")
Fonts and text representation	UTF-8 text format, where text presentation, downloading, rendering and placing are defined
Colour representation	sRGB (as defined in IEC 61966-2-1)
Application-specific presentation	Java JDK 1.1, features such as lightweight rendering and user interface presentation
DVB-HTML	HTML for broadcast use
Teletext	ETS 300 706
Subtitles	Based on language selection and different presentation settings

package requires a certain representation and encoding in textual or binary formats, as part of the physical layer. On the image layer a multimedia content repository stores, distributes and manages each physical metadata asset. Both lower layers focus on the basic processes related to dealing with SVG and X3D, such as transcoding, encoding, decoding, browser software. The functionality on higher software layers addresses issues of what to do with all those metadata and how to apply data structures. On object layers, synchronization and perceptive metadata involvement are performed. Relating real-time video to SVG files is part of the module functionality. On service layers, appliances are addressed. As an example, advertisements are embedded to video content and open an Internet connection to the seller. Most complex functionality is to be performed on narrative layers, by involving personalization algorithms and narrative structures.

10.7 SVG Implementation of Hyperlinked TV

A screenshot of the rendered SVG source code presented in Table 10.2 is shown in Figure 10.10. The lightweight implementation of an SVG-based hyperlinked TV implementation is very simple: frequent updates of images annotated with SVG metadata are sent from the BSP to the consumer terminal over the broadcast channel.

Several modes of delivery as defined in DVB profiles are enabled. A virtual file system mechanism as part of the object carousel (DSMCC) definitions is utilized for reading related files from the broadcast stream. If the application is in hyperlinked mode, the image is displayed and SVG metadata descriptions are rendered. By clicking on the rectangle, an event is triggered, the rectangle highlighted and an

Table 10.2 SVG source code for hyperlinked TV

```
<?xml version="1.0" encoding="iso-8859-1"?>
<!DOCTYPE svg PUBLIC "-//W3C//DTD SVG 1.0//EN"
       "http://www.w3.org/TR/2001/REC-SVG-20010904/DTD/svg10.dtd">
  <svg xmlns="http://www.w3.org/2000/svg" version="1.0">
    <image xlink:href="…Fig_10_SVG_Example.gif"
       width="352" height="280" x="0" y="0"> </image>

    <!-- ECMAScript -->
    <script type="text/ecmascript"><![CDATA[
       function Highlight(evt) { … }
       function Unhighlight(evt) { …}
    ]]></script>

    <rect fill="none" y="200px" x="190px" width="40px" height="75px"
       stroke-width="5" style="stroke: #0000FF" id="r1"
       onmousedown="Highlight(evt);" onmouseout="Unhighlight(evt);"/>
    <rect … />
    <rect … />

    <text id="r1text" x="20" y="310" text-anchor="middle"
       visibility="hidden">Original fishing coffee tea cup.</text>
    <text … >Fisher bag cheapest seen at Fish Oy.</text>

    <text id="r1desc" x="195" y="215" text-anchor="middle"
       visibility="visible">1</text>
    <text … >2</text>
</svg>
```

Original fishing coffee tea cup.

Figure 10.10   PC-based demonstration of the rendered SVG file.

action performed. Actions could be displaying a text describing the content of the rectangle or opening of the feedback channel leading to a company Web portal for buying goods.

10.7.1 SVG Metadata Description

The metadata description based on SVG 1.0 (see Table 10.2) consists of an ECMA script part, description of the position of hyperlinks in the form of rectangles, textual descriptors of text to be displayed upon clicking on hyperlinks and additional text describing hyperlinks in textual form. Each element is uniquely identified by its identifier. The overall metadata description is fairly simple and its most significant elements consist of the following:

- `rect`, defining a uniquely identified area for a hyperlink as contained in the image. Its attributes are x- and y-coordinates, width, height, style, stroke-width and i.d.
- `image`, indicating the image file path, position, size and rendering properties.
- `text`, defining position, size and rendering properties of text to be displayed if a hyperlink is activated, or as textual description of a hyperlink.
- `ECMA  script`, for the definition of dynamic behaviour in a scripting language. Its support depends greatly on client performance and is currently not part of the implementation owing to a lack of computational power on embedded digiTV systems. Each rectangle defines an action to be performed upon a mouse click or remote control input is stated.

10.7.2 Lightweight Client Implementation

The implementation is based on a Java version specially designed for embedded systems. Figure 10.11 shows the whole class diagram of our lightweight implementation. In addition to the typical digiTV APIs, JDOM APIs for parsing SVG metadata and selected SVG classes are implemented. SVGMain is extended from a more

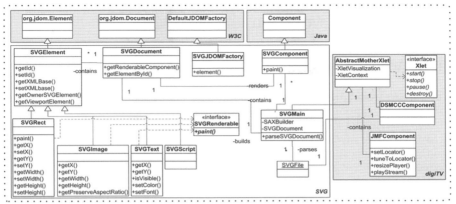

Figure 10.11 Class diagram for a lightweight implementation of hyperlinked TV.

general class combining digiTV features such as application life-cycle management, object carousel access and tuning system. Four states in the life-cycle of a digiTV application are applicable: running, paused, stopped and destroyed. A tree structure representation in the form of a JDOM tree is obtained by reading the SVG file from the object carousel. Each SVG document consists of renderable (e.g., rectangles) and non-renderable elements (e.g., scripting support). The whole SVG document is rendered in a container.

10.8 Related Work

Related works have mostly been cited within the scope of this chapter. As a starting point for the exploration of digital interactive TV we can consider several DVB and MHP standards (European Telecommunications Standards Institute, 2002a, b). General issues of digiTV and its future capabilities were addressed by Van Ossenbruggen et al. (2001) and Wallich (2002). Content encoding, layering and transmission were covered by Muller and Tan (1999). Other valuable reports of service scenarios and applications are those by Samsel and Wimberley (1998), Muller and Tan (1999), Christel and Huang (2001), Rafey et al. (2001), Van Ossenbruggen et al. (2001) and Vaughan-Nichols (2001). The third generation of multimedia also requires packaging structures for digital content. We have addressed this issue in other scientific contributions, such as that by Lugmayr et al. (2002), where the Digital Broadcast Item approach based on MPEG-21 was first introduced. For excellent coverage of digital narratives, see Ryan (2001).

10.9 Summary

This chapter introduced a generic architecture for digiTV and its essentials, and presented scenarios and applications of the third generation of Web-based multimedia in terms of new audiovisual content models. As a TV tells narrative in a virtual story space, the introduction of the narrative cube should help to align services according their narrative character. Furthermore, example scenarios of

SVG and X3D have been introduced. This work should be a starting point for further exploration of SVG and X3D capabilities in digiTV.

10.10 Acknowledgments

The authors would like to thank all colleagues at Tampere University of Technology for their help, support and discussions. Many thanks are due to Prof. Frans Mayra of the Hypermedia Laboratory (Tampere University) for discussions about interactive, narrative media. Samuli Niiranen greatly supported this work with proof reading and suggestions. Without his encouragement and lengthy discussions of various scientific work many of our ideas would not have been developed. Jussi Lyytinen is thanked for the development of the vision mouse for digiTV, discussions and input during the finalization of this chapter. Especially thanks go to Peter Dean for proof reading the chapter and also to Marie-Laure Ryan for the provision of her research material covering digital narratives during our research work. Thanks also go to Artur Lugmayr's brothers Martin and Robert, with good luck for their wide open futures. Finally, Martin Aichner (necropolis@gmx.de) is thanked for providing excellent 3D graphics models. Some more of his work can be found at http://www.3dluvr.com/necro/.

References

Christel M and Huang C (2001) SVG for navigating digital news video. In *Proceedings of the Ninth ACM International Conference on Multimedia*. Ottawa: ACM Press, pp. 483–485.

European Telecommunications Standards Institute (2002a) *Digital Video Broadcasting (DVB) Standards*. Available: http://www.dvb.org

European Telecommunications Standards Institute (2002b) *Digital Video Broadcasting (DVB) Multimedia Home Platform (MHP) Specification 1.0.2*. TS101.812, Edition 1.2.1. Sophia Antipolis: EBU/ETSI.

International Organization for Standardization (1994) *Generic Coding of Moving Pictures and Associated Audio Recommendation H.222.0 (Systems)*. ISO/IEC 13818–1. Geneva: ISO/IEC.

Lugmayr A, Niiranen S, Mailaparampil A, Rautavirta P, Oksanen M, Tico F and Kalli S (2002) Applying MPEG-21 in digital television – example use scenarios: epostcard, egame and eticket. In *Proceedings of 2002 IEEE International Conference on Multimedia and Expo*. Lausanne: IEEE.

Muller H and Tan E (1999) Movie maps. In *Proceedings of IEEE International Conference on Information Visualization*. IEEE, pp. 348–353.

Rafey R, Gibbs S, Hoch M, Le Van Gong H and Wang S (2001) Enabling custom enhancements in digital sports broadcasts. In *WEB3D'2001*. Paderborn: ACM.

Ryan M-L (2001) *Narrative as Virtual Reality*. Baltimore: John Hopkins University Press.

Samsel J and Wimberley D (1998) *Writing for Interactive Media – The Complete Guide*. Allworth Press.

SUN Microsystems (2002) *Java APIs*. Available: http://java.sun.com

Van Ossenbruggen J, Geurts J, Cornelissen F, Hardman L and Rutledge L (2001) Towards second and third generation web-based multimedia. In *Proceedings of the Tenth International Conference on World Wide Web*. New York: ACM Press, pp. 479–488.

Vaughan-Nichols S (2001) Will vector graphics finally make it on the web?. *Computer*, 34(12), 22–24.

Wallich P (2002) Digitv hubbub. *IEEE Spectrum*, 39(7), 26–31.

Chapter 11
Knowledge Visualization Using Dynamic SVG Charts

Nikolas A. Rathert

11.1 Introduction

The Internet has emerged as the most widely used and accessed media of our time. It is used by large global organizations and individuals both to disseminate and to collect information. The latest and most exciting standard in the field of open-source graphics standards is SVG (Jackson et al., 2002a, b).

Considering that this standard is widely accepted and with the increasing number of applications, this type of graphics generation tool is useful for knowledge management applications in two ways: first, SVG is used for the presentation of the collected data, and second, the first Web-based application with an entirely SVG-based graphical user interface could be developed.

Knowledge management is widely understood as an IT-supported process in an organization that will prevent the loss of information triggered by the loss of employees. The need for methods and tools for the preservation of knowledge is increasing. Companies are willing to invest in new applications that allow them to collect, classify and structure the knowledge of their employees. In recent years some ambitious projects have commenced to bridge the gap between the company's knowledge and the knowledge of each employee.

The Fraunhofer Institute for Computer Graphics in Darmstadt, Germany initiated a project, KAM.com, focusing on methods for knowledge detection and preservation and the implementation of a Web-based application for analysis of distributed knowledge. The research and implementation of prototypes for this project commenced in 2001. At that time, the only way of generating dynamic SVG charts within a Web-based client–server application was to use the framework that will be described later in this chapter. In the meantime, JFree Charts offers a Java class that produces these charts in a more effective manner.

This chapter starts with a brief overview of the project KAM.com for which SVG and XML are used. In order to give a clear view of the context in which the SVG prototype is used, an application scenario is presented together with the technology behind dynamic SVG charts including a short overview of the different types of charts used in the KAM.com prototype. The prototype itself will be presented focusing on manipulative and interactive features of the SVG charts. At the end of the chapter, an outlook on SVG on mobile devices and application fields of the future will be given.

11.2 SVG and Knowledge Management

Knowledge management applications consist of different modules. Examples of "classic" modules are document containers accessible via the intranet and used for sharing explicit and reproducible knowledge. Examples of more "advanced" modules are, for example, mechanisms for the gathering of knowledge and mechanisms for the presentation of knowledge maps or other kinds of displays. These modules often include components that are able to generate charts or other kinds of overview graphics for analysis of data collected by consultants during an assessment within a client company.

SVG is a versatile technology for a variety of application fields. Graphics generated with SVG technology could be used either offline or online. This graphics standard allows the user to generate charts from constantly changing dynamic data sources or from static data depending on the context of the application. The prototype for knowledge collection and rating presented in this chapter is set up as a highly dynamic Web-based application.

Most of the existing software systems dealing with knowledge management are used to manage different kinds of knowledge flows. The majority of these software systems are in fact document management systems, or used for information and document retrieval. They are largely confined to codified knowledge and knowledge prepared as documents. An important point missing here is the gathering of the knowledge that is in the employee's memory. Recording this knowledge and visualizing it in different ways is the aim of the knowledge management project KAM.com.

One of the most interesting challenges was the creation of appealing, manipulable and easy-to-use visualizations for collected rating data in consulting firms dealing with knowledge management issues. Here, a tool was needed that would support the consultants in their daily work, visualize the collected data in an appropriate and easy-to-understand manner and that could also be used on different mobile devices.

In order to identify the exact needs of the potential end users, interviews with the consultants were carried out.

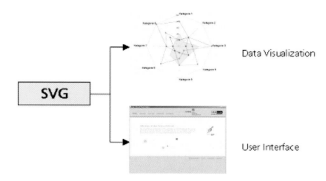

Figure 11.1   Use of SVG within the knowledge management project "Knowledge Asset Management – KAM.com". Here SVG is used both for the visualization of data and as the technology for the presentation of the user interface.

Figure 11.1 shows the usage of SVG technology for two different purposes:

1. for the presentation of rating data with the help of a variety of SVG-based charts
2. for the development of the user interface.

At the start of the project in 2001, SVG emerged as a popular standard in a variety of applications. Some graphics-oriented sciences, e.g., geographical information systems, started to use it to present, for example, vector-based Web cartography (Neumann, 2000). A Web-based application dealing with dynamically generated charts should rely on a reliable technology. SVG met this requirement.

The project was a pioneer in the development of front-end applications that are entirely based on SVG technology.

Every developer who produces Web applications that present data through dynamically generated images has to consider two important points. First, he/she has to decide on the technology to be used. Second, he/she has to consider the requirements that have to be met for the graphical output. Most applications that have been developed so far are intelligent environments for exchange, archiving and searching documents. There are many research activities on how to organize and visualize data within large knowledge domains and how document retrieval could be done more intelligently.

In the current knowledge management application, the data that should be presented in a more convenient way does not consist of isolated pieces of information like documents in a database. Here, data is collected during an assessment and consists of numbers that will be manipulated mathematically. For the knowledge management application prototype, SVG was chosen as the technology to produce graphical representations because there are some advantages compared with other technologies, which include:

- The output graphics could be generated on-the-fly via a simple transformation.
- A high grade of manipulation of the generated images is possible (such as zooming and panning).
- SVG could be used both for desktop systems and for mobile systems (SVG Basic, SVG Tiny).
- The files are small and easy to handle (e.g., editing is possible with any text editor).
- Most of the required technology is on the server side, the user just has to install a plug-in, which is very powerful.

The most crucial work that has to be done after choosing SVG as the technology for the generation of dynamic charts is to develop algorithms for the mathematical calculation of different kinds of charts. These depend on the actual application field and the way in which the users want to work with the prototype. Here, there are two important questions to be answered: first, who is the primary user of the application?; and second, what types of diagrams are necessary?

11.3 Application Scenario

In order to give the reader a better idea of the environment in which SVG is used, a brief description of a scenario enhancing the previously given information will be given below. This scenario aims to clarify the context in which the application is used:

The main target group for this application is consulting companies. One of these companies has a number of consultants who work in isolation from each other outside the headquarters at customer locations. Their daily work consists of interviews and they have to plan assessments, prepare the questionnaires carefully, carry out the interviews and do the analysis of the gathered data together with the client in order to find an appropriate solution for the identified problems. The devices that the consultant uses during his/her work are a portable computer (laptop, notebook) and an ordinary Ethernet card or a wireless LAN card. The application the consultant uses on his/her devices provides all necessary tools he/she needs for the fulfillment of his/her task. The easy-to-use SVG graphical user interface (GUI) leads him/her through his/her workflow. The process of the analysis will be supported by an SVG-based component that could be used for the generation of different kinds of visualizations using the gathered data. The customer is given a set of these diagrams and will be coached by the consultant concerning the next steps in order to improve results next time. In most cases the consultants will develop action plans together with the managerial level of the customer company. To assess if the scheduled activities have been successful, another rating or assessment must be held some time later.

Starting from this point, a conceptualization for the application could be noted. As stated above, the main focus is to develop different possibilities of visualizing the rating data. Therefore, it was important to examine the existing data. A survey was carried out in order to find the appropriate types of diagrams focusing on those types that allow one to present the data in an easy and understandable way. Second, it was necessary to find out if it was possible to create those types of diagrams with SVG technology. Furthermore, it was necessary to determine what kinds of manipulation and interaction features were needed. These interaction features and their feasibility had to be determined. These features offer manipulative capabilities according to ergonomic human–machine communication strategies. The design and development of the entirely SVG-based GUI commenced in parallel.

11.4 Technology Behind Dynamic SVG Charts

Using SVG for dynamically generated charts is more suitable than other technologies. The technology behind the automatic generation is generally standardized. With a set of standard and well-functioning tools consisting of a Web server, an application server, a database and an XML handler, the knowledge management application may be implemented (see Figure 11.2).

From a technical perspective, data transformation is of most interest. Basically, this is done using an XML transformation with the help of a Cocoon framework. Cocoon is part of the Web development environment utilized. Cocoon is the integral component for XML publishing on the Web and provides the possibility for handling XML transformations via Extensible Stylesheet Language for Transformation (XSLT). A stylesheet is used to transform the data into SVG (Mansfield and Fuller, 2002).

In addition to transforming the data into SVG, there are other transformation possibilities: regardless of user or application file format requirements, the XML data can simply be transformed into, for example, HTML, PDF or SVG. The Cocoon framework is useful for development processes in which people with different kinds of expert knowledge are involved. The consequent separation of management, logic, content and style provides the possibility of allocating different tasks to individual

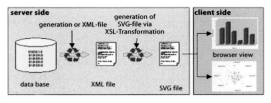

Figure 11.2   Schematic view of the data flow process – from database to image. The data that will be visualized by the system and presented in various diagram types is stored in a database. On request, an XML file containing the data will be generated and transformed into a SVG image with the help of XSLT. All components of the logic are located on the server side. The client is responsible only for the presentation of the images.

development team members, where each member needs only to concentrate on his or her own part.

This is the setting for the creation of dynamic Web content. Delivering dynamic Web content on request is something that is becoming more and more important in the world of in-time and on-demand online publishing. Additionally, Web Services are constantly increasing in number on the Web and more and more applications use this new technology. Some time ago, Web sites used to consist of a limited number of static pages programmed in HTML. As the service aspect of the Internet came to fruition, the functionality to provide dynamically created pages became progressively more important. The idea of integrating dynamic content on corporate Web sites is increasing and therefore new forms of information delivery are being established (e.g., Web Services).

The appearance of a simple HTML page will be enhanced by the use of dynamic content. The most obvious advancement is implemented by the use of dynamically generated graphics. Most commonly used raster graphics formats on the Web are static. The other main graphics format is not static but dynamic: vector graphics allow interactive manipulation by the user on the one hand and role-specific or even user-specific content that could be presented in a customizable way on the other. Another great advantage is that the use of SVG graphics format is not proprietary.

Using SVG means using XML. If a developer is familiar with XML, the gap towards SVG is not unbridgeable. The integration of dynamically created SVG graphics in different Web sites is a matter of developing XML and suitable XSLT-files – one for each transformation – leaving it to the customer to decide the process to achieve the desired results.

The implementation of Web-based applications including dynamic chart generation with the help of SVG involved the combination of existing tools and applications, which are all standard and freely available technologies.

In the meantime, research has led to mechanisms that simplify the process of generating charts, the most common being the JFree Chart Library, which provides easy chart generation using Java (Gilbert, 2003). These Java classes can be recommended for developments where applications are written in Java and involve many types of charts.

11.5 Charts

Appropriate presentations for the collected rating data were done by experimenting with different features including different aspects of interactivity. A study was

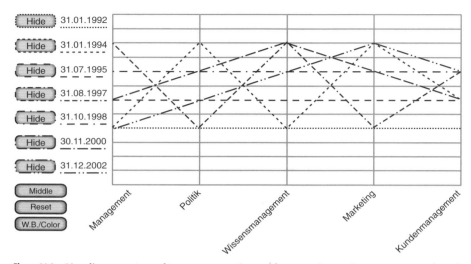

Figure 11.3   Line diagrams are used to compare continuous data over time against a common scale and are ideal for showing trends. This diagram shows the values of seven ratings each consisting of five categories. The colour scheme could easily be changed via the control panel on the left side.

carried out with an initial focus on four different types of diagrams. Considering the user of the system, his/her background, the context and the nature of the provided data, four types of commonly used charts were chosen: line charts, bar charts, pie charts and radar charts.

11.5.1 Line Charts

Line charts compare continuous data over time against a common scale and are ideal for showing trends. Line charts differ from X–Y charts in that the x-axis intervals are automatically created. The key concept for line charts is "progress". Data sets can be rendered as a series of symbols, connected by lines, with the area beneath filled in. Line charts are used in order to show the actual status of knowledge within the organization and to provide prognostic trends over a certain period of time.

The line diagram in Figure 11.3 compares seven ratings. Some interaction and manipulation features are implemented in this type of chart. The panel on the left gives the user the possibility to choose the rating he/she wants to see by clicking the "Display " or "Hide" buttons. The arithmetic mean may be displayed and the colour scheme may be changed from colour to black-and-white. All other manipulation features provided by the Adobe SVG Plug-in (Adobe Systems, 2001a, b) are also available here.

11.5.2 Bar Charts

Figure 11.4 shows visualized rating data using a bar chart. Bar chart diagrams are mainly used to show differences in different assessments. A 2D bar chart is useful for the presentation and comparison of different values derived from different assessments in different categories. Presented in this chart is the data drawn from

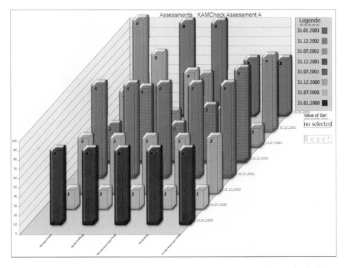

Figure 11.4   Data visualization using an SVG-generated bar chart. It includes eight different ratings with each rating consisting of values in five categories. Some interactive functionalities have been implemented to make the graph more informative for the user.

five categories and eight different ratings. On the right, a legend explains the different colours corresponding to different ratings. The control panel allows the user to display/hide the different ratings. By clicking on the different columns the absolute value appears (see Figure 11.4). This feature permits effective comparison of the different ratings for the user.

Image manipulation is not a common task for users of such applications; therefore, evaluation studies were carried out in order to determine the combinations of diagrams and interactions that could best fit the purpose of visualizing rating data in the case of this particular application.

In addition to the previously mentioned types of charts (line chart, bar chart) many other charts exist. The KAM.com prototype is additionally capable of producing both pie charts and radar charts. These are explained in the following sections.

11.5.3 Pie Charts

Pie charts are the most commonly used types of charts. Pie charts are used when focusing on one data series is important. With a pie chart, the relation of one data point to the rest of the data series can easily be visualized. The area of each slice or segment of the pie is the same percentage of the total circle as the data it represents. Figure 11.5 shows an example pie chart. By clicking on the legend on the left side or on the different coloured areas, the user is able to hide or display the different ratings.

11.5.4 Radar Charts

The most sophisticated type of chart within this knowledge management application is the radar chart (Figure 11.6). In order to provide a clearer view of the

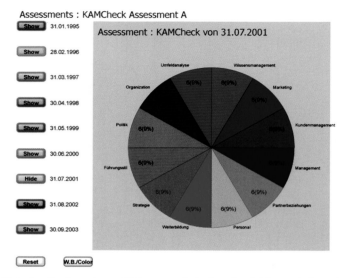

Figure 11.5 Data visualization using an SVG-generated pie chart. By clicking on the legend or on the different coloured areas, the user is able to hide or display the different ratings. This functionality is useful for comparisons and eases interpretation issues.

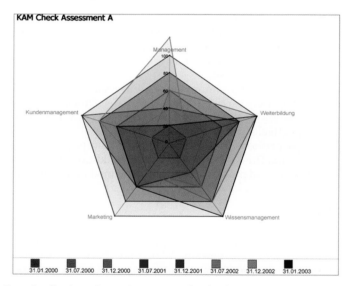

Figure 11.6 Data visualization using an SVG-generated radar chart. This is an original SVG-generated view on the data consisting of eight ratings where each rating includes five categories. The user could show the different ratings by clicking on the colours below.

different ratings in this chart, among other useful features, a display or hide functionality for the different ratings and the option to show the arithmetic mean are implemented. The radar chart is especially useful for showing different data derived from different assessments and provides an easy visual means for comparison of data.

There are many more types of diagrams apart from the four types discussed above. With the exception of the radar charts, the above charts and a few more can also be produced using the Jfree Chart Library (Gilbert, 2003). Currently, further work is being carried out in order to add further charts for visualization in the KAM.com knowledge management prototype.

11.6 Manipulation and Interactivity

Another advantage in using vector-based format SVG in knowledge management applications is the chance to provide many interactive features to the users. SVG itself is made for interaction and the Adobe SVG Viewer comes with a set of standard manipulation tools. Despite these features, additional features were developed and integrated into the graphics.

Visualization of data through charts can often be optimized by presentation of additional information and detail that may be achieved through activation hotspots within the generated diagrams. These features are therefore also integrated in the application. Basically the same interaction modes and animations are possible as those offered by other vector-based formats such as Flash, therefore making it possible for a specific diagram type to be accompanied with an animation that shows the rating data. This feature is useful, for example, in the presentation of the data in non-Web-based environments (e.g., embedded within a slide show).

In short, the data visualization manipulation functionalities developed for this application are as follows:

- switching between the different diagram types
- display or hiding of every single rating
- display of the arithmetic mean
- display of trends
- display of percentage and absolute values.

These features should be simple and self-explanatory. The user is invited to play with these functionalities in order to choose the kind of visualization he/she finds best suited to his/her needs.

Additionally, maximum support for users and their tasks in interpreting the result diagrams should be achieved by presenting a set of manipulation features. The following functionalities are therefore integrated in the user's working environment:

- saving facility for the diagram to any desired location
- conversion mechanism to other document formats (e.g., PDF, EPS)
- import and export of the graphics between different applications
- an editor for the definition of formulae that can be added to the diagrams
- additional editing possibilities for the rating values via a drag and drop mechanism.

11.7 Charting Anywhere

Knowledge management applications are increasingly being used on the move. One the one hand, this is due to the decreasing size of devices. On the other hand, it is more convenient for the customers if consultants are able to do their assessments on location without having to disrupt the workflow of their customers work processes.

SVG as a standard was originally developed for the use with desktop computers. Currently available common computer hardware mostly meets the requirements defined in the standard of W3C (Jackson et al., 2002a), but what about smaller, portable devices that do not have the capability of laptops? Smaller devices, especially devices such as personal digital assistants (PDAs) and cell phones with enhanced and Java-enabled operating systems, offer the possibility to install and run such software but require some modification. The SVG graphics may be displayed on these smaller devices only with limited features and a subset of the commands (Hayman, 2002). To meet these special requirements of smaller devices, the W3 Consortium has produced two special documents dealing with the specification of small mobile systems (Capin, 2002). The most important issue in dealing with mobile hardware with limited capability of displaying graphics is performance. Despite the small displays with which such devices are normally equipped, 2D graphics may be displayed on them but during the development process of the application the loading times should be considered (Robinson, 2002). The advantage is clear and could be derived from the above scenario: the chance to visualize data on small devices will increase the ubiquitous usability of the knowledge management application and any other application including the rating modules. Access to the server will be granted by modern wireless protocols (e.g., WLAN, Bluetooth). Short up- and download times will lead to highly convenient usage of the introduced knowledge management application and a broader acceptance as these devices will also be used at the workplace.

The main advantages of a small device, location-independent rating system are as follows:

- collect data anywhere
- no need for interference with the production chain
- meet your interviewees anywhere necessary
- more flexibility.

The knowledge management application has been tested on the new generation of Tablet PCs running a special edition of Microsoft Windows XP. On this device the application may be used more freely, as the device is portable and a pen is used as input device (a medium with which everyone is familiar).

11.8 Future Work

The presented knowledge management application with dynamic SVG charts is a prototype. There is still much work to be done. Future efforts will concentrate on

- development of more types of diagrams
- enhancement of the interactivity and manipulation functions for the user
- porting of the system on mobile devices and developing a possibility for remote working and synchronizing with a database running on a central server
- developing of additional output formats.

In parallel with these enhancements and advancements, the assessment tool and the tool for the visualization of the data will be optimized for use in other application areas, such as:

- e-learning
- e-government and
- other knowledge management applications.

The application itself should be transformed both into a module that could easily be integrated into different applications and into a stand-alone application that provides the possibility for easy questionnaire development and result display by the help of dynamically generated SVG diagrams.

11.9 Summary

In this chapter, we have demonstrated the usage of dynamically generated SVG charts within a Web-based knowledge management application. The main focus has been set on the development of different types of diagrams and their interactive potential. The example presented illustrated the broad variety of possible presentations and gave an insight into how the generation of dynamic charts will evolve. The Semantic Web will no longer be restricted to cable-bound desktop computers but be expanded by new and upcoming devices, which are able to communicate via wireless protocols.

11.10 Acknowledgments

The author would like to thank the State of Bavaria, which supported part of the research work in the framework of "HighTech-Offensive Bayern". Additional thanks go out to the core developing team and to the people who supported and helped in carrying out all the tasks necessary for this research and implementation.

References

Adobe Systems (2001a). *Current Support Documentation Version 3.0*. Available: http://www.adobe.com/svg/viewer/install/

Adobe Systems (2001b). *Adobe SVG Viewer for Windows Version 3.0 Release Notes*. Available: http://www.adobe.com/svg/viewer/install/

Capin T (ed.) (2002) *Mobile SVG Profiles: SVG Tiny and SVG Basic*. W3C Proposed Recommendation. Available: http://www.w3.org/TR/SVGMobile/

Gilbert D (2003). *The JFreeChart Class Library. Version 0.9.8. Installation Guide*. Simba Management Limited. Available: http://www.jfree.org/jfreechart/jfreechart-0.9.8-install.pdf

Hayman J (2002). *The Suitability of SVG for Deploying Wireless Applications*. Available: http://www.svgopen.org/papers/2002/hayman__suitability_of_svg_for_wireless_applications/

Jackson D (ed.) (2002a) *Scalable Vector Graphics (SVG) 1.2*. W3C Working Draft. Available: http://www.w3.org/TR/SVG12/

Jackson D (ed.) (2002b) *SVG 1.1/1.2/2.0 Requirements*. W3C Working Draft. Available: http://www.w3.org/TR/SVG2Reqs/

Mansfield PA, Fuller DW (2002) *Graphical Style Sheets – Using XSLT to Generate SVG*. Available: http://www.schemasoft.com/gcatools/gca2html/Output/05-05-02.html

Neumann A (2000) *Vector-based Web Cartography: Enabler SVG*. Available: http://www.karto.ethz.ch/neumann/index.html

Robinson B (2002). *Creating and Implementing Mobile SVG*. Available: http://www.svgopen.org/papers/2002/robinson__csiro_svg_mobile/

Chapter 12
Using SVG and XSLT to Display Visually Geo-referenced XML

Timothy Adams

12.1 Introduction

In the relatively short period following the release of SVG there has been growing interest in the format as a means of displaying maps. Numerous projects have been undertaken to develop techniques to achieve this and there have been some notable successes. Although many other uses for SVG are also under investigation (as is evident from other chapters in this book), those using it for cartographic purposes form a significant sub-group. The number of papers relevant to the Web-mapping topic which were presented at the SVG Open Conferences of 2002 and 2003 is evidence of the strength of this sub-group. The projects to date are far too numerous to list, but a few can be identified as notable examples of the techniques that have been developed so far. For each example identified, another of equal merit can be found. The list of links at http://www.carto.net/papers/svg/links/ is a good place to commence a search for alternatives.

The Ridley Creek Riparian Assessment Web site is a client-side implementation, available at http://www.greenworks.tv/eac/ridleycreek/maps/mappage.html, that displays numerical and textual information by use of JavaScript. This is achieved by storing the relevant information directly within the JavaScript as an array of variables. The Map Browser Web site at http://www.mycgiserver.com/~amri/mapbrow.html also makes use of JavaScript on a client-side operation but the information to be displayed is stored in separate XML files from where they are called as and when needed. Yet another client-side operation is the Tuerlersee project as described by Isakowski and Neumann (2002) and available at http://www.carto.net/papers/svg/tuerlersee/. This holds attribute data within the SVG map itself that is accessed by ECMAScript. A number of other interactive techniques are also successfully employed. Particularly noteworthy is the Tuerlersee map's use of SVG GUI features that negate the need to embed the SVG within an HTML page. This latter technique is often utilized in order to make use of the HTML form functionality, although it is widely expected that future updates of SVG will support the XForms language. The Tyrol Atlas at http://tirolatlas.uibk.ac.at/ is an interesting example of the server-side generation of SVG from a Postgres database as described by Forster and Winter (2002). When considering server-side projects, the work of Cecconi et al. (2002) is of particular importance. Their prototype makes use of traditional LOD techniques in combination with on-the-fly generalization with the express hope that the latter will become increasingly useful as the algorithms increase in efficiency.

Projects with a different purpose and aim are those engaged in the conversion of Geographic Markup Language (GML) data into SVG. GML is primarily regarded as a data storage language and as a means of interoperable data transfer. It is not a display format but, since GML and SVG are both forms of XML, it is possible to transform the former to the latter by using XSLT. SchemaSoft have been highly active as developers of this technique (Fuller et al., 2002) and Ordnance Survey have useful examples at http://www.ordsvy.gov.uk/os_mastermap/xml/. Ordnance Survey became one of the first data providers to use GML when they released their MasterMap product in November 2001. It is therefore not surprising that they should be early advocates of using XSLT to transform their data into SVG in this way.

Although it is clear that these examples do display external information with a variety of methods, the primary impetus of these projects has been the display of topographical data, thereby producing a map, and the development of the means to interact with these maps in various ways. The adoption of XML technology has been steady, unlike the meteoric acceptance of some predecessors. However, it is likely to continue to grow in importance as disparate groups come to terms with the advantages which semantic control gives them. Where XML data contains geo-referencing there will be a demand for the ability to display this data graphically within a pre-existing map. This chapter concentrates on the use of XSLT to achieve this. It can also be achieved by manipulating the DOM with JavaScript or ECMAScript, but this is not shown as many examples can already be seen in operation on the Internet (a few have already been cited above). For those wishing to pull XML data from an online server using PHP, Advanced Webmapping with SVG (Held et al., 2003) is as good a place to start as any.

12.2 Combining XML Files with XSLT

Geo-referencing is a grand-sounding term, but it only means that the information in question contains a cross-reference to a geographical entity. This may be a point, line or area, and may be a grid reference, a place name or a code such as a postcode. When a file is geo-referenced, one would expect to find this in the metadata; if it is an XML element which is geo-referenced, it would be reasonable to find it as an attribute. Of course, it is possible and often likely that a compound geo-reference is available, in which case the element would contain several attributes. For the purposes of demonstration, however, the examples have been kept as simple as possible.

Listing 12.1.   A simple geo-referenced xml file containing fictional data

```
<!-- data.xml -->
<farmsie>
  <Hectares name="New Farm">100</Hectares>
  <Hectares name="Pear Tree Farm">300</Hectares>
  <Hectares name="Crossways Farm">200</Hectares>
</farmsize>
```

The code in Listing 12.1 uses XML syntax but has no DTD and is therefore undeclared XML. It provides us with a statistical figure in hectares for three farms and therefore a measure requiring to be displayed as an area. We do not know the shape of the farms, areas and, although since the farm names are geographic entities the

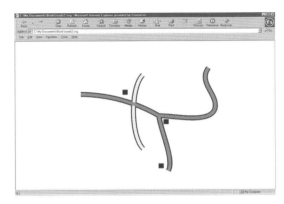

Figure 12.1   The original SVG image (farms.svg).

data is geo-referenced, we do not know any coordinates by which we can map the data in a vector format. If we are to map this data we have to make some early design decisions on the accuracy which is required and the availability of a map to meet this requirement. Let us assume that the simple map shown in Figure 12.1 is the only one available to us. The SVG code for this image is shown in Listing 12.2.

Listing 12.2.   A simple SVG map displaying the three farmhouses (farms.svg)

```
<!-- farms.svg -->
<svg xmlns:xlink="http://www.w3.org/1999/xlink">

<g id="Allroads" style="fill:none;stroke:black;
  stroke-width:10">
<path id="r1" d="M178 189 C233 190 285 205 331 233"/>
<path id="r2" d="M429 136 C409 164 442 186 442 212
  C442 253 360 232 331 233"/>
<path id="r3" d="M349 345 C361 322 335 266 331 233"/>
<path id="r4" d="M300,150 C275,175 275,275 300,300"/>
</g>

<g id="Broads" style="fill:none;stroke:yellow;
  stroke-width:6">
<use id="Back Lane" xlink:href="#r4"/>
</g>

<g id="Aroads" style="fill:none;stroke:red;
  stroke-width:6;">
<use id="High Street" xlink:href="#r1"/>
<use id="Low Road" xlink:href="#r2"/>
<use id="New Street" xlink:href="#r3"/>
</g>

<g id="farms">
<rect id="New Farm" x="330" y="330" width="10"
  height="10"/>
```

```
<rect id="Crossways Farm" x="340" y="240" width="10"
  height="10"/>
<rect id="Pear Tree Farm" x="260" y="180" width="10"
  height="10"/>
</g>
</svg>
```

This image displays the required farmhouses by use of a black rectangle as a symbol. We do not have the areal coordinates for each farm but we can display the statistics as scaled symbols centred upon the point coordinates of the farmhouses. It is possible to achieve this by merging the two files. When using XSLT, this can be done by making use of the document() function. The SVG file does not have a DTD. If one were present, the processor would attempt to validate the data.xml file when parsed by the document() function and consequently reject the file as invalid SVG.

It is not possible to tell an XSLT processor to work on more than one file at any time. If an additional file needs to be read, it can be done by using the document() function within the XSLT stylesheet. In our case, we need to use this function in combination with the xsl:key instruction and the key() function so that the two sets of information merge.

Although it is assumed that the reader has an awareness of both XSLT and XPath syntax, it is also assumed that both the document() and key() functions are new concepts. Since a number of things are happening when Listing 12.3's XSLT, an explanation of the individual steps will follow.

Listing 12.3. XSLT that inserts the data file into the SVG file

```
<!-- addData.xsl: adds data.xml into farms.svg to create
  new.svg-->
<xsl:stylesheet xmlns:xsl="http://www.w3.org/1999/XSL/
  Transform" version="1.0">
  <xsl:output method="xml" omit-xml-declaration="yes"/>

<xsl:variable name="dataDocCall" select="document
  ('data.xml')"/>

<xsl:key name="placeKey" match="Hectares" use="@name"/>

<xsl:template match="svg">

<svg xmlns:xlink="http://www.w3.org/1999/xlink">
  <xsl:apply-templates select="$dataDocCall"/>
  <xsl:apply-templates/>
</svg>
</xsl:template>

<xsl:template match="farmsize"/>

<xsl:template match="rect">
  <xsl:variable name="farmName" select="@id"/>
  <xsl:variable name="farmX" select="@x"/>
  <xsl:variable name="farmY" select="@y"/>
    <xsl:for-each select="$dataDocCall">
```

```
      <xsl:element name="circle">
<xsl:attribute name="id"><xsl:value-of
select="$farmName"/></xsl:attribute>
<xsl:attribute name="style">fill:lime; opacity:0.5
  </xsl:attribute>
<xsl:attribute name="cx"><xsl:value-of
select="$farmX"/></xsl:attribute>
<xsl:attribute name="cy"><xsl:value-of
select="$farmY"/></xsl:attribute>
<xsl:attribute name="r"><xsl:value-of
select="key('placeKey',$farmName)"/></xsl:attribute>
      </xsl:element>

      </xsl:for-each>
      <xsl:apply-templates/>
</xsl:template>

<xsl:template match="@*|node()">
  <xsl:copy>
    <xsl:apply-templates select="@*|node()"/>
  </xsl:copy>
</xsl:template>
</xsl:stylesheet>
```

Even the most casual observer will see that the stylesheet contains several templates. Before the first template is declared, we can see that a variable is created which is named "dataDocCall" in which the data.xml file is called via a document() function. It is not strictly necessary to call the XML file in this way. We could call for this file each time we need it using that same function, but by declaring it as a variable the call only has to be made once, which therefore increases efficiency of the ensuing transformation. Underneath this is a statement creating a key called "placeKey" and declaring this key's first parameter as the "name" attribute within the XML file. The key and the variable are the two important factors in making the transformation that we require.

Within the first template we can see that the data.xml file is read and parsed as an XML file by using the "dataDocCall" variable. It is read into the SVG document as the template is matched to the root element. Since this match will prevent the <svg> tag from being processed, it has to be reapplied within the template. The second template suppresses the <farmsize> element from the XML file in a similar way as it is not needed and would make the new.svg file invalid SVG.

The third template is where the really important changes take place. By matching the <rect> elements, the symbols which show the location of the farms are suppressed from the final readout. The "dataDocCall" variable is selected "for each" of these rectangle elements and the information within those elements which will be reused later is stored as variables named farmName, farmX and farmY. A <circle> element is created for each of the original rectangles and the appropriate attributes are added. The two data sources are combined by use of our key() function within the circle's "r" attribute. This key takes the "name" attribute from the XML file and looks through the rectangle "id" attributes to find those that match. When a match is found, the contents within the <Hectares> element of the XML file is returned.

The last template selects all the nodes and attributes with the exception of those already processed above, copying each of them into our final result. When all these templates are run together by an XSLT transform engine, the output will be as shown in Listing 12.4.

Listing 12.4.   The output created by xslt transform (new.svg)

```
<!-- farms.svg -->
<svg xmlns:xlink="http://www.w3.org/1999/xlink">
<!-- data.xml -->
<g id="Allroads" style="fill:none;stroke:black;
  stroke-width:10">
<path id="r1" d="M178 189 C233 190 285 205 331 233"/>
<path id="r2" d="M429 136 C409 164 442 186 442 212
  C442 253 360 232 331 233"/>
<path id="r3" d="M349 345 C361 322 335 266 331 233"/>
<path id="r4" d="M300,150 C275,175 275,275 300,300"/>
</g>
<g id="Broads" style="fill:none;stroke:yellow;
  stroke-width:6">
<use id="Back Lane" xlink:href="#r4"/>
</g>
<g id="Aroads" style="fill:none;stroke:red;
  stroke-width:6;">
<use id="High Street" xlink:href="#r1"/>
<use id="Low Road" xlink:href="#r2"/>
<use id="New Street" xlink:href="#r3"/>
</g>
<g id="farms">
<circle id="New Farm" style="fill:lime; opacity:0.5"
  cx="330" cy="330" r="100"/>
<circle id="Crossways Farm" style="fill:lime; opacity:
  0.5" cx="340" cy="240" r="200"/>
<circle id="Pear Tree Farm" style="fill:lime; opacity:
  0.5" cx="260" cy="180" r="300"/>
</g>
</svg>
```

Although the Listing 12.4 code appears to be correct, the problem with this image can clearly be seen in Figure 12.2. The coordinate system of the original SVG does not integrate well with the data that has been introduced, leading to an unclear display of that data. When mixing two distinct datasets, it is extremely likely that one or other of the datasets has to be manipulated in some way in order to achieve clarity. It is important that great care is taken when manipulating data if we are to avoid distortion of the data, an understanding of Tufte's *The Visual Display of Quantitative Information* (Tufte, 1983) being particularly useful. However, Monmonier (1991, p.1) argues that "Not only is it easy to lie with maps, it's essential. To portray meaningful relationships … a map must distort reality."

The example as shown in Figure 12.2 contains a distortion of the data as the hectare figure is used to generate the radius attribute of the circle symbol and therefore exaggerates the difference in size between the farms. We can overcome this by

Visualizing Information Using SVG and X3D

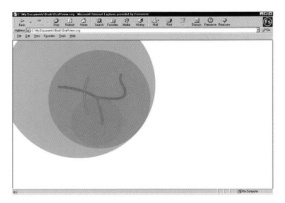

Figure 12.2 The image from Listing 12.4's code.

halving the total hectare figure. This can be easily achieved by revising the third template of the original XSL to that shown in Listing 12.5.

Listing 12.5. A revised third template which will manipulate the xml data

```
<xsl:template match="rect">
  <xsl:variable name="farmName" select="@id"/>
  <xsl:variable name="farmX" select="@x"/>
  <xsl:variable name="farmY" select="@y"/>
    <xsl:for-each select="$dataLookupDoc">
    <xsl:variable name="newData" select="key
      ('placeKey',$farmName)"/>

    <xsl:element name="circle">
<xsl:attribute name="id"><xsl:value-of
select="$farmName"/></xsl:attribute>
<xsl:attribute name="style">fill:blue; opacity:0.8
  </xsl:attribute>
<xsl:attribute name="cx"><xsl:value-of
select="$farmX"/></xsl:attribute>
<xsl:attribute name="cy"><xsl:value-of
select="$farmY"/></xsl:attribute>
<xsl:attribute name="r"><xsl:value-of
select="$newData*0.50"/></xsl:attribute>
    </xsl:element>

    </xsl:for-each>
    <xsl:apply-templates/>
```

Whereas in the original stylesheet the key() function is used directly within the statement which creates the circle's "r" attribute, the function is now a variable named "newData". When this variable is applied to the "r" attribute, it is multiplied by 0.50 and therefore halves the hectare number. If this template is used instead of that originally given, we have the image produced in Figure 12.3. We can perform a multitude of mathematical operations at this point depending upon what is required. Figure 12.4 shows the image produced if we arbitrarily multiply our hectare

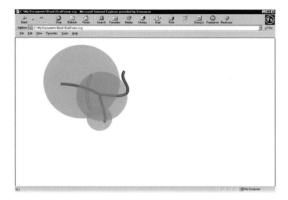

Figure 12.3   Original XML data halved by using Listing 12.5's template.

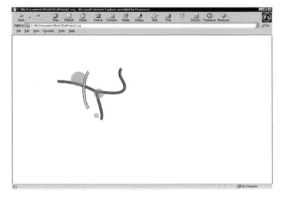

Figure 12.4   Original data arbitrarily multiplied by 0.1 to produce a meaningful image.

figure by 0.10 and therefore produce an image conveying the relationships between the farms.

Experienced GIS operators will know that it is often necessary to make use of an intermediary file when mapping data. A common example would be the display of data geo-referenced by postcode. This data will be first joined to a dataset containing details of the x,y coordinates for the centroid of each postcode area. It is only after the original data has an attached x,y reference that it can be displayed upon a topographic map. This process can be achieved using an expanded version of the techniques shown above as the document() function can be used to call several files into the xslt processor and several different key() functions can be used within the same stylesheet.

12.3 Problems and Potential

The potential for using these functions for the visualization of XML data is vast. However, there are some problems which need to be addressed. The major problem is that it relies upon the matching of geo-referencing attribute between the data file and the SVG map file or the gazetteer file. In theory this should not be a problem as we can use an XML search engine to search for an appropriate file with a matching reference. Hence, if the XML file contains data referenced to a particular street in a particular town, we can search for a file that contains the same street and use this map to plot our data. This requires a variety of SVG maps/XML gazetteers to be available on the Internet, which are not available at present, although this is likely to improve over time, particularly once the One Map Project develops (Misund and Johnsen, 2002). Specialist gazetteers are likely to be developed which will allow the cross-referencing of attributes. An example would be the mapping of historic data in which archaic spellings for geographic entities are used. The Virtual Norfolk Web site is a good example of the existence of XML in such a format. This Web site contains many examples of original historic documents in XML format, including a population survey of 1752 giving statistics by parish, but using original spellings for the parish.

Another problem is a direct consequence of the very utility of this process. XSLT allows us to make use of data from a wide variety of sources and plot them together within a single map or chart. However, each file will require a different XSLT code and the more differences between the files the more changes will have to be made. Even though it is possible to build a library of XSLT functions to avoid duplication of code, the necessary changes will take time and skill. Holman (2000) understates the task when he tells us that "writing a stylesheet is as simple as using mark-up to declare the behaviour of the XSLT processor, much like HTML is used to declare the behaviour of the web browser to paint information on the screen." Much closer to reality is Mansfield (2001), who states that "code to produce a visualization requires real programming. Not only is it real programming, it's programming in an obscure programming language (XSLT) without the aid of a debugger." Although the time and effort to produce a graphical visualization might seem to be an insurmountable problem, it is interesting to note the recent development of WYSIWYG XSLT editors (Microsoft, 2002; Ono et al., 2002). Even if such an application were to be developed specifically for our task it seems unlikely that it would totally eliminate the need for hand coding of SVG, XML and XSLT, although we live in hope. In the foreseeable future, these skills will be a necessary prerequisite for undertaking the process.

"The objective of scientific visualization, as it interacts with cartography, is the development of ideas and hypotheses about spatial information" (Fisher et al., 1993). It can therefore be considered to be a subset of the broader technique known as Exploratory Data Analysis. It will therefore always be a minority activity as specialist knowledge is required, such as cartographic, statistical and subject skills. Since ideation is one of the objectives of visualization, flexibility is one of the fundamental aspects of the technique as we do not know the potential outcome of our own data-mining. When we use a computer to aid us in our visualizations, we can gain more flexibility by utilizing a low-level programming language. In the case of XSLT, we have greater flexibility as we take direct control over the process which transforms raw data into a graphical image. There is, however, a direct trade-off. The lower the level of language we use, the more flexibility we gain, but using that lower level language also requires more time and higher skills. XML gives us a relatively high level of interaction, while XSLT is roughly at mid-range. Using these technologies gives the user the flexibility that is often not available when using window operating systems. The adoption of XML has been steady, unlike the meteoric acceptance of some earlier languages. However, it is likely to continue to grow in importance as disparate groups come to terms with the advantages which semantic control gives them. As XML use grows even further, it will also become more important to those seeking ideation and hypotheses since the pool of disparate data will increase accordingly and the ability to display that data via the use of XSLT will be a valuable skill.

References

Cecconi A and Galanda M (2002) Adaptive zooming in Web cartography. *1st SVG Open Conference Papers 2002.* Available: http://www.svgopen.org/papers/2002/cecconi_galanda__adaptive_ zooming/ [10 September 2003].

DuCharme B (2002b) *Reading Multiple Input Documents.* Available: http://www.xml.com/pub/a/ 2002/03/06/xslt.html [10 September 2003].

Fisher PF, Dykes J and Wood J (1993) Map design and visualisation. *Cartographic Journal,* 30, 136–142.

Forster K and Winter A (2002) The atlas of Tyrol. *1st SVG Open Conference Papers 2002.* Available: http://www.svgopen.org/papers/2002/foerster_winter__atlas_of_tyrol/ [10 September 2003].

Fuller D, Lindgren J and Mansfield P (2002) Rapid development and publishing of custom SVG maps using graphical stylesheets: unleashing the XML power of GML. *GML Developers Conference Papers 2002.* Available: http://www.gmldev.org/presentations/MakingMapsfromGML/fuller/gml.html [19 January 2003].

Held G, Schnabel O and Neumann A (2003) Advanced Webmapping with SVG. *2nd SVG Open Conference Papers, Vancouver, July 2003.* Available: http://www.svgopen.org/2003/courses.do [10 September 2003].

Holman GK (2000) *What is XSLT?* Available: http://www.xml.com/pub/a/2000/08/holman/index.html [10 September 2003].

Isakowski Y and Neumann A (2002) Interactive topographic Web-maps using SVG. *1st SVG Open Conference Papers 2002.* Available: http://www.svgopen.org/papers/2002/isakowski_neumann__ svg_for_interactive_topographic_maps/ [10 September 2003].

Mansfield P (2001) Graphical stylesheets. *XML 2001 Proceedings.* Available: http://www.idealliance. org/papers/xml2001papers/tm/web/05-05-02/05-05-02.htm [10 September 2003].

Map Browser. Available: http://www.mycgiserver.com/~amri/mapbrow.html [10 September 2003].

Microsoft (2002) *XML Editing: A WYSIWYG XML Document Editor.* Available: http://msdn.microsoft. com/library/default.asp?url=/library/en-us/dnxml/html/xmldocedit.asp [10 September 2003].

Misund G and Johnsen K-E (2002) The One Map Project. *GML Developers Conference Papers 2002.* Available: http://www.gmldev.org/GMLDev2002/presentations/MakingMapsfromGML/johnsen/one_ map_misund_johnsen.html [31 January 2003] and http://globus.hiof.no/gw3/Archive.html [10 September 2003].

Monmonier M (1991) *How to Lie with Maps.* Chicago: University of Chicago Press.

Ono K, Koyanagi T, Abe M and Hori M (2002) XSLT stylesheet generation by example with WYSIWYG editing (abstract). *Symposium on Applications and the Internet 2002.* Available: http://www. computer.org/proceedings/saint/1447/14470150abs.htm [10 September 2003].

Ordnance Survey. *GML and XSLT.* Available: http://www.ordsvy.gov.uk/os_mastermap/xml/ [10 September 2003].

Ridley Creek Riparian Assessment. Available: http://www.greenworks.tv/eac/ridleycreek/maps/ mappage.html [10 September 2003].

SVG Maps. Available: http://www.carto.net/papers/svg/links/ [10 September 2003].

Tuerlersee Project. Available: http://www.carto.net/papers/svg/tuerlersee/ [10 September 2003].

Tufte E (1983) *The Visual Display of Quantitative Information.* Graphics Press.

Tyrol Atlas. Available: http://tirolatlas.uibk.ac.at/ [10 September 2003].

Virtual Norfolk Web site. Available: http://virtualnorfolk.uea.ac.uk/long18thcent/introduction/ historicalgeography/popn.src.html [10 September 2003].

Chapter 13
Using Adobe Illustrator to Create Complex SVG Illustrations

Sara Porter

13.1 Introduction

Graphic designers are the next group of people starting to take an interest in SVG. We have grown accustomed to using robust design software that allows us to create graphics that range from simple to intricate. We can create everything from static raster and vector files for print, static and animated raster files for the Web, and animated vector files for the Web. The time has come to make static vector files for the Web.

The decision, by designers, to use Adobe Illustrator for creating SVG images is beneficial in many ways. We are used to the interface; we do not have to let go of this security blanket and be forced to learn yet another new software package. We have the ability to generate complex designs with Illustrator. Some other SVG imaging software is less complicated and has weaker tools; a designer would feel like their hands are tied when using this basic software. We can set up our SVG files so that a programmer can go back into the mark-up and further manipulate the file. Some designers might be intimidated by this fact. They may also not want to let their vector creations be made available to the entire world.

Anyone who right clicks an SVG image can copy that image to their personal computer. In the age of Napster, Morpheus and illegal file sharing, designers know that the 14-year-old who copies their SVG image for personal use will probably not ask the designer for permission. Copyright protection will be further tested with the emergence of SVG on the Web. A question to the programmers here: do you begin to see the designer's hesitancy at accepting an open source graphic? It would mean a potential loss in income. A question to the designers: what are you going to do? Acknowledge that as new technology emerges, you either re-skill yourself or be left behind. Consider the fact that SVG files are loaded with advantageous traits that will be exploited on the Web, in mobile platforms, in networking, in wireless, and certainly in future devices that have yet to be invented. Simply stated, by becoming more than a designer who simply creates pretty pictures, you can increase your marketability.

All SVG files created in this chapter were made using Adobe Illustrator 10.0.3 on the Windows platform. All SVG files were tested on Internet Explorer with ASV version 3. Although other vector illustration software exists that can create SVG files, I feel that Adobe Illustrator is the preferred choice for graphic designers (note: Macromedia Freehand is also an excellent software for vector imaging, but does not currently support SVG in any way). Furthermore, the decision to use both IE and ASV 3 was made because these are majority use vehicles.

This chapter is intended for those users who have experience with Adobe Illustrator and would like to use it to create visually appealing and dynamic SVG files. We shall start by creating the illustration in Illustrator and then, in some cases, go back and examine the Illustrator-generated SVG code. A warning to those who have not seen SVG mark-up before: the code created by Illustrator is not exactly the place to start learning the "how to's" of SVG – do this by creating hand-coded SVG files in a text editor. With Illustrator, we shall simply be dipping our toe into the vast world of mark-up creation and acknowledging the fact that cooperation between designers and programmers can result in elaborate and attractive SVG files.

13.2 Vector Designs

13.2.1 Vector and Raster Files

As designers, we know that Adobe Photoshop is the ultimate software for raster file creation. Blurring, textures, feathering and photo-realism are all created in this environment. However, any designer knows that they must be the two-handed gunslinger … raster on your right, vector on your left. If a design lends itself to the raster environment, use the appropriate tool. For vector file creation (and SVG file creation), we shall arm ourselves with Adobe Illustrator. We know that vector files are primarily lines, shapes, and paths. They can be filled with colour, scale, resize, incorporate text and even include embedded raster files. The main goal when creating vector images should not solely be duplicating raster appearances. If a raster file is better suited for the project, use it. However, if a vector file is warranted (e.g., if your file needs to be resolution independent, or scalable, or be integrated with a database file or other XML languages), use SVG.

13.2.1.1 Complex Shapes

True, SVG images can be created through hand coding (there are probably examples of this elsewhere in this book), but designers might not be impressed at the primitive shapes created. How many Web graphics are simple rectangles or circles? Even a toolbar graphic could involve much SVG hand coding. Also, designers would not possess enough patience to hand code it when they know they can use Illustrator and simply save files as SVG. Therefore, to create any SVG images that are more than simple primitive shapes, start by creating it in Illustrator.

13.3 Fonts

13.3.1 Limited Number of Fonts

Most professional designers follow the unwritten rule of using less than three fonts per design. Just because you have the ability to select and use 10 000 fonts does not mean that you should do so. Too many fonts on any design will make it appear like a ransom note. This is just a good design rule in general.

13.3.1.1 Typeface Choices

SVG files preserve text as text, as opposed to raster graphics that change text into pixel-generated shapes. In Illustrator, when you save your SVG graphic with text, the mark-up generated for the text tag will include your font name, size of font, boldness, etc. You do not have to change your text to paths (in fact, it is preferable not to change them to paths as this will only add to the number of existing paths within your file, thereby increasing your file size). Even though Illustrator claims to embed your fonts within your SVG file, I advise you to choose conservative and well-known fonts such as Arial, or Helvetica, or Times New Roman. Sometimes the embed feature does not work properly with more elaborate, unknown fonts. If you must use an exotic font for the sake of your design, be safe and convert it to paths. If you are using your font for simple descriptive text, select a known typeface.

13.4 Colour

13.4.1 RGB Colour Mode

Designers love colour, and Illustrator eloquently feeds this passion. Illustrator allows the user to pick a colour (whether it be a fill or stroke) through its colour mixer. As SVG files output to monitors and screens, use the colour mixer when it is set to RGB or HSB. Do NOT worry about Web-safe colours; simply ignore that little "out of Web colour" warning that Illustrator may give you. SVG files do not sit on a Web server as a bunch of coloured pixels; they are stored as text-based commands. They are called upon by the viewer and rendered on that viewer's computer monitor, cell phone screen, PDA screen, etc. Hence SVG colours are not limited to the very limited 256 Web-safe colours that designers have had to work with when using raster images. Freedom! Now go out there and exploit this perk. (An unfortunate note: the use of mesh gradients within Illustrator results in rasterizing of the vector file.)

13.4.1.1 Efficient Colouring

If you do not need to use a stroke (in the case where the fill and stroke are the same colour, for instance), leave the stroke out. It just makes the computer have more to compute when building the SVG image.

13.5 Layers

13.5.1 Not Truly Hidden

Designers that have experience with Photoshop should be comfortable using the layers within Illustrator. When we use Photoshop, we do not worry about deleting our hidden layers, but when using Illustrator and saving to SVG, these hidden layers are saved in the mark-up along with the visible layers. Visible layers are defined by a <g> tag with their display set to "yes". The only difference in the mark-up with hidden layers is that their display is set to "none". Naturally, this adds unnecessary data and increases the file size. It also allows those precocious users learning SVG by viewing the source of on-line SVG images to see the data that was originally intended to be hidden. Therefore, be sure to delete all hidden layers in Illustrator before saving to SVG, unless you hide the layers intentionally.

13.5.1.1 Layer Naming

Good general advice regarding setting up your Illustrator files is to strive for excellent organization. Group elements accordingly. Create layer names that convey meaning and can be understood by programmers when looking back into the file markup. Designers think graphically. Programmers are more literal. Do not use spaces in your layer names as XML tags cannot have spaces. Start thinking like a programmer and creating your layer names either with no spaces (e.g., "LayerName") or with underscores between words (e.g., "Layer_Name"). By keeping the names of the layers without spaces, it becomes much easier to search for these layers when looking at the SVG code.

13.6 Primitive Shapes

Illustrator CS supports the use of SVG primitives. Versions 9 and 10 do not. Primitive shapes are circles, ellipses, polygons, polylines and rectangles. Upon saving your AI file to SVG, they are all converted to paths. To help reduce the size of your SVG file, you can go into the mark-up and rename the paths back to their primitive tags. To do this, start by opening the Transform palette (under>Window>Transform) while in Illustrator. Then place the primitive object on to a layer by itself and name the layer something like "Rectangle_x218_y288_w144_h105". Remember to not have any spaces in your layer names. Also remember to have your document set to pixels, not inches. This descriptive layer name is extremely useful when changing the mark-up from paths to primitives, as all the element description is in front of you.

13.7 Filters and Effects

13.7.1 Differences of Filters and Effects

Illustrator allows the designer to apply both Filters and Effects to their vector files. The differences between the two are that Filters are permanent to the artwork, whereas Effects are not. You are able to edit the objects below the Effects at any time. In both the Filter and Effects menu, do NOT use the options below the final grey line as these result in rasterizing your image. This concept is easy to comprehend to those users who are proficient with Adobe Photoshop: the names of the Illustrator Filters that rasterize vector objects are the same names of Filters available in Photoshop (e.g., "Blur", "Pixelate", "Sharpen", "Sketch").

13.7.2 SVG Filters

SVG Filters are under the "Effects" menu. As an Effect, they are applied over your artwork, not to it. They do not permanently change your artwork; the underlying object remains editable. However, I suggest applying SVG Filters immediately before saving your file as SVG. This is because SVG Filters are applied to the object in the browser, not in the Illustrator file. You want the effect at the bottom of the Appearance palette (above the Transparency listing) in order to avoid rasterizing the file rather than simply changing its appearance. Also, if you use an SVG Filter, use it sparingly and as an accent, not as the primary focus applied to a large object. This may stall or completely quit your viewing software. In addition, using SVG Filters can dramatically increase your file size. Personally, I am not thoroughly impressed with the look created by any of the filters beyond "Gaussian Blur."

13.8 Interactivity and Animation

Users of Illustrator will probably be familiar with Macromedia Flash and of its capabilities. Some argue that Flash is a direct competitor to SVG. I would argue that this is not so. Flash clearly exhibits superior animation ability. Although SVG files can be animated, Illustrator does not support this; animation must be done through the hand coding of SVG files, and even this is difficult to do efficiently. As such, we shall not be creating animated movies with our SVG examples. Use Flash for this (and pre-pare to hear the programmers complain about the proprietary software format).

Where SVG lacks in animation (compared with Flash files), it excels in interactiv-ity and flexibility. SVG files have the potential for complex database integration; they can dynamically scale to fit a Pocket PC screen; they are editable through front-end software such as Illustrator, and further enhanced through back-end hand coding. In my opinion and based on my business experience, Flash files are excellent mar-keting and advertising vehicles. SVG files are (and should be) more serious in purpose, further supporting the fact that SVG is not, and will not be, a passing trend.

13.9 Rasterization

Designers know that Photoshop is the master tool for creating raster files. Raster files are beautiful and have many advantages over vector images. However, SVG is a vector format. Even though you have the ability to import a raster image in Illustrator and save this (now) Illustrator file as SVG, the raster image still main-tains its raster qualities. Also, we want to work with vector now, not raster. So let us be clear about this – if you import a raster file into Illustrator for any reason (such as using it to trace), you simply MUST delete this raster image before you save your Illustrator file to SVG. To answer a couple of questions regarding this issue:

- Question: Can't I import a raster image into Illustrator so that it changes to vec-tor? Answer: No. It is still raster; it still composed of pixels. It is only embedded in the vector file. You must either use a conversion software or retrace the raster image with the magnificent and much understated/extremely important Pen tool.
- Question: What happens if I leave my embedded raster image in Illustrator and save the file as SVG? Answer: Your SVG file size increases astronomically. You will also have the negative raster traits to deal with such as inability to scale, loss of quality when zoomed and resolution dependence.

13.10 Working with Non-AI Files

Illustrator can import other various file formats by using the "Place" command and/or simply opening the file with>File>Open.

13.10.1 Raster Files

Most raster files are imported into Illustrator for tracing purposes. As mentioned earlier, you have the ability to save the embedded raster file within Illustrator, thereby creating an SVG file. However, this is not smart SVG file creation; the file size is huge and you still have to deal with raster properties such as pixelation of your image. For efficient SVG files, delete all raster elements. So, with this point clearly understood, let us further discuss how to trace raster images placed within Illustrator. The first step to tracing a raster image is to set it to a new layer and then dim that layer (in the Layers palette, click the flyout and choose "Options for Layer", then click the "Dim Images to" box and type in 30–40 percent). Create another layer on top of the raster layer so that you may trace it using the Auto Trace tool, the Magic Wand tool, the Pencil tool, and/or the Pen tool. Most designers would agree that the Pen tool gives the user the most control. However, there may be times when a quick auto trace does the job efficiently (especially if the raster image has no background to it). The tutorial in Section 13.15 provides further tips on tracing a raster image.

13.10.2 DXF Files

Anyone working with, or within, a company that has an engineering department creating product DXF files should immediately develop a bridge between themselves and the engineers. Why? Because DXF files are also vector files (albeit incredibly deep vector files). If you can use a DXF file as the first step when creating your AI file, most of the line work is done for you. Illustrator opens DXF files with a simple >File>Open. You are then presented with options concerning layers, fitting, and closing of paths. Experiment with each of these settings to see which file is brought into Illustrator the cleanest. That is what you will be doing to the DXF file the most, "cleaning" it. You will be deleting miscellaneous lines; your text may be split and have to be retyped; your paths may need to be simplified; you will probably have to delete information that is too technical for the target audience (they do not need to see every single filleted edge of the product, do they?). You should ask the engineer to send you a TIF file along with the DXF file so that you can reference the data that is lost or shifted in the vector-to-vector transition. Regardless of all of this, those glorious lines and paths are waiting for you, and ready to be made into something colourful and SVGish. Figure 13.1 illustrates how DXF files opened in Illustrator with their original paths are too complex for marketing means. After a quick deletion of paths, as shown on the right, the SVG file size drops by 100 kb. CAD files show the depth of the object with numerous lines spaced closely together to indicate each surface change. With Illustrator, you can indicate this change and show depth with colour. This allows you to delete some of the original, intricate DXF paths.

13.10.3 Enhancing Vector Images

Using colour to indicate shading and highlights is one way to give dimensionality to a flat graphic file. Pick an imaginary light source directed on to your graphic object. When light strikes a 3D object, there exists a light side of the object in which highlights directly face the light source, a shadow side of the object where darker values turn away from light source, reflected light represented by light being cast

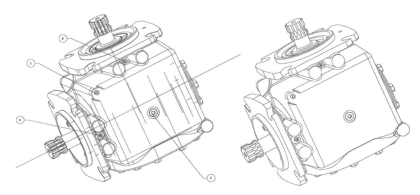

Figure 13.1 An example of a large DXF file (on the left) simplified by deleting excessive details (on the right).

back from a nearby surface and cast shadows represented by dark values cast by the object upon the surface or ground.

Additional traditional sketching techniques can further be applied to your Illustrator/SVG file to make it appear to have depth. Overlap foreground elements to suggest that these are in front of the background elements. Illustrate perspective of blur and atmospheric perspective by having a lack of focus on the background elements while keeping the foreground elements sharp. Pay attention to the vertical location of your graphic in the visual field; along with decreasing the size of the graphic, move the graphic up on the page (or monitor) to signify that it is further away.

13.11 Positioning

Those who are familiar with using Illustrator have grown accustomed to the artwork printing as specified by the location on the page. When saving as an SVG file, the Illustrator file's page size becomes irrelevant. The only things that will be printed are the objects within the artboard's black boundary lines (do not worry about the grey lines as these are also for printing). Illustrator sets the 0,0 coordinates of its exported graphic based upon the top-left edge of the artwork's bounding box. If you have any hidden layers that go outside of the visible artwork's position/bounding box, do the following:

1. Temporarily make your hidden layers visible.
2. Create a new layer and call it "Boundingbox". On this layer, draw a rectangle around all of your artwork; give it a stroke and fill of "none".
3. Go back and hide your hidden layers.

This ensures all artwork fitting into the viewbox display when it saves as SVG.

13.12 Saving Your File

13.12.1 Good File Management

A common saying when dealing with computers is "Save often; save early". This certainly holds true for all files created within Illustrator and saved as SVG.

I suggest saving multiple versions of your graphic file at these particular points:

1. Save your file as .AI with all of its information. This may include any raster images, extra line drawings, anything off of the artboard and hidden layers and paths that have not yet been cleaned.
2. Save your file as .AI without extraneous information. This should be the final Illustrator file before it becomes an SVG file. No unnecessary information should be in the file.
3. Save your file as .SVG with the "Preserve Illustrator Editing Capabilities" box checked.
4. Save your final SVG file with the "Preserver Illustrator Editing Capabilities" box unchecked.

13.12.2 Minimizing File Sizes

When you save your Illustrator file as SVG, you are presented with the "SVG Options" box. Certain selections within this box can greatly impact your file size:

1. "Font Subsettings" include the options of "None" (in case you used no fonts within your design), "Only Glyphs Used" (saving only the specific characters that have been used in the file), "Common English" (for the basic characters used in the English language), "Common English and Glyphs Used" (for the basic characters plus special characters), "Common Roman" (common English plus characters with accents used in other languages), "Common Roman and Glyphs Used" and "All Glyphs" (the complete font set). In most cases, you will choose "Common English". Do not be too cautious and readily choose "All Glyphs", as this will result in a considerably larger SVG file.
2. You also have the choice of whether to embed your font or store it separately from the SVG file. Sometimes this feature is buggy; the resulting SVG files do not always have the fonts embedded in them even if directed to do so. Be sure to check your SVG file with multiple users located on multiple machines.
3. When you go to save your final Illustrator file as SVG, uncheck the "Preserve Illustrator Editing Capabilities" box. If left on, you keep the ability to edit your SVG file within Illustrator later on as the Illustrator-only features are retained. However, be warned, keeping this box checked results in a large amount of CDATA within your SVG file (take a look at the mark-up in each scenario). This is why you uncheck the box at your last Illustrator-to-SVG save.
4. In the SVG Options box under the "Advanced" button, try keep the "Decimal Places" set to "1". If you do not like the look of your SVG image at this setting, increase the value to "3" or "4". If you are creating a vector image where details are imperative (such as in a map), raise the setting to "7". The higher the decimal places setting, the slower is the rendering but more accurate the image.

13.13 Review

The following is a brief review highlighting the major points of this chapter before we proceed to creating SVG files:

1. Save multiple Illustrator and SVG files throughout your entire process of your design project.

2. Minimize the final SVG file size by saving the SVG file appropriately (see above section).
3. Become an expert at organizing your illustration with appropriate layers and layer names.
4. Do not have spaces in layer names.
5. Delete hidden layers unless intentional; realize that hidden data is not hidden from "view source".
6. Delete any raster images imported/placed into a final Illustrator-to-SVG file.
7. Use standard, reliable fonts.
8. Try to keep text as text (rather than convert to paths).
9. Use filters as small accents, and not on large objects.
10. Exploit colour uses whenever possible, but do not use mesh gradients.

13.14 Tutorial: Creating a Simple Image Map

The objective is to create a simple graphic button that has a rollover cursor change and hyperlink to a new Web page (see Figure 13.2).

1. Create a new file in Illustrator; RGB colour mode; size is not very important but could be 200 × 200 pixels.
2. Display your "Tools", "Layers" and your "Colour" options.
3. To make the button graphic:
   (a) Draw a small square (a little less than ½ inch in size is fine). Give it no "Stroke", and a "Fill" of a two-colour linear gradient. Choose the gradient colours from the RGB colour system (the colour systems are changed by pressing the small flyout arrow button located in the upper right-hand corner of your colour options box). Go ahead – pick a colour, any colour! To help display depth, choose a light colour and a darker colour.
   (b) Make the gradient "Angle" = 30 degrees.
   (c) "Copy" (>Edit>Copy) the square and "Paste In Front" (>Edit>Paste In Front). "Paste In Front" places the copied square directly on top of the original.
   (d) Double click the "Scale" Tool, and choose 75% Uniform.
   (e) Go back to the "Gradient" palette and change the "Angle" to −120 degrees. It is starting to look like a button with some depth – correct?

Figure 13.2   An example of the finished tutorial.

4. To add the "Play" icon to the button:
   (a) Click and hold on the "Rectangle Tool" and select the "Star Tool".
   (b) Click once on your artboard to get the "Star Tool Options" box. Change the number of "Points" to 3. Hit "OK".
   (c) "Rotate" the triangle 90 degrees. Give it no "Stroke" and a yellow "Fill" (or any other contrasting colour). I chose to change the yellow colour "Saturation" to 30 percent. To do this, click on the flyout button in the colour options box, as shown in Figure 13.3, and choose "HSB". You can change the "Saturation" by moving the slider bar or by typing in the percentage.
   (d) Scale the triangle to fit within the centre of the button; position it accordingly.
5. To add the interactive elements:
   (a) Select the three graphic elements that make-up your button and "Group" (>Object>Group) them. In your "Layers" palette, double-click on the "Layer 1" name to rename the layer to "PlayButton" (remember, do not have spaces in your layer name). Deselect all artwork.
   (b) Next we add the "Image Map" by "targeting" the layer as opposed to "selecting" every element within the layer. There is a difference between "selecting" a layer and targeting one. To "select" a layer, click to the furthest right point on the layer name. Your mouse cursor will change to a hand and a square graphic appears, as seen in Figure 13.4. If held long enough, you should see a pop-up that says "Indicates Selected Art". For adding a URL, you would rather "target" the layer than "select" it. "Targeting" allows you to

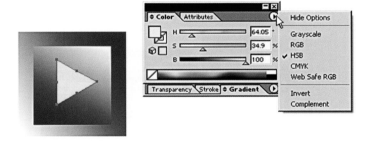

Figure 13.3   By clicking the flyout button, you are able to change the colour systems.

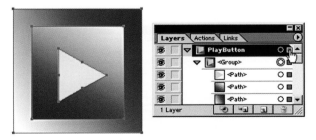

Figure 13.4   Select your artwork by clicking to the right of the circle.

specify the desired behaviour on a set of objects as a group, rather than on the individual objects within the group. It also allows you to be assured that every graphic element within the layer becomes part of the "Image Map". Therefore, click the hollow circle in the "PlayButton" layer name, as seen in Figure 13.5.

(c) Change to your "Attributes" palette. On the "Image Map" drop-down area, choose "Rectangle". In the case of SVG files, it does not matter whether you choose "Rectangle" or "Polygon" as primitive shapes, in Illustrator 9 and 10, once saved to SVG, are converted to paths. Type in the exact name of the Web page you wish to hyperlink (you may want to create a test HTML page for the sake of this tutorial). Be sure to type the exact file name and extension (.HTML versus .HTM). Figure 13.6 shows an example of this step.

6. Save your file as SVG (>File>Save, then change the "Save as Type" to "SVG"). In the SVG options box, set the "Fonts Subsetting" to "none" and uncheck the "Preserve Illustrator Attributes" box. Click the "Advanced" button and set the "Decimal Places" to 1. Hit "OK" twice.

7. To test your SVG file (make sure you have the ASV plug-in installed), either open your browser and do a >File>Open and browse for your SVG file – making sure that your "Files of Type" is set to "All Files", or simply double click on the SVG file icon). Notice that even though you did not assign it, your mouse cursor automatically changes to a hand cursor when rolling over the button.

8. This tutorial created an SVG graphic that will, most likely, be used within a traditional HTML page. A means to get an SVG image within an HTML page is to use the <embed> tag. For my example, I would put the following line within the body area of an HTML page: <embed src="playbutton.svg">

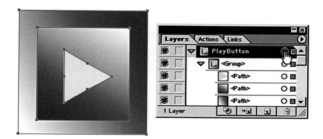

Figure 13.5   Target your artwork by clicking on the circle.

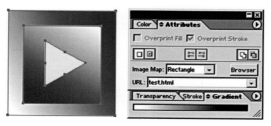

Figure 13.6   An example of the Attributes panel and test URL.

13.15 Tutorial: Tracing a Raster Image – Adding a Mouseover Event

The objective is to trace an existing raster graphic and create an SVG image with mouseover events that displays various text callouts (see Figure 13.7).

Most inexperienced designers do not fully understand the basic make-up of a raster graphic versus a vector graphic. Raster graphics are composed of pixels. The collection of pixels, or points of light, form to create the image. A vector graphic describes specific objects by defining their size, position and geometry. Examples of common vector objects are lines, circles and curves. The vector line, then, is an absolute line that is connected by at least two points. The vector information for this object is mathematical; it is not stored as a series of pixels like that of a raster graphic. Think of it in this way – raster graphics are "dumb" whereas vector graphics are "smart". Therefore (to make this point again), when the questions are asked, "Can't I just place a Photoshop/raster file into Illustrator/vector software? Won't it become vector?", the answer is "No. Illustrator simply embeds the raster image; it does not convert it to vector". To put it another way, it is easy to make a vector file dumb; it is difficult to make a raster file smart. There is commercial software available that generates raster-to-vector conversion, but telling a designer to use one of these packages is like telling a racecar driver to drive a manual transmission car. You are ultimately stripped of control.

The ultimate control tool when tracing most raster images is the "Pen" tool. For tracing raster images that contain simple profiles without any background elements, try using the "Auto Trace" tool. This tool generates quick paths that, in most cases, need to be edited beyond their worth. Hence, I suggest selecting the "Pen" tool and becoming a master at creating paths and Bezier curves. Once learned, these skills will be utilized in almost every other design software (Photoshop, Director, Flash and Freehand all have vector imaging tools that behave exactly the same as Illustrator's "Pen" tool).

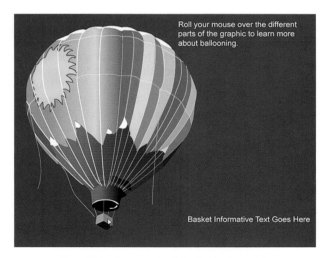

Figure 13.7   An example of the finished tutorial.

In this tutorial, we shall start by tracing a raster image in Illustrator. We shall then apply mouseover events to make the vector file more interactive. Such interactivity could be used in cases where the user is allowed to roll the mouse over a certain area in the SVG image, and some type of change to the SVG graphic would result. The change can generate descriptive text; it can change the colour of part of your graphic; it can change the size of your graphic.

In the last tutorial, you worked with the "Attributes" palette to add an Image Map to your Illustrator/SVG file. You will need to start working with the "SVG Interactivity" palette and using JavaScript. JavaScript can be either internally embedded within an SVG file or externally linked to an SVG file. If you suddenly think that you need to buy a JavaScript book and learn everything about it, do not fret: free JavaScript code can be borrowed (with the owner's consent, of course) from a trusted Web source (e.g., www.adobe.com and www.javascript.com) and used within your Illustrator/SVG design.

1. Create a new file in Illustrator with an RGB colour mode; size of file is "Letter".
2. Display your "Tools", "Layers", "Rulers", "Colour" options, "Type" and the "SVG Interactivity" palette.
3. Tracing a raster image:
   (a) "Place" (>File>Place) your raster image within your Illustrator file. For this tutorial, I am tracing a photograph of a hot air balloon.
   (b) In the "Layers" palette, double click on the layer name to generate the "Layer Options" window. Change the layer name to "Raster". Click the "Dim Images to" box and type in 40 percent. This step is shown in Figure 13.8.
   (c) In your "Layers" palette, lock your raster layer. Then create a new layer and name it "Lines" or "Paths". A good habit to get into is to keep a backup of your original trace lines that have no fill to them in case you need to copy elements of your original trace lines later.
   (d) Now begin to trace the raster image. Create paths with no fills, only strokes. You will quickly realize that lines are the most important and most tedious elements to create within vector images. Be careful to close all paths that you wish later to fill with colour. Depending on your experience with the "Pen" tool, you can either quickly draw your path and add (by clicking) various anchor points, or you can create your paths slowly by drawing your path and click-and-holding your anchor points. This will add handles, or direction lines, to your points. Either way, the most time will be spent adjusting your lines with the "Direct Selection" tool (the white arrow), converting your corner points to curve points with the "Convert Anchor Point" tool, adding or deleting points with the various "Add" and "Delete Anchor Point" tools, and splitting (with the "Scissor" tool) and joining (>Object>Path>Join) your paths to

Figure 13.8   The "Layer Options" box is where the layer can be both renamed and dimmed.

create closed shapes. A final note about the number of points to add to your path – use points where they matter; do not over-point your paths. A path with numerous points takes longer to generate as an SVG image than a path with a few, efficiently used points. Once you are satisfied with your line drawing, move it (by selecting the layer) next to raster image, as seen in Figure 13.9. For safety's sake, create another layer and copy and paste the entire no-fill-only-stroke layer to it as a backup. Then move the backup layer off of the artboard.

(e) Unlock your "Raster" layer and uncheck the "Dim Images to" box (double click on the "Raster" layer name to bring up the "Layer Options" box) so that you can see its full colour. Consult this image when adding colour to your vector shape. Even though you understand that this is a vector environment rather than raster, you can still add some three-dimensionality to your graphic by considering its depth cues. Where is the light source? How much shadow can I add? Can I create colour depth by applying simple gradients to a shape? Can I show depth by drawing shadows with my "Pencil" tool and filling them with a darker colour?

(f) If you have more than a simple illustration, separate the different graphic elements of your colour vector image into different layers and name them appropriately. For my balloon image, I have layers named "basket", "ropes" and "sky" (see Figure 13.10). Make sure the names of the layers have no spaces.

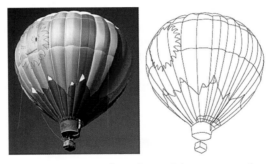

Figure 13.9 Always keep a copy of your line work in case you need to return to it.

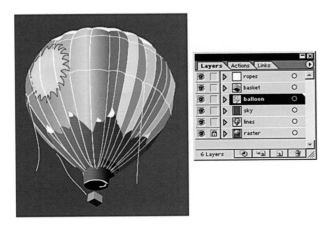

Figure 13.10 Use layer names with no spaces to help organize the different details in your graphic.

Congratulations! You are about 75% of the way. Now you have to think about what you want to happen to your graphic once a user rolls the mouse over certain areas. For my balloon graphic, I want informative text callouts to appear when the user rolls over the balloon portion or the basket portion (see Figure 13.3). To do this in Illustrator, I will create and position my callout text, then make it invisible, then add scripting (by way of the "SVG Interactivity" palette) to my balloon layer and basket layer. As mentioned earlier, you can embed JavaScript into an SVG image by typing it directly into the space next to the word "JavaScript" in the "SVG Interactivity" palette, but if you are not fluent in the ways of JavaScript, you can externally link a JavaScript file. I am going to externally link a JavaScript file named "Events.js" that came from the Adobe Web site (http://www.adobe.com/svg/illustrator/interactivity_palette/index2.html) and is approved for sharing by its creator. Before we start, go back to any one of your other vector layers and type in some informative help – something like "Roll your mouse over the different areas of the graphic to see more information on them". Now we can begin.

4. Create a new layer and call it "Callouts". On this layer, create all of your text callouts, and name each sublayer appropriately (need I say it? – do not use any spaces in the sublayer names). You might need to toggle on and off the eye/visibility icon if multiple callouts appear in the same X location (but will appear at different rollover times). Use guides to help you line up your graphic elements. Use "Paste In Front" for perfect text alignment. Choose a common font such as Arial or Times New Roman. When you are satisfied with the positioning and design, make the sublayers hidden (my sublayers are called "ballooncallout" and "basketcallout"), but keep the "Callouts" layer visible. This is shown in Figure 13.11.

5. Linking to an external JavaScript file:
    (a) On the "SVG Interactivity" palette, click on the folder icon. Figure 13.12 shows where the icon is located.
    (b) Click on the "Add" button.

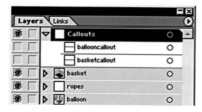

Figure 13.11   Hide the sublayers but keep the Callouts layer visible.

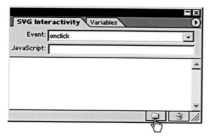

Figure 13.12   Click on the folder icon to link an external JavaScript file.

    (c) In the "URL" text field, locate your external JavaScript file. For my example, I can either type "events.js" or locate it through the "Choose" button. Note: if your external JavaScript file is not located in the same directory as the SVG file, add its relative path.

    (d) Click the "OK" button and then click the "Done" button.

6. Add mouseover scripting that will show callout text.

    (a) Target (circle icon instead of square) your layer that holds your graphic elements. In my example, I shall first target the "Balloon" layer.

    (b) On the "SVG Interactivity" palette, I shall select "onmouseover" from the "Event" drop-down menu.

    (c) In the "JavaScript" text field, I type "elemShow(evt, 'ballooncallout')". (Note: 'ballooncallout' is the name I gave my sublayer.) Be careful about spacing here, the only space I have is after the comma. Also, be careful about typos and be sure to include the quote marks. Picky – but this is where most errors occur. See Figure 13.13 for the exact text.

    (d) Hit "Enter" after you have inputted the JavaScript text.

    (e) Next I shall select "onmouseout" from the "Event" drop-down menu.

    (f) In the "JavaScript" text field, type "elemHide(evt, 'ballooncallout')" and press "Enter".

    (g) To add my text callout when rolling over the basket area of my image, I will target my basket layer, and then repeat steps (b)–(f) changing the 'balloutcallout' to 'basketcallout'. See Figure 13.14 for exact text necessary for interactivity.

7. For safety's sake, save your file as .AI – save everything in the file.

8. Next, delete your raster layer and your no-fill-only-stroke backup layer. Save your file as SVG (>File>Save As, then change the "Save as Type" to "SVG"). In the "SVG Options" box, set the "Fonts Subsetting" to "Common English" and

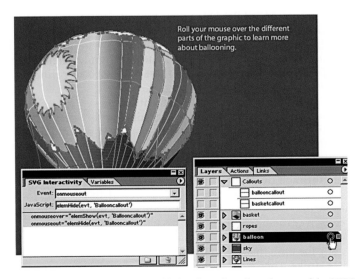

Figure 13.13 Mouseovers and Mouseouts are added to the Balloon layer by way of the SVG Interactivity Palette.

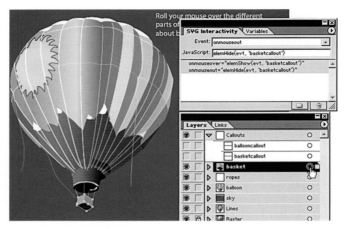

Figure 13.14   Similar actions are performed to make the Basket layer interactive.

make sure the "Preserve Illustrator Attributes" box is unchecked. Click the "Advanced" button and set the "Decimal Places" to 1. Hit "OK" twice.

9. Now test your SVG file. Right click on your SVG image and "View Source". It is not immediately apparent, but you should be able to decipher the different layers based on your layer names.

10. This SVG image is complex enough to stand alone rather than be embedded within an HTML document. To give it an added bonus, we shall make the file centre itself and resize automatically no matter what the viewer's display size may be. Here is how this is done:

   (a) When you initially save your Illustrator file to SVG, Illustrator writes a set width and height in the mark-up.

   (b) Open Notepad and>File>Open your SVG file (you may have to change the "Files of type" to "All files").

   (c) Near the beginning of the mark-up, find the width and height settings (they should be before the viewbox setting). Simply delete them. This sets the default width and height to be 100% of the browser window, regardless of its size.

   (d) Resave your file; do not forget to name it "name.svg".

   (e) Test your work by viewing the SVG within your browser at maximum size (does the SVG centre itself?) and then scaling your window down slightly (does the SVG resize and centre itself again?). I do not know about you, but this feature just thrills me!

After going through the steps of this tutorial, what if you would like to change the colour of part of your image when rolling over it? In my case, I would like to have the outline of the balloon and basket change to a 4-point yellow stroke when the viewer rolls over them (see Figure 13.15).

I go back to my saved Illustrator file that has the no-fill-only-strokes layer off the artboard. I copy the lines that I wish to change to 4-point yellow and give them all a 4-point yellow stroke. Then I put them as additional sublayers under my "Callouts" layer. To add these effects, I group each of my changes (the callout and the new yellow outline) in a group and name the group something like "balloonchange"

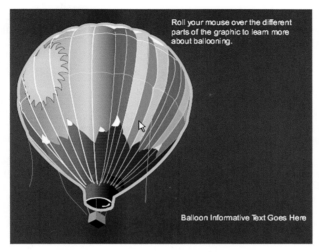

Figure 13.15   An example of an additional occurrence (the yellow stroke appears in addition to the call-out text) when the viewer rolls the mouse over the graphic.

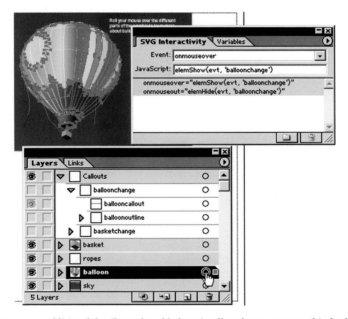

Figure 13.16   Additional details can be added to visually enhance your graphic further.

and "basketchange". I make sure to turn the group sublayers invisible and the "Callout" layer visible. Then I change the JavaScript in the targeted "balloon" and "basket" layers to "elemShow(evt, 'balloonchange')" and "elemHide(evt, 'balloon-change')", etc. Figure 13.16 shows one more way to add further visual interest in your graphic file.

Are you now impressed with Illustrator's capability of generating SVG files? If you are, share your artwork and designs with the rest of the SVG community. And welcome to the SVG party!

References

Eisenberg, DJ (2002) *SVG Essentials,* 1st edn. Sebastopol, CA: O'Reilly and Associates.

Laaker M (2002) *Sams Teach Yourself SVG in 24 Hours,* 1st edn. Indianapolis, IN: Sams.

Saliger J and McDonald G (2003) Adobe Illustrator 10: *a Step-by-Step Approach*, 1st edn. Morton Publishing.

Teague JC and Campbell M (2003) *SVG for Web Designers,* 1st edn. Indianapolis, IN: Wiley Publishing.

Trippe W and Binder K (2002) *SVG for Designers,* 1st edn. Berkeley, CA: McGraw-Hill/Osborne.

Watt A (2002), *Designing SVG Web Graphics,* 1st edn. New Riders Publishing.

Chapter 14
X3D-Edit Authoring Tool for Extensible 3D (X3D) Graphics

Don Brutzman

14.1 Purpose and Basic Usage

X3D-Edit is a graphics file editor for Extensible 3D (X3D) that permits simple, error-free editing, authoring and validation of X3D or VRML scene-graph files. Context-sensitive tooltips provide concise summaries of each VRML node and attribute. These tooltips simplify authoring and improve understanding for novice and expert users alike. Figure 14.1 shows the X3D-Edit interface for a typical "Hello World" example, shown in Figure 14.2 with spinning globe and animated text. Help information and links to installers, updates, viewers and content archives are available online at http://www.web3d.org/x3d/content/examples/help.html.

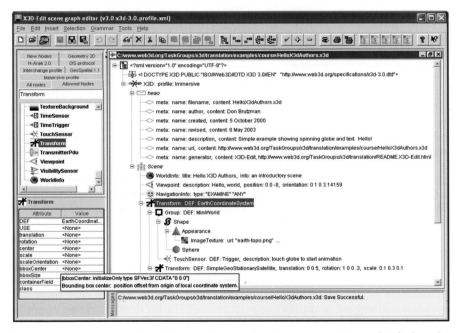

Figure 14.1 X3D-Edit screen layout for example scene, showing context-sensitive tooltip for bounding box centre.

Figure 14.2 Animating text of an X3D "Hello World" scene, converted into VRML encoding and launched into a Web browser's standard VRML plugin.

14.2 VRML/XML Quicklook

X3D is a scene-graph architecture and encoding that improves on the Virtual Reality Modeling Language (VRML) international standard (VRML 1997). X3D uses the Extensible Markup Language (XML) to express the geometry and behaviour capabilities of VRML. Now entering its third generation, VRML is well known as a highly expressive 3D interchange format that is supported by large numbers of tools and APIs (Lansdale, 2002). In addition to being able to express diverse geometry and animation behaviours, scripting (in Java or EcmaScript) and node prototyping provide excellent support for scene-graph extensions. Despite intermittent industry support, VRML has persisted and remains the most widely supported non-proprietary scene format.

The X3D specification is an exciting new area of work, expressing the geometry and behaviour capabilities of VRML using the Web-compatible tagsets of XML. Scene graph, nodes and fields correspond to document, elements and attributes, respectively, in XML parlance. The X3D Working Group continues to design and implement updates to the next-generation X3D graphics specification (www.web3D.org/x3d). XML benefits are numerous: customized metalanguages for structuring data, easily read by humans and computer systems, validatable data constraints, etc. XML is licence free, platform independent and well supported (Bos and W3C Communications Team, 2001). Together, these qualities can ensure that the VRML ISO standard is extended to match functionally the emerging family of next-generation XML-based Web languages.

X3D attributes include far simpler validity checking of content, componentized browsers for faster downloads, flexible addition of new hardware extensions, a lightweight Core Profile and better script integration. Numerous (over 2500) example scenes exercize most 3D and animation aspects of these scene-graph specifications, demonstrate syntax checking during autotranslation to VRML encodings and provide a challenging conformance/performance site for demonstrating exemplar high-end content. Both VRML- and XML-based syntax are valid ways to encode the information in an X3D scene.

14.3 IBM's *Xeena* Tool Builder and X3D-Edit Design

IBM's *Xeena* tool (IBM, 2002) is an interface-building tool written in Java that uses designer-produced XML profile configuration files to create customized tree-based editors for arbitrary XML languages. This is a powerful approach that has allowed extensive development and testing of X3D's XML encoding, which corresponds to the functionality of the VRML encoding. Thanks to a Java implementation, the tool is reasonably platform independent, with successful results reported under Windows, Macintosh and Linux.

Authoring-tool features available through the *Xeena* configuration are numerous. Student authors consider the user interface (shown in Figure 14.1) to be intuitive and powerful. Design of actual functionality flows from the design of XML-encoding relationships for X3D itself. The primary determinant of node relationships is determined by the rules expressed in the X3D Document Type Definition (DTD), which is the classical method for defining XML tagsets. As a result, the tool always creates well-formed scene graphs, and new nodes only fit into the scene graph where allowed. Componentization rules allow subset validation for X3D scenes conforming with the VRML 97, Core and other profiles. Adding node-specific icon images further improves scene-graph authorability and author comprehension.

While modifying a tree view of the scene graph, authors can automatically translate each X3D scene into the VRML encoding and launch a plugin-enabled Web browser to view the results. A huge set of publicly available X3D scenes provides well-documented exemplars, including translated X3D versions of all examples in the *VRML 2.0 Sourcebook* (Ames et al., 97). An independent NPS effort named Scenario Authoring and Visualization for Advanced Graphical Environment (SAVAGE) has utilized and tested all of these constructs (Blais et al., 2001). We have further seen significant improvements in our ability to teach the principles of 3D graphics, enabling students in any major subject to become effective authors with no prior programming experience. Our teaching experiences are documented further in papers on development of the Kelp Forest Exhibit (Brutzman, 2002a, b).

X3D extensibility includes capabilities to identify profiles, each corresponding to a common palette of nodes for lightweight, intermediate or fully capable content. This allows browser Profiles including Interchange (lightweight core content), Interactive (addition of keyboard and wand/mouse capabilities), Immersive (roughly equivalent to VRML97 scene graph) and Full (all nodes). Extensions allow authors to indicate that the contained scene includes intermediate levels of node capabilities. Designating profiles and components in scene headers allows more effective extensibility in 3D browsers, both for current content and for future capabilities.

Other syntactic changes in X3D include changing the Scripting protocol keyword from `javascript:` to `ecmascript:` at the beginning of ECMAScript scripts. Access type enumerations have been renamed (with essentially identical semantics) as follows: *inputOnly, outputOnly, initializeOnly* and *inputOutput* replace *eventIn, eventOut, field* and *exposedField,* respectively. Semantic changes are few. Script nodes are now allowed to have *inputOutput* field connections, the scripting event model has been made more consistent, and a Scene Authoring Interface (SAI) has eliminated major differences between internal and external scripting.

Node-selection panels provide full X3D-Edit support for numerous X3D extensions, including:

- Distributed Interactive Simulation (DIS) nodes specified by the DIS-Java-VRML Working Group (http://web.nps.navy.mil/~brutzman/vrtp/dis-java-vrml).
- GeoSpatial Profile nodes from GeoVRML 1.0 specification (http://www.geovrml.org/1.1/doc).
- Humanoid Animation (H-Anim 2001) Specification and backwards-compatible support for H-Anim 1.1 profile (http://h-anim.org).
- Non-Uniform Rational B-Spline (NURBS) parametric surfaces.
- LatticeXvl parametric surfaces (http://www.lattice3D.com).
- New X3D nodes: TriangleSets, LoadSensor, KeySensor, StaticGroup, Sequencers for output of discrete values in a manner similar to Interpolators, Boolean/Time event utilities, and others.
- Inline scenes have field extensions for event passing with parent scenes: IMPORT and EXPORT.

14.4 Stylesheet Conversions

The Extensible Stylesheet Language for Transformations (XSLT) is used for conversions from X3D form to various other encodings. For example, converting the original X3D source scene using stylesheet *X3dToVrm97.xslt* produces the VRML scene shown in Figure 14.2. Numerous scene-graph checks are also performed. A similar stylesheet, *X3dToXhml.xslt,* is used to convert source X3D scenes into HTML output. This is a helpful capability to ensure that users can obtain colour-coded documentation regardless of their system's XML-editing capability. The

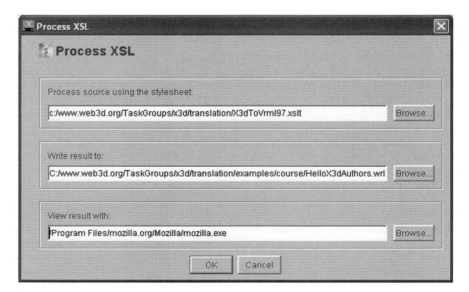

Figure 14.3   Stylesheet interface to invoke *X3dToVrml97.xslt*, converting X3D source scene to VRML encoding.

Xeena/ X3D-Edit interface for HTML conversion appears in Figure 14.3. An excerpt HTML-styled output in given in Listing 14.1.

Listing 14.1.   HTML presentation of X3D source, produced from the X3D (XML) encoding by *X3dToXhtml97.xslt* stylesheet

```
<?xml version="1.0" encoding="UTF-8"?>
<!DOCTYPE X3D PUBLIC "ISO//Web3D//DTD X3D 3.0//EN"
"http://www.web3d.org/specifications/x3d-3.0.dtd">

<X3D profile='Immersive' xmlns:xsd='http://www.w3.org/2001
/XMLSchema-instance'
xsd:noNamespaceSchemaLocation='http://www.web3d.org/speci-
fications/x3d-3.0.xsd'>
 <head>
   <meta name='filename' content='HelloX3dAuthors.x3d'/>
   <meta name='author' content='Don Brutzman'/>
   <meta name='created' content='5 October 2000'/>
   <meta name='revised' content='8 May 2003'/>
   <meta name='description' content='Simple example show-
   ing
      spinning globe and text. Hello!'/>
   <meta name='url' content='http://www.web3d.org/x3d/
   content/examples/course/HelloX3dAuthors.x3d'/>
   <meta name='generator' content='X3D-Edit,
   http://www.web3d.org/x3d/content/README.X3D-Edit.html'/>
 </head>
 <Scene>
  <WorldInfo info='an introductory scene' title='Hello X3D
    Authors'/>
  <Viewpoint description='Hello, world' orientation='0 1 0
    3.14159' position='0 0 -8' centerOfRotation='0 0 0'/>
  <NavigationInfo type='"EXAMINE" "ANY"'/>
  <Transform DEF='EarthCoordinateSystem'>
    <Group DEF='MiniWorld'>
      <Shape>
        <Appearance>
          <ImageTexture
            url='"earth-topo.png" "earth-topo.gif" "earth-
            topo-small.gif" "http://www.web3d.org/x3d/con-
            tent/examples/course/earth-topo.png"
            "http://www.web3d.org/x3d/content/examples/cou
            rse/earth-topo.gif" '/>
        </Appearance>
        <Sphere/>
      </Shape>
        <TouchSensor DEF='Trigger' description='touch
        globe
          to start animation'/>
    </Group>
  <Transform DEF='SimpleGeoStationarySatellite' rota-
  tion='1 0
    0 .3' scale='0.1 0.3 0.1' translation='0 0 5'>
      <Shape>
```

```
        <Appearance>
          <Material diffuseColor='0.9 0.1 0.1'/>
        </Appearance>
        <Text string='Hello X3D Authors !!'>
          <FontStyle size='3'/>
        </Text>
        </Shape>
      </Transform>
    </Transform>
    <TimeSensor DEF='OrbitalTimeInterval'
      cycleInterval='12.0' loop='true'/>
    <ROUTE fromNode='Trigger' fromField='touchTime'
      toNode='OrbitalTimeInterval' toField='startTime'/>
    <OrientationInterpolator DEF='SpinThoseThings' key='0.00
      0.25 0.50 0.75 1.00' keyValue='0 1 0 0, 0 1 0 1.5708,
      0 1 0 3.14159, 0 1 0 4.7123889, 0 1 0 6.2831852'/>
    <ROUTE fromNode='OrbitalTimeInterval' fromField=
      'fraction_changed' toNode='SpinThoseThings'
      toField='set_fraction'/>
    <ROUTE fromNode='SpinThoseThings'
      fromField='value_changed' toNode=
      'EarthCoordinateSystem' toField='rotation'/>
  </Scene>
</X3D>
```

14.5 Tooltips and Internationalization (I18n)

A particularly powerful capability that derives from using *Xeena* is the availability of tooltips for each element and attribute. Tooltips provide authoring hints that pop up in context of use, helping authors learn and understand how VRML/X3D scene graphs really work. A typical tooltip consists of a few concise sentences describing purpose, allowed values, example use and caveats. Originally derived from the VRML 97 specification, the tooltips have been repeatedly refined based on student questions and recommendations. An example tooltip for the bboxCenter attribute of the Transform node is shown popped up in the lower left-hand quarter of Figure 14.1.

Tooltips are now a valuable resource in their own right. The English-language profile has been translated into French and German, allowing the creation of X3D-Edit variants that edit syntactically identical scenes but provide customized tooltips in alternative languages. Tooltips are further available as standalone documents, organized by nodes and formatted for ready reference using a tooltip-generation stylesheet. Multilingual tooltips are available at the following Web pages:

http://www.web3d.org/x3d/content/X3dTooltips.html
http://www.web3d.org/x3d/content/X3dTooltipsChinese.html
http://www.web3d.org/x3d/content/X3dTooltipsFrench.html
http://www.web3d.org/x3d/content/X3dTooltipsGerman.html
http://www.web3d.org/x3d/content/X3dTooltipsItalian.html
http://www.web3d.org/x3d/content/X3dTooltipsPortuguese.html
http://www.web3d.org/x3d/content/X3dTooltipsSpanish.html

Figure 14.4   Catalogue pages are rapidly autogenerated to account for large archives of example scenes.

14.6 Construction of Example Archives

The rapid page-generation capabilities of XSLT and the inclusion of document metadata via HTML-like "meta" tags are powerful capabilities. This combination allowed the development of archive-generation stylesheets to make over 2000 example scenes available.

Archive design for lots of content is accomplished as follows. First, file and directory names are carefully chosen to be concise, descriptive and without abbreviations. Camel-case capitalization is applied to the first letter of each word (e.g., *Universal MediaPanoramas*). An XSLT stylesheet is then able automatically to build tables of contents, chapter contents and individual scene pages to present all content in an intuitive, cross-referenced fashion. An example scene page appears as Figure 14.4.

Archives of example scenes are available as follows:

- X3D Software Development Kit (SDK) CDs are online at http://sdk.web3D.org
- X3D Examples are at http://www.web3D.org/x3d/content/examples/contents.html
- X3D versions of VRML 2.0 Sourcebook examples are at http://www.web3D.org/x3d/content/examples/Vrml2.0Sourcebook/contents.html
- VRML/X3D Conformance Suite Examples are at http://www.web3D.org/x3d/content/examples/Conformance/contents.html
- NPS Scenario Authoring and Visualization for Advanced Graphical Environments (SAVAGE) library is at http://web.nps.navy.mil/~brutzman/ Savage/contents.html

14.7 Conclusions and Future Work

X3D-Edit is an effective authoring tool that significantly improves our ability to author interactive 3D scenes and teach the principles of 3D graphics to new students. XML provides significant capabilities for scene validation, effectively eliminating most of the "garbage in, garbage out" pathologies that might otherwise exist undetected in large content archives. Future work will include merging all node-relationship rules, complex types and multilingual tooltips into a single XML-based X3D Schema that will provide similarly strong functionality in any XML Schema-based editing tools.

14.8 Acknowledgments

The author and the Web3D Consortium gratefully acknowledge the support of IBM in licensing *Xeena* for unrestricted X3D development and use, and further thank the IBM Haifa team for technical support. Tooltip translations were performed by Yiqi Meng of Nanjing Art Institute, China, Frederic Roussille of Ecole National des Ingenieurs de Tarbes (ENIT), France, Raimund Dachselt and Johannes Richter of Dresden University of Technology, Germany, Roberto Ranon of L'Universita degli Studi di Udine Italy, Luciano Pereira Soares of the Universidade de São Paulo Brasil, and Guadalupe Muñoz Martín of Universidad Rey Juan Carlos, Madrid, Spain. Tooltip inputs were provided from dozens of hardworking NPS graduate students. James Harney and Jeff Weekley produced the autoinstallers for Windows, MacOS, Linux and Solaris operating systems. All contributions are greatly appreciated.

References

Ames A, Nadeau D and Moreland J (1997) *VRML 2.0 Sourcebook*, 2nd edn., New York: Wiley.
Blais C, Brutzman D, Horner D and Nicklaus S (2001) Web-Based 3D technology for scenario authoring and visualization: the SAVAGE project. *Interservice/Industry Training, Simulation, and Education Conference (I/ITSEC) 2001*, Orlando, FL, November 2001. Available: http://web.nps.navy.mil/~brutzman/Savage/documents/WebBased3dTechnology-Savage-IITSEC2001.pdf
Bos A and W3C Communications Team (2001) *XML in 10 points*, revised November 2001. Available: http://www.w3.org/XML/1999/XML-in-10-points
Brutzman DP (2002a) Teaching 3D modelling and simulation: virtual kelp forest case study. *Web3D/VRML Symposium*, Tempe, AZ, February 2002.
Brutzman D (2002b) *X3D-Edit for Extensible 3D (X3D) Graphics README*. Available: http://www.web3D.org/TaskGroups/x3d/content/README.X3D-Edit.html
Extensible 3D (X3D) Graphics, Working Group Home Page. Available: http://www.web3D.org/x3d.html
IBM (2002) *Xeena XML Editor*. Available: http://www.alphaWorks.ibm.com/tech/xeena
Lansdale R (2002) *VRML2 is an Excellent Conversion Route from Many CAD Packages*. Press release, Okino Computer Graphics, January 2002. Available: http://www.okino.com/press/vr012202.htm
VRML (1997) *VRML 97 International Specification (ISO/IEC 14772-1)*, December 1997. Available: http://www.web3d.org/x3d/specifications/vrml/ISO_IEC_14772-All
World Wide Web Consortium (W3C). *Internationalization (i18n) Home Page*. Available: http://www.w3.org/International

Chapter 15
Concluding Remarks

Vladimir Geroimenko and Chaomei Chen

In this monograph, we have investigated several significant topics in the leading-edge research area of Information Visualization using SVG and X3D. These native XML-based technologies will play a crucial role in visualizing machine-understandable Web data on the Second-generation Web that is at this time becoming a reality. The new version of the Web requires and stimulates the development of novel visualization techniques and metaphors. It is really difficult or even impossible to predict what these techniques and metaphors will look like because they depend heavily on how the real-life progress of the Semantic Web will turn out. Because of this, drawing a more or less detailed picture of the new research area will be possible only as a result of several years of thorough exploration, and we hope that with this pioneering book we may help to make it happen sooner. As with any novel area, we have tried our best to investigate the topics that seem to be of primary importance at this moment in time. We think that in general we have achieved our goal and that the reader will not judge us too severely for not presenting those aspects that could not be covered today because they require research that can be done only after the main structure of the XML-based Web has been implemented.

It is obvious that the next-generation Web will be rich both semantically and visually. Since XML separates content from presentation rules, any form of presentation has "equal opportunities", but SVG and X3D have a better chance of being implemented in semantic human–computer interfaces because they are native to the XML family and also allow the development of graphical 2D and 3D interfaces that are visually rich and highly interactive. The intensive use of semantics will change the nature of the visual aspect of the Web. In addition to today's images, pictures and animations, the future Web will permit the user to visualize much more conceptual things such as the meaning and structure of Web data. The next generation will be not only the Web of formalized meanings, understandable by machines, but also the Web of visualized meanings that increase human understanding of Web data. In other words, computers will be able to comprehend the future Web because it includes machine-processable semantics; humans can better comprehend this Web because of the use of visualized semantics.

On the emerging Semantic Web, SVG and X3D will allow Web developers to produce visually rich 2D and 3D worlds that are in essence the worlds of meanings. Such worlds will comprise a variety of different levels and forms of metadata – from simple domain-specific XML documents and RDF Schemas to complex ontologies based on OWL and similar technologies. They will allow the user to interact with data and metadata in an efficient and desirable way (for example, navigate, manipulate, transform, zoom and filter). Visual interaction with Web data, metadata, schemas

293

and ontologies will be effectively used for a wide variety of purposes, such as searching the Web using semantically enhanced search engines, customizing Web pages and Web sites on-the-fly, instructing autonomous software agents, navigating through huge sets of data and metadata and accessing any part of any Web document.

The new generation of the Web is changing the nature of images that we are used to seeing on the current Web. Presented in SVG and X3D, they will be put to active use, similar to any other XML documents. This means that computers will be able to understand the meaning of not only Web data but also Web images. Since they will be written in XML-based plain text format, both computers and humans can access any parts of such images, "recognize" them by their XML tags, find them on the entire Web, compose new images on-the-fly using XSLT and other technologies and also do many other things that are impossible on the current HTML-based Web. SVG and X3D are not a simple replacement for GIF/JPG and VRML. They introduce a new generation of computer-understandable Web graphics that are native to both the XML family and the Semantic Web and therefore they are the Information Visualization technologies of choice for years to come.

Index